ENVISIONING THE FUTURE OF DOCTORAL EDUCATION

ENVISIONING THE FUTURE OF DOCTORAL EDUCATION

Preparing Stewards of the Discipline

Carnegie Essays on the Doctorate

Chris M. Golde, George E. Walker, and Associates

o

CARNEGIE CENTENNIAL
1905 — 2005

JOSSEY-BASS
A Wiley Imprint
www.josseybass.com

Published by Jossey-Bass
A Wiley Imprint
989 Market Street, San Francisco, CA 94103-1741   www.josseybass.com

Limit of Liability/Disclaimer of Warranty: While the publisher and author have used
their best efforts in preparing this book, they make no representations or warranties
with respect to the accuracy or completeness of the contents of this book and specifically disclaim any implied warranties of merchantability or fitness for a particular
purpose. No warranty may be created or extended by sales representatives or written
sales materials. The advice and strategies contained herein may not be suitable for
your situation. You should consult with a professional where appropriate. Neither
the publisher nor author shall be liable for any loss of profit or any other commercial damages, including but not limited to special, incidental, consequential, or other
damages.

Readers should be aware that Internet Web sites offered as citations and/or sources
for further information may have changed or disappeared between the time this was
written and when it is read.

Jossey-Bass books and products are available through most bookstores. To contact
Jossey-Bass directly call our Customer Care Department within the U.S. at
800-956-7739, outside the U.S. at 317-572-3986, or fax 317-572-4002.

Jossey-Bass also publishes its books in a variety of electronic formats. Some content
that appears in print may not be available in electronic books.

Library of Congress Cataloging-in-Publication Data

Golde, Chris M.
 Envisioning the future of doctoral education : preparing stewards of the discipline
Carnegie essays on the doctorate / Chris M. Golde, George E. Walker, and associates
  p. cm.
 Includes bibliographical references and index.
 ISBN 0-7879-8235-0 (alk. paper)
 1. Doctor of philosophy degree. 2. Universities and colleges—United States—
Graduate work. I. Walker, George E. II. Title.
 LB2386.G64 2006
 378.24—dc22

                                                                    2005028350

Printed in the United States of America
FIRST EDITION
HB Printing   10 9 8 7 6 5 4 3 2 1

CONTENTS

PART FOUR
Conclusion

THE AUTHORS

Joyce Appleby, a retired professor of history at UCLA, has studied the early modern period in England, France, and the American colonies over a long career. Appleby—a teacher of American history—has focused on the American Revolution and the U.S. constitution, as well as the early national period, in her published work, with special attention to Thomas Jefferson and the party he founded. In her work on seventeenth-century England, she investigated the way that progressive changes in economic life fostered new theories about human nature and the cohering forces in human society. The way that the French revolutionaries used the founding ideas of the United States drew her to French history. She has also examined changes in how historians have approached their subject over the past fifty years. Appleby, founder of the History News Service—an informal syndicate of historians writing op-ed essays that use history to illuminate contemporary issues—has long advocated closer relations between professional historians and the reading public.

Hyman Bass is the Roger Lyndon Collegiate Professor of Mathematics and professor of mathematics education at the University of Michigan. He is past president of the American Mathematical Society. He recently chaired the Mathematical Sciences Education Board at the National Academy of Sciences and the Committee on Education of the American Mathematical Society; he is currently president of the International Commission on Mathematics Instruction. His mathematical research is in diverse areas of algebra, with connections to topology and geometry. During the past ten years he has been conducting collaborative research on the mathematical knowledge and resources entailed in the teaching of mathematics at the elementary level. In all of this work, a major challenge has been to build bridges between diverse professional communities, especially mathematicians, and stakeholders involved in mathematics education.

Thomas Bender is University Professor of the Humanities and professor of history at New York University, where he currently directs the International

Center for Advanced Study. He has twice served as chair of the history department, as well as dean for the humanities. He is an intellectual and cultural historian of the United States, with particular interests in histories of cities and city culture, the history of intellectuals, the arts, and academic disciplines.

Bender is also interested in historiography and questions of narrative, and he has increasingly focused his attention on transnational approaches to American history. His books include *New York Intellect: A History of Intellectual Life in New York City, from 1750 to the Beginnings of Our Own Time* (Knopf, 1987), *Community and Social Change in America* (Rutgers University Press, 1978), and *Intellect and Public Life: A Social History of Academic Intellectuals in the United States* (Johns Hopkins University Press, 1993). He was coeditor (with Carl E. Schorske) of *American Academic Culture in Transformation* (Princeton University Press, 1998) and *The Unfinished City: New York and the Metropolitan Idea* (The New Press, 2002). He was editor of *Rethinking American History in a Global Age* (University of California Press, 2002), coauthor (with Colin Palmer and Philip M. Katz) of the American Historical Association study of doctoral education titled *The Education of Historians for the Twenty-First Century* (University of Illinois Press, 2004), and author of the *La Pietra Report* (2000)—a report of the Organization of American Historians on internationalizing the study of American history.

Bender is committed to a public role for scholarship; he has served as chair of the New York Council for the Humanities, and he writes frequently for newspapers and other publications for a general audience.

David C. Berliner is Regents' Professor of Psychology in Education and of Educational Leadership and Policy Studies at Arizona State University. He is past president of the American Educational Research Association and of the Division of Educational Psychology of the American Psychological Association. His achievements in educational psychology include coauthorship (with N. L. Gage) of six editions of the textbook *Educational Psychology* (Houghton Mifflin, 1998) and coeditorship (with R. C. Calfee) of the *Handbook of Educational Psychology* (Erlbaum, 1996). He is author, coauthor, or editor of over 150 articles, chapters, and books, earning him the E. L. Thorndike Award in educational psychology and both the Distinguished Contributions Award and the Outstanding Book Award (for the *Manufactured Crisis*, coauthored with B. J. Biddle [Perseus, 1995]), from the American Educational Research Association. In 2003 he won the Brock International Prize in education. Berliner is a member of the National Academy of Education and a fellow of the Center for Advanced Study in the Behavioral Sciences.

Ronald Breslow is the Samuel Latham Mitchill Professor of Chemistry and University Professor at Columbia University in New York. He received his undergraduate and graduate training at Harvard University, where he received an A.B. summa cum laude in chemistry and an A.M. in medical science before he did his Ph.D. research with Professor R. B. Woodward.

Breslow's research interests can be described generally as involving the design and synthesis of new molecules with interesting properties and the study of these properties. In his early work he synthesized the simplest aromatic system and demonstrated the phenomenon of antiaromaticity. His major emphasis in recent years has been on the synthesis and study of molecules that imitate enzymatic reactions. Recently, he has developed a new group of cytodifferentiating agents, with potential use in cancer chemotherapy.

He is the author of over four hundred publications and winner of two dozen awards, including the U.S. National Medal of Science. He has been elected to the U.S. National Academy of Science, the American Philosophical Society, the European Academy of Science, and the Royal Society of Great Britain; he holds honorary membership in the Indian Academy of Science, the British Royal Society of Chemistry, the Japanese Chemical Society, and the Korean Chemical Society. In 1996 he served as president of the American Chemical Society, where he focused the society's attention on doctoral education.

Tony F. Chan is professor of mathematics and dean of the Division of Physical Sciences at UCLA. Prior to becoming dean, he served as director of UCLA's Institute for Pure and Applied Mathematics (IPAM). Chan has been an active member of the Society of Industrial and Applied Mathematics and the American Mathematical Society. His general research interest is interdisciplinary mathematics. Specific current projects include differential-equation-based image processing and computer vision, multiscale computational methods, and optimizational and algebraic multigrid methods for VLSI circuit layout.

William Cronon is the Frederick Jackson Turner Professor of History, Geography, and Environmental Studies at the University of Wisconsin–Madison. In 2003 he was also named Vilas Research Professor at UW-Madison—the university's most distinguished chaired professorship. At the University of Wisconsin he served as director of the Honors Program for the College of Letters and Science from 1996 until 1998, and from 1997 until 2000 he served as the founding faculty director of the Chadbourne Residential College. He served as vice president of the American

Historical Association from 2002 until 2005 and as president of the American Society for Environmental History from 1989 until 1993. He holds a doctorate (D.Phil) from Oxford University in British urban and economic history and a Ph.D. in American history from Yale University, where he also served as a faculty member.

Cronon studies American environmental history and the history of the American West. His research seeks to understand the history of human interactions with the natural world: how we depend on the ecosystems around us to sustain our material lives, how we modify the landscapes in which we live and work, and how our ideas of nature shape our relationships with the world around us. His books include *Changes in the Land: Indians, Colonists and the Ecology of New England* (Hill & Wang, 1983), *Nature's Metropolis: Chicago and the Great West* (W. W. Norton, 1991), and *Uncommon Ground: Rethinking the Human Place in Nature* (W. W. Norton, 1995). He is currently at work on a history of Portage, Wisconsin, that will explore how people's sense of place is shaped by the stories they tell about their homes, their lives, and the landscapes they inhabit. He is also completing a book titled *Saving Nature in Time: The Past and the Future of Environmentalism* on the evolving relationship between environmental history and environmentalism, and what the two might learn from each other.

David Damrosch is professor of English and comparative literature at Columbia University, where he has taught since 1980. He has served as department chair and as director of graduate studies, and is a past president of the American Comparative Literature Association. His books include *Meetings of the Mind* (Princeton University Press, 2000), *We Scholars: Changing the Culture of the University* (Harvard University Press, 1995), on conference culture, and *What Is World Literature?* (Princeton University Press, 2003).

Yehuda Elkana became rector and president of the Central European University (CEU) in Budapest, Hungary, in 1999. The CEU draws more than one thousand students from sixty countries and one hundred professors from thirty countries. Prior to his role at the CEU, Elkana was professor of philosophy and social studies of science at the Eidgenössische Technische Hochschule Zurich, as well as professor at the Cohn Institute for the History of Philosophy of Science and Ideas at Tel Aviv University. Since 1987 he has been a permanent fellow of Berlin's Wissenschaftskolleg. Elkana has taught at the Hebrew University, where he was chair of the Department of History and Philosophy of Science. He earned his

Ph.D. from Brandeis University in 1968 and subsequently taught at Harvard University. From 1968 to 1993, he was director of the Van Leer Jerusalem Institute.

Chris M. Golde is a senior scholar at The Carnegie Foundation for the Advancement of Teaching, where she is research director for the Carnegie Initiative on the Doctorate. For the last decade her research has focused on doctoral education, particularly the experiences of doctoral students. Her dissertation work was on doctoral student attrition, and she is the lead author of *At Cross Purposes: What the Experiences of Today's Doctoral Students Reveal About Doctoral Education*—the 2001 report of a national survey funded by The Pew Charitable Trusts (available at www.phd-survey.org).

Before joining Carnegie, she was a faculty member at the University of Wisconsin–Madison. She received a Ph.D. in education in 1996 and an M.A. in sociology in 1993, both from Stanford University. She is also a graduate of Brown University (B.A. in linguistics, 1982) and Columbia University Teachers College (M.A. in student personnel administration, 1984).

Gerald Graff is professor of English and education at the University of Illinois at Chicago (UIC). Earlier he taught for twenty-five years at Northwestern University, where he chaired the English Department and served as director of the Northwestern University Press. In the 1990s he taught at the University of Chicago, where he directed the Master of Arts Program in the Humanities. For the last three years he served as dean of curriculum and instruction in the UIC's College of Liberal Arts and Sciences.

Graff is the author of several influential books, including *Professing Literature: An Institutional History* (University of Chicago Press, 1987) and *Clueless in Academe: How Schooling Obscures the Life of the Mind* (Yale University Press, 2003). In December 2005 he and his wife, Cathy Birkenstein-Graff, published a textbook, *They Say/I Say: The Moves That Matter in Academic Writing* (W. W. Norton).

Zach W. Hall is president of the California Institute for Regenerative Medicine. Previously, he was senior associate dean for research and acting director of the Zilkha Neurogenetic Institute at the Keck School of Medicine of the University of Southern California. In 2001–02, he was president and CEO of EnVivo Pharmaceuticals, Inc.—a biotechnology company for the discovery and development of pharmaceuticals for central nervous system diseases. Prior to that, he was executive vice chancellor and professor of physiology at the University of California, San Francisco (UCSF), where he led the development of a forty-three-acre basic science campus at Mission Bay. Hall served as director of the National Institute of Neurological Disorders and Stroke at the National Institutes of Health from 1994 until 1997. He also served on the faculties of the Harvard University Medical School and UCSF. His undergraduate degree is in English from Yale University, and his Ph.D. is in biochemistry (medical sciences) from Harvard University in 1966.

Hall has made fundamental contributions to the investigation of the neuromuscular junction. He is the author and editor of *An Introduction to Molecular Neurobiology*, has published more than one hundred original papers and reviews, and was a founding editor of *Neuron*. He is an elected member of the Institute of Medicine, the American Academy of Arts and Sciences, and the American Neurological Association; he is also a fellow of the American Association for the Advancement of Science. In 2003, he received the Purkynje Medal for Scientific Achievement from the Czech Academy of Science.

Steven E. Hyman is provost of Harvard University and professor of neurobiology at Harvard Medical School. From 1996 to 2001 he served as director of the National Institute of Mental Health (NIMH)—the component of the National Institutes of Health charged with generating the knowledge needed to understand, treat, and prevent mental illness. Prior to assuming his position at NIMH, Hyman was professor of psychiatry at Harvard Medical School and director of psychiatry research at Massachusetts General Hospital. His laboratory focused on mechanisms by which the neurotransmitter dopamine produced long-term changes in brain function by regulating the expression of genes. He codirected the basic graduate course in neurobiology at Harvard Medical School and was actively involved in the doctoral program. He also served as the first faculty director of Harvard University's interfaculty initiative in mind, brain, and behavior. He is editor-in-chief of the *Annual Review of Neuroscience*. Hyman is a member of the Institute of Medicine of the National Academy of Sciences and is a fellow of the American Academy of Arts and Sciences.

Hyman received his B.A. from Yale in 1974 and his M.A. from the University of Cambridge, where he was a Mellon fellow studying the history and philosophy of science in 1976. He received his M.D. degree from Harvard Medical School in 1980. Following an internship in medicine at Massachusetts General Hospital (MGH), a residency in psychiatry at McLean Hospital, and a clinical fellowship in neurology at MGH, he was a postdoctoral fellow at Harvard in molecular biology.

Alvin L. Kwiram is professor of chemistry and vice provost for research, emeritus, at the University of Washington. Kwiram has published over seventy papers in the field of physical chemistry, emphasizing the development of novel magnetic resonance techniques designed to probe the electronic structure of molecular systems in the solid state. He has served in leadership positions in the American Chemical Society (including service on the Graduate Education Advisory Board), the Council for Chemical Research, the Council for Research Policy and Graduate Education (of the National Association of State Universities and Land-Grant Colleges), and the American Association for the Advancement of Science. He has also served on a number of not-for-profit and for-profit boards. He is currently serving as executive director of the National Science Foundation's Center for Materials and Devices for Information Technology and Research.

Andrea Abernethy Lunsford is currently the Louise Hewlett Nixon Professor of English and director of the Program in Writing and Rhetoric at Stanford University. She has designed and taught undergraduate and graduate courses in writing history and theory, rhetoric, literacy, and intellectual property. Before joining the Stanford faculty, she was Distinguished Professor of English and director of the Center for the Study of Teaching of Writing at The Ohio State University. Professor Lunsford's interests include rhetorical theory, women in rhetoric, collaboration, cultures of writing, style, and technologies of writing. She has written or coauthored fourteen books. She has also served as chair of the Conference on College Composition and Communication and chair of the Modern Language Association Division on Writing, and as a member of the MLA Executive Council.

Kenneth Prewitt is the Carnegie Professor of Public Affairs, School of International and Public Affairs, at Columbia University. Previous positions include director of the U.S. Census Bureau, president of the Social Science Research Council, senior vice president of the Rockefeller Foundation, and director of the National Opinion Research Center. He taught for fifteen years at the University of Chicago and, for shorter periods, at Stanford University (where he received his Ph.D.), Washington University, the University of Nairobi, and Makerere University (Uganda). Among his awards are a Guggenheim Fellowship, honorary degrees from Carnegie Mellon and Southern Methodist University, a Distinguished Service Award from the New School for Social Research and The Officer's Cross of the Order of Merit from the Federal Republic of Germany, and various awards associated with his directorship of the U.S. Census Bureau. He is a fellow of the American Academy of Arts and Sciences, the Center for Advanced Study in the Behavioral Sciences, the Academy of Political and Social Science, the Russell Sage Foundation, and the American Association for the Advancement of Science. He recently published *Politics and Science in Census Taking* (Russell Sage Foundation and Population Reference Bureau, 2003).

Virginia Richardson is professor of education and chair of the Department of Educational Studies at the University of Michigan. She is an active member of the teacher education faculty and teaches in the certification and Ph.D. programs. She is the author of several books, including the fourth edition of the *Handbook of Research on Teaching* (2001, American Educational Research Association), as well as many articles and chapters related to teacher beliefs, change, and the fostering of moral virtues in the classroom.

Angelica M. Stacy is professor of chemistry at the University of California, Berkeley. She received her Ph.D. from Cornell University. Her research interests are in the synthesis and characterization of new solid-state materials, with an emphasis on electronic and magnetic applications. Her research group is known for using molten salts for the synthesis of copper oxide superconductors and for the preparation of numerous new metal oxide phases. Currently, Stacy's attention is directed toward nanowire arrays for thermoelectric and magnetoresistance applications.

Stacy is well known for her work in chemistry education. Her contributions include studies of student understanding, and she is developing ChemQuery—a criterion-referenced assessment for tracking student learning. Numerous students have already benefited from a new high school chemistry curriculum she developed, called Living by Chemistry. She is in the process of publishing this curriculum.

Stacy also serves the UC Berkeley campus as the associate vice provost for faculty equity. This office develops and oversees policies and programs dealing with faculty recruitment, development, and retention. She has won numerous awards, including the Francis P. Garvan–John M. Olin Medal from the American Chemical Society, a Faculty Award for Women Scientists and Engineers from the National Science Foundation, the Iota Sigma Pi Award for Professional Excellence, and the James Flack Norris Award for Outstanding Achievement in the Teaching of Chemistry.

In 2005 she was named one of seven National Science Foundation Director's Distinguished Teaching Scholars, recognizing her groundbreaking results in research, her strong teaching and mentoring skills, and her major educational contributions.

Catharine R. Stimpson became dean of New York University's Graduate School of Arts and Science in January 1998, after directing the MacArthur Foundation Fellows program for four years. At Rutgers she was first a professor and director of the Institute for Research on Women, then dean of the graduate school and vice provost for graduate education. Stimpson is a former president of the Modern Language Association, former chair of the New York State Humanities Council and the National Council for Research on Women, and former president of the Association of Graduate Schools. She authored a novel, books on feminism and the work of Gertrude Stein, and over 150 monographs, essays, stories, and reviews in *The Nation* and *The New York Times Book Review*, among others. Stimpson earned her Ph.D. at Columbia University, received Fulbright and Rockefeller humanities fellowships, and has been awarded several honorary degrees.

Crispin Taylor is currently executive director of the American Society of Plant Biologists (ASPB). After spending ten years climbing up the trunk of the academic career tree, he left academia as a postdoc to pursue a career in the not-for-profit publishing arena, working initially as a science writer at *The Plant Cell,* which is published by ASPB. In 2000 he joined the staff of Science's *Next Wave*—an online career-development magazine for scientists published by the American Association for the Advancement of Science, where his interests in providing practical and well-informed career advice to other up-and-coming scientists were amply met. After spending his last year at *Next Wave* as its editorial director, in 2004 he returned to ASPB and his disciplinary roots in plant biology. Taylor serves on the advisory board of the National Postdoctoral Association, and he is a member of the board of the Boyce Thompson Institute.

George E. Walker is a senior scholar at The Carnegie Foundation for the Advancement of Teaching, where he directs the Carnegie Initiative on the Doctorate project. He is a theoretical physicist and a fellow of the American Physical Society. He received his bachelor's degree from Wesleyan University and the M.S. and Ph.D. from Case Institute of Technology. Walker was a faculty member from 1970 until 2004 and an administrator at Indiana University for fifteen years. He twice won awards for contributions to graduate education. Before coming to Carnegie, he was vice president for research and dean of the graduate school at Indiana.

Walker has been active in many of the national organizations related to graduate education and research administration. A selected list of past national offices includes chair of the Council of Graduate Schools, chair of the Midwest Association of Graduate Schools, chair of the National

Association of State Universities and Land-Grant Colleges (NASULGC) Council on Research Policy and Graduate Education, and president of the AAU Associations of Graduate Schools. He currently serves as chair of the N-Division Technical Review Committee and chair of the Physics and Advanced Technologies Directorate Review Committee at Lawrence Livermore National Laboratory.

ENVISIONING THE FUTURE OF DOCTORAL EDUCATION

PART ONE

INTRODUCTION

PREPARING STEWARDS
OF THE DISCIPLINE

*Chris M. Golde, The Carnegie Foundation
for the Advancement of Teaching*

*We view the doctorate as a degree that exists at the junction
of the intellectual and moral. The Ph.D. is expected to serve as
a steward of her discipline or profession, dedicated to the
integrity of its work in the generation, critique, transformation,
transmission, and use of its knowledge.*

—Lee S. Shulman, President, The Carnegie Foundation
for the Advancement of Teaching

THE FIRST DOCTORATE in the United States was awarded in 1861; by
1900 a total of about 3,500 doctorates had been granted, and by 1960
the annual production exceeded 10,000 per year. Now, at the start of the
twenty-first century, more than 40,000 doctoral degrees are awarded
annually. The number of universities granting doctorates has grown from
14 in 1920 to over 400 today. Whereas Americans once went to Europe
for the doctoral degree, now people come from around the globe to pursue the doctorate in the United States. By many measures, this is a tremendous success story.

By other measures, the story is not so clearly one of unqualified success. Indeed, throughout this century of maturation, the purpose of the

doctorate has been questioned, beginning with William James's essay "The Ph.D. Octopus," in which he warned against the development of "a tyrannical machine with unforeseen powers of exclusion and corruption" (1903, p. 152). Although there is strong evidence that doctoral recipients trained in the United States are excellent researchers and scholars and can look forward to rewarding careers, it is important to continue to strive to make doctoral education the best possible preparation for the next generation of disciplinary leaders. Disciplines continue to change, as do universities, the job market, the character of professional work, and the student population. Over time, changing conditions may mean that doctoral programs no longer effectively meet their purposes, as some practices are rendered obsolete. In fact, doctoral education may have lost sight of its central purpose.

Some of the most important changes in the context of graduate education include:

- *Time-to-career continues to increase.* In the sciences, the current expectation is that a new Ph.D. must complete one or two postdoctoral positions before being eligible for a permanent position. Likewise, humanities Ph.D.'s are likely to take a series of temporary positions before securing a tenure-track job.

- *Every discipline is evolving, with its boundaries expanding and changing.* The resulting redefinition of intellectual identity is often fraught with tension. The challenge for doctoral education is to help students be flexible and interdisciplinary, and to balance this with the enormous amount that students are expected to know.

- *Financial support for doctoral students is a complex and dynamic ecosystem, dependent on changing federal and state priorities.* In the science fields, students are supported on a faculty entrepreneurship model, in which externally funded research supports graduate students as well as faculty. In the humanities, students are supported by a combination of university fellowships, teaching positions, and debt. There is considerable difference among universities and departments in whether and how students are supported.

- *Although research is largely an international enterprise, federal policies affect flows of students into and out of the United States.* Currently, the number of international graduate students coming to the United States is shrinking. At the same time, other countries are reaching out to those students, and many national systems are being systematically improved.

Although conditions are changing, some vexing problems seem to perpetually plague American doctoral programs. Studies and reports of the 1990s echo their counterparts from the 1970s and 1980s, emphasizing ways in which conventional doctoral programs do not meet the needs of students, employers, and society.

- *Many Ph.D. recipients are ill-prepared to function effectively in the settings in which they work.* Many new faculty members do not feel ready to carry out the range of roles asked of them, particularly those related to teaching. Ph.D. recipients who work outside the academy struggle to make that transition. In most departments, the most visible and valued career path for doctoral students is into the professorate, even in fields that have historically had many students move into government or industry settings.

- *In most disciplines, women and ethnic minorities are underrepresented among doctoral students.* There seem to be systematic biases in doctoral training that deflect some kinds of students from entering doctoral study, successfully completing it, and entering faculty careers.

- *Doctoral student attrition in many departments approaches (or even exceeds) 50 percent.* This loss of talent is particularly troubling when the decision to leave (by the student or the department) occurs after several years of study. Too many departments do not have accurate records and are unable to discern rates or patterns of attrition.

------- ○ -------

We began our work on the doctorate at The Carnegie Foundation for the Advancement of Teaching by posing the question: *What is the purpose of doctoral education?*

We propose that the purpose of doctoral education, taken broadly, is to educate and prepare those to whom we can entrust the vigor, quality, and integrity of the field. This person is a scholar first and foremost, in the fullest sense of the term—someone who will creatively generate new knowledge, critically conserve valuable and useful ideas, and responsibly transform those understandings through writing, teaching, and application. We call such a person a "steward of the discipline." The idea of stewardship is at the heart of The Carnegie Foundation's work on doctoral education and is explored in the essays collected in this volume.

The Carnegie Initiative on the Doctorate

In 2001, The Carnegie Foundation undertook a five-year project—the Carnegie Initiative on the Doctorate (CID). The CID is an action and research project focused on aligning the purpose and practices of doctoral education in six disciplines. After elaborating on the idea of stewardship, which is described in more detail shortly, we began the activities of the initiative. With a goal of examining and improving doctoral programs at institutions across North America, the CID works in partnership with departments committed to restructuring their doctoral programs to better prepare their graduates as stewards of the discipline.

The CID Project

The CID focuses its work in six disciplines that span a range of disciplinary areas and traditions.

THE DISCIPLINES. Chemistry, education, English, history, mathematics, and neuroscience are the fields on which the CID concentrates. Focusing on a few disciplines allows us to get to know a discipline very well, understand the nuances of the differences between departments and subfields, and appreciate the marked differences among them.

As we considered the many fields where we might concentrate the work of the CID, we took into account several factors. Not only is the knowledge base, by definition, in every discipline different from others but the ways in which knowledge is created and shared are different. Inevitably, then, doctoral education is different among the various fields of study. The history of fields differs: some were part of the academy from the very beginning, such as mathematics or history; others are recent creations, such as neuroscience, women's studies, or computer science. The career paths of graduates may lead nearly exclusively to the academy, as in English, or to a broad range of careers, as in chemistry and education. The size of the enterprise varies: fewer than sixty doctorates are granted per year in classics and nearly two thousand in chemistry. On many other measures—time-to-career, attrition rate, funding patterns, demographic diversity of students, scope and structure of a dissertation—there is considerable variation among the fields.

We deliberately chose fields that grant a sizeable number of doctorates. We also chose these six disciplines because they represent both core liberal arts fields and emergent interdisciplinary fields. They span the humanities, the professions, and the physical and life sciences; only the social sciences are under-represented, although they are present in some parts of history and education.

THE DEPARTMENTS. We selected eighty-four departments that had applied to participate in the CID. Participating departments are committed to designing and implementing doctoral programs that foster stewardship of the discipline. Department members—faculty and students—are engaged in a process of reflection, implementation of program changes, and assessment that will lead to strategies for the creation of stronger doctoral programs, both in the participating departments and in each discipline.

The premise of the CID is that doctoral education will be improved if conversations about the purpose of, mechanisms for, and the particular elements of doctoral education and mentoring become routine and public.

Products of the CID

Throughout the initiative, The Carnegie Foundation and the participating departments are distilling the results of discussions and research and sharing them with the doctoral education and disciplinary communities. The Carnegie Foundation is studying the design experiments and preparing to share the lessons learned in order to catalyze change more broadly. A variety of products will result from the initiative, including models of experimental doctoral programs, research and analysis of the experiments and deliberations, and institutional and policy recommendations.

This book of essays is the first product of the CID. Each of the sixteen essays commissioned by The Carnegie Foundation for the CID addresses one of the six disciplines spanned by the CID. Taken together, the essays in the volume provide opportunities to compare and contrast doctoral education among the disciplines. The essays provide ideas for fruitful practice, a perspective on doctoral education as a larger enterprise, and visions of the possible.

Assumptions of the CID

The CID is an exercise in field building and knowledge building. The strategies of the initiative rest on four assumptions about doctoral education and how to catalyze change in doctoral education:

GROUND THE WORK IN DISCIPLINES. As already described, the CID is focusing on six disciplines in order to gain specific understanding and to have a disciplinewide impact. Consequently, we foreground the expertise of disciplinary leaders and disciplinary societies. The Carnegie Foundation and our educational researchers are given a back seat to the voices and perspectives of leaders in the disciplines. Whether it is the definition of problems or solutions, chemists speak to chemists and historians to historians.

GROUND THE WORK IN DEPARTMENTS. Not only do we focus on disciplines but within disciplines we assume that the key educational community is the academic department—the nexus of the discipline and the institution. Some of the institutional characteristics that shape all departments in the institution include financial resources, institutional prestige, geographic location, institutionwide policies, and institutional mission. The discipline also shapes the department, particularly through the shared disciplinary norms, intellectual core, nature of work, and job market of the field. Not only is the department uniquely the product of its discipline and institutional home, it is also molded by its history and current members. The members of the department shape the culture, climate, and lived practices of the department.

Individuals and departments who organize and implement graduate education programs are, for the most part, thoughtful and committed to creating a high-quality education for their students. Nevertheless, program development often takes place without collective deliberation and documentation, and may rely more on tradition than on a shared vision of the purpose of doctoral education. Consequently, the practice of doctoral education advances more slowly than is necessary and can be out of synch with the developmental needs of students.

IDEAS ARE POWERFUL INCENTIVES FOR CHANGE. Big ideas are more compelling and more persuasive than either financial incentives or lists of "best practices." Academics, perhaps more than average Americans, are captivated and moved by important ideas. Puzzles, tensions, paradoxes, visions of the possible, and difficult challenges—all of these motivate and engage the lively and sophisticated minds that make up today's academic departments. The structure of a doctoral program is a defined set of strategies in service of larger goals: teaching, research, and stewardship. Therefore, thorough discussions of the purpose of doctoral education must be at the heart of efforts to change American doctoral education.

OTHER DISCIPLINES HAVE MUCH TO OFFER. We also recognize that there is much that those in one field can learn from another. Here our attention is not so much focused on the kinds of learning that come from multidisciplinary explorations (where one field learns the tools, techniques, or paradigms of another) but from investigating the same question of making doctoral education as effective as possible. Every field has strategies for doctoral education that serve remarkably well, and other disciplines can learn from these practices.

----------- o -----------

Given these four core assumptions, our first step was to commission essays for each of the six disciplines on the challenges of doctoral education in that field. The essays speak to doctoral education in that particular discipline and capture the nuances of that field. Written by leading scholars within the field—stewards of their disciplines—the essays focus on ideas, not solely on technical details, and provide valuable models to readers from other fields.

Charge to the Essayists

Essayists were invited to reconceive or reinvent the forms and structures of doctoral education in their particular discipline. We offered a framing question: If you could start *de novo*, what would be the best way to structure doctoral education in your field?

The idea that the purpose of doctoral education is the preparing of stewards of the discipline raises several related questions:

1. What constitutes knowledge and understanding in the discipline?
2. What is the nature of stewardship of the discipline?
3. How ought Ph.D.'s be educated and prepared?

The essayists also received a longer description of stewardship, similar to the one that follows.

Roles and Skills of a Steward

What does it mean to be a steward of the discipline? Stewardship encompasses, on the one hand, a set of roles and skills, and, on the other, a set of principles. The former ensure competence, and the latter provide the moral compass. Stewardship establishes the purpose of doctoral education.

Regardless of whether or not one sees the doctorate as a professional degree in the strictest sense, there are parallels between the doctorate and the learned professions. The goal of professional education is to inculcate those we educate with the highest levels of competence and integrity.

Upon entry into practice, all professionals assume at least a tacit responsibility for the quality and integrity of their own work and that of colleagues. They also take on a responsibility to the larger public for the standards of practice associated with the profession. Likewise, we believe that Ph.D. recipients bear responsibility for the integrity of their discipline. Just as a lawyer is not only an advocate for clients but an officer of the court, and a doctor is responsible for the health of the patient as well as the health of the commons, so, too, a Ph.D. is a steward of the discipline, not simply a research specialist in one subfield.

The doctorate should signal a high level of accomplishment in three facets of the discipline: generation, conservation, and transformation. A Ph.D. holder should be capable of *generating* new knowledge and defending knowledge claims against challenges and criticism, *conserving* the most important ideas and findings that are a legacy of past and current work, and *transforming* knowledge that has been generated and conserved by explaining and connecting it to ideas from other fields. All of this implies the ability to teach well to a variety of audiences, including those outside formal classrooms.

GENERATION. The Ph.D., at its heart, is a research degree. Demonstrating the ability to conduct research and scholarship that make a unique contribution and meet the standards of credible work is the culminating experience of the Ph.D. This accomplishment is traditionally displayed in the dissertation. The Ph.D. signifies that the recipient is able to ask interesting and important questions, to formulate appropriate strategies for investigating these questions, to conduct investigations with a high degree of competence, to analyze and evaluate the results of the investigations, and to communicate the results to others to advance the field.

A steward is expected to conduct investigations according to accepted standards of rigor and quality. Commensurately, she is obliged to read and assess others' work critically, according to these standards, to ensure the quality of scholarly work. This means that a steward not only strives for excellence but also understands how irresponsible work or conduct is identified. For example, in chemistry, good research meets the standard of experimental replicability; researchers share enough data, methods, and results that others can determine the accuracy of conclusions. For historians, scholarly integrity emphasizes triangulation of data sources and the interpretation of primary texts.

CONSERVATION. Another facet of stewardship is an understanding of the history and fundamental ideas of the discipline. Disciplines evolve continuously, and stewards have responsibility for maintaining the continuity, stability, and vitality of the field. Every scholar and steward must strike a balance between mastering breadth and depth in the discipline. Typically, doctoral students learn a small area in great depth, but this deep understanding must be placed in context. Once students understand the historical context of the field—how and when important ideas, questions, perspectives, and controversies arose or fell (or were overturned)—then they can grasp the span and sweep of the field and locate themselves and their work in the disciplinary landscape. Moreover, stewards should understand how their discipline fits into the larger intellectual landscape, have a respectful understanding of the questions and paradigms of other disciplines, and understand how their discipline can speak to important questions.

What constitutes a balanced command of breadth and depth differs by discipline. For example, in physics it requires understanding the prevailing theories and worldviews but does not require more than a passing understanding of prior theories that have been overturned or supplanted. In English, stewards are expected to have a thorough knowledge of the canon broadly construed; the catchphrase "from Beowulf to Virginia Woolf" gives some flavor of the breadth of understanding expected of students before they begin their dissertations.

Conservation, as we use the term, is not intended to imply only the preservation of the ideas of the past. It does mean that disciplinary stewards are aware of the shoulders on which they stand and are able to judge which ideas are worth keeping and which have outlived their usefulness.

TRANSFORMATION. Knowledge, understanding, and insight have little meaning by themselves. The third facet of stewardship—transformation—speaks of the importance of representing and communicating ideas effectively and clearly. *Transformation* encompasses teaching in the broadest sense of the word. Those who are expert practitioners of their field will be called upon to teach, regardless of their work setting. Whether one is a classroom teacher or is working in a government laboratory, industrial setting, or policy arena, the steward must be able to convey information clearly. Stewards want others to value their knowledge and skills, which requires the ability to communicate effectively to a variety of audiences in oral and written forms.

These audiences include the disciplinary community, the community of those who are formally instructed (ranging in sophistication from graduate students to those taking one introductory course), and society at large. The steward of the discipline has responsibility for transforming knowledge and communicating to each of these communities, although each may require a different approach.

In many fields, knowledge is also applied: it is generated in the service of problem solving or greater understanding. Stewards have a responsibility to apply their knowledge, skills, findings, and insights. This might be as direct as cleaning up an oil spill or influencing legislation or helping create a museum exhibit. It may include creating and inventing, as well as patenting discoveries.

The idea of transformation also suggests that stewards must understand other disciplines, know the differences between disciplinary views of the world, and be able to appreciate and communicate across traditional boundaries.

Principles of Stewardship

The use of the label steward is deliberately intended to convey a role that transcends a collection of accomplishments and skills. It has an ethical and moral dimension. Definitions of stewardship suggest core principles of stewardship that inform the term steward of the discipline. It calls to mind various historical uses and definitions.

The *Merriam-Webster* online dictionary (www.m-w.com) defines stewardship as "the careful and responsible management of something entrusted to one's care." Emphasis is on the idea that one has been entrusted with the care of something valuable on behalf of others. A steward is a forward-looking manager. A steward of the discipline is entrusted with care of the discipline by those in the discipline on behalf of those in and beyond the discipline. Stewardship is a professional responsibility that comes with being accorded professional benefits.

Originally, the steward, or "keeper of the hall," was the official in a medieval household who was responsible for its management. The *Oxford English Dictionary* (online at dictionary.oed.com) defines stewardship as the "conduct of the office of steward; administration, management, control." The emphasis is on a broad oversight of the whole, comprising many smaller parts and functions. A steward of the discipline thinks broadly about the entire span of the discipline and understands how its constituent parts fit together.

There is an ecclesiastical definition of stewardship befitting the ecclesiastical origins of many universities. The OED says: "The responsible use of resources, especially money, time and talents, in the service of God." The origin is the Parable of the Talents, in which a man gave three of his servants each some coins to take care of in his absence. Two of the servants traded with the coins and doubled their holdings; the third was fearful of the master and buried the coins. Those who had taken risks and used the coins were rewarded; the one who had simply saved the money was punished. Here the emphasis is on investing, risk taking, and putting talents (whether coins or abilities) to work, not on hoarding and saving. A *steward of the discipline* considers the applications, uses, and purposes of the discipline and favors wise and responsible applications.

The contemporary environmental movement has adopted the word steward by focusing on sustainable resource management, so that environmental resources will be available for many generations into the future. Here the emphasis is on people living in concert with the environment and on preservation with an eye toward the future. Stewards think into the future and act on behalf of those yet to come. A steward of the discipline, then, thinks about the continuing health of the discipline and how to preserve the best of the past for those who will follow. Stewards are concerned with how to foster renewal and creativity. Perhaps most important, a steward considers how to prepare and initiate the next generations of stewards.

By invoking the term steward, we intend to convey the sense of purpose that guides action. Self-identifying as a steward implies adopting a sense of purpose that is larger than oneself. One is a steward of the discipline, not simply the manager of one's own career. By adopting as a touchstone the care of the discipline and understanding that one has been entrusted with that care by those in the field, on behalf of those in and beyond the discipline, the individual steward embraces a larger sense of purpose. The scale is both temporally large (looking to the past and the future) and broad in scope (considering the entire discipline, as well as intellectual neighbors).

There are conservative aspects to the term, implying the preservation of the past. A steward thinks about how to preserve the heart and essence of the field. But there are also important forward-looking meanings, as stewardship does not imply stasis. A steward is a caretaker who trains a critical eye toward the future. A steward must be willing to take risks and move the discipline forward.

Development of Stewards

We believe that the term *steward of the discipline* should be applied to all doctorate holders. It is not a "Hall of Fame" title reserved for the rare individual who excels in all domains of action.

Instead, stewardship comprises a set of qualities that can be developed; it is not an innate gift. We believe that defining the *development of stewards* as the purpose of doctoral education reframes the educational mission in a more constructive direction than the current unexamined default that defines success as securing an academic position or tenure. Returning to the analogy of the legal profession, the goal of legal education is to prepare lawyers who serve as officers of the court. Not all lawyers may meet this standard, but no law school aims to prepare ambulance chasers. Only a few lawyers will become officers of the court of the caliber of Learned Hand or Louis Brandeis, but it is a goal to which all should aspire. Not all scientists will be admitted to the National Academy of Sciences nor will all scholars be named Teacher of the Year, but Ph.D.'s can work to balance the roles of generation, conservation, and transformation in ways that serve the discipline with integrity. If all doctorate holders are admitted to the guild of stewards, then it is useful to consider how members can continue to grow and mature as stewards throughout their career.

The most important period of a steward's formation occurs during formal doctoral education. "Generation" has been the most thoroughly developed aspect of doctoral education. Nevertheless, we often do not deliberately consider or explicitly articulate our theories and strategies on the pedagogy of research for developing excellent researchers. Development of the skills, knowledge, habits, and abilities of conservation and transformation is even less systematic.

In reading the essays that follow, it is important to recognize that the formulation of what *stewardship* means is discipline-specific. What it means to be a steward of chemistry differs from, say, English or mathematics. By drafting this general formulation of stewardship, we intend to provide a framework for discipline-specific conversations.

Within a particular discipline, what shape do generation, conservation, and transformation take? How are the various facets of work undertaken with integrity and with the principles of stewardship in mind? What are the responsibilities to the field? How are stewards of the discipline best developed? The preparation of stewards is the central issue of this volume. It was the guiding issue before the essayists whose views make up the bulk of this volume.

The Essays and Essayists

The charge posed to the essayists was, "If you could start *de novo*, what would be the best way to structure doctoral education in your field?" Essayists were to accept that a key purpose of doctoral education is the development of "stewardship of the discipline." Each author took the spirit of our inquiry and shaped a highly personal answer. This makes the collection lively and nuanced. The style and format of the essays reflect the habits of mind that are inculcated in each field. The individuality of the essays is one of their great delights.

The Essayists

In each of the six disciplines, we commissioned two, and sometimes three, authors to provide multiple and diverging perspectives. In selecting the essayists, we sought the voices of those with prominence and standing in their field and who had already shown themselves to be thoughtful about doctoral education. Our decision is not without its critics. Indeed, by selecting leading scholars, many of whom are toward the end of their career, we created a collection with a conservative bias.

We do not directly reflect the perspectives of students or newly minted scholars. Arguably, those would be the individuals who most clearly understand the shortcomings of prevailing approaches to doctoral education. Not only does this collection lack a diversity of generational voices, it also reflects a conservative institutional perspective. This betrays not a bias of The Carnegie Foundation but rather the strong prestige and status pressures that continue to operate in American higher education. Whether leading scholars are recruited to a small group of institutions or whether those at the elite institutions are automatically believed to be "leading scholars," the institutional biases of this collection are clear. The authors are senior faculty members at AAU-member universities. And the constraints of the project meant that only two or three essayists were tapped in each field; consequently, there cannot be adequate subdisciplinary representation. (This is most obvious in history, where three Americanists are writing.) Still, with all these caveats and with all the potential conservatism and complacency that one might expect, the collected essays certainly fill their intended goal of provoking and stimulating.

Organization of the Volume

The sixteen essays at the heart of this volume are organized according to discipline, and each discipline is introduced with a short overview of doctoral education in the field. Before delving into the essays, however, readers will find three commentaries that look across the broad themes of the essays and consider the implications for action. These commentaries consider the implications of the essayists' ideas for various constituencies. Doctoral education is an enterprise with many stakeholders whose interests sometimes compete and sometimes converge. Putting the concerns of, in turn, institutional leaders (Ken Prewitt), faculty members (David Damrosch), and graduate and postdoctoral students (Crispin Taylor) at the center provides three different lenses for viewing the disciplinary essays.

These overview commentaries follow immediately after this introductory chapter and provide tantalizing glimpses of the essays that we hope will tempt the reader to move well beyond his or her home field. Indeed, in our experience, many readers will find in the offerings from other fields fresh descriptions of familiar problems and new slants on possible solutions.

To help set the larger context and offer further challenges to thinkers and practitioners, an essay on the broad area of the sciences (Yehuda Elkana) introduces the collection of essays.

Working by discipline from science to the humanities, we start with mathematics (Hyman Bass and Tony Chan), then chemistry (Alvin Kwiram, Ronald Breslow, and Angelica Stacy), followed by neuroscience (Zach Hall and Steven Hyman). Education (Virginia Richardson and David Berliner), like neuroscience a multidisciplinary field of study, is next. We follow these with essays from history (Thomas Bender, Joyce Appleby, and William Cronon)—part social science, part humanities—and then English (Andrea Lunsford and Gerald Graff). An essay focusing on the humanities (Catharine Stimpson) follows.

The concluding essay, written by George Walker, the CID project director, poses a number of provocative questions. He invites readers to conduct a "thought experiment"—his model for creating the energy and momentum that help transform ideas into action. He challenges departments, or at least a critical mass of their faculty and graduate students, to engage in serious deliberation and creation of their own vision of the future. This is not easy. It involves looking forward and not being overly concerned with the constraints and obstacles that seem so difficult to overcome.

Learning from the Essays

The goal of these essays is to start a conversation. We think it terribly important that every graduate faculty and every doctoral student consider, individually and collectively, the purpose of doctoral education and the characteristics of a doctoral recipient. All too often the assumptions are implicit and are never clarified or debated among faculty members; neither are they discussed with or among students. These tacit assumptions can lead to misunderstandings, as well as diffusion of purpose and even contradictory understandings and practices. Our starting questions— What is the purpose of doctoral education? and If you could start *de novo,* what would be the best way to structure doctoral education in your field?—are intended to prompt lively debates.

These essays should provoke. If they do their job, they will unsettle the reader. They call conventional practices into question. Just as often, they affirm conventional practices, which may be equally surprising. They should spark the reader's imagination and prompt consideration of other disciplines that can provide ideas and grist for the mill.

These essays are the *first* word in a discussion, not the last. They are *not* to be read as definitive proposals or recipes that will be adopted wholesale (although some authors may hope for such a response!). Nor should they be read as position papers advocating the stance of The Carnegie Foundation for the Advancement of Teaching.

How to Use the Essays

The effect of these essays has already been to spark debate and deliberation within a number of the doctorate-granting departments participating in the CID. Their experiences suggest ways to use the essays as part of a class, department retreat, conference panel, student event, or faculty meeting:

- Select a few essays as common starting points. Which points resonated? With which points do you disagree?

- Construct, for your discipline:

  A list of the shared values of disciplinary practitioners, like the detailed one in William Cronon's essay;

  A chart of the crucial elements of scholarly inquiry and student learning, like the one that appears at the end of Virginia Richardson's chapter;

  A list of "curricular enhancement" elements and when they should be incorporated into doctoral study, like the one Alvin Kwiram provides;

  A list of qualities or capacities of the professional who is educated for stewardship of the discipline, like the ones written by Thomas Bender and Hyman Bass.

- Select one or two ideas and conduct a thought experiment: What would the implications be of restructuring our program to incorporate (or eliminate) that feature or requirement? If the ideas come from quite divergent fields, the thought experiment can be friskier: What are the essential features of a "lab" that can translate from chemistry to English? Could one eliminate, or institute, several years of course work? What would a "contested ideas" course, of the sort proposed by Gerald Graff, look like in mathematics?

- Several authors (David Berliner, Ronald Breslow, Tony Chan, Gerald Graff) provide lists of specific practical suggestions. Can these translate to your department or discipline?

- Organize an introductory seminar for doctoral students around reading and debating the essays. First-year doctoral students have not yet been hardened into the norms and mores of the discipline. What ideas that are taken for granted seem dispensable? Which questions asked in a different discipline have resonance?

- Conduct the four-step thought experiment proposed by George Walker. What visions emerge? What answers to the many questions he poses become apparent?

Themes Across the Essays

One way of appreciating the shared challenges facing doctoral education is by looking at the ways similar problems are framed and resolved. The following ten issues are each discussed at some length in the listed essays (and others give them mention as well). This is not an exhaustive list but gives a flavor of the span of the essays; we hope it will encourage the reader to sample widely in the collection:

- The importance of preparing doctoral students in the art, craft, and science of teaching is addressed by ten of the essayists, who discuss this matter specifically: Appleby, Bass, Breslow, Bender, Chan, Cronon, Graff, Kwiram, Lunsford, and Stacy.

- As Cronon reminds us, "the tendency of all guilds is to turn inward," and several essayists specifically advocate for an increased emphasis on intellectual breadth and awareness of the larger disciplinary context: Bender, Breslow, Chan, Cronon, Hyman, Kwiram, and Stacy. Indeed, Hyman goes so far as to propose a "functional test" for breadth.

- The question, "Who should the next generation of graduate students be?" as Stimpson phrases it, is addressed by Chan, Lunsford, Stacy, and Stimpson.

- The future of the discipline and the new intellectual problems with which it must contend are challenges ("Grand Challenges," Breslow calls them) explicitly articulated by Bender, Breslow, Chan, and Hall. Graff's essay details an important object lesson: it is too

easy to meet new challenges by adding new faculty or new programs; it is much harder to make choices among competing
visions.

- Engaging with "large questions and projects," to use Lunsford's
phrase, whether in "contested issues" courses (Graff) or emphasizing "big ideas" (Berliner) as a way to inculcate students into
important disciplinary conversations is included in the essays by
Appleby, Berliner, Elkana, Graff, and Lunsford.

- The role and responsibilities of advisers and mentors—an issue
often raised by students—is discussed by Bender, Chan, Cronon,
Elkana, and Stacy.

- The development of "practical knowledge," to use Richardson's
label, or "professional skills," Breslow's term, in the curriculum
and through mentoring, is a specific concern raised by Breslow,
Chan, Kwiram, and Richardson.

- The creation, using Stimpson's words, of "academic citizens, members of a public," through engagement with policy and practice in
the larger world, is addressed by Appleby, Bass, Berliner, Elkana,
and Stimpson.

- Richardson calls for inculcating values and integrity, as do Breslow
and Kwiram, who focus on ethics.

- The diversity of career paths, or what Hall calls the "recent expansion of professional opportunities," and the attendant challenge
for doctoral programs, is tackled in the essays by Bender, Chan,
Graff, Hall, and Stimpson.

Finally, and perhaps most centrally, many of the essayists focus on the
challenges involved in preparing excellent researchers. While arguing that
most research preparation in U.S. doctoral programs is of high quality,
specific challenges emerge: maintaining rigor and quality (Elkana and
Hyman), developing independence and creativity (Breslow, Stacy), fostering curiosity (Appleby, Stimpson), addressing the challenges of collaboration (Lunsford), encouraging risk taking (Elkana), making better use of
the high stakes and intellectual challenges of problem and project selection (Cronon, Elkana), and understanding the importance and difficulties
of working interdisciplinarily (Bender, Cronon, Hall, and Stimpson).

As I said at the start of this chapter, graduate education faces changed
circumstances, whether we wish to recognize them and whether our doctoral programs respond to them or not. Globalization of knowledge, as
Yehuda Elkana describes most forcefully, is one of these. New practices

may include coauthored dissertations, such as Andrea Lunsford describes, and similar adaptations to the changed ways in which interdisciplinary science is done.

This book articulates many questions regarding the future of doctoral education that have been raised in the last fifteen years and begins to provide some answers to them. Those who take the challenges seriously and deeply can consider the possible strategies suggested by these essayists and will then have the opportunity to create new forms of doctoral education that will truly create stewards of the discipline. The issues are complex, and solutions require deep thinking, hard work, and the goodwill of many people. We are encouraged that so many faculty, students, staff, administrators, and postdocs find these matters worth taking seriously. We invite you to join the conversation.

Acknowledgment

Before the reader turns to the essays, I want to conclude with a thank you. This volume owes a great deal to Ellen Wert. She served as the editor for each of the essays. A good editor is like a gem cutter. She looks at a diamond in the rough and sees its potential. She works carefully, but with a sure hand, to help the sparkling essence emerge. She both shapes and polishes. Ellen's light touch, deft editing suggestions, and deep knowledge of doctoral education allowed the core ideas of each author to shine. We are greatly indebted to her for making this collection a set of jewels.

REFERENCES

James, W. "The Ph.D. Octopus," *Harvard Monthly,* Mar. 1903, 149–157. Reprinted in *William James, Writings 1902–1910.* New York: Library of America, 1987, 1111–1118.

PART TWO

COMMENTARIES

2

WHO SHOULD DO *WHAT?*

IMPLICATIONS FOR INSTITUTIONAL
AND NATIONAL LEADERS

Kenneth Prewitt, Columbia University

IF THE *WHAT* IS REFORMING DOCTORAL TRAINING, the *who* are higher education's institutional and national leaders. Reforming doctoral training will falter unless those who control entry into doctoral training, fellowship and research funds, postdoctoral positions, tenure criteria, career options, publication outlets, awards and prizes, and related gate-keeping resources deploy them in ways that urge the array of reforms our essayists bring to the fore. Incentive systems etch the pathways that reforms follow. If needed reforms are best fashioned by those close to the practices that need changing, appropriate modification of the incentive systems is more of a top-down effort, carried out by leaders who look across the entire landscape and see how the elements fit together.

The genius of doctoral training in American higher education is that *no one is in charge.* The hold of this fundamental principle on our thinking is implicitly revealed in the sixteen essays collected in this volume. They are bold in the reforms recommended. But they are timid, in fact mostly silent, about who will have to align institutional habits, budgets, rules, and incentives if the reforms are to move from pages in this volume to practices in research universities. That no one is in charge cannot be taken to mean that no one above the faculty level has responsibilities.

In higher education, reform co-evolves as a process that joins ideas from students and faculty with incentives designed by institutional and national leaders. Reform does not happen dissertation by dissertation or even department by department. It happens because criteria by which applicants are selected for doctoral training link to the curriculum, mentoring, funding, and dissertation work that make up graduate training, which in turn feeds into the career paths, research opportunities, teaching roles, and stewardship responsibilities that make up the mature professional life. It is a system. At issue is whether it is coherently and self-consciously assembled or accidentally so, with incentives that pull in contradictory directions. The essayists repeatedly say that doctoral training should prepare for teaching as well as research, and then just as frequently tell us that incentives work against this obviously desirable outcome. The essayists do not say why this is so. But when goals and incentives are misaligned, a prime suspect is leadership failure.

I risk oversimplifying when I say that the reforms urged in the essays call for attention either by disciplinary leaders (and are mostly about content or *what* is taught) or by university leaders (and are mostly about process or *how* it is taught). An example of the former is a seminar on improving time-to-degree—something we would expect chairs, rather than deans or provosts, to take responsibility for. An example of the latter is interdisciplinary research with multiple supervisors—something hard to engineer at the departmental level but possible (perhaps) with strong leadership by a dean or provost. It would not do to push the distinction too far, for many of the reforms require action at more than one level. An example is the call for doctoral-level team research, which would have to be engineered at the department level but would also require new university rules about what is acceptable as a dissertation—a policy for the provost's office.

Still, it will be convenient to sort through the changes that primarily involve disciplinary leadership and those that involve transdisciplinary leadership. In both categories, there are local and national leaders; disciplinary leaders are not just department chairs. They include officers of discipline-based professional associations such as the American Chemical Society or the Modern Language Association, as well as editors of the disciplinary journals. Similarly, transdisciplinary leadership is not limited to university officers. It includes those in charge of a wide range of national scholarly and scientific associations, ranging from funding institutions such the National Institutes of Health, National Science Foundation, and National Endowment for the Humanities to membership institutions such as the American Association for the Advancement of Science to honorific organizations such as the National Academies of Science and the American Academy of Arts and Sciences; leadership also includes the editors of journals that draw from many disciplines; examples are *Science, Daedalus,* or the *American Scholar.*

Disciplinary Challenges

The disciplines range from neuroscience, presented by Zach Hall and Steven Hyman as a discipline (or maybe a field) that is still in its early formation and emerging from as many as half-dozen or more existing disciplines, to English, where, as Gerald Graff notes, a traditional core has given way to intellectual disagreements and turf conflicts which, he recommends, should now be self-consciously taught as a way to reconfigure the discipline ("teach the conflicts"). Catharine Stimpson echoes this in celebrating the "messiness" of the humanities. Yehuda Elkana extends Stimpson's point to the sciences as well, though other essays, particularly for chemistry and math, suggest greater certainty about core methodologies and research agendas. They nonetheless share in the larger project of how best to reconfigure their boundaries in order to connect with other disciplines.

History occupies a somewhat different space, because there was and continues to be good historical writing that owes nothing to doctoral training. It is, in this regard, both a discipline defined by its doctoral programs and a body of literature whose ever-changing interpretations cannot be limited to the professionally trained historian. Education, notes Virginia Richardson, also has a hybrid nature. It is part discipline and part profession and exists, like the profession of law or business, only in relation to the world of practice that it engages. In education, then, stewardship implies responsibility toward the enterprise of education generally, as well as focus on doctoral programs.

Although distinctions among the disciplines matter for how doctoral training can be reformed, I pay less attention to these distinctions than to the themes common to all the disciplines represented in the project. Prominent among the issues that appear across the essays is the lament that doctoral training is poorly aligned with the careers actually available to a large number—in some instances the majority—of those who earn the Ph.D.

Elkana notes that "a vast majority of those with a doctorate in science will not remain within academe. Perhaps not more than 10 percent will be faculty at elite universities, and around 40 to 50 percent in any academic institution." The rest find nonacademic employment. This is not a new assertion and perhaps is all the more devastating because it has been around for some years. In Alvin Kwiram's essay on chemistry, lack of fit between training and career is the central theme: "All the tasks the [recent Ph.D.] now faces are ones for which she has had no formal preparation. This approach is not optimized to ensure success. Indeed, the mismatch between training and task is glaring."

Kwiram differs from his fellow essayists only in the amount of attention he gives to misalignment. Scattered across the other essays, as in many preceding reports, are numerous references to non-teaching but professionally meaningful careers for which the doctorate is the entry degree: neuroscientists and chemists in industry, historians in museums, mathematicians in federal agencies, educational psychologists in think tanks, and humanists in publishing and film. And for every discipline there is the option of intensive teaching in colleges, which allows little time for the laboratory and the library. Seldom does doctoral education give sustained attention to the skills appropriate to these careers, even though these are destination points for a large number of Ph.D.'s. Career preparation is not even satisfactory for the new Ph.D.'s who get tenure-track positions in research universities. Although prepared to do original research, they seldom are adequately prepared for their teaching duties or their more general professional obligations. Notes chemistry professor Angelica Stacy, "None of us are prepared to teach." Beyond teaching and research, "there remain numerous other basic professional functions for which little or no mentoring may have been provided." This is a similar observation from Hyman Bass about mathematics; he includes a list of such topics as writing research proposals and preparing peer-review evaluations. Again, these are not new complaints and thus are all the more troubling.

Of all the tasks that await our disciplinary leaders, perhaps nothing is so pressing as to take a hard look at how doctoral training can be better designed to teach the skills and instill the habits of mind that, in fact, will increase the odds of career success, whether the career is in a research university, teaching college, or outside the academy. Close reading of the essays offers many practical design elements, suitably adjusted to the particularities of different disciplines. They do so without in the least giving away the core of doctoral training. It is a research degree and can remain so, even when careers do not call for a life dedicated to original research. William Cronon, writing about history, takes a position echoed across the essays: "The reform of doctoral training should focus on improving rather than replacing its research component," and this training should explicitly address "the different venues and audiences in which historical knowledge is conveyed." Put concretely, historians should know something about how documentary films are made or historical Web pages are constructed because there are rewarding career opportunities in such venues.

Every reader can bring examples to mind: successful foundation officers, academic publishers, museum curators, industrial science managers,
undergraduate teachers, and government civil servants who are good at
what they do *because* they earned a Ph.D. and then applied their training
in careers outside the academy. But examples are often the exception. The
question before disciplinary leaders is whether the exceptions can become
the rule, whether career success outside the academy can be extended,
reproduced, and generalized by reconfiguring elements of doctoral training with a view to where many of its graduates are headed.

The essays emphasize that doctoral training does not align with career
practice in another way, though now they have in view the failure to produce Ph.D.'s who can link disciplinary knowledge to public benefit. The
intellectual historian Joyce Appleby makes the point forcefully. She writes
of how historical research "impinges on the sensibilities and convictions
of the public" and then goes on to argue that the "history doctorate
should be configured for the future against this background of history's
new prominence in the public realm."

Echoes of her general point appear in the discussion of chemistry and
mathematics, where it is less the sensibilities than the economic welfare
of the public that is at issue. Tony Chan writes that society supports
mathematics and science, in part, because of its "impact on the economy
and furthering national goals [in], for example, national defense." Bass is
explicit about mathematicians contributing "advice or service in policy
environments." In a sentence you would not expect to see in an essay on
chemistry, Stacy suggests options for chemistry doctorates to go into
"public policy, social sciences, education, and business." In education,
writes David Berliner, one of the tasks is to engage policy debates and
"address the needs of society in order to make it better." Thomas Bender,
with history in mind, urges that "the public as well as peers" be taken as
an audience for the results of research.

The idea that disciplines are prominent "in the public realm" and have
"an audience" beyond disciplinary borders is coupled with the lament that
doctoral training does a poor job of preparing its Ph.D. candidates to engage
the public in any meaningful way. Candidates need to be taught a way of
thinking that will connect with responsibilities beyond the classroom, even
beyond disciplinary boundaries. Appleby's injunction that doctoral work
be configured against a background of engagement with the public realm is
a powerful challenge to disciplinary leaders, not just in history.

With respect to the more specific point about career preparation and
the more general point about responsibilities beyond the discipline, the
first order of business is to give serious attention to what is taught. Here
the essays are consistently suggestive, often bold. They do not hesitate to

argue for curricular change, new pedagogic strategies, and even different allocations of that most scarce of all resources—the graduate student's time. These are changes that, in principle, can be carried out at the level of the individual department.

If instituted only at that level, however, they will falter. An example suggests why. Several of the essayists worry about the pipeline for doctoral candidates, noting, as Andrea Lunsford does, that demographic diversity is less advanced in practice than in rhetoric. Or, from another angle, the pipeline in science and math has proportionately fewer and fewer Americans on their way to doctoral programs.

Pulling these strands together, we might imagine a mathematics doctoral candidate at a leading university who spends several hours a week working with the chess team in a nearby urban high school. She does this because she likes it, and when some of the chess players show promise as mathematicians, she gives them extra time. Though not self-consciously, this doctoral candidate is (1) encouraging minority students to strengthen their math skills and (2) increasing the odds that Americans will find a career in math and science. Incidentally, she is meeting another test of stewardship: public service. She is encouraged by her dissertation adviser who, fresh from writing a National Research Council report on the pipeline crises, sees her extracurricular work as helping to further needed reforms.

So far, this is one of those vignettes that the department will brag about in its promotional material but perhaps is not the rest of her story. The candidate completes her doctoral work with distinction and enters the job market. Despite strong departmental backing, she loses out when it comes to tenure-track positions. Colleagues in the hiring departments are asked why, and the report comes back that she looks great but has her name on fewer publications than did her competition.

This hypothetical case illustrates the difficulty of reforming doctoral education. It cannot happen one student, or even one department, at a time. Incentive and reward systems have to shift so that the candidate ahead of her times is not penalized, as is our mathematician, by hiring criteria rooted in pre-reform practices. This is where national leadership steps in. The resources they control—special fellowships, postdocs, prizes, publication opportunities—can signal that time spent in extracurricular but professionally relevant activities will not be penalized. The incentive system has to be designed so that what we now casually label "extracurricular" is no less curricular than the research seminar that would have produced one more published article and perhaps the tenure-track appointment. In the absence of this co-evolution of reform-in-practice at the individual level and alignment-of-incentives at the institutional level, next year's doctoral cohort will not produce someone eager to help the chess team.

The responsibility of leaders to align incentives with reforms is even clearer if we turn from the discipline as our unit of analysis to some of the transdisciplinary reforms embraced by the essays.

Transdisciplinary Challenges

None of the essayists were able to imagine a *de novo* start without quickly formulating an argument about the need to cross disciplinary boundaries. The essays—all written from within a discipline and all charged with answering discipline-specific questions (What is knowledge in your discipline? What is stewardship for your discipline? How should doctoral candidates in your discipline be trained?) come back time and again to formulations that refuse to accept disciplinary boundaries. These boundaries, on the testimony of our essayists, are there to be crossed, blurred, merged, reconfigured, and even ignored. There is no neuroscience without cognitive science, no history without demography, no chemistry without biology, no education without sociology, no mathematics without computational sciences, no humanities without the arts, and on and on.

To take boundary transgression seriously means, among other things, graduate courses taken in departments other than one's own, seminar assignments that work equally well for students steeped in the discipline and those with an outsider's view, dissertations read by faculty from more than one discipline, cross-department lab rotations, joint-degree programs, and joint appointments of faculty. These are familiar to us, and we know them to be more or less successful, depending on whether institutional incentives impede or promote them. We also know how hard it is to get the incentives right. Tub-on-its-own-bottom budgeting, for example, produces wrangles about how to credit the professor who offers lectures in another department and about allocating tuition funds paid in one school to another when students migrate to popular courses outside their school or department. Such budgeting has its virtues, or smart institutions would not adopt it, but easing disciplinary boundary crossing is not one of them. Even without such budget rules, there are fears that largely hidden patterns of cross-subsidization help "them" but not "us."

Other examples proliferate: taking the seminar in an adjacent discipline is great but will be avoided unless departmental prelims are capaciously written; joint appointments are applauded until conflicting tenure criteria are brought to bear and the provost has to adjudicate between a no from one department and a yes from another. So it goes, across university practices that grew up in a time of less boundary crossing than today's scholarship requires.

The old practices have a lot of staying power. Witness the revealing fact that none of the essayists, although being asked to imagine a *de novo* start and despite their repeated emphasis on boundary crossing, suggest that their department be closed down as a way to reconfigure intellectual boundaries. (To be fair, Hyman shows a tolerance for neuroscience clusters in a number of departments and schools, though he does want it to have a core departmental home as well.)

Even allowing that the departmental structure, modified with dozens of cross-departmental centers and programs, is not about to be radically transformed, the ambitious call for learning and training that will break through disciplinary boundaries requires equally ambitious changes in administrative and budgeting structures. This is not news to deans, vice presidents, and provosts. And every major research university struggles with how to design budgets and administrative practices that will encourage rather than impede new intellectual groupings. It remains to be seen whether our faculty-run research universities will cooperate as more far-reaching changes are implemented to achieve the array of curricular and appointment reforms on offer in the essays. But certainly this is an area in which aligning incentives with reforms falls to university and not just departmental leadership.[1]

Another and, as it turns out, related theme in the essays is collaboration or team research. We expect this in the sciences but note with interest that its importance is cited also in the humanities. Stimpson writes: "Collaborative practices, common to the sciences, must now take hold in the humanities. It can be done within a field, or among fields, or among arts and sciences and the professions." Lunsford believes that rethinking the Ph.D. in English involves "introducing our graduate students to the possibilities and potential of collaborative research and offering them a means of engaging in it productively." Even history, where, notes Cronon, "extreme individualism" is the norm, is pointing some of its graduates to careers in public history, "for which collaboration is essential." Working out the practicalities of collaboration in the humanities and social sciences can benefit by borrowing practices from the sciences. In chemistry, for example, Stacy informs us that "students have also done joint theses, with two advisers assisting with the same research project or two separate projects, one with each of the two advisers." Both Hall and Hyman describe "umbrella" arrangements that have allowed neuroscience to draw from numerous disciplines—arrangements that might be transferable to the humanities and social sciences.

The practical and intellectual challenges are notched up a level if collaboration is also interdisciplinary. Ronald Breslow sees the future as follows:

> [I]n the ideal Ph.D. program in chemistry, some of the research would be interdisciplinary and would involve collaboration with scientists outside the special field of the principal research sponsor. Students would learn to appreciate the expertise of scientists in other fields, while developing self-confidence as they see how their own expertise is valued by others.

This is especially important for Ph.D.'s going into chemically related industries where "it is necessary to work in teams with other scientists," and the new recruits will have "a great advantage if they have already done so as part of their graduate work." Bass makes a similar point: mathematical activity in nonacademic settings "tends to be interdisciplinary" and is "often part of a collaborative team effort" for which graduate programs should be a preparation.

Breslow, in urging Ph.D. "interdisciplinary project[s] with more than one supervisor," reaches further than the other essayists in this regard, but the sentiment behind his proposal would not, I believe, get an argument from any of his fellow essayists. The model Breslow holds out for chemistry can make inroads in many departments and disciplines, with enormous positive consequences for doctoral training and the nation's production of new knowledge.

At present, of course, the promise of doctoral preparation that is collaborative and interdisciplinary is hostage to a reward system tailored to individual achievement within a discipline. Modifying this reward system is slow going, as we know from tenure review discussions about how much credit should be given to the candidate under consideration when so much of the work is coauthored. If assessment is hard even for established scholars, assessing contributions to team research or team teaching is harder yet at the graduate-student level. It is made more difficult when collaboration is multidisciplinary but being evaluated by faculty in only one of the represented disciplines. The fact that it is difficult is no reason to avoid it, however. On the testimony of the Carnegie Essays on the Doctorate, building doctoral training around practices that are *interdisciplinary and collaborative* is our future. Funding agencies such as the pioneering effort by the National Institutes of Health for neuroscience or the National Science Foundation more generally can lead the way by rewarding collaborative and cross-discipline proposals. Aligning grant criteria with research frontiers and with institutional-practice frontiers is a powerful incentive that works its way back into doctoral training.

Doctoral Reform as Disciplinary Stewardship

I conclude with one redundant and one fresh point. I noted at the outset that the "no one is in charge" principle has guided doctoral training for a century. It is a good principle, not one to be casually tampered with. But in the vision of the CID and on the testimony of the sixteen powerful essays in this volume, doctoral training is due for some fundamental reforms. I offer the simple observation that reform occurs at two levels: (1) from students and faculty we get new ideas about how doctoral training should be reconfigured; (2) from leaders we get adjustment to the incentive systems that allow those reconfigurations to occur. This co-evolution is required, whether the reform is discipline-specific or crosses disciplines. The "no one is in charge" principle will have to make room for some strong university and national leadership.

Finally, a fresh point is illustrated with disciplines as seemingly distant from each other as the newest of the represented disciplines (neuroscience) and the oldest (history). Thirty-five years ago, there were no neuroscience doctoral training programs in the United States. Now there are nearly two hundred. Hyman writes persuasively that this new discipline faces basic questions about what constitutes neuroscience knowledge, but of one thing he is certain: the "key to coalescence of a new discipline is the graduate program." His neuroscience colleague Zach Hall agrees. He describes graduate students as the "vectors of information, skills, and ideas not only within programs but also across them."

Recorded history goes back to Herodotus. As a discipline, history shares with neuroscience porous borders and an aversion to monopolistic thinking. Yet, Cronon tells us, it is important to professional history that Ph.D.-granting activities draw "a boundary around an intellectual community" and define the "circles within which disciplinary communication takes place." Both neuroscience and history are telling us that even as (and because) the disciplines cross borders, they need an intellectual center of gravity. It is the doctoral program that defines and protects this center.

If doctoral training is intellectually sloppy or administratively incoherent, we fail our students. Our essayists say this, but then they say something that reaches further. In anchoring the disciplines in doctoral programs, the essays tell us that the disciplines are not going to be better than their doctoral programs. If we do not take care of our students, we do not take care of our disciplines. If we do not take care of our disciplines, we fail as stewards of knowledge generation, which is, after all, why we were once students ourselves and why today we read and write essays about improving doctoral programs.

NOTES

1. Shortly after completing my essay, I discovered a summary of research directly related to how university incentives often operate as barriers to interdisciplinary research. The project examined six National Science Foundation Environmental Research and Education centers. The principal investigator, Diana Rhoten, focuses on three factors that affect interdisciplinary collaboration: (1) the motivation of individual scholars, (2) the support of funding agencies, and (3) what she labels the "middle level" or university-based practices. Her key finding is that it is at this middle level that cross-boundary collaboration fails. Universities, she finds, rename but don't redesign. This failure has "actually created incentives that are inherently incapable of achieving the very goals they seek to accomplish" (p. 9).

REFERENCES

Rhoten, D. "Interdisciplinary Research: Trend or Transition?" *Items & Issues,* 2004, *5*(1–2), pp. 6–11.

3

VECTORS OF CHANGE

David Damrosch, Columbia University

THE SIXTEEN ESSAYS at the center of this volume reveal commonalities that are at once inspiring and depressing. It is inspiring to see a broad convergence across widely disparate disciplines, as the essayists discuss their different institutional situations in very compatible ways. Given the infrequency with which humanists and scientists interact, it is striking to find many comparable ideas for structural reform percolating on both sides of the divide of the "two cultures," as well as among the social sciences in the methodological borderlands in between. With virtual unanimity, our essayists praise the growth of interdisciplinary work and discuss the need to find a new balance of disciplinary rigor and cross-disciplinary breadth; they promote the value of team teaching, and they advance ideas for new sorts of collaborative work, whether in labs or on dissertations. Taken together, these separately written essays reveal nothing less than an emerging pedagogical "consilience," to use Edwin Wilson's term, which suggests the outlines of a substantial shift in the goals and methods of graduate education.

Yet the very similarity of so many proposals in essay after essay is depressing as well: if everybody knows what needs to be done, why are so few programs doing it? Not only are the present essays largely in agreement; very often, they echo recommendations already made by panels in their discipline a decade ago (Breslow, for instance) or even half a century ago (Kwiram). For all our awareness of living in a time of rapid change, these essays suggest that many of our graduate programs do not run so very differently than they did when our own teachers were graduate students. As the riddle goes, "How many Princeton professors does it take to change a light bulb?" The answer (to be given in a tone of bemused incredulity): "*Change?*"

I was told this joke by a Princeton professor, who may have felt that his institution has a special claim to its punch line, but probably most academics would find many ways in which it could resonate on their own campuses as well. This resonance too has a long history: think of F. M. Cornford's brilliant satire *Microcosmographia Academica,* published in 1908 and reprinted many times since, which dissects the machinations of the faculty at turn-of-the-century Cambridge as they strove to preserve the status quo. A series of major reforms had recently been stifled there, and Cornford shows how factions like the Liberal Conservatives and the Conservative Liberals combine to prevent any change at all from occurring on their campus, wielding such arguments as the unanswerable "it has never been tried" and (equally unanswerable) "it was tried in 1867."

Why is change so difficult to achieve? We are not talking about the weather, after all, but our graduate programs, over which faculty have retained an exceptional degree of control, even as many other areas of academic management have devolved to the full-time administration. As Tony Chan says in his essay, "There is no shortage of ideas about *what* we need to change. We have to decide whether or not we *want* to change." The following pages will describe some of the constraints on change and some real opportunities that our collected essays suggest. "It is not enough to rethink the doctorate," as Yehuda Elkana says in his bracing essay. "We have to rethink the faculty."

Limitations of Success

There are serious constraints on our ability to rethink the faculty. The first is that we academics are better placed to solve the world's problems than our own. It is hard to get an analytical purchase on the situation in which we are immersed. We thus face, in a heightened form, the problem of the "participant observer" that has generated so much discussion among anthropologists. Moreover, our immersion is deepened (and our observation accordingly obscured) by the fact that tenured faculty are prime beneficiaries of the present system, profiting from graduate students' labor in many ways large and small, from research assistance to paper grading to routine lab work to the sheer opportunity to teach our favorite research subjects at an advanced level. Even the dysfunctions of the current system have their silver linings—not for the students but for the faculty. Ph.D. programs can live for decades at a time with attrition rates of 50 percent or more, for example, in part because a high level of attrition is doubly beneficial to the faculty, giving us a plentiful supply of beginners to teach (and to do our grading), while sparing us a corresponding overload of dissertation advising at the other end of the program. No faculty member would make a direct calculation of such a cost-benefit ratio, but we are so used to the system that we can readily avoid facing its real problems when they do not impinge on us, and all the more if they silently benefit us in unexamined ways.

Our ability to confront the limitations of our programs is further diminished by the fact that the tenured faculty at doctorate-granting institutions are all people for whom the present system has worked well. Possibly, we could wish to move to some more prestigious institution or have some added benefits where we are, but these are minor adjustments in a context of overall success. Universities offer few rewards greater than tenure at a Research I institution (where the majority of doctorates are granted), and the chief beneficiaries of a system are rarely the best people to reform it. As living proof of the system's success, tenured faculty may have little awareness of what the system's disadvantages may have been for the unlucky few—in fact, the many—who have dropped out along the way or who have failed to find a job they like. Many others have been served adequately, not optimally, by their graduate training and may have good ideas for what could have been done better, but they are now employed at an undergraduate institution or outside academia altogether; they no longer have any direct say in the governance of a graduate program. At the very point at which people can look back at their graduate experience and assess it fully, a few years out, most people who would advocate real change are no longer part of the discussion.

Many who go on to work in two- and four-year colleges, in high schools, and in nonacademic careers are, of course, very happily employed in such venues, but graduate programs are generally not very good at keeping in touch with alumni. We know that people who have adapted well to careers beyond the research university often have a lively sense that their graduate training didn't prepare them very well for their actual professional lives. This is yet another way in which the reproductive model of mentoring pervades our system, as we train our students largely for jobs in programs like our own, even though doctorate-granting institutions will only be able to employ some 10 percent of our graduates. Several of our essays touch on this problem, but it cannot be solved only by introspection on the part of the minority who have found employment in doctorate-granting schools. We need to broaden the conversation as much as possible—intellectually, experientially, and even in basic personal terms.

I have argued elsewhere that our long apprenticeships, first as graduate students and then as untenured faculty, serve to weed out people who
are not happy with the present system and to select for people who work
well in an atmosphere of heightened individualism and lowered intellectual sociability (1995). As Catharine Stimpson puts it in her essay, "The
humanities are hardly an activity that encourages only the Little Mary
Sunshines of any gender to enroll in graduate school." Perhaps the
humanities attract a specially antisocial group (Stimpson speaks rather
alarmingly of "the acerb and the cruel . . . the passive-aggressive and
manic-depressive"), yet in all fields the American university system has
long rewarded an entrepreneurial spirit and a drive to advance one's own
research that often leave tenured faculty with little time or patience for
the hard collective work needed for major programmatic reform.

It has not only been people like Cornford at "conservative" institutions
who have lamented faculty resistance to changing a system that has served
its survivors well. Similar regret has been voiced by no less a figure than
Clark Kerr, who was so influential in the expansive, progressive California
system during the postwar era. In the first edition of *The Uses of the University* (1963), Kerr celebrated the entrepreneurial system he was helping
to build—a "multiversity" far more dynamic than the cloistered colleges
of the past.

Yet a decade later, in a postscript to the second edition of his book
(1972), he gave a far more somber assessment of his efforts at reform. By
this time he had resigned as chancellor of the University of California at
Berkeley, after a series of conflicts culminating in the student protests of
the late sixties. These had included demonstrations against government-
sponsored university research, led by students wearing T-shirts proclaim-
ing "Forward Under Clark Kerr"—with the capital letters arranged to
give a pointed anagrammatic message of quite different force. Though the
student protests garnered the media's attention, Kerr focused more on his
problems with the faculty:

> It is remarkable not how much has changed but how little has changed
> on so many campuses in those areas that are under faculty control and
> where the faculty feels strongly about its control. The more the envi-
> ronment has changed, the more the organized faculty has remained the
> same. It has been the greatest single point of institutional conservatism
> in recent times, as it has been historically. Little that it has held dear
> and that it could control has been allowed to change (pp. 130–131).

A decade later, in a postscript to the third edition of his book (1982),
Kerr's administrative depression had only deepened, and again the faculty
led his list of resisters to change:

The three fundamental changes attempted over the past twenty years have largely failed. Academic reform was overwhelmed by faculty conservatism. Efforts to turn the university into a direct instrument for social change were thwarted by institutional autonomy. . . . Changes in formal governance have generally made little difference and, when they did, mostly for the worse. All that effort, all that passion, all that turmoil was mostly for naught, but it was also mostly inevitable given the conditions of the times (pp. 180–181).

Clearly, even the best intentions cannot be realized by administrative fiat; a new approach is needed, and our collected essays can help us work this out.

A New Relation

The heart of Ph.D. training is the relationship between mentors and students. Real change must involve rethinking this relation, and yet, as Angelica Stacey notes in her essay, the subject of adviser-advisee relationships "is awkward because it is about people, relationships, and money. And so it is really about power." As Clark Kerr learned to his sorrow, the faculty are tremendously protective of their powers, and although faculty power may have eroded in other spheres, it remains decisive when it comes to the training and advising of graduate students. This fact of academic life may seem discouraging, but in fact it has great potential: if the faculty want to make changes, they can. Idealism or moral exhortations will only get us so far, though. The changes that really stick are those that serve the faculty's needs as well as those of the students. Enlightened self-interest is a powerful force for change, and it can certainly be brought to bear on faculty-student roles. What several of our essays suggest is that faculty stand to gain as much as students from a new approach to graduate training—one that emphasizes collaboration instead of the top-down, authoritarian model inherited from the nineteenth-century German university.

The old model presupposed a one-to-one relationship between student and sponsor, actually called the "*Doktorvater*" in German, as though the patriarchal sponsor was supposed to give birth, parthenogenetically, to the newborn Ph.D. For many reasons, this old model no longer works well for many students—or even for many faculty. The rapid growth of fields and of interdisciplinary work, of which many of our essayists speak, means that incoming students often do not have interests that map closely on to those of a single faculty member: hence several essays call for opening up the system to more varied, multiple advising. The matching of students and advisers is further complicated to the extent that more and more students are coming in with very different personal backgrounds from those of their advisers, whether in terms of gender, ethnicity, or nationality. In an ideal world, all such personal differences might fade away in the clear light of the intellect, but given the close relation of mentor and graduate student, it appears to be a fact of life that the intellectual can never be entirely divorced from the personal. A reproductive model of mentoring subtly reinforces social as well as intellectual conformity, and this surely contributes to the pattern that several of our essays note: greater diversity among undergraduate majors than among graduate cohorts, a further decrease in diversity among the ranks of assistant professors, a further decrease still among tenured ranks.

Faculty often invest a great deal of time and effort in mentoring students, and the rewards flow both ways when the relation works well. As Zach Hall says, graduate students are prime "vectors of information, skills, and ideas," and faculty can learn as much from their advanced students as the students learn from them. Faculty have long recognized this in principle, and in various ways in practice as well. As Steven Hyman observes, "the key to coalescence of a new discipline is the graduate program" and the leaders of new disciplines have made sure to embody their ideas in graduate form. Yet the strength of such new programs and their ability to survive the founding generation can be limited when faculty cling to a purely reproductive model of training. All too readily, a scholar's insights can pass through what's been described as "the five stages of fame":

1. Who is So-and-so?

2. *Get* me So-and-so.

3. Get me someone *like* So-and-so!

4. Get me a *young* So-and-so. . .

5. Who is So-and-so?

As in some Shakespearean tragedies, the third act is the high point, where the hero is so dominant as to be almost unreachable. By the time the call goes out for a "young So-and-so," the moment of eclipse is near. This was made clear to me some years ago when I was on a search committee for a junior position, and we received a letter from a leading figure in the field in question, strongly supporting his favorite student. Seeking to impress us with his protégé's special status, he ended his letter by roundly declaring: "This is my Oedipal son." The application was dead in the water after that. As much as we admired the sponsor, we really weren't interested in hiring his Oedipal son. The fact was that the candidate's writing sample looked all too much like a pallid version of the sponsor's work, set off by fitful expressions of the anxiety of influence. The sponsor's recommendation crystallized our own doubts about the candidate's work.

My point is that such Oedipal relations are no better for the sponsor than for the student. We, as sponsors, will learn more from students who have some independence from us, who bring to bear a more varied set of perspectives than we alone can give, and who can work with us on a basis of greater freedom than the older model supposes. Already in 1908, Cornford was fully aware of the patricidal dangers latent in the Oedipal model of scholarly training, and he lays this out for us without any reference to the theories of his contemporary Sigmund Freud, apparently purely from his own observation of the rising academic generation in England. He warns his supposed reader (Cornford, 1954)—"the young academic politician"—of the dangers that await him if he manages to achieve tenure and "nestle down into a modest incompetence."

> While you are young you will be oppressed, and angry, and increasingly disagreeable. When you reach middle age at five-and-thirty, you will become complacent, and in your turn, an oppressor; those whom you oppress will find you still disagreeable; and so will all the people whose toes you trod upon in youth. . . . If you persist to the threshold of old age—your fiftieth year, let us say—you will be a powerful person yourself, with an accretion of peculiarities which other people will have to study to square you . . . and from far below you will mount the roar of a ruthless multitude of young men in a hurry. You may perhaps grow to be aware what they are in a hurry to do. They are in a hurry to get you out of the way (pp. 2–3).

This is not a pleasing sound for senior faculty to contemplate, and the scholarship of young and older scholars alike will benefit if we can develop a stewardship of the discipline that entails a more mutual relation and less anxiety of influence, less need to overthrow the last generation's—or last year's—theories, methods, and sponsors.

Program Revision in Practice

Our essayists advance a range of ideas for opening out the mentor-advisee relation in fruitful ways, including giving students more leeway to formulate their own topics (in fields in which topics are now often assigned), encouraging them to get a solid background in other disciplines, and working with multiple advisers throughout graduate school. In order to bring about such changes, a serious revision to the graduate program is likely to be needed, and for this to work it is important to have very active involvement by graduate students in the assessment of the current program and the planning for revisions. It would be odd, after all, if a move toward a less hierarchical structure were itself to be imposed in a top-down fashion, and the Carnegie Initiative on the Doctorate has built graduate student participation into the fabric of the project. Their involvement is somewhat obscured by the fact that only faculty—and senior faculty at that—have been commissioned to write essays for this collection, one small sign of the pervasive updraft that silently reinforces our profession's built-in hierarchies. The essays themselves, in turn, tend to assume that programmatic change comes purely through faculty initiative. In these essays, graduate students' needs are sympathetically evoked, but the general emphasis lies on what *we* (tenured faculty? colonial administrators?) should do for *them* (students? natives?). This tacit perspective confuses the faculty's overall responsibility with the separate issue of how changes are best planned and then put into place.

A close involvement by graduate students is essential, both to improve the substance of changes and to help see them realized in practice. My department engaged in an extended process of self-study during the academic year 2003–04, which resulted in a broad program of changes (more than fifty separate items altogether). This process began with an extensive survey of our current students, asking eighty questions covering every facet of the program and its requirements. We had hoped as well to survey our graduates of the past decade, but, all too typically, neither our department nor the graduate school had any adequate record of our graduates' addresses, much less those of people who had left the program before graduation. Even so, the dozens of responses we received from our current students provided a wealth of statistical information and many thoughtful, creative ideas for change, many of which made their way into our final package of reforms. There is no better way to begin studying a program than with a survey of this sort.

Those of us who have been involved in administering graduate programs know that our faculty colleagues are often blissfully unaware of many of our own programs' requirements, and our colleagues typically have only scattered, anecdotal information on students' difficulties and concerns. Even their own favorite students may not want to trouble them with issues not related directly to their work together, and faculty typically hear little from students who are not their own protégés, though it is precisely the students who have not settled into a close working relationship with their sponsors who are likely to see most clearly what could use changing. So I was not at all surprised that our survey revealed many issues that needed to be brought to my colleagues' attention. What I had not expected, after seven years as director of graduate studies and three as department chair, was how many of the students' concerns came as a surprise to me. I had no idea, for example, how many hours a week the students in our "fully funded" Ph.D. program were working off-campus just to make ends meet (typically fifteen and often more); my surprise on this would have been less if I had not been several years out of date in what I thought the university was charging for graduate-student housing.

Although I had known of various areas of concern, I found that students had substantive issues, even in several areas that I thought were working well, such as our introductory M.A. seminars and our overall course offerings. We have tended to take a laissez-faire approach to course selection, for example, assuming that our knowledgeable, independent-minded students will survey their options and take what they like. Our survey, however, revealed widespread dissatisfaction with the lack of advice on courses. Our advising got weak reviews at all levels, but by far the lowest marks went to course advice—an area I had never thought needed attention at all. Fifty students replied to the question, "How would you describe the advising you receive in choosing your courses?" Of these fifty, exactly *zero* listed "excellent," only nine listed "adequate," fourteen listed "somewhat adequate," and an outright majority of twenty-seven listed the bottom category—"inadequate."

Their problem, furthermore, was not only confusion over the sheer embarrassment of riches we were offering. We have a large graduate program and as a result can offer many graduate courses, mounting a good range of offerings in all the fields important to our students. Or so I thought. Our surveyed students registered a broad concern that our offerings have been weighted too heavily toward the faculty's own research preferences, giving insufficient training in their field as a whole. Only 13 percent of our respondents described themselves as "very satisfied" with the course offerings; 35 percent were "satisfied," 37 percent were "somewhat satisfied," and 15 percent were "dissatisfied." More people, in other words, chose the lower two categories than the higher two. We had asked our students in recent years to tell us what they would like to see offered and had usually added one or two courses a year in response, but this modest level of responsiveness didn't seem overwhelming to them. Asked about graduate students' role in determining course offerings, no respondents at all listed the highest category ("just right"). A mere 12.5 percent listed the next category ("adequate"); 18.5 percent listed the third choice ("somewhat adequate"); a large majority—69 percent—listed the lowest category ("inadequate").

Not only can a survey reveal surprises even to the most hardened (or clueless) directors of graduate studies but the students' responses were powerful factors in persuading both the faculty and the administration of the importance of change. We now have put in place an ambitious set of procedures for advising at every stage of the program, and we've made many other changes along lines our students have recommended to us. Student input is also important in knowing what *not* to change. Several of our faculty in traditionally crowded fields have long felt that our large program should be smaller, both in view of faculty workload and in terms of job placement. What was really decisive in the discussion of program size was the input from our graduate students, who strongly supported retaining our present size. Many said that they had chosen us over the smaller programs at peer institutions precisely for the greater range and stimulation of the large cohort, as against what they perceived as the potential claustrophobia of smaller programs.[1]

The Vital Center

As important as graduate student involvement is, students are no more able to get a full picture of their situation than are tenured faculty, all the more as they are caught up in a process of training and acculturation whose outcome they do not yet know. Further, as relatively powerless members of the community, they have a reciprocal bias to that of tenured faculty; they are not yet able to fully assess the benefits or disadvantages of the hurdles they are in the process of surmounting. In structural terms, the real lynchpin of graduate program reform is to be found in the generation in between the graduate students and the senior faculty. The untenured faculty and the recently tenured associate professors represent the best hope for sustained and meaningful reform. This is the group who has had some time out in the profession and can look back at their graduate training, still fairly fresh in their minds, with a realism tempered by experience. They are not so deeply embedded in the professorial ranks as are their senior colleagues, so they are the faculty most likely to retain a sense of the realities of graduate student life. They are also most often closest, as a group, to new directions in their fields, and their mentoring relation to the new generation of students is often different in kind from that of their more powerful senior colleagues: less like a parent than like a supportive older sibling to whom confidences are more likely to be told.

Written entirely by well-established senior scholars, our collected essays often speak of graduate students as the future of the field and the prime bearers of new ideas and perspectives, but it is notable that nowhere do these essays discuss the role of untenured and recently tenured faculty.

Instead, we find a binary opposition between "faculty" and "students," and if junior faculty are implicitly included in the faculty ranks, they are not shown to have any special perspective or role. Here again, our attention drifts upward in the ranks, and the junior and recently tenured faculty come to seem an occluded, if not excluded, middle. It is certainly true that our graduate students are in a general sense the future of our disciplines, yet the fact is that almost all of them will go on to teach in other schools than our own or will leave academia altogether. It is our junior colleagues who are the very real future *of our own departments,* and reforms are best conceived and best carried out when these colleagues are centrally involved every step of the way.

The granting of tenure is, of course, a major academic rite of passage, one with very real material and intellectual consequences. (As a friend of mine once remarked: "They get tenure, and then they become knowledgeable about wine.") Newly tenured faculty have a special status as people in whom the department has recently and explicitly vested its future. Generally, though, there are broad commonalities in the perspectives of all those who have been teaching for, say, three to ten years beyond the receipt of the Ph.D. (allowing that it takes at least a couple of years for new Ph.D.'s to adjust to faculty life and begin to learn where the department's bodies are buried). I would argue that, taken together, our advanced junior faculty and recently tenured faculty form a distinct cohort—the vital center of any program revision. This is the group that can best balance idealism and pragmatism, mediating between the competing and at times conflicting perspectives of the generations above and below them.

To this basic model, which applies to all departments, it would be important to add consideration of adjunct and other non-tenure-track faculty, depending on the particular circumstances of each program. This is a matter, not only of the relative numbers of each group in a given place but also of the particular history and ethos of each department or program, as well as the expectations and roles of the non-tenure-ladder faculty themselves. In some places, adjunct or other non-ladder faculty ought to be closely involved, reflecting their active work with graduate students or the possibilities for new involvements they have not yet had; in other cases, they could logically be spared a heavy dose of committee work of no special relevance to their own situation. It is important for any program revision to begin by considering its constituencies and making thoughtful (and explicit) decisions about who should be involved in assessing the program and putting changes into place.

None of these remarks is meant to denigrate the key role of senior faculty, whose longer experience brings an important depth of perspective into the discussion and whose involvement is needed for purely pragmatic reasons as well. Senior faculty do not take well to any feeling of being ganged up on, as I have found every time I have tried. Reforms won't pass at all, much less last over time, without the agreement of the senior faculty, given their numbers in general and their overall responsibility for their programs. In my department's program revisions, we had some heated discussions in faculty meetings over various of our proposals, with the senior faculty generating most of the heat. Heat, but also some light, and a fair number of proposals were substantially modified or even dropped in the process. In the end, the fifty-plus surviving proposals all passed, typically by margins of 90 percent—an extraordinary result in a department not known for intimate harmony and in a profession whose faculty are often deeply wedded to their particular ways of doing things. "We've been doing it this way since 1867" is as powerful an argument for the status quo as, "It didn't work in 1867."

A full involvement by graduate students and younger faculty is an essential counterweight to all appeals to how things were or were not done a generation ago, even as, conversely, the stewardship of our disciplines depends crucially on the long memories of those who have managed the household over many years. In his essay, Steven Hyman speaks of the need for "Janus-like interactions" between specialized knowledge and the broader community beyond one's discipline. As we contemplate our programs and their discontents, we equally need a Janus-like historical and generational perspective: our best hope for change is to keep past and future always in view.

NOTE

1. Our Carnegie Committee further eased the faculty's concerns by conducting our own careful statistical work, showing that our placement rate was actually much better than most of us had thought, and showing as well that the "overworked" faculty were recalling historical imbalances that had been addressed a decade earlier and that no longer applied.

REFERENCES

"Columbia University English Ph.D. Program Revisions." Available at www.columbia.edu/cu/english/grad_studnews.htm.

Cornford, F. M. *Microcosmographia Academica*. (5th ed.) Cambridge: Bowes and Bowes, 1954. (Originally published 1908.)

Damrosch, D. *We Scholars: Changing the Culture of the University*. Cambridge, Mass.: Harvard University Press, 1995.

Kerr, C. *The Uses of the University*. (3rd ed.) Cambridge, Mass.: Harvard University Press, 1982. (Originally published 1963; 2nd ed. 1972.)

4

HEEDING THE VOICES
OF GRADUATE STUDENTS
AND POSTDOCS

Crispin Taylor, American Society of Plant Biologists

THE ESSAYS IN THIS VOLUME have, as their major objective, to determine what it takes to become a steward of a discipline—an objective that the Carnegie Initiative on the Doctorate (CID) is addressing, at least in part, by analyzing the extent to which today's doctoral programs are—or are not—adequately preparing such stewards.

However, if we start, instead, with the assumption that doctoral education is not only about the discipline and advancing knowledge but also about the people—all of the people—who are engaged in those activities, we would examine the adequacy of doctoral programs, not from the perspective of those who are already stewards of the discipline but from the perspective of the programs' major constituent: the everyman-everywoman doctoral student.

When we look at doctoral programs from this perspective, we see that the programs—and those seeking to reinvent them—ought to put students front and center. They should do so not simply because it is the right thing to do to nurture and grow our successors but also because the discipline is not anything if it cannot engage the people who aspire to join it. Thus those responsible for creating, evaluating, or modifying doctoral programs should directly and explicitly broaden their focus by thinking about the ways in which departing students go out into the world to develop and transform their discipline by applying the knowledge, skills, and experiences they acquire as doctoral students.

If Ph.D. programs are doing a good job in this regard—and are perceived to be doing so—they will continue to attract individuals who have the capacity to become disciplinary stewards, whether they grow into that role while working in academia, government, or the private sector. If our efforts to develop doctoral programs that will adequately prepare Ph.D. students—as many as possible, not just the few stars—to become disciplinary stewards are to succeed, we will need to focus the bulk of our attention on those future stewards and their wants and needs. Our goal should be practical: How do we prepare as many as possible Ph.D. humanists and scientists in as many as possible disciplines for rewarding careers in as many arenas as feasible?

If we really do take stewardship in the discipline seriously, and if we really want to create student-centered doctoral programs, we should consider these issues among the most important to address:

- We are, and have been for a long while, graduating many more Ph.D.'s than there are fulfilling jobs available in academia—the traditional bastion of the disciplines. Are doctoral programs adequately preparing students to face and surmount this reality and establish rewarding careers within—or, more likely, outside—the academy?

- How do we go about informing doctoral students of their post-Ph.D. options and preparing them for as many such options as possible? And what is the role of individual faculty members in this endeavor?

- How can we ensure that the major demographic shifts that are under way in the United States will not render doctoral programs increasingly irrelevant? Or, to put it another way, how can we engage populations that are unfamiliar with doctoral education and thereby ensure that our disciplines remain both healthy and representative?

- What can we do to modify the existing faculty reward structures and financial incentives that work as counterweights to preserve the currently inadequate status quo, thereby increasing the chances that any fixes—either those that I propose here or anyone else's—stick?

As you may have gathered from the preceding list, my main worry is that today's Ph.D. programs are not adequately preparing their doctoral students for successful careers. Why? Well, it is more or less impossible to become a disciplinary steward if one is not successful and fulfilled in one's career. *Success* and *fulfillment* are, of course, subjective terms. But let us consider defining success for the newly minted Ph.D. as "acquiring a rewarding position that offers legitimate opportunities for professional advancement," whether or not that job happens to be in academia. Naturally, in defining success in this way, we also accept Elkana's assertion that one does not have to be an academic to be a disciplinary steward.

Further, with the exception of some disciplines—notably chemistry, in which doctoral students have for years been groomed for rewarding careers in industry—few students now enter doctoral programs with the expectation that they will be able to bypass some form of post-Ph.D. training. And so, in examining doctoral programs, I suggest we include the various post-Ph.D. "apprenticeship" structures that, regardless of the discipline, have relatively recently become de facto rungs on the career ladder: the postdoc in the natural sciences, primarily, and the potpourri of temporary, junior, and adjunct positions that are increasingly the immediate post-Ph.D. destination of many in the humanities. A science postdoc is analogous to a humanities adjunct position only insofar as both have come to be accepted as steps on the ladder to a full-time tenure-track position.

Finally, in addition to looking forward at the destinations toward which they propel their students, doctoral programs should also look backwards, at the places from which those students have come. All of education is a continuum, and although there is certainly value in the reductionist approach of addressing single, bite-sized components (the Ph.D., for instance), that value is markedly increased if we ensure that our more focused analyses are embedded in as many as possible of the components that precede and succeed the one we are examining.

Viewing the situation from the perspective of the doctoral student, let us evaluate the ideas and recommendations in the essays in this volume, as well as the assumptions behind them. Will the ideas work? Will they gain credence and traction among today's and tomorrow's scholars as they struggle to satisfy program requirements, make financial ends meet, and balance their careers with their personal lives? And what is skimmed over or missing altogether from the analyses?

Multiple Successful Outcomes (Or "What Is a Ph.D. Good For?")

The fundamental problem with doctoral education, as I see it, is that it tends to be divorced from post-Ph.D. reality. Despite the occasional "alternative" career seminar or workshop, in most departments and in most disciplines (chemistry again being an exception), the prevailing sentiment is that doctoral students are being prepared for careers in academia and that anything else is second-best.

As most of the essayists acknowledge, albeit in passing, the difficulty with this perception is that there are not enough permanent jobs in academia to keep all the Ph.D. graduates satisfactorily employed. As a consequence, the Ph.D., in and of itself, is increasingly considered to be insufficient preparation, and some subsequent period of post-Ph.D. apprenticeship has become *de rigueur* in the sciences and in the humanities. Although many Ph.D. holders do find rewarding work in other arenas, the feeling that they have failed to live up to their mentors' highest expectations is a difficult one to shake. More to the point, the steady shift toward adjunct and part-time "faculty" appointments is, in my opinion, bad for the academy and bad for the vast majority of individuals so employed. These positions stifle creativity and, although there are certainly some happy and fulfilled adjuncts, in many instances this construct places rootless, disaffected, and (occasionally) bitter individuals directly in front of the next generation of potential scholars and stewards.

Given that there is currently a substantial disconnect between the number of graduating Ph.D.'s and the number of "real" jobs available in academia, I think it is essential to explain to prospective and incoming students exactly what kinds of post-Ph.D. career outcomes they may pursue. Providing due consideration to the career—the vehicle via which the steward will advance the discipline—is one important example of the kind of topic that doctoral programs would address directly and creatively if they really had students at the center.

For example, faculty might share with prospective and incoming students a joint report by the European Science Foundation (ESF) and the Human Frontiers Science Program (HFSP) (Krotoski, 2002). This report offers a striking visual analogy that, although rooted in the experiences of natural scientists, is, I think, transferable to other disciplines. The diagram depicts the major rungs on the academic ladder—bachelor's, master's, Ph.D., and post-Ph.D. apprenticeship (in this case, the postdoc)—as the trunk of the tree. On each side of the tree, deriving from specific rungs along the trunk, branch out a broad spectrum of careers. Those on the right are in education—everything from primary education (which, in this European analysis, branches from the master's level) to the upper echelons of academia, which can be reached only after climbing the trunk as far as the postdoc. On the left is everything else—industry, law, journalism, politics, government—similarly organized in terms of how far up the academic trunk one must climb in order to branch off into specific careers.

Most of the careers depicted on this diagram are not scientist-specific; that is, there is no reason why someone with a Ph.D. in English or history cannot work in the government or become a journalist. Sure, one may choose to quibble with the details, but this is an elegant, useful, and descriptive model. Particularly telling is the fact that the branches on the right-hand side of the tree—those that lead toward careers in academia and teaching—are fewer in number than those on the left.

Citing data from the federal government, Elkana notes that few of today's science Ph.D.'s will become faculty. So given that most Ph.D. programs focus on preparing individuals for careers in academia, most particularly for jobs in Ph.D.-granting institutions, and allowing for a similar discrepancy between the number of Ph.D.'s trained and the number of available full-time academic jobs in the humanities, well over half the people going through Ph.D.'s are being inadequately prepared to maximize their own future potential. (Arguably, even those who do find rewarding careers in academia are also inadequately prepared. More on that in a bit.)

But is it not the job of the doctoral program to provide "education" in the grander sense rather than some kind of vocational "training"? Well, yes—and no. In my experience, most individuals who wish to pursue a Ph.D. are motivated by the desire to learn—to deepen their understanding of the world around them and humankind's place in it. So education is a fundamental and important part of the equation. But many potential students are also increasingly motivated to better themselves and their families financially—and to find post-Ph.D. jobs that allow an appropriate balance between professional and personal responsibilities. Doctoral programs should pay attention to both kinds of motivation; they neglect to react and respond to the growing prominence of the latter at their peril.

That a career trajectory ought to be thought of more like a tree than a pipeline—albeit a tree whose trunk is represented by the conventional rungs on the academic ladder—is not a new idea. But what does it mean for the doctoral students coming through our programs?

What it means is that we ought to be thinking about how to develop doctoral programs that effectively prepare students for as many different career trajectories as possible. For many careers, as the ESF-HFSP career tree illustrates, an additional post-Ph.D. "apprenticeship" period may be necessary. But for others, there is no need to pursue a postdoc or to spend time in an adjunct position—appointments that, with depressing frequency, can become semipermanent "holding patterns." If doctoral students are sufficiently well informed early enough in their programs about their options and what it takes to pursue them, those students will be able to make rational decisions and choices about their post-Ph.D. steps, rather than allowing themselves to be herded down well-worn default paths that are not necessarily appropriate prerequisites for their defined professional objectives.

Broadly, then, I agree with Hyman: doctoral programs ought to be training T-shaped individuals. As represented by the vertical stroke of the "T," such people would, by the time they receive their Ph.D.'s, have sufficient depth of knowledge in some fairly narrow area (which is defined by their thesis)—to be able to advance scholarship and understanding in that area. These are the strong foundations on which a discipline's long-lasting knowledge structures are necessarily built; by maintaining its current emphasis on depth, Ph.D. education can remain both "faithful to its origins and appropriate for its times" (Berliner, this volume). But, as represented by the horizontal stroke of the "T," Ph.D.'s should also have sufficient breadth, in both skill sets and general knowledge, to apply themselves in a range of different areas that include, but are by no means restricted to, academic research, teaching, or scholarship.

This will not just happen, of course, and paying pedagogical attention to both strokes of the "T" simultaneously is going to take some doing. Nevertheless, inculcating and teaching skills that include critical and independent thinking, effective written and oral communication, project planning and execution, time management, and networking from the earliest days of the Ph.D. will, I am sure, generate doctoral students who are not only more effective in the short term but also better prepared to succeed in the long term.

Although my remarks might sound like a radical departure from the current status quo, I do not think they are, in fact, so far off the mark. The world is increasingly dependent on "knowledge workers," and high-powered consulting companies have recognized for years that employees with Ph.D.'s come with some decidedly useful transferable skills. Accordingly, essayists Breslow and Graff both address creating (and, in Breslow's case, actively supporting) ways to help students develop professional skills. But, typically, the kinds of skills I outlined have not been taught, and they have not been presented as legitimate learning outcomes for the Ph.D. program. That is not to say they cannot be picked up; they can be. But at this point, it tends to happen on an ad hoc, erratic, and fragmented basis.

Take networking, which Richardson specifically mentions in her essay, along with the value for doctoral students of establishing direct professional relationships with the colleagues of their mentors. One way that doctoral programs can foster networking (at least, within academia) is through their seminar programs. But the robustness and networking merit of a seminar program will necessarily depend on its scope, which in turn will depend on the resources the department is able to devote to it. I was fortunate. I did my Ph.D. in a well-funded institute that many prominent scholars wished to visit. Moreover, the faculty encouraged the students to select and invite one seminar speaker each semester and to host that individual when she or he came to give the talk (as Breslow urges in his essay). Imagine our surprise when we learned that distinguished scholars were more inclined to accept a speaking invitation when it came from students! And imagine how much more we were able to realize from the interaction when it was our responsibility to chaperone the speaker throughout the visit. Those quiet, one-on-one moments that are impossible to make happen in public arenas were much easier to come by, and anyone who wanted to could grab a little quality time with the speaker.

Another example is communication skills. An established tradition in my institute was for the more senior doctoral students and postdocs to give regular departmental seminars, formally placing their thesis work (or postdoctoral research project) in the broader context of related work in the field and describing their progress to date. In addition to obliging one to generate sufficient data to discuss on a fairly regular basis, this venue provided a familiar and supportive environment in which to hone speaking skills. Although the audiences were friendly, they were not easy, and the tough questions from peers and faculty were great preparation for learning how to think on your feet. Breslow suggests this practice, and Lunsford writes a bit about the value of the informal (or semiformal) departmental seminar in helping students to organize their thoughts and get used to presenting their ideas in a public setting—a practice she cites as common at universities in Europe and Canada.

As a doctoral student, I was also given the opportunity to serve as an elected member of the student body on a number of the committees that governed the institute in which I was working. But it was not just me. The institute emphasized including a doctoral student and a postdoc representative on all its governance committees, from the building affairs committee (which, in my time, worried about assigning planting space in institute-owned growth chambers and greenhouses) to the faculty committee and even an ad hoc committee charged with identifying a new director for the entire laboratory. What an education that was for those of us fortunate enough to have the opportunity to serve. It taught us how to work in a team environment of a very different kind and how to get our points across effectively in groups composed of individuals with diverse backgrounds and perspectives. And what an important principle— that of inclusiveness—it demonstrated.

The thesis is—and ought to remain—a critical component of the Ph.D. Through their theses, doctoral students help add to the intellectual foundations of a discipline. Also, as several essayists describe, the processes of developing, planning, and executing a thesis, when done well, afford many additional skills to the student. For Ph.D. students, learning how to think—and being rewarded for doing so independently—will have the most potent and long-lasting benefits, regardless of the career the individual chooses to follow.

As Elkana points out, the humanities and education generally favor greater independence in thesis problem choice than do the sciences, where the trend (driven, I expect, by funding priorities, funding mechanisms, and faculty reward structures) has been toward principal investigators (PIs) developing "carve-off-able" pieces of work for students (and also postdocs) that dovetail with the overall direction in which the PI's projects are moving. Elements of both approaches have merit, but I think both are tending toward extremes rather than toward happier (and more valuable to the student) mediums. For example, being handed a thesis project on a plate, as happens with increasing frequency in the sciences, may mean that students obtain their Ph.D.'s more quickly (which, in turn, likely means that their PI's next grant is also awarded more quickly). But the students may lack intellectual engagement with their project, and it may take them longer to develop the facility for independent, strategic, and constructively critical thought that is a vital component of any doctoral program worth its salt. However, providing too little guidance can leave Ph.D. students feeling rudderless and frustrated and has the inevitable consequence, seen all too frequently in the humanities and education, of markedly increasing time-to-degree.

Up to this point I have focused implicitly on doctoral programs as preparation for careers outside the academy. But the skill sets I have described are valuable in any career, including the more traditional academic ones. Who would not want a faculty colleague who is an effective communicator, a fine team player, and also broadly informed? But just as I do not think doctoral programs are doing a very good job of preparing today's Ph.D.'s to succeed in the full range of careers that are available to them, neither do I think we are doing a particularly good job of training future faculty.

As Kwiram mentions, if only a subset of doctoral students really intend to pursue academic careers, then it makes sense to provide that subset with a more explicit apprenticeship period, during their postdoc (in the sciences) or during an adjunct appointment of narrowly defined length (in the humanities), that is focused on their facility to hit the ground running once they achieve, in Kwiram's words, that "coveted academic job." Although creativity of thought remains important for faculty, particularly, but not exclusively at Ph.D.-granting institutions, they typically spend increasingly less time engaged in research and scholarship as they move up the ranks. Instead, they become managers, evaluators, and leaders whose direct participation becomes increasingly vicarious. So teaching these individuals effective project and personnel management skills would seem to me to be a good idea, too. In other words, if among some subset of doctoral students there is a strong and obvious commitment to aspire to join the faculty and some reasonable chance of success in this endeavor, then for goodness sake, let us provide these people with the tools they will need to succeed while they are students or, more likely, while they are engaged in their immediate post-Ph.D. apprenticeship.

To the best of my knowledge, few such programs exist, although there are some notable exceptions. On the funding side, private philanthropies and federal agencies that offer so-called "transition awards" to science postdocs do a lot to help a very small number of future academics get a huge lift in their efforts to find faculty positions at research institutions. And workshops and programs designed to inculcate academic management skills are, in my opinion, well worth the investment (see, for example, Burroughs Wellcome Fund and Howard Hughes Medical Institute, 2004).

Also of note are programs like Preparing Future Faculty (information available online), which, among other things, provide both experience and pedagogy aimed at improving doctoral student (and, by extension, post-Ph.D.) teaching. Aside from these, though, I am aware of few programs specifically aimed at helping doctoral students in the humanities transition into independent tenure-track faculty positions.

Truth in Advertising

Practicing empirical science requires that one develop hypotheses and gather data that test those hypotheses, refining them as necessary. Unfortunately, there are few comprehensive data indicating where doctoral students end up professionally; what is particularly lacking is any serious effort to engage many of those former students in the conversation about how to improve doctoral education.

In large part, that is because we lose track of them, either at the program level, the institution level, or nationally. That is a fixable problem and one that seems to be restricted to the academic disciplines. Professional schools of business and law, for example, take great pains to fol-

low the careers of their graduates and trumpet their successes in efforts
to recruit new students to their programs. To echo a point also made by
Prewitt, it would be imprudent (at best) not to track down alumni and
ask them what they did and did not get out of a doctoral program if one
is in the process of determining whether or not said program is meeting
the needs of its students and, more broadly, the needs of the discipline that
it represents.

And in any case, I honestly think that efforts to recruit students to doctoral programs in the disciplines represented by the CID would be assisted
by accurately representing what the graduates of those programs go on
to do professionally. So there ought to be an obligation (at the departmental level, presumably) to track and stay in touch with all Ph.D. graduates so that the departments can demonstrate to current students some
of the likely outcomes and career trajectories available to them post-Ph.D.

Indeed, I think it would be worth adding to the CID (or any of its successors) the requirement that participating departments locate as many as
possible of their recent graduates before soliciting those graduates' input
on the pros and cons of their Ph.D. program. To my mind, finding and
interviewing these people, although a decidedly nontrivial exercise, would
be well worth the effort because the data obtained would add temporal
depth to the department-by-department empirical analysis that the CID
is already undertaking. It would also help to address a point I made at the
outset: we ought to be looking at doctoral programs, not so much in isolated "snapshot" mode but as one component of an educational and professional continuum.

More fundamentally, recognizing the fallacy that all graduates of any
program will find successful (that is, tenure-track) positions in academia is
the first step toward encouraging Ph.D. students to think outside the
tenure-track box and to dispense with the unfortunate notion that a career
in any setting other than academia is a distant second-best. (Through conversations with many doctoral students and postdocs, it is clear to me that
this reality dawns on them much more readily than it does on faculty. I
remain hopeful, however, that today's junior faculty, many of whom have
come of professional age during a period of unprecedented competition
for faculty positions across the board, will be just a little more sensitive
to this issue than many of their more senior colleagues.)

An additional potential benefit of making the broad range of possible
post-Ph.D. career outcomes explicit to incoming or prospective doctoral
students is that it helps to address the generational shift in perceptions
about balancing work and personal life. Many of today's young people—
doctoral students included—are selecting fields of study and professional

positions based (in much larger part than would seem to have been the case thirty years ago) on considerations that include future earning potential and the capacity for personal time outside of work. Needless to say, traditional academic careers do not score well in either category, and many prospective doctoral students are acutely aware of this. In the sciences, for instance, it is common practice for senior undergraduates interested in careers in science to work at the research bench. Being surrounded by frequently disaffected doctoral students and postdocs in labs that are typically run by harried PI's who are on the road giving seminars three times a month and otherwise locked in their offices working on grant proposals, such promising potential scientists cannot fail to notice that academic research is a decidedly demanding calling. This is by no means a representative sample, but I know of many such individuals who, encountering the stark realities of a premier research lab, have, not surprisingly, opted for medical school, business school, or something else all together instead of pursuing a Ph.D.

Stimpson makes a similar point, but in her case, she is suggesting that economic realities may, in part, be behind the decrease in the number of undergraduates entering humanities programs. Perceptively, she embellishes this point with another: that investigating the longer-term economic consequences of choosing one or another course of study is likely to be a particularly prevalent practice among those individuals who "are new to the United States or new to higher education or new to both."

Indeed, the topic of ethnic diversity, which can only become increasingly important as the vast demographic shifts under way in this country continue to unfold, is touched on by several essayists, including Elkana, Lunsford, and Stacy. They point out that corporations take it for granted that a diversity of opinions and ideas, best achieved by employing a diverse workforce, is critical for sustained innovativeness and success. Lunsford, who recognizes the universality of this principle, favors supporting ethnic diversity in higher education, not only for its own inherent value (important though that is) but because if we fail to propagate diversity and ensure that our doctoral programs increasingly, rather than decreasingly, reflect the ethnic diversity of the country (and also the balance of men and women), they will become increasingly unwelcoming, unimaginative, and, ultimately, irrelevant.

Home Truths and Next Steps

As the numbers of individuals engaged in doctoral education and post-Ph.D. apprenticeships continue to increase, we will find ourselves in a career economy in which there is an ever-ballooning glut of talent. Indeed, most doctoral students, adjunct faculty, and postdocs that I have spoken with opine that the country is already awash with Ph.D. talent and that there are many more well-qualified and highly capable people than there are respectable jobs.

Clearly, one immediate consequence of this situation is that it keeps salaries low, which at the macro level benefits the institutions at which these people work, the departments in which they are training, and (in the sciences, in particular) their faculty advisers. Put bluntly, doctoral students, postdocs, and adjunct faculty do good and important work well and cheaply, which means that for as long as supply exceeds demand, universities will get more and better workers for less money. The medium- and long-term consequences of the current imbalances are less clear but might include turning large numbers of talented people away from doctoral programs and research all together, simply because the economic disincentives (Kwiram cites economist Richard Freeman's publications on this topic) do not outweigh the innate intellectual curiosity that drove them toward doctoral study in the first place.

In other venues, Freeman (2002) has pointed out that the typical economic cost-benefit equations do not apply in doctoral education because most of the funding comes, directly or indirectly, from governments. The more cash a federal agency puts into the system, the more students (or postdocs or adjuncts) can be recruited. As it is currently constructed, this continued injection of funding is undeniably a good thing in terms of the knowledge it helps to generate, but it is a decidedly bad thing for the economic well-being of doctoral students and, ultimately, many others in the academy.

So I think it ought to be incumbent on the bar setters and funders to at least think about—if not explicitly articulate—what kinds of professional opportunities will exist for the people who will be recruited as doctoral students to do the work they are funding after that funding has gone away. Is their only option to take, depending on the discipline, a postdoc or two (or three) or a series of part-time or adjunct teaching positions? Or will the training and expertise they obtain during the course of executing the funded work stand them in good stead to advance their career to the next level, whether it is within the academy or without?

Appleby also argues that in constructing a history Ph.D. program *de novo*, it "would probably be a good idea to limit the number of entrants to the funds available to sustain them during a five- or six-year period." Indeed. But I would suggest taking that a step further not only by thinking about available funds but by considering reliable (or, at least, well-informed) estimates of the likely future demand for the program's graduates. The connection between the former and the latter has been lost in biomedicine, to the short-term detriment of the overqualified and underemployed Ph.D.'s and the (possible) long-term detriment of the arena as a whole (as the word gets out and fewer and fewer domestic students—of any ethnicity—pursue Ph.D.'s in the biosciences).

Although many might say that all such efforts at prediction have failed in the past, I would note that in some instances, the predictive efforts were, in part, politically motivated and thus almost bound to fail. More to the point, we now have the capacity, if we only choose to exercise it, to develop much more sophisticated models of the knowledge workforce and the ebbs and flows among it. Engaging *all* the employers of Ph.D.'s to learn about their short-, medium-, and long-term hiring expectations, as well as their criteria for developing those expectations, is bound to help—a task that would be facilitated by ensuring that we can keep track of many more of the extra-academic career trajectories being pursued by the Ph.D.'s we are training.

At the micro level and perhaps rather more subtly, the professional reward structures within the academy also tend to bolster a status quo that does not serve doctoral students well. As Bass and several other essayists point out, reward structures that strongly emphasize research over teaching and service tend to favor the glut economy of students and postdocs. The more knowledge that the faculty member produces, the more successful he is considered; similarly, the more grants the faculty member receives or the more papers and books she writes, the quicker her promotions and the higher her accolades.

I have no doubt that reward structures are currently a big driver of the problems with doctoral education. However, I think they are also a critical part of the solution. Because so long as funding and reward structures drive accepted practice, the most lasting way to effect change or otherwise influence those practices is to change the underlying funding mechanisms and other reward structures. In other words, tangible rewards and incentives are more potent agents of change than intellectual arguments, no matter how eloquent and well thought out those arguments may be.

So, if we want to make changes in doctoral education, in addition to ensuring that there is some articulation between funding mechanisms and output of Ph.D.'s, we will also need to find ways to reward individual faculty, departments, and universities for preparing well-rounded people who are equipped to apply their skills in a broad range of professional arenas.

Faculty are also a problem at another level: they are generally expected to be experts, and when it comes to careers, unless they are particularly enlightened or have themselves spent a portion of their careers outside the academy, they are largely uninformed regarding the diversity of career trajectories that are available to their protégés and thus ill-prepared to adequately counsel their students. This is an eminently solvable problem. If a department is investing time and effort in tracking (or tracking down) its earlier Ph.D. graduates, then it might want to invite back those engaged in diverse careers for presentations and networking with students and faculty on a departmentwide "career day." (This seems to me to be something that the CID might want to strongly encourage among the departments it is working with most closely.) In addition, individual faculty should become better informed about the various careers sites and services that are available on the Web. And university careers centers, which for the most part focus on the needs of undergraduates, should develop support structures for doctoral students, too.

New Ideas from Abroad

Let us not forget the value of looking outside the United States for potential solutions to problems in graduate education. I was struck, for instance, by Elkana's suggestions regarding a shift toward a dialogical approach toward learning in Ph.D. programs, as opposed to "frontal" teaching, not only because it is a good idea (it is!) but because this is precisely the approach from which I benefited as a senior undergraduate in the United Kingdom. There, a great deal of emphasis is placed on tutorials (at least it was when I was in my teens and early twenties), and even now, most British Ph.D. programs do not require formal class work; instead, they rely on tutorials and other forms of dialogical learning.

Of course, this approach is viable in Britain (and, as Kwiram points out, in many other countries) because most people entering doctoral programs have acquired a more complete intellectual grounding in their discipline as undergraduates than have their American counterparts. Because less time must be spent ensuring that all students in a program have achieved some minimal intellectual proficiency, Ph.D. programs can be shorter. Moreover, there is a greater emphasis on the fundamentals: exams tend to rely more on essays and written arguments and less on multiple choice and memorization. I mention this only because by shifting initial efforts to teach these skills in the undergraduate realm in the United States, we can spend more time during the Ph.D. years working on aspects that are the unique requisites of becoming a disciplinary steward.

Nevertheless, the United States is not alone in examining how doctoral programs integrate with the rest of the educational continuum or whether or not they are adequately preparing the knowledge workers of tomorrow. And yet the majority of the essayists chose to focus their comments more or less exclusively on the situation in this country. This parochialism—a facet, it seems, of the United States, which has a general predisposition toward inward-looking, introspective analysis to the frequent exclusion of international comparisons—struck me, particularly, as many of America's most prestigious and well-known academic institutions are busy opening campuses overseas. Will these universities learn from intellectual practices in the countries in which they are now operating, or will they endeavor to export an arguably out-of-date system?

Other countries are looking outward. The Japanese government, for example, is more than halfway through a five-year review of doctoral education and training in that country. This analysis takes as its context current national needs and projected future needs for highly trained, capable, flexible, and insightful thinkers, strategists, and managers.

The Most Important Next Step

Ultimately, however, it is vital to actively engage doctoral students and recent Ph.D.'s in the process of reform. Tomorrow's stewards—that is, today's doctoral students and immediately post-Ph.D. apprentices—must be comprehensively engaged in efforts to address any deficiencies in doctoral education.

Many of the essayists recognize the perils of exclusivity. They mention that, when asked for their input, doctoral students always have valuable insight to offer. Damrosch, another commentator, also states that meaningful change in individual doctoral programs and in general requires the participation of doctoral students. In the individual programs that the CID is exploring, this is happening.

But there are no doctoral students, postdocs, or adjuncts on the advisory board to this project. Why is that? Is it because they are too busy doing the tenured (and tenure-track) faculty's grunt work to serve in this way? Or is it because these junior cohorts have not been sufficiently exposed to the kinds of opportunities necessary to develop the intellectual and dialectic tools required to participate meaningfully in a conversation of this caliber? Of course not. Such notions about doctoral students are fallacious. So whether in discussions of doctoral curricula and basic departmental management or in efforts to increase representation on national bodies and disciplinary society committees, the best way to ensure lasting positive change in doctoral programs is to seriously, deliberately, enthusiastically, and comprehensively engage the current students—the up-and-coming undergraduates who might well become tomorrow's doctoral students and, to the fullest extent possible, those who have recently passed through our doctoral programs.

If I had to make a prediction, it would be that doctoral students fully engaged in developing reforms would suggest creating a core Ph.D. curriculum that would require all students to achieve basic knowledge and skills in fundamental transferable skills, such as communication (written and oral), management (project, personnel, and financial), and constructive, strategic thinking. With this knowledge and these skills, with objective information on career trajectories, and with careful mentoring in the kinds of options available, students would be able to deepen their emphasis in areas that make best sense to them while simultaneously engaging in the research, teaching, and related work necessary to complete their degree. And above all else, the doctoral students would be able to do this at a point in their education when they still have the opportunity to change tacks, acquire extra skills, and learn from their mistakes, well before they find themselves languishing in a dead-end job. But as a number of other essayists and I have said repeatedly, we cannot get there from here without comprehensively engaging our disciplines' future stewards, heeding their voices, and acting on their suggestions.

REFERENCES

Burroughs Wellcome Fund and Howard Hughes Medical Institute. *Making the Right Moves: A Practical Guide to Scientific Management for Postdocs and New Faculty.* Research Triangle Park, N.C.: Burroughs Wellcome Fund and Howard Hughes Medical Institute, 2004. Available at www.hhmi.org/labmanagement.

Freeman, R. "Thanks for the Great Postdoc Bargain." *Science's Next Wave,* 2002. Available at nextwave.sciencemag.org/cgi/content/full/2002/08/23/4.

Krotoski, D. "Toward a New Paradigm for Education, Training, and Career Paths in the Natural Sciences." Reports on the Meeting on International Training and Support of Young Investigators in the Natural Sciences. Human Frontiers Science Program and the European Science Foundation, 2002. Available at www.hfsp.org/pubs/Position_Papers/FundersReport2002.pdf.

Preparing Future Faculty Program. Available at www.preparing-faculty.org.

PART THREE

THE ESSAYS

5

UNMASKING UNCERTAINTIES AND EMBRACING CONTRADICTIONS

GRADUATE EDUCATION IN THE SCIENCES

Yehuda Elkana, Central European University

MY APPROACH TO THIS ESSAY is deeply imbued with thoughts and theories of the late Robert Merton, long-time, much-admired friend and colleague (what I did, by not mentioning his work in the text, was to supply a very good example of what Merton called "obliteration by incorporation"); my argument can actually be described as "social epistemology"—a happy term that I borrowed from Harriet Zuckerman.[1]

Much of what follows applies, with some modification, to the continued education of postdoctoral fellows. This is, however, another topic to be discussed elsewhere.

The Argument[2]

1. There is far more fundamental controversy within the sciences than its practitioners are prepared to confront. Doctoral students need to understand that much of modern science still must confront basic epistemological issues of knowledge and knowing. These range from questions of knowledge organization and images of the possible to arguments about method, precision, and rigor. The contradictions and inconsistencies of

science must be cherished. Seminars should emphasize the examples of instances where the favored theories simply will not work.

2. Doctoral education in the sciences must emphasize the personality, character, habits of heart and mind, and general scholarly dispositions of the steward of the discipline. Being a steward of the discipline involves generation, conservation, and transformation (the educational and pedagogical functions of the scientist), as well as understanding the public context of scientists' work. Toward this goal, doctoral programs must encourage risk taking and intellectual adventurousness, while fostering the importance of precision and rigor.

3. The single most significant and pivotal process in science training is finding, choosing, and defining a problem and locating the problem on the larger map of one's field. Problem choice should be a major focus of the entire doctoral program—a primary responsibility for the candidate to exercise. The program should focus more work—course work, colloquia, formal and informal conversations—on the state of the field and its controversies more generally, always with problem choice at the heart of this work.

4. Doctoral programs should devote far less attention to work within the boundaries of a discipline's subfields and far more attention to the broader questions of the philosophical, sociological, and methodological contexts of work, thus combating overspecialization. This must be repeated regularly at all the important choice points in a doctoral program.

5. Doctoral education needs to "go meta" and encourage and guide the students to step back, look reflectively and critically, contemplate how it might be otherwise, and critically examine the weaknesses of the "mainstream" of the discipline, however well respected and well funded it might be.

6. Leaders in the disciplines must understand the critical roles of curricular and pedagogical work in their field and how deeply these functions are affected by the same epistemological understandings that relate to the research role. They must recognize, empirically, that most of those who earn the doctorate will spend far more time teaching and engaging with a variety of publics—in industry, policy, and community settings—than they will at the frontiers of science. Doctoral education must equip students to work in these settings.

7. Science is inexorably intertwined with the world, which today is globalized to an unprecedented degree. Doctoral students must have opportunities to explore the implications of this.

8. We must be willing to rethink the features of our doctoral program so that we are focused on doing what is necessary to produce stewards of the discipline.

Understanding and Cherishing
the Contradictions in Science

The doctorate in the natural sciences is *seemingly* in a much better shape than are the much-debated doctorates in the social sciences and the humanities. It is much less controversial, and its objectives are less often questioned, for the scientific community indulges in a greater sense of consensus than is the case in the professional communities in other areas of academe.

Why do I say "seemingly"? The problem lies exactly in the reasons it looks so unproblematic. There is, in fact, far more fundamental controversy within the sciences than its practitioners are prepared to confront. This leads to doctoral preparation of the next generation that leaves students and new Ph.D.'s living in a dream world of putative consensus and shared premises. They need to understand that much of modern science still must confront basic epistemological issues of knowledge and knowing, ranging from questions of knowledge organization and images of the possible to arguments about method, precision, and rigor.

Elsewhere in this volume, Catharine Stimpson tells us that the humanities are messy, pointing out the double sense of their messiness: turmoil, disorder on the one hand, and healthy complexity on the other. The same is true about the natural sciences. Just as in the humanities and the social sciences, there are no complete theories of anything in the sciences: the theoretical structures are far from complete; the foundations abound in internal contradictions and rapidly changing presuppositions. But whereas the social sciences and the humanities accept incompleteness and contradiction as a given, perhaps even welcome it, most of the natural sciences ignore it, claiming that incompleteness and the accompanying contradictions do not affect the daily work of the scientist, neither in experimental work nor in theoretical deliberations, for they are considered unimportant passing phenomena—actually, mere noises—on the long and uninterrupted road toward certain and complete knowledge and Truth.[3]

It would be presumptuous on my part (or, for that matter, on anybody's part) to make general statements and suggest correctives or changes in the scientific contents of the doctorate in the different disciplines. This essay will, therefore, concentrate on aspects of the doctorate that are, although inseparably connected, beyond the narrowly understood scientific content of what is being taught, transferred, and internalized by doctoral students.

So now we are in the domain of epistemology, even though the working scientist wants to think this domain away from the center of the scientist's attention. That was not always so. There is no nineteenth- or early-twentieth-century textbook that does not start with an extended epistemological chapter, dealing exactly with the question, What constitutes knowledge in this discipline? This is especially important if we think of the multivolume compendia, or "Vorlesungen," covering whole disciplines. It served a good and very educational purpose, in that the same scientist was supposed to cover the whole of physics or the whole of biology. In the process of doing that, contradictions came up, competing paradigms became inescapable, and even if the self-chosen task of the writer was to eliminate such disturbing "noises," they had to be dealt with nevertheless.

With increasing specialization, this tradition disappeared, and the need to confront inconsistencies between and among subfields disappeared with it. Imagine that today the repeated and deep disagreement on the foundations of physics between Philip Anderson and Steven Weinberg (perhaps the two most important Nobel Prize–winning leaders of the profession) would not come out in little-read "philosophical" asides of the two. Neither would it emerge through the contradictory advice they might offer to a Senate committee deciding whether or not to fund the multi-billion-dollar superconducting supercollider. Instead, each would be expected to write a comprehensive, five- to six-volume textbook of the whole of today's physics, each writing about elementary particle *and* solid-state physics. These two series would then be the ideal training for the doctoral student in physics, regardless of the student's specialization in either elementary particle *or* solid-state physics.

Would Anderson and Weinberg disagree on the body of knowledge in physics? No, they would not. They would disagree over a question that is much more fundamental: Could it possibly be that different levels of organization of matter (subatomic, atomic, molecular, cellular, and so on) obey different sets of laws that are not necessarily reducible to each other, as Philip Anderson (1972) dares to ask? Or, on the contrary, as Weinberg (1992) has been consistently claiming for several decades, are we indeed approaching the final theory?

To understand such a debate, we must indulge in interpretation, which is part of a theory of meaning. Yet it is clear to all what enormous differences these are and how much is at stake.[4] Nonetheless, consensus among the community of scientists has been an ideal, or even an ideology, ever since the emergence of modern science in the 1660s in London and Cambridge. Like every other intellectual movement, even if it is formulated in terms of nonpolitical, objective, value-free, context-independent scholarship, science emerged in the framework of a given political context. That political context influenced, to a great extent, the socially determined confines of the movement, even though it did not influence the very content of the ideas involved.

Be assured that I am not claiming that the content of knowledge is socially determined.[5] Mine is not a facile postmodernist and rather primitive claim of the sort that invited the no less facile and primitive "science wars," culminating in the Sokal Affair (described in some detail in Chapter Twenty). What I claim is that we must not ignore what follows from serious contextual history: modern science emerged after the painful and cruel wars of religion that killed off a substantial part of the population of Northern Europe. The worried scholars—helpless observers—became more and more convinced of the need to create a new type of knowledge that would continue to serve the glory of God but not be dependent on the differences between the various religious movements. They had, if you will, a strong urge to establish value-free, objective, rationally based knowledge; they had an ideological need for what became modern science.

That urge did not influence the content of knowledge; there are no socioeconomic roots of Newton's *Principia*. But it did set the context in which such a science would emerge.[6] The tradition of consensus was very strong among the first modern scientists and was verbalized repeatedly by Robert Boyle, who helped formulate the ideology of the Royal Society. This tradition is now deeply ingrained in the training of scientists and is part-and-parcel of doctoral training. Whereas in the humanities and in the nonquantitative social sciences, disagreement on basics is considered an intellectual desideratum, in the sciences, it is not.[7] The quest for consensus in the sciences is at the root of the fact that very often students in the early years of their studies are not being told expressly that still, as of today, there is a fundamental theoretical and empirical contradiction between the standard model and gravitational physics. In many cases this contradiction is a revelation to the doctoral student.

Why does this embrace of consensus persist? One recent influence comes from the philosophy of science. Although philosophy of science never had any significant influence on the growth or direction of change in science, the ideas put forth by Thomas Kuhn in his *Structure of Scientific Revolutions* were most widely read and reflected upon since its publication in 1962 (Kuhn, 1996).

Kuhn's resulting influence was twofold. First, Kuhn articulated and strengthened the view that was already shared by most scientists: when a science becomes mature, it becomes mono-paradigmatic, and then it is as nearly consensual as is possible. Change comes uncontrollably in the form of a "scientific revolution." One cannot prepare for it, and thus one need not educate for it. If we agree with this view, doctoral training in the sciences is just right as it is.

Another important influence of Kuhn is on our conception of science as an integral part of culture in general (science as a cultural system) and on science studies; a more important influence has been on science policy (including policies of granting agencies). Kuhn opened the door for serious discussion of how the social context influences the growth of knowledge. The new and rich research area of science studies (which combines history, philosophy, and sociology of science, obviating the need to distinguish between them as separate disciplines), although far beyond what Kuhn found acceptable, contributes to a much deeper understanding of the historical and social conditions under which new disciplines and new problem areas emerge.[8]

Most of those who read Kuhn were historians, philosophers, sociologists of science, and the educated public. Perhaps most important, politicians and those engaged in science policy also read it. It had, however, very little influence on working scientists. (Steven Weinberg puts this point very strongly: "We learn about the philosophy of science by doing science, not the other way around" [2001, p. 84].) However, it is interesting that most scientists agree with Kuhn, and having found reassurance for their initial beliefs, often claim (albeit, ceremonially, in valedictory speeches or while opening and closing public addresses) to have been influenced by him. (Weinberg, of course, disagrees with Kuhn and asserts that no science is ever in a mono-paradigmatic stage: competing paradigms always exist, and the fights among them are being conducted by the leaders of the field, sometimes at the forefront but more often in relative obscurity.)

What else contributes to this sense of consensus and avoidance of the contradictions in science? Avoidance of contradictions follows from the antidialectical nature of science. When the emerging corpus of modern science in the seventeenth century evolved, emphasizing strongly its consensual nature, there was no place in it for dialectical thinking. A dialectical approach suffers contradictions and allows for the fact that different formulations of a question may yield different answers. Rhetoric is dialectical; so is legal thinking; so is a basic approach like that of Philip Anderson, according to whom different levels of organization of matter may be guided by different sets of basic laws, which are not reducible to each other. Also "dialectics" reminds us of "dialectical materialism," namely Marxism, which has no place in the body of science, and thus the wrong gut reactions come to the forefront when a "dialectical approach to science" is mentioned.

Another barrier to exploring contradictions (and even controversial new ideas) is the abhorrence of contradictions in a rationally built up corpus of arguments. Science is considered the rational field of inquiry *par excellence*, and a rational argument does not suffer contradictions—an idea that is very close to the Kuhnian claim that a mature science is practically mono-paradigmatic. If two contradictory theories come to be discussed in a scientific discipline, it is presupposed that at least one of them is false. Moreover, it is also presupposed that a mature science offers a complete overview of its domain. As this thinking goes, there are minor, not-yet-solved problems, but because knowledge is cumulative, these minor gaps will be filled in due course, and the newly acquired additional knowledge will find its rational and coherent place in the corpus.

We are even lulled into thinking (and telling the public, and, worse, teachers of science) that we are unified in our approach to our work, for we are at all times following the "scientific method." In truth, as Weinberg (2001) observes, "We do not have a fixed scientific method to rally round and defend . . . most scientists have very little idea of what the scientific method is, just like most bicyclists have very little idea of how bicycles stay erect" (p. 84). Ever since William Whewell's *History of the Inductive Sciences from the Earliest to the Present Time* (1858), many students of science have made this very same point, not the least of whom was Albert Einstein.

Implications for Doctoral Education in the Sciences

Without calling it philosophy of science, most doctoral students in the sciences tend to internalize a sense of consensus in the sciences because the great majority of their supervisors, without much critical reflection, hold this notion. And this view leads supervisors to hold the notion that it is efficient, from the point of view of the economy of time, for the speed and depth of the training of the doctoral student, not to waste time on contradictions in the field. As a result, critical preparation for the possibility of new thinking at the very foundations is often absent from doctoral training. Rather, the attitude is this: if and when a real genius appears on the scene, he or she will know what to do.

However, it is important historical information that no scientific theory in any discipline has ever been complete. We never had a complete theory of life; that is, we never had a complete biology. Nor did we ever have a complete physics or a complete economic theory—to say nothing of a complete theory of the human being (a complete psychology) or a complete theory of society (a complete sociology). We have partial theories. We have competing paradigms underlying our partial theories. Yet if we do not tolerate contradictions, then we must always decide which partial theory is to be discarded, thus greatly impoverishing our ability to reflect critically and comparatively on our intellectual options.

Understanding different paradigms should be made part of doctoral education in the sciences. I find it patronizing and condescending to doctoral students not to do so, and I believe we have a moral obligation to acquaint our students with all the nonconsensual elements of the state of the art in their chosen field. I do not accept that it is more efficient to neglect these aspects of the sciences. **Doctoral training in the sciences should include a serious study of the foundations of the disciplines, the internal contradictions, incompleteness of prevailing theories, and competing paradigms. The approximate degree of intellectual security and the meaning of taking intellectual risks in the disciplines should be verbalized as part of doctoral education. The contradictions and inconsistencies of science must be cherished.**[9]

How best to do that? Certainly not by preaching. Nor can one make sure that every department has among its faculty one of the leaders of the field, whose very thinking would include everything suggested here. What remains is the rhetorically efficient and strong means of engaging in controversies: dialogue. To facilitate this pursuit, the relevant literature is always available, and whether the doctoral supervisors master that literature or will be exposed to it on equal footing with the doctoral students is immaterial. Perhaps there are advantages to students and their teachers being confronted *together* with new thoughts and approaches.

Ongoing critical reflection in the form of a departmental seminar on the state of knowledge in the discipline must be an integral part of doctoral training. Seminars should emphasize examples of times when the favored theories simply will not work. For example, to strengthen the students' ability to think dialectically, a course parallel to the basic course on the elementary theory of the discipline should be given; in this course, students would explore a theory that does not work. This is as possible in physics as it is in economics. A seminar could address different formulations of a partial theory, showing how they are actually the same discipline. For example, Goldstein, Poole, and Safko's classical textbook, *Classical Mechanics* (2002), can be understood as basically the same body of knowledge as Lanczos's *The Variational Principles of Mechanics* (1986). This is usually done for the Schrödinger formulation and the Heisenberg formulation of quantum mechanics, and that is extremely healthy for doctoral students. When, following the launch of Sputnik, new approaches to teaching science were developed, different versions for teaching biology emerged: a molecular, an evolutionary, and an environmental approach. No effort was made to show that these approaches each teach and study the same subject matter. Equivalents can be thought of in other disciplines.

Guiding Principles for Developing Stewards of the Sciences

The training of doctoral students is unquestionably meant to educate scholars who are professionally well equipped, are aware of the human and social side of the life of their profession, can cope with rapid changes in the problem areas and in the very foundations of their discipline, and can become, in due course, stewards of their discipline. In addition, and not less important, they have to be complex and many-sided individuals who can grapple with the myriad aspects of modern life.

Actually, the need to discuss the nature of stewardship as part of our mandate in these essays is much deeper than the question of whose task it is to be a steward of the discipline. Obviously, there are many social institutions that can and do take it upon themselves to lead, shape, and protect—that is, to serve as stewards of a given discipline. These may be private and public granting agencies, university administrations, and national institutions such as the National Science Foundation, the National Institutes of Health, and the National Academy of Sciences; sometimes individuals' achievements and status make them de facto institutions. But what concerns us here is this question: What in the education of the doctoral student prepares him or her for becoming a steward of the discipline and profession?

Doctoral education in the sciences must emphasize the personality, character, habits of heart and mind, and general scholarly dispositions of the steward of the discipline. Doctoral programs must ask how they can encourage risk taking and intellectual adventurousness while fostering the importance of precision and rigor. For rigor must not be permitted to dominate the personality of a future investigator so that the speculative and conjectural courage needed to do good science is destroyed. Programs must model, practice, and reward risk taking.

Let us consider the education of the doctoral student toward the four aspects of stewardship: generation, conservation, transformation, and responsibility for the field.

Generation

EMBRACING RISK AND RIGOR. Considering the notion of stewardship brings us to the most important and yet the most imponderable part of the education of any scholar, specifically of a scientist: how to educate a daring, risk-embracing scholar, whose flight of imagination is untrammeled and who is daring yet responsible, risk-embracing without being a Don Quixote, and self-confident in rational limits without overestimating his or her intellectual powers? If the young scholar is to err, it is better to be too confident than too risk-averse.

Here we are on very sensitive ground. We wish to educate a generation of scholars who are considerate, egalitarian, democratic, modest, and so on. Yet in my opinion, the greatest deficiency a young scholar can have is being so cautious that scientific endeavor is paralyzed. Applying relent-lessly the critical mode of reflection, not taking anything for granted, not accepting that any past achievement or authority should remain unques-tioned is the sine qua non of doctoral training. But all these attributes come in as secondary requirements. If I were to formulate it in a slogan, the doc-toral student's attitude should be "It is so. But it could be otherwise."[10]

This not only is a controversial formulation but, even if agreed upon, is extremely difficult to achieve. Moreover, by the time the undergradu-ate budding scientist becomes a doctoral student, it is very often too late. So much in the undergraduate training in the sciences is typified by huge floods of material to be mastered, and so much of it is accompanied by being humiliated by better students and often by faculty, that many of the bright freshmen who come with myriad questions on arrival at the uni-versity have, by their third year, only a repertoire of answers, having for-gotten to ask questions or to question what is being fed to them. Yet this is, in my eyes, the most central aspect of producing a steward of the dis-cipline. I shall not try to indulge here in penny psychology as to how to achieve this goal. Let me leave it at this: **difficult as it may be, developing critical thinkers must become an integral part of the intellectual climate of a doctoral program.**

Actually, much of what I expect should be the task of undergraduate education. By extending this argument we could reach the conclusion that social awareness, moral responsibility, and knowledge of the real world could have been the task of high school. Let us instead concentrate on doctoral training here. The readiness to challenge established ideas should have been achieved already in the student's undergraduate education, but the readiness to challenge advanced theoretical foundations or emerging new paradigms on the level of cutting-edge research is definitely a new ballgame and clearly belongs to doctoral training. **The difficulty lies in developing students' ability to do independent research, to solve theoret-ical or experimental problems on their own, with all the confidence and positive verve this takes, and yet to retain the critical, questioning eye for their own ideas and those of peers and superiors. This can be achieved only in informal discussions, small seminars, interdisciplinary discussion groups—in short, in the dialogical mode.** A precondition for such a dia-logue is a nonhierarchical climate. What must count is what is said rather than who says it. I admit that this is much more of a problem in Europe than in the United States, but even here it is often an issue.

It is common wisdom to say that "one responsibility that a steward has to the disciplinary community is to conduct their own research and schol-arship according to accepted standards of rigor and quality" (Carnegie

Initiative on the Doctorate, available online). These words sound good, yet they are very problematic. It is precisely in inculcating the doctoral student with demands of rigor and quality that supervisors, believing that they know what the scientific method is, exactly, and that their chosen method is identical with quality and rigor, stifle all budding attempts at risk-embracing questioning.

This is more easily demonstrated in some areas of scholarship than in others. For example, in philosophy, especially in the philosophy of science, it was once an accepted rule that only analytical methods can guarantee rigor. Now, when many leading philosophers have realized that there are no sound analytical ways to approach the most important aspects of life—love, religion, and ethics—many have embraced these major existential questions by abandoning all rigor. But one could illustrate this also from the natural sciences. For example, what would constitute rigorous research in evolutionary biology? Surely, much that is learned in molecular biology does not apply. At the same time, it is being realized more and more that training on the doctoral level should not allow a cleavage between these two branches of biology. What will count as rigor in such a "combined" department? What do we do with the criterion of predictivity, for example?

Clearly the concept of rigor is all-important. It has to be reflected upon in terms of critical thinking, which takes nothing for granted. Yet being rigorous does not mean that *nothing* is taken on authority or trust; there is no way to put to the test all the accumulated knowledge before applying it. So quality and rigor will have to mean that whenever an experiment based on previous knowledge fails to yield the predicted result, not only the technical details or the calculations but the previously accepted knowledge on which the experiment has been based have to be questioned. Although in principle this is self-evident and would always be acknowledged by any scientist in a ceremonial address or an introductory lecture, it is very rarely encouraged in a busy laboratory. Yet this is exactly when daring and readiness for risk taking should come into play.

Even in specific recommendations for rigor, some critical approach is mandatory. Let us touch, for example, on experimental replicability—in principle, of course. Rarely do we have to repeat de facto experiments, unless there are recurring problems with the theory or with related experiments. However, take the enormous number of data that have to be collected when deciding that, indeed, a new elementary particle has been discovered. Do we really mean that such a series of measurements, often involving hundreds of scientists, technicians, engineers, and hundreds of thousands of pictures, will be repeated simply for the sake of rigor? At the same time we must be able to know when scholarship is irresponsible.

There are no simple recipes for discovering sloppy or irresponsible work. **But rigor should be critically discussed, and different possible ways of being rigorous should be integrated into lectures and laboratory settings.**

CHOOSING PROBLEMS. If there is a single most significant and pivotal process in science, it is *finding the problem.* A scientist must define his or her problem and locate it both on the map of his or her field and in the broader landscape of science, beyond the traditional boundaries of the field. In doctoral education, too often the chance to learn this process is absent altogether; the mentor assigns the problem or a problem is engaged quite uncritically.

Instead, problem choice should be a major focus of the entire doctoral program—a primary responsibility for the candidate to exercise. The student should choose, defend, critique, and examine how it might be otherwise. The student's peers should be invited to examine the problem with the student, as he or she will do for them. **The program should focus more work—course work, colloquia, and formal and informal conversations— on the state of the field and its controversies more generally, always with problem choice at the heart of this work.**

Indeed, unless we accept the anti-intellectual habit in some of the disciplines, in many of the less elite academic institutions and in the more hierarchically organized universities in Europe (including Eastern Europe), that the supervisor allocates the topic of the dissertation, *problem choice is the most crucial point in a doctoral program.*

Why do I believe this? Knowledge, and even more important, understanding, in the discipline is more complex than is obvious. The obvious approach is to master the theoretical and empirical body of knowledge, the usual technical know-how to operate the equipment needed in the discipline, the assessment of data and how to choose appropriate controls, techniques of calculation relying on the appropriate and sufficient knowledge in mathematics, and the tacit knowledge that is typical to the group or the team of the laboratory.

But doctoral education should go beyond the obvious. Students should be getting acquainted with the foundations that are not often referred to or not even mentioned in the course of the daily work of the research team. They should be aware of the underlying disagreement and competing paradigms, should realize to what extent the consensus on the "correct" methodology is local, and should understand that in a different lab or within a different group, even if everyone is working on the same problem (or seemingly the same problem), the method to which all adhere might be quite different. They should have encountered the basic paradigm decisions that may have preoccupied the previous generation of scientists but are now all resolved, at least until the next difficulty occurs. And above all, the students should have arrived at the moment of problem choice after deep and exhausting deliberation of alternatives and after a thorough check and balance on all levels of the final choice: doability, chance of innovation, risks involved, costs and continuous fundability, and opportunities for the topic to broaden into other areas of research.

In many disciplines, the chosen topic involves working with models. A model is a simplified picture of, we hope, reality, in which many parameters that were too numerous to be accounted for have been eliminated. It is rarely the case in the process of the doctoral studies that prime time and attention is spent on parameters that should be retained or eliminated and on what the problem would look like if the choices had been different. Once the model is in place, it is often presumed that the limitation of computing capacity is the only criterion for deciding within which limits the parameters are to be taken into account. That means that the real scientific considerations for deciding the breadth of the spectrum of permissible values are neglected, and the limitation of the machinery is allowed to make the decision. Needless to say, this is anti-intellectual, and it is behind much conventional and not very high-level work in thousands and thousands of doctoral theses. Possibly, the supervisor has gone through such considerations. If so, the quality of the work may be secured, but certainly the training of the doctoral student isn't. Closely related but different are the questions of when and to what extent to rely on models, and when confrontation with the real world is indispensable. These questions should be crucial considerations as the doctoral student chooses a problem.

The process of choosing a problem should be deeply complex. Although it should not be determined solely by the adviser, it should not be chosen by the doctoral candidate alone. **The process of choosing a problem should be an example of interdisciplinary teamwork par excellence. It would be useful to involve with this team an expert in the comparative study of methodology (even if, heaven forbid, this would involve a philosopher of science). Further, the problem and the process leading to its delineation should be discussed at a departmental seminar, with the faculty and other doctoral students present.**

EXPLORING THE BOUNDARIES BEYOND SPECIALIZATION. The superhuman pressure under which doctoral students in most elite departments labor leads to an ever-narrower, highly competent specialization. The sheer quantity of the material to be mastered is ever growing, and the graduate student is trained to be a perfect problem-solving apparatus in a particular narrow, very well-defined area. This type of training is, from the earliest moment onward, considered as an integral part of a goal-oriented, often ritualized career structure—much like the careers of young instrumentalists in music, who are becoming ever better technically and less and less capable of a broad, enjoyable roaming in the full spectrum of diverse musical styles, genres, and abilities. There is no place in this training for doubting, rethinking, slowing down, meditating, meeting neighboring problem areas, or reflecting on the great existential questions of life. In short, it is the perfect intellectual straitjacket.[11] It is believed that any pause in the race will endanger the career.

This attitude is inculcated during the doctoral training and is, in my opinion, a disaster both for the development of the individual scholar and for the development of the profession. In today's world, the rapidity of changes in the body of knowledge and the globalization factor make it necessary for individuals to be well prepared for sharp and quick changes in their research program and frequent physical relocations to new and different social and academic milieus. The broader the training, the better the acquaintance with the varieties of cultures in general and academic cultures in particular. The more flexible the mental habits, the better the chances for leading a successful professional life. If the present style of training and of career structure is good for anybody at all, it can be appropriate only for the very few who will end up in an elite institution, in a high position, and stay there for their entire academic career. The others are programmed for unhappiness and disappointment. So much for individuality.

Historically, it is well known in all areas of scholarship, the sciences included, that many of the most important new ideas and new discoveries occurred at the border between neighboring disciplines and very rarely at the center of well-defined areas of knowledge. This phenomenon was called "alien wisdom" by the great humanist-scholar Arnaldo Momigliano. Yet in this race, doctoral programs devote far too much attention to work within the boundaries of a discipline's subfields and far too little attention to the broader questions of the philosophical, sociological, and methodological contexts of work. **Addressing the broader questions and contexts takes time. It is not a task that can be completed with an introductory seminar (although the design and teaching of such courses are very important) but must be repeated regularly at all the important choice points in a doctoral program: after qualifying exams, at the time of problem formation, and during the dissertation process.**

As for the future of the profession—in Kuhnian language we could say that this training and career structure prepares exclusively for what seems to be "normal science." I use "seems to be" because, if indeed no science is ever mono-paradigmatic, the need to rethink the foundations is much more frequent than what we take into account in the training of graduate students. **Moreover, due to the rapidity of changes occurring in the body of knowledge, it would be self-evident that every two years (and that would mean in the midst of doctoral training) the student takes time to reassess the problem in the context of the map of the field.** I am not suggesting that students should change their research topic in the middle—that would be detrimental—but should rethink the exact place of the chosen problem in the discipline; this indeed could—and should—influence the final formulation of the results.

In general, doctoral education fails to "go meta" in encouraging and guiding the students to step back, look reflectively and critically, contemplate how it might be otherwise, consider the disciplined eclectic of the middle range as against the oversimplification of the single, dominant paradigm, and critically examine the weaknesses of the "mainstream" of the discipline, however well respected and well funded it might be.

Doctoral training in the sciences should also emphasize the need to reassess, periodically, the place of the problem in the discipline. Doctoral students should be encouraged to accept the idea that it is not a waste of time to stop the hectic activity and take some time off to think, meditate, recharge the batteries, and indulge in reassessment.[12]

Conservation

Related to exploring the boundaries of the disciplines and subdisciplines is students' need to balance breadth and depth in the field.

The inherent tension between depth and breadth must be addressed in all the science disciplines, not just in typically interdisciplinary fields (although more and more areas of research are of this nature).

In this volume there are two important essays dealing with neuroscience. One is by Steven Hyman, a neuroscientist who was at the helm of several leading institutions that were instrumental in shaping the emergence and growth of this flourishing interdisciplinary academic pursuit. Therefore, it is very important to note that although he analyzes and emphasizes the need to go into depth and breadth simultaneously, he does not come up with practical suggestions for building a doctoral program that deals with the problem.

Indeed, there is no recipe to indicate the exact (or even approximate) amount of depth or breadth that doctoral training in any of the sciences should involve, nor is there a way to calculate how much to sacrifice the completeness of training that is the goal of existing, classical disciplines (depth) and replace it with a broad view across disciplines (breadth).

There is no way to foretell how much breadth across disciplines or historical knowledge of a discipline a student will need in order to achieve the necessary depth for solving a problem. It depends on the specific problem and, even more, on the stage of the problem-solving process.

The other essay, written by Zach Hall, gives some practical solutions. He suggests that laboratory rotation is an absolute prerequisite for training doctoral students in interdisciplinary areas, that it helps promote both breadth and depth. I would add another experience, beyond the laboratory rotation: every doctoral student should spend at least six months in a different department, either in the same or "neighboring" discipline but definitely in a different culture.

Another practical approach: when students are choosing a subdiscipline to concentrate in or the problem for the thesis, they should survey the discipline and try to locate the subdiscipline or problem in the whole picture. This will help identify the amount of breadth and historical knowledge the problem will require.

Clearly, much of what I have said so far is indispensable for the young scholar who has just finished the doctorate. He or she must have an overview of the field—its foundations and methods, objectives, and research agenda. And on top of that, as I discuss next, the student must have a moral and social understanding of the role that the given discipline is capable of and meant to play in academe and society at large—a tall order but not impossible. Once the mental habit of critically and reflectively investigating every aspect of the chosen field of study becomes second nature, it is no longer a question of how much time to dedicate to such issues but rather an almost automatic reflex of critical inquiry.

The process of critical inquiry should include reviews of the older literature. Encouraging doctoral students to refer to older literature—well beyond what is on the Internet—is not an antiquarian taste. We do know how many important discoveries were made as a result of "aimless" meandering among books or older articles, or simply by serendipity (Merton and Barber, 2004).

To foster that sense of the role and habits of critical inquiry, I would add to doctoral training a critical study of selected biographies of past caretakers of the profession. It should be made an enjoyable part of the doctoral training; it should not be an exercise in hagiography but definitely a normatively constructed series of critical case studies.

Transformation

It is the task of a steward of the profession to be able to communicate the knowledge of the field to others in an understandable and thought-provoking, critical, reflective, and dialogical mode. We can understand this by considering the professional as teacher and the professional who contributes to the public understanding of science.

This role of the steward involves transformation (the educational and pedagogical functions of the scientist), as well as integration and review—work that is generally dismissed or ignored. Leaders in the discipline must understand the critical roles of curricular and pedagogical work in their field and how deeply these functions are affected by the same epistemological understandings that relate to the research role. They must recognize, empirically, that most of those who earn the doctorate will spend far more time teaching and engaging with a variety of publics (industry, policy, and community settings) than they will at the frontiers of science. Doctoral education must equip students to work in these settings.

Moreover, all doctoral students in the sciences should understand, with respect to communication, whether among peers or to the public, that "the standard scientific article" is, in the words of Nobel laureate Peter Medawar, actually a fraud. It gives a rational description of how a discovery should or could have been made, not how it was actually made. All the judgment, false turns, and errors are eliminated.[13]

CLASSROOM TEACHING. The most neglected part of the training of scientists is their training as teachers. It is usually presupposed—obviously wrongly—that knowledge is itself sufficient for its communication. Second (and this is even worse), it is presupposed that communicating or teaching involves mere didactics, simply using educational gimmicks; teaching and learning are not considered a science (one of the main areas of advanced research of The Carnegie Foundation); neither is the question of how to teach or communicate subject matter considered an epistemological question. And because the question of how to teach or communicate anything at all is, in fact, an epistemological question, the content of knowledge has to be thought of in different terms when its communication is at stake. As a result, gaining a new, insightful way of thinking about the body of knowledge of a discipline enriches the scientist's understanding.

In most good doctoral programs, the students are expected to serve as teaching assistants; they often conduct exercises or even give advanced courses on the topic of the doctorate, in which they are expected to be unique experts. Also in good doctoral programs, the department is aware of the need to teach well, and some attention is paid to that aspect of the faculty's work. My main point here is not the moral notion that this is, indeed, the obligation of a faculty. What I want to stress is that if the principles of rethinking for teaching purposes are not considered—that is, if the process of rethinking the place of cognitive results in the corpus of the discipline is not a systematically studied process—the whole effort is in vain. Unlike some of my recommendations, which involve special seminars, for this purpose I do not necessarily suggest a special course. **Rather, I suggest an awareness of the need and the readiness to integrate a study of teaching into *all courses*. It can be done by bringing historical examples, by inventing special illustrations, by including some philosophical or epistemological asides, or by telling the students what thought processes the teacher has to go through when preparing to communicate a body of knowledge.**

Doctoral training must involve a realization by the faculty that teaching and learning is a science, that teaching poses epistemological problems, and that the reflection on these problems will yield a deeper understanding of the body of knowledge and thus has to be made an integral part of the program, whether in formal courses, informal seminars, or, even better, any dialogue with the students about the topic under discussion.

COMMUNICATING TO THE PUBLIC. Contributing to what is called "public understanding" of science is not tantamount to giving a simple explanation of technical details. The public's ability, for example, to evaluate the necessity, desirability, or risks of nuclear reactors will not be developed through technical explanations of the functioning of nuclear reactors. The ability to assess the dangers involved (or not involved) in consuming genetically manipulated food will not be achieved by studying an accessible explanation of the principles of genetic engineering. Scientists need to be able to convey to the public the arguments for and against the use of these devices and materials and to have some understanding of medicine and ecology, even if on a popular level. This is quite different from "transforming" the science into easily understood descriptions. **A scientist needs to be able to rethink the foundations of a given science in its social context. Communicating in this way to the public should be part of the training of the doctoral student.**

Who would train them? Alas, few scientists, not even the leaders, are capable of this type of thinking. Doctoral training in any science should involve social thinkers with sufficient scientific literacy who can discuss with the faculty and the students the kind of arguments needed in order to communicate the discipline to the public.

Responsibility for the Field

Hyman Bass, in his thoughtful essay in this volume, when speaking of the stewardship of the discipline distinguishes between mathematics (or any other field) as a discipline and as a profession. I fully endorse what he says there, but I want to draw attention to another aspect of being a professional. Early on, doctoral students correctly internalize dedication and loyalty to the profession—to its institutions, its ritualized methodologies, its professional ethics, its authorities. This professional loyalty is so strong that it often overshadows or eliminates any loyalty to the academic institution the doctoral student will serve later as a faculty member. This is becoming part of the behavior pattern in the process of building up a professional career, and it results in many phenomena that can be described as character damaging. Although we preach values of collegiality, "communism" (one of the old Mertonian values), sharing of information, and openness of competition in a friendly way for the benefit of science, at the very same time we encourage a cut-throat, competitive, inconsiderate career-mindedness that only loyalty to the profession seems to justify. It is, again, an aspect of the doctoral training for which there is no recipe, and yet it is important enough to be discussed and suggested for integration during doctoral training.

Our current training of stewards of the discipline is successful in one way: doctoral students internalize very early, as part of their ambition for a successful career, the value of becoming referees of papers, editors of journals, or advisers to granting agencies; they aspire to serve on the appointment committees of future colleagues, receive grants and prizes, and, ultimately, if they are ambitious enough, win the Nobel Prize, the Wolff Prize, or the Fields Medal.

The reverse side of this success is the fact that a thin layer of academics fill *all* these positions. Members of that relatively small group referee the journals, receive the grants, advise governments and granting agencies, and sit on the appointment committees of elite universities. And in recent years, much more than before, the pressure for accountability is such that the gatekeepers of the profession either genuinely or hypocritically claim that they cannot afford the risk of irresponsible ideas, let alone to take the risk of charlatanry, because they are the guardians of public money. And thus the chances for a new, controversial, or countertrend idea to receive a hearing or a grant become miniscule.

This success is a direct invitation *not* to support any idea that is beyond the intellectual horizon of referees or grant advisers. Yet we know that, by definition, any new idea *is* beyond the intellectual horizon of the gatekeepers: it may be close enough to the received view that the seniors recognize it as feasible, doable, or reasonable, even if it had never occurred to them, or, it may be far-fetched enough to be really beyond their intellectual horizon. Is there a danger of supporting a stupid or irrational proposal, or, heaven forbid, an idea that is fake? Yes, there is. Is there a recipe to prevent such occurrences? Only if those ideas that are within the intellectual limits of the seniors, that is, of the previous generation, are accepted exclusively.

My solution: training doctoral students should involve historical case studies pointing out innovations that were strange and unacceptable to the leaders of the older generation but later turned out to be the new truth—ideas that were rejected by the gatekeepers (the negative example) or accepted in spite of the risk (positive example).

UNDERSTANDING CONTEXTS. At the opening of this essay, I discussed the social embeddedness of science. The point I made was that the context does not determine the contents of science—ideas are not created by societies—but the context determines the necessary conditions for the possibility of ideas to emerge. A steward of the discipline understands the contours of the context.

The sociopolitical context of contemporary science and scientific research has changed in recent years, and it is critical that students be given opportunities to explore and understand how the globalization of knowledge has changed scientific discourse and changed the way scientists engage with the world.

More than half of those with a doctorate in science will not remain within academe.[14] Of those with doctorates in science and engineering who are currently faculty members (about 46 percent), half are in research universities and half are in other academic institutions (National Center for Education Statistics, 1999). The remaining working scientists and engineers are employed in government, industry, finance, business, transnational corporations, security-related research, and legal firms dealing with the growing issue of intellectual property rights.

This fact is intimately connected with globalization. We live in a world where not only markets and information technology are globalized but knowledge, even ideas at the basis of political systems, are globalized. At the same time, in all societies those aspects of local life that do not touch on the market tend to become stronger: there is a renewed emphasis on local languages, religions, and other dimensions of culture. In all extra-academic activities (but also in academe) the fresh Ph.D.'s who enter the job market will encounter all these characteristics of real life. Doctoral programs must consider how to prepare their doctoral students for this new and changing context. Although doing so might entail supplying the students with technical know-how, it is of greater importance to influence their mode of thinking about the world. At the end of their studies, doctoral students should be encouraged—and helped to spend some time in an internship in a nonacademic milieu, preferably abroad. This experience will also strengthen the student's understanding of what is meant by the "international character" of science (Biddle, 2002).

Moreover, there is another, albeit imponderable, aspect of the thinking and attitude of scientists: their widespread and well-documented "angst" about being contaminated by politics and social problems. Regardless of whether this attitude is being artificially fostered by the intellectual climate in science departments, or, possibly, is a side effect of the very nature of preoccupation with ideas about Nature and the pursuit of objective Truth, it has to be directly confronted. As Helga Nowotny has phrased it so aptly, not only do we have to educate the doctoral student to become a steward of the discipline but also, and no less important, to become "a steward of public interest" (personal communication, 2004). What must be understood about the "local" in order to function intelligently and efficiently in scientific areas, which are seemingly independent of the cultural elements of life? Clearly, most of the answer is nongeneralizable and belongs to the vast domain of "tacit knowledge" (Polanyi, 1966). Yet as multinational companies and even security-driven Western interventions have taught us, there is much in the "local" that has an impact, or at least should have an impact, on the way we handle situations.

UNDERSTANDING THE ANTAGONISM TOWARD SCIENCE.   In her essay, Stimpson enlarges on the defensive, self-deprecatory self-image of the humanities and the prevailing anxiety of being threatened by the social sciences, but even more by the natural sciences. This anxiety has many dimensions: poverty of means in numbers and in moral support by the public. Fear of and antagonism toward the sciences is rooted in the claim of the sciences for monopoly on truth, or rather Truth.[15]

Indeed, there is ample literature that makes this point about the sciences' claim that they have a monopoly on Truth.[16] But without getting into the merit of the humanities' argument with the sciences, what is important for us is to recognize the fact that the sciences are on the defensive, too, and much of their insistence that they have the monopoly on Truth stems from their own anxiety about losing means, moral support of the public, and recognition of their achievements. Although the number of doctorates in the sciences and engineering outnumber those in the humanities and social sciences,[17] and although the financial support of the sciences from both public and private sources still overshadows that of the humanities, and although technology and industry continue to rely on basic training in the sciences, popular support, if not yet declining, is certainly being repeatedly questioned. This has been going on for several decades. The sharpness of the "science wars" can be attributed, at least in part, to the prevailing angst about irresponsible postmodern influences.[18] The defensive literature stresses the danger of the growth of public embrace of a great variety of "irrational" preoccupations such as astrology, Lysenkoism, creationism, parascience, and UFO-ology.

Whatever the reason for the anti-science phenomenon, it is a fact to be reckoned with. Society cannot afford a serious decline of science; too much of our daily life is dependent on a steady supply of experts in science and technology and of new ideas to cope with the steady flow of new problems, even if it is true that some, or even most, new problems are created by our very progress and efforts to solve previous ones. Thus the defensiveness of the scientific community is understandable. Awareness of the problem must be an integral part of scientific education. Moreover, science is a product of the inquisitive human mind, on a par with the social sciences and the humanities. These pursuits must be protected and their support made secure together, as part of one and the same enterprise.

If the argument is about economic relevance, many of the scientific disciplines and mathematics are as vulnerable as the humanities. However, the consensus among scientists and their reliance on the lack of technical understanding among the representatives of many of the granting agencies help hide this vulnerability.

But even more specifically, "if science cannot claim preeminence for its intellectual virtues or *an excellence for its methodologies and sense of design,* then it will have great difficulty laying claim to a rational share of the nation's resources for its perpetuation" (Gross, Levitt, and Lewis, 1996, p. x). Indeed, every doctoral student, whether in the physical, biological, earth, or health sciences, will find these remarks on scientific methodology familiar and congenial—perhaps too familiar. **Most doctoral programs in the sciences give a seminar or course on the scientific method. The course should be made critical and reflective, comparative, and deliberately controversial. This goal could best be achieved if several scientists, preferably from different disciplines and with diverging methodological convictions, would co-teach such a course.**

MAKING COMMON CAUSE WITH THE HUMANITIES. There is a tacit presupposition that the "culture wars" of the 1960s and 1970s (not the same as the "science wars") had primarily to do with the humanities. As described in Stimpson's essay, the culture wars were waged around four issues: "the nature of the United States and its role in the world . . . race and race discriminations; gender and gender discrimination, and sexual norms." It is easy to overlook the fact that all these issues touch on the education of the natural sciences, too, both externally and in the body of knowledge.

Externally, such issues have a decisive influence on who is going to do a doctorate in the natural sciences. Creating equal chances for daring to start on a doctorate and then succeed in it for minorities, be it for women or for people of color, is of major importance. The problem of the role of the United States in the world is more relevant today than ever. Will a patriotic American who goes along with the neoconservative, or even Bushian, ambition of acting as policeman of the world, and who sees his or her role as an exporter of democracy, human rights, or anticorruption policies, go and study languages, cultures, or comparative religion rather than the natural sciences? Or, alternatively, will those who reject this role for the United States turn more than ever to the arguably "value-free," "objective," and "rational" natural sciences? In the body of knowledge, has the gender-equality revolution weakened the typical male presupposition that because a woman takes care of children, she might spend less time in a lab, and it is therefore much more risky and wasteful to employ her in the experimental sciences? Moreover, has the sexual revolution succeeded in demoting the myth that the thinking of women is inferior and less rational and, especially, that fewer women are able to think mathematically than men? Whatever the answer to these questions, it has a major influence on who goes into a doctoral program in science, and, in the end, how the doctoral training is undertaken.

The usefulness of Stimpson's points in understanding the situation for the sciences suggests that the different emphases between the natural and the social sciences and humanities be integrated during doctoral training. Good arguments should replace the habitual labeling and mutual recriminations. For example, theories of the beautiful are as much part of physics, of complex systems, and of evolution and cosmology as they are of literary studies. Rather than trying to define what the "beautiful" is, let us consider the power of the argument that a theory is beautiful: it actually obviates the need for critical reflection. Indeed, mathematicians and theoretical physicists often announce the beauty of a new theory with prophetic fervor. We encounter the same uncritical attitude to concepts like simplicity or, on the contrary, complexity. The greatest minds indulged in this. For "simplicity," one might think of Einstein; for "complexity" one could invoke Niels Bohr, Kepler, and many others since, for arguing the truth-value of a theory from its beauty. **The doctoral student should acquire a critical ability to reflect on the pet beliefs of the best and brightest.**

Scientists who think in terms of beauty and methodological values should not hide these thoughts in their secret minds nor relegate them to their memoirs, written after retirement, or to ritual public addresses. They should make them themes of doctoral education. **Every doctoral student** should be able to conduct an argument on the meaning of the claim, be it in physics, biology, or any other science, that symmetry rules are beautiful, and, as such, have claim on truth value.

There are other areas in which one field can learn from the other. Whether in physics or in biology, the question of the possibility of reduction of different levels of organizations, one on the other, and thus of explanations, is fundamental and should be made part of the education of the doctoral student in all the sciences.[19] A new development, stemming from Jerome Bruner's work, is the emphasis on narrative as a cognitive process. To study narrative is to study the interpretive stance, whether in law, medicine, or any other area (Bruner, 1990, 2002). Case studies in law would not immediately seem relevant for the training of scientists, but consider that Columbia's medical school, under the guidance of Rita Charon, set up a department of narrative medicine. Students deduce, through studying the structure of the story of the patient by means of literary theory, how the story might influence the diagnosis. And thus the "scientific method" of medicine becomes deeply involved with literary theory. Narrative in meaning-making is also central to problems of relativism and constructivism, which all impinge on the training of doctoral students in the sciences.

One final thought on this matter: one of the foremost intellectuals of our time, the anthropologist Clifford Geertz, suggests that culture can best be studied by breaking it down into "cultural systems." Geertz wrote several magnificent studies: "Religion as a Cultural System" (1973a), "Art as a Cultural System" (1983a), "Common Sense as a Cultural System" (1983b), and others. Unfortunately, he never wrote a "Science as a Cultural System," but as a commentator on my lectures with this title at the Boston Colloquium for the Philosophy of Science, Geertz did not distance himself from the idea that science is also a cultural system. In "Thick Description," Geertz says that "man is an animal suspended in webs of significance he himself has spun . . . culture [is] those webs, and the analysis of it [is] . . . therefore not an experimental science in search of law but an interpretative one in search of meaning" (Geertz, 1973b, p. 5).[20]

Practical Matters: Rethinking the Features of a Ph.D. Program in the Sciences[21]

The question posed to me was, If you could start *de novo*, what would the features of a Ph.D. program in science be? Next I offer some practical recommendations in addition to those I offered earlier. Among other features, I would add to the doctoral training process two intensive, eight-week-long periods. However, the vexing problem of doctoral education in the sciences is that the doctoral studies already take too long. So, as I discuss features of the doctoral program, I offer a way to shorten the process, even while adding the activities I suggest.

Training the Newcomers

Upon their acceptance to the graduate program, before the course work normal to most U.S. doctoral programs, all new and continuing graduate students and their faculty should participate in a twice-weekly, intensive seminar, where all the issues mentioned in this essay are systematically touched upon, accompanied by the relevant literature, appropriate case studies, and frequent oral reports by the incoming graduate students. Alternatively, a well-structured course, richly accompanied by an appropriate bibliography, could be developed. The presence of the older graduate students and of the faculty is very important, even if those would speak against some, or even many, of my suggestions and observations. The very discussion of such matters would achieve the degree of awareness that I consider essential for graduate training. At the end of such an intensive course, the student will have been made aware of the "truths" to question, criticize, contextualize, reaffirm, or abandon. This could be the course that Catharine Stimpson has called "General Education for Graduate Education" (Stimpson, 2002).

Course Work

In general, the less frontal teaching the better. Although students must master some basic material, whether they are in a well-defined discipline or in typically interdisciplinary fields, as far as possible the mode of their studies should be dialogical, that is, small discussion groups, shared problem solving, and discussion of papers by the students themselves and from the printed literature. It is of major importance that such discussions take place in a strictly nonhierarchical atmosphere (what counts is what you say, not who says it), in the presence of faculty (preferably representing several disciplines) and older graduate students.

After the Comprehensive Exams

The period after the student passes the comprehensive exams and is starting the search for a research topic is a most formative one. I consider this period the most important and intellectually most taxing part of a doctoral training period. It should be used carefully to develop the student.

Let me make it very clear once more: simply distributing research topics among the incoming batch of new doctoral students is one of the most anti-intellectual, and even morally least acceptable, aspects of otherwise very efficiently organized departments. When topics are assigned, the only point of view is the immediate need of a professor or of a research team for solving a scientific problem, which, in itself, can be very important in the body of knowledge and also relevant for society at large. To be given a topic and thus to be used as a minor technician in a huge machinery is the opposite of being trained for intellectual risk taking. Unfortunately, it is common to structure the long period of the doctoral training so that the student spends too much time as a technician (half a year or even a year of "apprenticeship," depending on the discipline) as a minor cog in a big wheel.

The economic argument that some huge research projects can be financed only if a large number of underpaid graduate students are employed is unacceptable from the educational point of view; in the long run, it is also wrong economically, if the future productivity and efficiency of the graduate student for the profession and the country that is subsidizing the research is taken into account.

Instead, after passing the comprehensive exams, the doctoral student should spend an eight-week period searching the literature, thinking through the foundations of the field, and mapping the problem areas to be worked on in order to zero in on an interesting, important, innovative, and doable research topic. This is a process of intensive, individual, critical reflection, of absorption of great amounts of new material. It is also an important social-educational-collegial process. In such a process, other graduate students at the same stage, advanced graduate students who have embarked already on working on their chosen topic, and the faculty of the department should be actively involved. Moreover, experts in modeling, in techniques of computing, and in planning experimental set-ups should also participate.

The student should prepare his or her idea about problem choice in as much depth as possible at this stage, accompany it with an appropriate bibliography, and present it to the others in a seminar, with faculty and other graduate students present. The student and the doctoral committee should discuss the idea critically and receive from their colleagues encouragement to continue or advice to abandon the topic.

Finding Time by Putting Learning at the Heart

Finally, let me touch on an all-important issue that is also raised by Hyman Bass in his essay. He says, "[A]n obvious and fundamental dilemma. Reform agendas . . . typically know how to add but not subtract. To an already demanding model . . . we have proposed added conditions of performance. Yet the traditional model has already been criticized for the excessive time required."

How true. Bass talks about mathematics, but the argument applies to all disciplines. He has no obvious or simple solution to offer. Let me stick my neck out and propose a solution, which is not necessarily obvious but is very simple. Abandon the conventional wisdom that good preparation of a scholar means that the university has actually taught all the knowledge necessary for the future scientific work of the Ph.D.

The conventional approach suffers from the usual malaise of most educational and instructional theories: it looks at the input and not the output. In other words, we measure our success in preparing the students by what we taught (the input) and not by what they learned, or, even more important, are capable of learning in the process of problem choice—the actual work on the chosen topic (the output). Programs must insist that the students attend only a minimal number of courses to acquire the tools to learn from books or observation. I presume that in general; obviously, the specific list of courses will be discipline-specific. However, by following this recommendation, programs can drop at least half of the obligatory courses, possibly even more.

Rethinking the Faculty

There is one additional important and very complicated issue: whatever is being recommended here can happen only if the relevant faculty play along. Or, in other words, it is not enough to rethink the doctorate. We have to rethink the faculty. This cannot be done by mere preaching, although it is possible to argue and demonstrate that whatever is suggested for the training of the doctoral students will be beneficial for the profession, and, ultimately, for the individual faculty member. A central feature of these recommendations is that they are not realizable in bits and pieces. It is a somewhat different approach to department life altogether, and thus a doctoral training based in the final account on a nonhierarchical atmosphere—a critical, reflective, and dialogical mode for conducting intellectual work.

Acknowledgments

I am appreciative of and grateful for the many useful critical comments, a great many of which I have adopted, from the following colleagues: Aziz Al-Azmeh, Daniel Dor, Chris Golde, Gerald Holton, Szilvia Kardos, William Newton-Smith, Helga Nowotny, Gottfried Schatz, Lee Shulman, Catharine Stimpson, Günter Stock, Ellen Wert, and Harriet Zuckerman.

NOTES

1. For the origins of Merton's powerful ideas, see *Social Theory and Social Structure* (Merton, 1968). See also "Analysis and the Complex Problem of Intellectual Influence. A Comment on 'Testing the Ortega Hypothesis: Facts and Artifacts' by M. H. Macroberts and B. R. Macroberts" (Zuckerman, 1987, p. 331).

2. Before the abstract came to be a common prelude to a paper, authors would provide a summary of the argument the readers would find. This seventeenth-century strategy seems highly advantageous, and I offer it here.

3. The biological sciences are much more open to admitting internal contradictions and incompleteness in their theories than are the physical sciences. Of course, whether it is the state of the art in the biological sciences that invites more admitted "messiness" than do the physical sciences is an arguable point. Nevertheless, the biological sciences are much more flexible, open-ended, contradiction-tolerant, and context-dependent than are the physical sciences. Because much of the future lies with biology, the strength of the argument in favor of awareness of context dependence may be a battle half won.

4. Similar deep divides are prevalent in the debates between molecular biologists and evolutionary experts, much as the state of the art is pushing them toward problem areas where the distinction becomes redundant. In the final account, whatever the explanatory framework, the experimental work will have to be conducted more on the molecular or more on the holistic level.

5. I do not do so, either in terms of the famous 1930s formulation of "The Socio-Economic Roots of Newton's *Principia*" (Hessen, 1971) or in terms of the 1970s and 1980s "Strong Programme in the Sociology of Science." See, for example, *Scientific Knowledge: A Sociological Analysis* (Barnes, Bloor, and Henry, 1996).

6. Nor did this happen for the first time. When Plato introduced epistemic knowledge and fought tooth-and-nail the "metic" (that is, cunning reason) kind of knowledge that was being pursued in the poleis on the Agora, he was doing so in the framework of a strong antidemocratic, aristocratic bias. The great intellectual debate between the Augustinians and the Thomists, from the fourteenth century but especially in the fifteenth and the sixteenth centuries, was conducted in the context of the Reformation and Counter-Reformation.

7. I stress the nonquantitative social sciences, because the quantitative ones are keen on aping the natural sciences, thus their reliance on methodological individualism. The commitment to the belief that because we cannot rigorously study societies, we must study the individual and then try to extrapolate from the individual to the group, is an invitation for consensus.

8. However, emphasizing the necessary conditions (never the sufficient ones) for such developments, some claims about science as a cultural system go beyond what I would call acceptable rational limits: there is an attempt to "relativize" the results of scientific research, explaining scientific activity merely in terms of power, interests, and status, forgetting about the formative role of human curiosity and the dimension of scientific knowledge—clearly absurd.

9. Throughout this essay, concrete recommendations appear in boldface.

10. This was the title of the inaugural lecture that Helga Nowotny and I gave when being appointed to the Feyerabend Chair in Theory of Science at the ETH Zürich in 1993. Later it became the title of a short book by Helga Nowotny (1999).

11. I have been a Permanent Fellow at the Institute of Advanced Study in Berlin for many years and thus a participant in their selection process for fellows. We are encountering greater and greater difficulty convincing gifted young researchers, especially in the sciences and, worst of all, in the medical sciences, to benefit from the offer to take a year off under ideal conditions and lean back and think or write or just meditate.

12. If this training is successful, the fresh Ph.D. will dare to "stop the clock" from time to time during the immense pressures of an academic career.

13. The literature on this issue is ample. See, among others, Peter Medawar's "Is the Scientific Paper a Fraud?" (1963/1990), Richard Feynman's Nobel address, "The Development of the Space-Time View of Quantum Electrodynamics" (1966), and above all, see Merton's masterly "Afterword" to *The Travels and Adventures of Serendipity* (Merton and Barber, 2004, pp. 269–278).

14. According to data from the 2001 "Survey of Doctorate Recipients," the employment sectors of science and engineering doctorate holders were 45.8 percent education, 9.5 percent government, and 44.7 percent industry; see "Employment Sector, Salaries, Publishing, and Patenting Activities of S&E Doctorate Holders" (Hoffer, 2004).

15. Stimpson here quotes an excellent essay, "The Sokal Affair and the History of Criticism" (Guillory, 2002).

16. Actually, scientists very rarely claim absolute truth, yet it has become a widespread belief that they do claim that.

17. In 2003, 48.1 percent of doctorates were awarded to students in the broad areas of physical and life sciences and engineering combined, whereas 46.2 percent were given to students in the fields of humanities, social sciences, and education (Hoffer, 2004).

18. It is, as usual, difficult to pinpoint exactly when and how a public debate started, yet let us start with two books: *Higher Superstition: The Academic Left and Its Quarrels with Science* (Gross and Levitt, 1994) and *The Flight from Science and Reason* (Gross, Levitt, and Lewis, 1996). Then came Sokal's hoax article in 1996. I would recommend two good readers to every doctoral student: *The Sokal Hoax: The Sham That Shook the Academy* (The Editors of Lingua Franca, 2000) and *The One Culture? A Conversation About Science* (Labinger and Collins, 2001), which is reviewed in detail in *Social Studies of Science* (Stolzenberg, 2004).

19. Much as I would consider relevant to the training of the doctoral student to get a glimpse into the prevailing theories of mind, I admit that this would be too far-fetched for most doctoral programs in the sciences.

20. See also my "A Programmatic Attempt at an Anthropology of Knowledge" (Elkana, 1981) and the recent "Rethinking—Not Unthinking—the Enlightenment" (Elkana, 2000).

21. The need to rethink the doctorate should not come as a surprise to anybody. The literature is quite extensive. One of the revealing research reports is a survey initiated by The Pew Charitable Trusts (Golde and Dore, 2001). The survey stresses how uninformed many doctoral students are about the various stages of doctoral training, about the details of professional practice, and also of ethical issues. Above all, many students are without any accompanying help in navigating the training process. See also the report "Assessing Research-Doctorate Programs: A Methodology Study" (Ostriker and Kuh, 2003). Unlike previous reports, here the needs of the students are treated as central.

REFERENCES

Anderson, P. "More Is Different." *Science,* 1972, *177,* 393–396.

Barnes, B., Bloor, D., and Henry, J. *Scientific Knowledge: A Sociological Analysis.* London, U.K.: Athlone Press, 1996.

Biddle, S. *Internationalization: Rhetoric or Reality?* ACLS Occasional Paper, No. 56. New York: American Council of Learned Societies, 2002.

Bruner, J. S. *Acts of Meaning.* Cambridge, Mass.: Harvard University Press, 1990.

Bruner, J. S. *Making Stories: Law, Literature, Life.* New York: Farrar, Straus & Giroux, 2002.

Carnegie Initiative on the Doctorate. "Stewards of the Discipline." Available at www.carnegiefoundation.org/cid/stewards.htm.

The Editors of Lingua Franca (eds.). *The Sokal Hoax: The Sham That Shook the Academy.* Lincoln: University of Nebraska Press, 2000.

Elkana, Y. "A Programmatic Attempt at an Anthropology of Knowledge." In E. Mendelsohn and Y. Elkana (eds.), *Science and Cultures: Anthropological and Historical Studies of the Sciences.* Dordrecht, Holland: D. Reidel, 1981.

Elkana, Y. "Rethinking—Not Unthinking—the Enlightenment." In W. Krull (ed.), *Debates on Issues of Our Common Future.* Weilerswist, Germany: Velbrück Wissenschaft, 2000.

Feynman, R. "The Development of the Space-Time View of Quantum Electrodynamics." Nobel lecture, Dec. 11, 1965. Published in *Science,* Aug. 12, 1966, *153,* 699–708.

Geertz, C. "Religion as a Cultural System." In *The Interpretation of Cultures: Selected Essays.* New York: Basic Books, 1973a.

Geertz, C. "Thick Description: Toward an Interpretative Theory of Culture." In *The Interpretation of Cultures: Selected Essays.* New York: Basic Books, 1973b.

Geertz, C. "Art as a Cultural System." In *Local Knowledge: Further Essays in Interpretative Anthropology.* New York: Basic Books, 1983a.

Geertz, C. "Common Sense as a Cultural System." In *Local Knowledge: Further Essays in Interpretative Anthropology.* New York: Basic Books, 1983b.

Golde, C. M., and Dore, T. M. *At Cross Purposes: What the Experiences of Today's Doctoral Students Reveal About Doctoral Education.* A Report to The Pew Charitable Trusts, 2001. Available at www.phd-survey.org.

Goldstein, H., Poole, C., and Safko, J. *Classical Mechanics.* (3rd ed.) Menlo Park, Calif.: Addison-Wesley, 2002.

Gross, P. R., and Levitt, N. *Higher Superstition: The Academic Left and Its Quarrels with Science.* Baltimore: Johns Hopkins University Press, 1994.

Gross, P. R., Levitt, N., and Lewis, M. W. (eds.). *The Flight from Science and Reason.* New York: The New York Academy of Sciences, 1996.

Guillory, J. "The Sokal Affair and the History of Criticism." *Critical Inquiry,* 2002, *28*(2), 470–508.

Hessen, B. "The Social and Economic Roots of Newton's *Principia.*" In *Science at the Crossroads: Papers Presented to the International Congress of the History of Science and Technology.* (2nd ed.) London: Frank Cass, 1971.

Hoffer, T. B. "Employment Sector, Salaries, Publishing, and Patenting Activities of S&E Doctorate Holders." *InfoBrief,* 2004. Washington, D.C.: National Science Foundation.

Hoffer, T. B., and others. *Doctorate Recipients from United States Universities: Summary Report 2003.* Chicago: National Opinion Research Center, 2004.

Kuhn, T. *The Structure of Scientific Revolutions.* (3rd ed.) Chicago: University of Chicago Press, 1996.

Labinger, J. A., and Collins, C. (eds.). *The One Culture? A Conversation About Science.* Chicago: University of Chicago Press, 2001.

Lanczos, C. *The Variational Principles of Mechanics.* (4th ed.) New York: Dover, 1986.

Medawar, P. B. "Is the Scientific Paper a Fraud?" In P. B. Medawar, *The Threat and the Glory: Reflections on Science and Scientists.* New York: Harper Collins, 1990.

Merton, R. K. *Social Theory and Social Structure.* (3rd ed.) New York: Free Press, 1968. (Originally published 1949.)

Merton, R. K., and Barber, E. *The Travels and Adventures of Serendipity: A Study in Historical Semantics and the Sociology of Science.* Princeton, N.J.: Princeton University Press, 2004.

Momigliano, A. *Alien Wisdom: The Limits of Hellenization.* Cambridge, U.K.: Cambridge University Press, 1975.

National Center for Education Statistics. "National Study of Postsecondary Faculty," 1999. Available at http://nces.ed.gov/dasol/.

Neurath, O., Carnap, R., and Morris, C. (eds.). *Foundations of the Unity of Science: Toward an International Encyclopedia of Unified Science.* (Combines the ten monographs of Vol. 1 and nine monographs of Vol. 2, formerly titled *International Encyclopedia of Unified Science.*) Chicago: University of Chicago Press, 1969–70.

Nowotny, H. *Es ist so, es könnte auch anders sein. Über das veränderte Verhältnis von Wissenschaft und Gesellschaft.* Frankfurt a.M.: Suhrkamp, 1999.

Ostriker, J. P., and Kuh, C. (eds.). *Assessing Research-Doctorate Programs: A Methodology Study.* Washington, D.C.: The National Academies Press, 2003.

Polanyi, M. *The Tacit Dimension.* Garden City, N.Y.: Doubleday, 1966.

Stimpson, C. R. "General Education for Graduate Education." *Chronicle of Higher Education,* 2002, *10*(49), pp. B7–10.

Stolzenberg, G. "Kinder, Gentler Science Wars." *Social Studies of Science,* 2004, *31*(1), 77.

Weinberg, S. *Dreams of a Final Theory: The Search for the Fundamental Laws of Nature.* New York: Pantheon Books, 1992.

Weinberg, S. *Facing Up: Science and Its Cultural Adversaries.* Cambridge, Mass.: Harvard University Press, 2001.

Whewell, W. *History of the Inductive Sciences from the Earliest to the Present Time.* (3rd ed.) New York: D. Appleton and Co., 1858.

Zuckerman, H. "Citation Analysis and the Complex Problem of Intellectual Influence. A Comment on 'Testing the Ortega Hypothesis: Facts and Artifacts' by M. H. Macroberts and B. R. Macroberts." *Scientometrics,* 1987, *12*, 329–338.

DOCTORAL EDUCATION IN MATHEMATICS

KNOWN AS "THE ENABLING SCIENCE," mathematics is a field with two faces. Pure mathematics is akin to an art; its problems and research strategies are not obvious to nonmathematicians. The layperson knows only that mathematicians write equations and that some problems remain unsolved for hundreds of years. Important areas of study include algebra, number theory, probability, analysis, logic, differential equations, geometry, and topology.

Applied mathematics—pure math applied to problems—is credited with many of the technical advances of the second half of the twentieth century, from airplanes to computers to Wall Street trading. Because mathematics has its own language, it is naturally able to be an international discipline. A large proportion of mathematicians working in American colleges and universities completed much of their education while living in other countries.

Mathematics is also one of the original and core liberal arts disciplines and is foundational for many other fields of inquiry. Therefore, it is taught at every educational level, including at nearly every institution of higher education. Mathematicians are also employed by the government and in a wide variety of business and industry settings. Because of its centrality, there has been a great deal of public concern about the quality of mathematics instruction at both the K–12 and the college level.

The stereotypes are that progress is the result of sudden breakthroughs, that genius shows itself in young mathematicians, and that mathematics, like the humanities, is an individualistic, thus lonely, pursuit. There may be truth to some of the stereotypes; graduate education in mathematics is often taken to task for being too isolating and competitive—an attitude that many believe discourages talented students. However, some aspects of mathematics are quite cooperative. In most departments, faculty members group themselves into one of a half-dozen areas of research in which the department is strong. Mathematicians routinely discuss with one another work in progress in front of a whiteboard. Nevertheless, there is room for improvement. The National Science Foundation–funded VIGRE (Vertical Integration of Research and Education in the Mathematical Sciences) program took as a charge to transform departments into "mathematical villages, blurring the distinction between traditional boundaries separating research and instruction, pure and applied math, and advanced and beginning students" (MacKenzie, 2002, p. 1390).

Currently, 178 departments in the United States offer doctoral programs in mathematics; there are 86 departments or programs in statistics and 20 departments of applied mathematics. These departments, combined, annually grant about 1,000 Ph.D.'s a year. Time-to-degree in mathematics is currently 6.8 years of registered enrollment; 70 percent of doctoral candidates majored in mathematics as undergraduates.

Mathematics has seen a particularly steep decline in the number of U.S. citizens among new Ph.D.'s: 80 percent of all Ph.D.'s were awarded to U.S. citizens in the 1970s; today it is less than 50 percent. Like most natural sciences, mathematics remains male-dominated; women today still represent just over a quarter of all U.S. Ph.D.'s in mathematics, although the percentage has been increasing. Among U.S. citizens, about 80 percent of Ph.D.'s in mathematics are white.

Most mathematics doctoral students spend their first two to three years taking specialized courses. Although they have some common course requirements, generally students have a great deal of latitude to select the courses that most interest them. Their course work typically culminates with qualifying examinations at the end of the first and second year, usually required in a selection of subfields. These exams can serve a gatekeeping function; they are notoriously difficult, and often students fail the exams and must retake them. Students typically begin working closely with an adviser or research mentor only after they have passed their qualifying exams. Identifying a dissertation topic then takes additional time and is done jointly with the adviser. Although dissertations in mathematics are often much shorter than those of other fields (many are under one hundred pages), they represent several years of work.

Most graduate students in mathematics spend several years working as teaching assistants, which is one of the primary funding mechanisms for their doctoral studies. This is due to limited research funding relative to other sciences and because math departments are service departments, teaching thousands of undergraduates in introductory-level mathematics courses. Just as English departments staff introductory writing courses with graduate students, likewise math departments staff their lower-level courses with graduate students. Nonetheless, several reports note that little attention is paid to preparing and supporting graduate teaching assistants.

The academy is the biggest employer of Ph.D. mathematicians. Fewer than one-third of Ph.D. mathematicians take jobs outside academia (non-U.S. jobs included). Among those nonacademic positions, the government employs a sizeable number of mathematicians. In recent years, both post-doctoral and temporary positions have become more prevalent. An increasing number of math Ph.D.'s are beginning their career in one-year positions. Possibly the only area of the job market in math where there is a shortage of suitably qualified candidates and a surplus of jobs is mathematics education—the study of how mathematics is learned and taught.

Doctoral education in mathematics faces a number of well-defined problems: (1) adjusting to shifts in the employment market for Ph.D.'s in math, (2) recruiting a more diverse population of candidates, (3) providing adequate training for teaching assistants, and (4) providing adequate financial and moral support for doctoral candidates and postdoctoral fellows. Less well understood are the difficulty of shifting from individualistic to team approaches for problem solving and the challenge of incorporating new experiences (for example, pedagogy, interdisciplinary studies, industry internships) into an already lengthy doctoral program.

These are challenges that the essayists face squarely and without hesitation. Hyman Bass begins his essay, "Developing Scholars and Professionals: The Case of Mathematics," by drawing an important distinction between mathematics as a discipline and mathematics as a profession. He argues that this has important implications for doctoral education. In fact, this distinction has conceptual application in other fields, and Bass's formulation deserves to be elaborated upon in other contexts. In "A Time for Change? The Mathematics Doctorate," Tony F. Chan calls on the mathematics community to embrace new strategies for graduate education in order to maintain the vitality of the discipline.

—— o ——

BIBLIOGRAPHY

Information and specific data were derived from the following sources:

Bass, H. "Mathematicians and Educators." *Notices of the AMS,* 1997, 44(1), 18–21.

Board on Mathematical Sciences. *Preserving Strength While Meeting Challenges: Summary Report of a Workshop on Actions for the Mathematical Sciences.* Washington, D.C.: National Academy Press, 1997.

Board on Mathematical Sciences. *Renewing U.S. Mathematics: A Plan for the 1990s.* Washington, D.C.: National Academy Press, 1990.

Bozeman, S., and Hughes, R. "Smoothing the Transition to Graduate Education." *Notices of the AMS,* 1999, 46(3), 347–348.

Directorate for Mathematical and Physical Sciences. *Graduate Education and Postdoctoral Training in the Mathematical and Physical Sciences.* Workshop Report. Washington, D.C.: National Science Foundation, 1995.

Ewing, J. (ed.). *Towards Excellence: Leading a Doctoral Mathematics Department in the 21st Century.* Providence, R.I.: American Mathematical Society, 1999.

Hoffer, T., and others. *Doctorate Recipients from United States Universities: Summary Report 2003.* Chicago: National Opinion Research Center, 2004.

Jackson, A. "Graduate Education in Mathematics: Is It Working?" *Notices of the AMS,* 1990, 37(3), 266–268.

Jackson, A. "Making Mathematics Work for Minorities: National Convocation Rallies Forces for Change." *Notices of the AMS,* 1990, 37(6), 666–668.

Jackson, A. "Perspectives on the Underrepresentation of Minorities in Mathematics: An Interview with James C. Turner, Jr." *Notices of the AMS,* 1994, 41(5), 448–450.

Loftsgaarden, D., Maxwell, J., and Remick, K. "2000 Annual Survey of the Mathematical Sciences: Second Report." *Notices of the AMS,* 2001, 48(7), 709–720.

Mackenzie, D. "NSF Moves with VIGRE to Force Changes in Academia." *Science,* 2002, 296, May 24.

Mathematical Sciences Education Board. *A Challenge of Numbers.* Washington, D.C.: National Academy Press, 1990.

McClure, D. "Employment Experiences of 1990–1991 U.S. Institution Doctoral Recipients in the Mathematical Science." *Notices of the AMS,* 1995, 42(7), 754–764.

National Research Council. *Educating Mathematical Scientists: Doctoral Study and the Postdoctoral Experience in the United States.* Washington, D.C.: National Academy Press, 1992.

Reys, R. "Mathematics Education Positions in Higher Education and Their Applicants: A Many-to-One Correspondence." *Notices of the AMS,* 2002, 49(2), 202–207.

DEVELOPING SCHOLARS AND PROFESSIONALS

THE CASE OF MATHEMATICS

Hyman Bass, University of Michigan

TO BEGIN, consider the following definitions from the *Oxford English Dictionary* (OED):

Doctor: (1) A teacher, instructor; one who gives instruction in some branch of knowledge, or inculcates opinions or principles. (2) One who, by reason of his skill in any branch of knowledge, is competent to teach it, or whose attainments entitle him to express an authoritative opinion; an eminently learned man.

Philosophy: (1) (In the original and widest sense) The love, study, or pursuit of wisdom, or of knowledge of things and their causes, whether theoretical or practical. That more advanced knowledge or study, to which, in the medieval universities, the seven liberal arts were recognized as introductory; it included the three branches of natural, moral, and metaphysical philosophy, commonly called the three philosophies. Hence the degree of Doctor of Philosophy. (2) That department of knowledge or study which deals with ultimate reality, or with the most general causes and principles of things.

Discipline: (1) Instruction imparted to disciples or scholars; teaching; learning; education, schooling. (2) A particular course of instruction to disciples. (3) A branch of instruction or education; a department of learning or knowledge; a science or art in its educational aspect.

Profession: (1) The declaration, promise, or vow made by one entering a religious order; hence, the action of entering such an order; the fact of being professed in a religious order. (2) The action of declaring, acknowledging, or avowing an opinion, belief, intention, practice, etc.; declaration, avowal. (3) A vocation in which a professed knowledge of some department of learning or science is used in its application to the affairs of others or in the practice of an art founded upon it. Applied specially to the three learned professions of divinity, law, and medicine; also to the military profession. (4) The occupation which one professes to be skilled in and to follow. Now usually applied to an occupation considered to be socially superior to a trade or handicraft; but formerly, and still in vulgar (or humorous) use, including these. (5) The body of persons engaged in a calling.

Mathematics as a Discipline and a Profession

Mathematics[1] is a *discipline*—a domain of knowledge, an intellectual heritage with ancient roots, with language and methods for analysis and understanding of aspects of the worlds that we inhabit and experience. And mathematics is now as well a *profession*—an intellectual community dedicated to knowledge generation, application, conservation, and transmission, and interacting with other domains and institutions of learning and with the larger society. My thesis is this: *historically, the disciplinary perspective of mathematics has dominated and largely shaped the design of doctoral programs.*

The professional aspects of mathematics have gradually come into prominence over the past half-century, sometimes haltingly and with mostly ad hoc adjustments in education and practice. Mathematics departments have mainly responded to immediate environmental pressures—resource availability and the professional marketplace—without much broad reflection on the proper meaning and purpose of the mathematics doctorate in today's world. I argue here that we should build on the proven strength of the discipline-focused doctoral training and develop scholars who are also professionals, with a sense of calling that I shall begin to elaborate. It is this view, rather than transient market and resource pressures, that can best guide our rethinking of the doctorate in mathematics.[2] The ideas advanced here are not so much conclusions as they are prompts for a broad-based professional conversation about the doctorate in mathematics.

What is driving the need for change? Partly responsible is the intellectual growth in the discipline, as new ideas, methods, and instruments open up unexplored mathematical landscapes of both theory and application. But at least as important are demographic and economic pressures. Mathematics and science undergird the growth and development of modern technology and industry. Everything from security to commerce to health now rests inextricably on scientific foundations. This involves mathematics, both as a direct producer of marketable ideas and applications and as an enabling discipline for all the other sciences—physical, life, and social. As the whole scientific enterprise thus expands and intertwines with economic and social needs, there is a corresponding growth in the building of human capital and thus of the professional communities webbed in this complex system. The professional mathematics community has fully participated in this growth. Moreover, it has been not only a protagonist but, more intensively than the other sciences, a primary resource and agent for quantitative education at all levels.

The human expression of this growth and evolution is, first of all, a long-term increase in the sheer numbers of persons who characterize themselves as mathematicians or as involved in mathematically intensive professions.[3] Second, the variety of professional environments in which substantial mathematics is practiced has greatly expanded well beyond the academic settings—themselves now more diverse—that historically employed the vast majority of mathematics doctorates. This demographic change alone calls for increased professional infrastructure and function (for example, expanded instructional mission, more publications and journals, more conferences, new institutes, more robust professional organizations, greater representation of mathematics in public arenas). In turn, there is a concomitant need for mathematicians to take professional responsibility for managing and supporting this more elaborate infrastructure and function. Our doctoral programs in mathematics have yet to prepare students for these expanded professional roles.

In this essay, I first offer a brief sketch of mathematics as a *discipline*. This perspective, whose validity endures but whose incompleteness for doctoral preparation is increasingly evident, has historically dominated thinking about the doctorate. Following that, I discuss the *profession* of mathematics as it has currently evolved. With this background, I then propose one vision of "stewardship" of mathematics. I deliberately choose not to say "of the discipline of mathematics"; I intend this concept of stewardship to embrace the professional, as well as disciplinary, aspect of the field. In a final section, I outline some implications of this perspective for the design of doctoral programs in mathematics.

The Discipline of Mathematics

The discipline of mathematics, as a deductive science, has its roots mainly in Greek antiquity. Geometry, for our Greek forebears, was considered empirical in content, being a theory of the physical space that we inhabit, but deductive in method. Euclidean geometry took as a logical point of departure a small set of propositions (axioms) deemed to be "self-evident" and then eschewing all reasoning that makes an appeal to physical sense or measurement. The extent to which Euclidean geometry models physical reality is a scientific, not a mathematical, question. But the deductive axiomatic method modeled by the intellectual development of Euclidean geometry remains a cornerstone of the mathematical paradigm. Mathematics today includes deductive explorations of its own internal worlds in their own terms. The extent to which these mathematical worlds reflect, or model, some natural reality may account for the external utility of the mathematics but is not essential to the logical coherence or significance of the mathematics within the discipline. Nonetheless, most mathematical theories have their historical roots in problems arising from empirical science, and even the "purest" of mathematical theories often reconnect in unanticipated ways with the external world, constantly reinforcing Eugene Wigner's evocation of the "unreasonable effectiveness of mathematics" (1960). We are repeatedly reminded that mathematics seems to be the spring of Nature's idiom.

The characteristic that distinguishes mathematics from all other sciences is the nature of mathematical knowledge and its certification by means of mathematical proof. On the one hand, it is the only science that thus pretends to claims of absolute certainty. On the other hand, this certainty, which is self-referential, is gained at the cost of logical disconnection from the empirical world. As Einstein put it, "As far as the properties of mathematics refer to reality, they are not certain: and as far as they are certain, they do not refer to reality" (1921/1983).

This explains a fundamental contrast between mathematics and the scientific disciplines. Mathematics and the physical sciences honor very different epistemological gods. Mathematical knowledge tends much more to be cumulative. New mathematics builds on but does not discard what came before.[4] The mathematical literature is extraordinarily stable and reliable. In science, in contrast, new observations or discoveries can invalidate previous models, which then lose their scientific significance. The contrast is sharpest in theoretical physics, which historically has been the science most closely allied with the development of mathematics. The mathematician I. M. Singer once compared the theoretical physics literature to a blackboard that must be periodically erased.

Some theoretical physicists (Richard Feynman, for instance) enjoyed chiding the mathematicians' fastidiousness about rigorous proofs. For the physicist, if a mathematical argument is not rigorously sound but nonetheless leads to predictions that are in excellent conformity with experimental observation, then the physicist considers the claim validated by Nature, if not by mathematical logic. For the physicist, Nature is the appropriate authority. The physicist P. W. Anderson once remarked, "We are talking here about theoretical physics, and therefore of course mathematical rigor is irrelevant."

On the other hand, some mathematicians have shown a corresponding contempt for this freewheeling approach of the theoretical physicists. The mathematician E. J. McShane once likened the reasoning in a "physical argument" to that of "the woman who could trace her ancestry to William the Conqueror, with only two gaps."[5]

The development of mathematics as a deductive science is more complex than my simple account suggests. Many central mathematical theories were first developed quite far, largely on the basis of deep physical or other intuitions, prior to being put on rigorous logical foundations. Moreover, even the foundations of mathematics and logic have weathered turbulent shocks and tensions, for example, from the work of Gödel and later the constructivist doctrines. But these foundational crises have not functionally undermined the basic deductive ethos of working mathematicians. The mathematician Andre Weil once characterized logic and foundations as the "hygiene" of mathematics, not its heart and soul.

A more recent development is the influence of technology and its essential use in the construction of some important mathematical proofs. The notion of mathematical proof is a precise theoretical construct, but it is quite formal, rule-bound, and ponderous. Mathematicians typically do not produce such formal proofs; rather, they convince expert colleagues that such a proof exists, the presumption being that the conviction carries the belief that, under duress and with sufficient time, such a proof could be supplied by the proponent. Here we glimpse the boundary of mathematics as a discipline—as a set of theoretical ideas, on the one hand, and as a profession—as a human practice—on the other. When a "proof" is reduced to checking a finite, but large, set of critical cases, and this checking is within range of machine computation but beyond reasonable human capacity, what then is the standing of the computer-reliant argument?

Notice that this question is not strictly a mathematical one; it is a question about the intellectual sociology, norms, and methodology of practice.[6]

So much for the deductive methodology of mathematics. What about the *content*—the subject matter of the discipline? How has that changed? Many mathematicians hold deep convictions about the fundamental unity of the discipline. The grand themes—number, space, change, and (more prominently in recent times) chance—are often just different perspectives on or representations of the same phenomena, focusing on somewhat different kinds of questions. These themes are sometimes associated with the respective names—algebra, geometry, analysis, and probability-statistics. What has changed is the appearance of new or rejuvenated areas of investigation within the discipline, as well as vastly expanded interdisciplinary interaction with other domains of science and technology.

Much of this has been spurred by the availability of powerful computers and sophisticated mathematical software for computation, exploration, modeling, and simulation. The latter, which are founded on mathematically designed software, have become a fundamental paradigm in virtually all of science and industry. For example, aircraft prototypes are now tested virtually on computer screens, not physically built and then tested in wind tunnels. It is easy to envisage the cost reductions and design leverage thus gained.

The new frontiers of mathematics investigation and application are too numerous to list, but we can mention a few noteworthy examples. The theory of dynamics and complex systems (studying the long-term evolution of systems governed by even relatively simple nonlinear laws) stalled in the 1920s for lack of computational capacity. The use of computers, comparable with the introduction of telescopes into astronomy, has supported an explosive rebirth and expansion of the subject, including the visual discovery of stunning fractal geometries. Coding theory and cryptology, dealing with historic questions of reliability and security in the public transmission of information, now rests on the use of sophisticated tools from number theory and algebraic geometry.

Theoretical computer science is founded on discrete mathematics and has given birth to the new mathematical domain of complexity theory, which offers precise mathematical measures of the difficulty of certain classes of computations, which in turn is one of the foundations for the design of public, key encryption systems. Quantum models of computation (not yet physically realized) are being theoretically developed and shown to support practical algorithms for problems known to be intractable by conventional computers.

Methods of geometry and analysis have supported the design of non-invasive medical diagnostics. Signal and image processing have achieved dramatic applications using methods from analysis and statistics. Mathematical biology now incorporates tools from fields like topology and dynamics, as well as traditional fields like fluid mechanics. Mathematics of finance has become a thriving field of application, providing widely used mathematical tools to Wall Street. And at the more theoretical end, there has been a virtual merger of fundamental particle physics with some of the most sophisticated branches of geometry and topology, with fascinating shifts in the traditional paradigms of knowledge generation.

The overriding message from all these developments is that mathematics is much more "out in the world" than it was even a quarter of a century ago. There are more directions of exploration within mathematics, with a greater diversity of tools and methods; there are substantial interdisciplinary interventions of mathematics in a variety of fields; the utility of mathematics for many problems of science and society is increasingly evident, and mathematics has a growing presence in administrative and policy environments, both in universities and at the national level. Finally, the mathematics profession has a growing responsibility for helping to improve the quality of quantitative education in the nation's schools—a task that can fruitfully be viewed as another site of interdisciplinary mathematics. Awareness of this outward reach must newly figure in the design of doctoral programs.

The Profession of Mathematics

Historically, the doctoral program in mathematics was designed to be an apprenticeship into the research practice of an academic research mathematician. Its general form, if not the fine details of its structure, was remarkably similar across research-intensive universities.

Mathematics Work Environments

Foundational knowledge, typically gained in the first year or two of courses, covered algebra, analysis (real, complex, functional, and differential equations), and topology-geometry. This knowledge was certified through qualifying examinations, and the student often earned a master's degree upon passing. The next stage was more advanced: taking elective courses and seminars leading to the selection of an area of research and an adviser, perhaps following a second preliminary examination. In the final stage, students framed a doctoral research project, carried out the research, and wrote the dissertation under the guidance of their advisers. In the past, there were also requirements for reading knowledge of as many as two of the major languages of the mathematical literature. These have recently been considerably relaxed, if not eliminated. The final passage is the dissertation defense, typically at the conclusion of four to seven years of study.

Imagine that this newly minted doctoral student gains a faculty position in a similar doctorate-granting, research-intensive mathematics department. What are the components of her professional work, life, and responsibility? First, and foremost in the culture of her professional formation, is the active production and publication of original mathematics research. Second, and at least as demanding in time and effort, is teaching—mostly undergraduate and frequently calculus. Other aspects of her scholarly work might eventually include participating in and running research seminars, mentoring graduate students, writing mathematics papers, interacting with journal editors, peer-reviewing papers and research proposals of others, keeping up with the research literature related to her field, preparing and submitting research proposals for funding support, participating in research conferences or perhaps helping to organize them, joining professional organizations, and writing reference letters for students and colleagues. She would be expected to serve on departmental or university committees and work on committees of state or national organizations. At later stages of her career she might take on major administrative responsibility in the department as chair or director of the graduate or the undergraduate program. She might also be enlisted as a journal editor, or for work in policy environments, or as staff in a federal research agency, or as an officer of a professional organization.

It is interesting for us to consider, along this spectrum of potential professional activities, those for which her doctoral program provided explicit and substantial preparation. Foremost is the preparation for doing original *research*: selecting and framing research questions, assimilating the immediately relevant literature, strategizing the work, using imagination, diligently and productively enduring frustration, and, finally, finding new results, organizing and clearly articulating them, and providing for them well-presented documentation and exposition. In the traditional value system of disciplinary mathematics, this performance of creative scholarship far outweighs all others combined. It is considered the most noble of professional achievements.

Teaching, which typically occupies about half of her working time, is belatedly gaining an improved status in the professional value system. But traditionally it was considered a professional duty (one spoke of "teaching loads" but not of "research burdens"), whose most dignified aspect was the instruction of mathematically talented and motivated students, whom one tried to nurture and induct toward advanced mathematics study. Currently, the quality of mathematics instruction for *all* students is taken much more seriously, not least because of external pressures. Mathematics faculty members are now expected to provide high-quality mathematics instruction across the board, and they are held accountable for this in the prevailing hiring, promotion, and reward system.

At the same time, it is often tacitly assumed that rigorous and deep understanding of disciplinary mathematics, coupled with injunctions to communicate it clearly and coherently to students, suffice to produce quality instruction. The "transfer model" of learning implicit in this Platonic way of thinking treats knowledge as a commodity that the professor carefully delivers to the student, considered as a vessel expectantly waiting to be filled. Until recently, it was hardly acknowledged that teaching entails knowledge and skills that are *more than* academic subject-matter knowledge combined with formally lucid exposition and a sympathetic disposition toward students. In fact, it involves a kind of knowledge of mathematics itself that is distinct from what research mathematicians require for their research or typically know. Moreover, it is only recently being recognized that this knowledge and skill can be taught and learned. Apart from a minimally mentored apprenticeship, through teaching assistantships or graduate instructorships, scant professional development for the work of teaching has been provided to doctoral students in most mathematics departments. Similarly, the skills of mentoring graduate students are, like those of teaching, typically (and imperfectly) gained by imitating the observed models of one's own mentors.

Beyond these two domains—research and teaching—what preparation was provided for the other aspects of our new Ph.D.'s professional life and work? A good initiation into tracking the research literature and participation in research seminars will have been provided. These activities, integral to the dissertation research, are among the vital practices of the ongoing intellectual life of a research mathematician. But there remain numerous other basic professional functions for which little or no mentoring may have been provided. These include the more refined skills of scientific writing, interacting with editors, preparing peer-review evaluations and letters of reference, and preparing and submitting research proposals. Some mentoring for these activities may be picked up as part of a postdoctoral appointment, but unevenly so. Virtually no preparation, nor even consciousness-raising, is made for possible administrative or other leadership or public roles. Nor is there much cultivation of an expected participation in the larger mathematics community, for example, in the professional organizations or as staff in federal research agencies.[7]

The preceding discussion was predicated on our new Ph.D. having joined a doctorate-granting, research-intensive mathematics department. Two other major kinds of career launches have to be considered as well: academic appointment in a less research-intensive mathematics department, for example, in a liberal arts college, or nonacademic appointment as a mathematics specialist in some industrial or other private sector setting. Moreover, her lifetime career trajectory may well include passages in a mix of such environments. They each place many of the same demands on our new Ph.D. that were discussed earlier but perhaps with different emphases and priorities. In the first example, research and intellectual vitality remain important, to varying degrees, but much greater emphasis tends to be placed on teaching, interacting with students, and service to department and the university or college. In the second, nonacademic, types of settings, the mathematical activity tends to be interdisciplinary, and then of course there is need to gain some functional knowledge of one or more outside fields of mathematical application. This kind of work is often part of a collaborative team effort, so that relational skills come into play. Moreover, the demands of effective communication of technical knowledge among others with a very different professional culture and language present a major challenge. It is worth noting that these demands are similar to those of effective teaching. Again, the doctoral program likely provided very little professional development for these kinds of skills, dispositions, and sensibilities.

Mathematicians in the World at Large

Our portrait of the professional life of a mathematics Ph.D. has consisted, so far, of a survey of the diverse demands and responsibilities of the kinds of *work environments* in which she would likely find herself. Missing from this is a sense of what is, or might be, the sense of personal agency and professional identity that our Ph.D. carries into the *outside world at large*. Neither our profession nor our doctoral departments have devoted much conscious reflection to these issues, and hence these have not been cultivated in our doctoral programs.

What professional identity does a traditionally trained mathematics Ph.D. carry, at least ideally? Being a mathematician incorporates a deep and expert knowledge of some significant domain of mathematics, including its epistemology and research methods. This is situated within a broader knowledge of the history and grand intellectual currents of the discipline, including their historic connections with the allied natural sciences, particularly physics. Today, more and more, the mathematician should have some functional knowledge of active interfaces with other disciplines and of important areas of application of mathematical methods. This ensemble of resources provides the mathematician with a rich cultural awareness of the discipline, with the tools and skills for the generation of new mathematical knowledge, and with the skills and expert knowledge for selected interdisciplinary work environments or institutional settings. Finally, the mathematician should be a competent teacher in academic settings and communicator in interdisciplinary settings. This collectively describes a professional identity founded on a deep enculturation into the intellectual traditions of the discipline and further expanded by the demands and vicissitudes of the job market, the mathematician serving as supplier of expert skill and communicator of technical knowledge to needy consumers.

This portrait includes some, but not all, of the roles that "stewardship of mathematics" might encompass. What significance does being a mathematician carry in the larger society and culture? In what ways does a mathematician function as a representative of the discipline in public arenas? What are its dimensions of social responsibility and of cultural and aesthetic expression? To prompt our thinking about these questions, we might consider other professions in which this sense of professional belonging, presence, and purpose is more easily recognized and appreciated. Medicine is a profession of health and healing guided by the Hippocratic Oath. Although each physician pursues a specialized practice, this practice is situated in a larger sense of belonging to a professional community with a collective social mission of human betterment, of which each practitioner is a contributor, advocate, and representative. Law is similarly a profession of diverse expert practices, which carries with it a sense of stewardship of the political institutions on which our system of social organization and justice is founded. Architects provide expert technical and aesthetic skills, but these are expressions of an ancient legacy of the design and function of public and private physical environments to support and harmonize with human need and social purpose. And, of course, creative artists—writers, composers, performers—have a deep sense of how their well-honed craft serves large goals and needs of human social and cultural enrichment, of awakening emotions, and of elevating an awareness of the basic human condition.

What is the larger social and cultural significance of mathematics that the public should know and appreciate and that professional mathematicians could represent? Many current conditions beg for some compelling answers to this question: the existence and growing scale of our professional community, which is supported by public resources; the pervasive, though not highly visible, enabling roles of mathematics in every domain of science and technology; the many years of mathematics instruction, as a basic literacy, required of all school children. These conditions all speak to the implied importance of mathematics. Yet few mathematicians can furnish intrinsic explanations of this that would be compelling to most well-educated adults, who, in the United States at least, often boast of their mathematical weakness. Indeed, mathematicians may well be challenged even to provide convincing arguments to themselves—arguments that go much beyond the comfortable celebration of the beauty and depth of the core ideas and intellectual architecture of mathematics.

This relatively undeveloped sensibility and skill among professional mathematicians is not merely a matter of benign neglect of their social development and responsibility. It has a direct bearing on the overall long-term well-being of the field and of the quality of mathematics education at all levels. It is at the root of the pressing problems of sustaining public resources and of enlisting more, and more diverse, domestic U.S. talent into mathematics and into mathematically intensive professions. It is certainly germane to any conception of "stewardship" of mathematics.

By what means could these larger senses of professional identity find expression, beyond the routines of professional practice? Expression can be found in many ways: op-ed pieces or other public writing and exposition; public presentations or performances; participation in civic enterprises, such as school boards or cultural organizations; or contributions of well-informed advice or service in policy environments and government agencies.

And, perhaps above all, mathematicians can serve through teaching and communicating with the same professional attention and skill that we dedicate to our scholarly research. In each of the instances mentioned, one crucial resource is having deep and well-articulated expert knowledge and communicating clearly how this knowledge bears on the issues at hand. But much more skill and sensibility, of a more subtle kind, come into play. This includes a sense of audiences, of their knowledge and beliefs, and of the kind of language, contexts, and representations that they can find comprehensible and persuasive. It includes a sense of norms for disciplined and respectful interaction with people very different from oneself. It includes an appreciation that, in civil or cross-disciplinary (as opposed to some scholarly mathematical) discourse, adversarial postures are not a primary virtue but are a last recourse, when constructive and collaborative approaches have failed.

Stewardship of Mathematics

As I emphasized at the outset, mathematics is both a discipline and a profession. On the one hand, the discipline of mathematics is a domain of knowledge, with finely developed methods of generation and validation of new knowledge, a noble intellectual heritage with ancient roots, and an unending source of language and concepts for quantitative description and understanding of the world. The profession of mathematics, on the other hand, is a community of human practice—one that generates, validates, synthesizes, conserves, and disseminates mathematical knowledge and practices. "Stewardship" of the field of mathematics must attend to both the strength and integrity of the disciplinary culture and to the health and integrity of the professional community. This may seem self-evident, as each essentially depends on and reinforces the other. However, a main purpose here is to give the professional face of this a visibility that has been largely lacking.

A steward of mathematics must have a deeply developed sense of intellectual and professional mission and community. This is operative in an expanding progression of spheres of professional life and activity.

At the most immediate and familiar level, a mathematician belongs to the community of *research* scholars in her area of *specialization*—colleagues with whom she intellectually identifies and communicates via correspondence, shared manuscripts, conferences, and so on. This is situated within the *larger mathematics research enterprise*. Although any single mathematician is active in no more than a small number of sites of this work, mathematicians recognize the global cohesion and interdependence of the ensemble of this work, and this manifests itself in the lack of parochialism in the advocacy (for example to federal agencies) of support for the field. One expression of this community participation is active membership in and support of the work of the professional organizations in the field.

In a similar vein, as a member of a *university mathematics department,* the mathematician faces a different terrain of collective mission, this time embracing not only diverse mathematical specialties but also interdisciplinary connections with other units and programs, the immense teaching enterprise for which every mathematics department is responsible, and the larger intellectual, instructional, and administrative needs of the university environment. The individual mathematician is actively engaged with only a few components of this vast portfolio of responsibilities. A mathematics department is not a single, purposeful agent with a focused agenda. What makes it a cohesive intellectual and professional community is that each member feels the collective responsibility for and commitment to the whole departmental mission, in the sense that each member respects and supports each aspect, whether directly involved in it or not.

Finally, the mathematician as scholar and teacher may function within the *larger society*, in diverse areas of policy and outreach: federal funding of research, and education at all levels, technical legislation and regulatory policies, and public communication about the nature, significance, and evolution of mathematics and its applications.

If doctoral programs are to produce "stewards of mathematics," what are the capacities that stewardship entails? In the view that I have espoused here, the following should be prominent in that list:

- Mastery of the core foundational knowledge of the discipline, including a broad sense of its historical evolution
- Command of the methods of mathematical inquiry and of certification of new knowledge
- A deep and expert knowledge of at least one specialized area of mathematics at a level supporting the capacity for original research and including a knowledge of how this area is situated in the larger mathematical landscape in relation to other fields, as well as a thorough knowledge of the immediately relevant literature
- A sense of discrimination and judgment of the significance and depth of new mathematical problems and results
- Skills of scientific documentation and written exposition
- Facility in the use of the mathematical literature, including an informed awareness of its scope, organization, and editorial and reviewing practices
- Knowledge (mastery in some cases) of some basic uses of technology in mathematics, including uses of the Web, electronic manuscript preparation, computationally supported research, and instructional uses of technology
- The ability to frame and draft proposed programs of research for outside funding
- Finely developed and adaptable skills for teaching mathematics at diverse levels, from introductory undergraduate courses to advanced graduate research courses and seminars
- The ability and disposition to mentor research students and young faculty
- A general cultural knowledge of the range of mathematically intensive fields and of the ways that mathematics is used in various

human endeavors and with what applications, perhaps including some in-depth knowledge in one or two cognate areas

- Skills of communication of and about mathematics to diverse audiences

Design of Mathematics Doctoral Programs

What does all of this say or imply about the design of doctoral programs in mathematics? Let us summarize some of the main features proposed here.

The strength and soundness of the traditional research training in the core areas of the discipline should be preserved. This is training that emphasizes both a broad and unified global view of the discipline and the need for deep knowledge and original scholarship in some specialized area. In addition, opportunities for interdisciplinary learning and research should be available and sanctioned, if not required. Because of the increasing role of data analysis in applications of mathematics, some exposure to probability and statistics should now be a part of every mathematician's preparation.

Doctoral programs should further recognize the critical role of teaching in a mathematician's career; for this, it does not suffice to provide graduate teaching experience. Much more serious attention needs to be paid to professional development for this work; the involvement of expertise from mathematics education would be useful and appropriate.

Development of competencies with the diverse uses of technology for document preparation, for research, and for instruction should be provided. Attention should be given to the development of skills of scientific documentation and written exposition. Students should learn to navigate and use the mathematical literature and the protocols of scientific publishing and reviewing. Mentoring should be provided for the process of framing a research program and of preparing and submitting a proposal to a funding agency for its support.

Students should be given more explicit awareness of the infrastructure of their diverse professional environments and of the resources and services that sustain them. This includes the mathematics department within the university environment, and, on the outside, the disciplinary community—its organized activities, and the organizations and institutions that sponsor them. Students should be able to anticipate and appreciate the professional roles that they will eventually play in these spheres.

Finally, doctoral programs should more self-consciously and creatively confer a strong sense of cultural awareness in students of the significance of their discipline in the larger worlds of science and society, and of the expectation that they will serve as emissaries of their discipline in the outside world. One concrete way that this might be done is in the form of a professional development seminar. The themes of the seminar could include questions in education, for example, a serious inquiry into the nature of teaching, learning, and assessment or critical evaluation of curriculum materials. Or the seminar might examine some current area of public policy of concern to mathematicians, in which assignments might include composition of an op-ed piece or a letter to a congressperson.

This ambitious list poses a challenging task of program design. Some, but not all, of the items can be treated in a curricular framework, through appropriate course or seminar development. Other aspects might more appropriately be addressed through other professional development kinds of formats. Possibilities include special supervised projects or brief internships, perhaps in the context of a one-credit professional development seminar. These might take such forms as immersion in an interdisciplinary project, time spent in an industrial setting or in a school mathematics program, or a small project of analysis and writing about some policy area, for example, in education, in research funding, about the infrastructure of the profession.

At this point, we must confront an obvious and fundamental dilemma. Reform agendas, of which this essay represents one, typically know how to add but not subtract. To an already demanding model of the mathematics doctorate, we have proposed added conditions of performance. Yet the traditional model has already been criticized for the excessive time required. This is a major design challenge. No simple solution exists. This difficulty cannot, however, be an excuse for inaction. The challenge merits broad discussion in the professional community, with perhaps the development of diverse models emphasizing different kinds of orientation. We can likely profit from a study of how other fields manage, within a fixed timeframe, to prepare doctoral candidates to enter the profession, as well as earn admission to the practice of the discipline.[8]

Stewards of the Profession

This essay argues that the traditional doctorate in mathematics has been fashioned almost exclusively on a *disciplinary* view of the field and that the strength of that model needs to be expanded to encompass the modern evolution of mathematics as a *profession*. Stewards of mathematics must attend not only to the traditional disciplinary missions of knowledge generation, validation, representation, and dissemination but also to the needs and infrastructure of the professional community of mathematicians, to the responsibilities of that community to the discipline, to the institutional environments in which it functions, and to the needs of the larger society.

Acknowledgments

I acknowledge, with thanks, the following colleagues whose comments helped inform this essay: Deborah Ball, John Ewing, Phillip Griffiths, and Virginia Richardson.

NOTES

1. Mathematicians are the primary among multiple audiences for this essay. This is my excuse for the occasional use of technical terms in an essay otherwise intended for a broad intellectual audience concerned with doctoral programs.

2. In the COSEPUP Report, *Reshaping the Graduate Education of Scientists and Engineers* (Committee on Science Engineering and Public Policy, 1995), a related distinction was made between preparation for academic research within the discipline and preparation for applied research in industry, government labs, and so on. That report similarly proposed a better integrated and more versatile preparation for these two kinds of career trajectories; see "Should Doctoral Education Change?" (Jackson, 1996). Earlier discussions of the mathematics doctorate can be found, for example, in "The Ph.D. Degree and Mathematical Research" (Richardson, 1936), "Are There Too Many Ph.D.'s in Mathematics?" (Duren, 1970), and "Graduate and Postdoctoral Mathematics Education" (Ewing, 2002).

3. From 1862 until 1933 there were about 1,300 U.S. mathematics Ph.D.'s earned. Only 16 percent of these published more than five papers, and more than half published none (Richardson, 1936). During the 1950s Ph.D. production increased sevenfold; during the post-Sputnik 1960s it increased from 500 to 1,250 annually. In the 1970s and 1980s there was retrenchment in response to funding reductions and a saturated academic marketplace. About 25 percent of the Ph.D.'s found positions in doctoral-granting departments, the others in liberal arts colleges and nonacademic settings. There was brief but aborted consideration of a nonresearch "Doctor of Arts" degree. 1,127 mathematics Ph.D.'s were earned in 1999–2000. Barely half of these were U.S. citizens, and many were Asian. The number of women is still too small but has been growing. There are hardly any blacks or Hispanics (Duren, 1970; Ewing, 2003).

4. This monumental growth of usable mathematical knowledge poses a major challenge for the scholar as well as the research student of mathematics. Relief is found in one of the essential tendencies of mathematics itself—the use of abstraction and generalization—whereby broad swaths of the subject are synthesized and distilled into simple unifying concepts and principles that encompass a variety of complex cases. This process has sometimes been called compression. Interestingly, this very effective epistemological process presents an obstacle to mathematicians as teachers, in which role they must "decompress" the subject matter in order to connect with their less initiated students. A more complex discussion of the growth of mathematical and scientific knowledge can be found in *The Nature of Mathematical Knowledge* (Kitcher, 1984, chapter 7).

5. This debate about the norms for mathematical claims based on sophisticated physical heuristics has been recently reawakened by the dramatic and paradigm-challenging co-mingling of fundamental particle physics with the most advanced levels of geometry. A remarkable record of views on this philosophical issue has been assembled in the *Bulletin of the American Mathematical Society*; see for example, Vol. 29, No. 1, July 1993, and Vol. 30, No. 2, April 1994.

6. See "On Proof and Progress in Mathematics" (Thurston, 1994) for an insightful reflection on these issues.

7. This portrait of traditional professional development in doctoral programs has been substantially improved in selected departments that have benefited from the National Science Foundation's VIGRE (Vertical Integration of Research and Education in the Mathematical Sciences) program. In fact the VIGRE program incorporates a vision of a departmental culture that resonates remarkably well with the vision of the CID. For an informative account and assessment of current implementations of the VIGRE program, see *The Report of the AMS, ASA, MAA, and SIAM workshop on Vertical Integration of Research and Education in the Mathematical Sciences* (American Mathematical Society, 2002).

8. Phillip Griffiths has suggested that we have something to learn here from the design of programs in the professional schools.

REFERENCES

American Mathematical Society. *The Report of the AMS, ASA, MAA, and SIAM Workshop on Vertical Integration of Research and Education in the Mathematical Sciences*. Reston, Va.: American Mathematical Society, 2002.

Committee on Science Engineering and Public Policy. *Reshaping the Graduate Education of Scientists and Engineers.* Washington, D.C.: National Academy Press, 1995.

Duren, W., Jr. "Are There Too Many Ph.D.'s in Mathematics?" *American Mathematical Monthly,* 1970, 77(6), 641–646.

Einstein, A. "Geometry and Experience. An Address to the Prussian Academy of Sciences, Jan, 27, 1921." In *Albert Einstein, Sidelights on Relativity.* New York: Dover, 1983.

Ewing, J. *Graduate and Postdoctoral Mathematics Education.* Providence, R.I.: American Mathematical Society, 2002. Available at www.ams.org/ewing/Grad-Education.pdf.

Jackson, A. "Should Doctoral Education Change?" *Notices of the AMS,* 1996, 43(1), 19–23.

Kitcher, P. *The Nature of Mathematical Knowledge.* New York: Oxford University Press, 1984.

Richardson, R.G.D. "The Ph.D. Degree and Mathematical Research." *American Mathematical Monthly,* 1936, 43(14), 199–215.

Thurston, W. P. "On Proof and Progress in Mathematics." *Bulletin of the American Mathematical Society,* 1994, 30(2), 161–177.

Wigner, E. "The Unreasonable Effectiveness of Mathematics in the Natural Sciences." *Communications in Pure and Applied Mathematics,* 1960, 13(1), 1–14.

7

A TIME FOR CHANGE?

THE MATHEMATICS DOCTORATE

Tony F. Chan, University of California, Los Angeles

ONE CAN ARGUE, with ample evidence, that in U.S. universities, the system of producing mathematics doctorates is doing very well and needs no major overhaul. It is widely recognized that however poor our K–12 mathematics education—and perhaps also our undergraduate mathematics education—might be, our graduate programs in mathematics are the best and the envy of the world. Top students from around the world are still beating on our doors to get into our doctoral programs. We train them well, and many of these students become international leaders in their research fields.

Take, for example, the two 2002 Fields medalists and the Nevalinna Prize winners. Even though the press (at least, the press in Beijing, where I read the news) referred to them as French, Russian, and Indian, two received their doctoral training at U.S. universities. We also seem to be succeeding in getting new support from the federal government for mathematical sciences. The recent increase in funding for the National Science Foundation (NSF) specifically targets the Division of Mathematical Sciences; doctoral training, in particular for U.S. students, is a core part of this new funding program. Even Hollywood seems to be working in our favor, in view of the generally positive image of mathematics generated by movies such as "A Beautiful Mind."

However, there are many signs that not all is well with our doctoral programs. Top, talented students, especially those born in the United States, are choosing fields other than mathematics for graduate study. Many mathematics departments, especially those outside the "top tier," are having trouble filling their graduate programs with reasonably prepared and talented students. As a field of science, mathematics is underfunded compared to other sciences. Most of our doctoral students are supported by teaching assistantships rather than by fellowships or research assistantships. Our doctoral students are taking too long to get their degrees, and they are not sufficiently and broadly trained for career paths outside academia. Other scientists and academic administrators perceive us as an insular—and worse, irrelevant—community.

None of these symptoms are new. Most are well documented in a series of nationally commissioned reports on the status and health of our community, from the 1984 and 1990 David Reports (both titled *Renewing U.S. Mathematics* [National Research Council, 1984; Board on Mathematical Sciences, 1990]) to the Odom Report (*Report of the Senior Assessment Panel of the International Assessment of the U.S. Mathematical Sciences* [Odom, 1998]), and *Towards Excellence: Leading a Doctoral Mathematics Department in the 21st Century* (Ewing, 1999). Indeed, over the last two decades, the mathematics community, perhaps more than any other science, has produced many national self-studies that urge fundamental changes to our doctoral programs.

Judging from the persistence and recurrence of some of the same main issues in these reports over a period of twenty years, one can only arrive at the conclusion that very little real change has been made. And recent attempts at change (for example, the NSF's VIGRE program—Vertical Integration of Research and Education in the Mathematical Sciences) have been met with controversy (Durrett, 2002a, 2002b; Mackenzie, 2002). Viewed against this background, the current Carnegie Initiative on the Doctorate (CID) comes at a critical juncture for our community.

Does U.S. doctoral education in mathematics need rethinking at this moment? There is no shortage of ideas about *what* we need to change. We have to decide whether or not we *want* to change.

Goals of and Context for Doctoral Education in Mathematics

In order to understand the need for change in the mathematics doctorate, let's consider the goals of and context for doctoral education in the discipline.

What are the overarching goals of U.S. doctoral education in mathematics? How does the context of the American university affect these goals? What perspective does each of the key stakeholders bring to doctoral education?

The U.S. doctorate system has its origins in the universities of Europe, especially those of Germany. In this context, our system is relatively new, and yet it has acquired certain distinguishing characteristics. One particular characteristic is how we fund our doctoral students. Most are supported by a mix of teaching assistantships (most mathematics departments are responsible for a large amount of service teaching on university campuses), federal research support (through grants to advisers and departments), and fellowships (through the federal government, private foundations, and universities). Thus, in addition to the faculty and the doctoral students, the federal government and the universities play important roles in shaping doctoral programs because each party brings particular goals and needs to the system.

Within the profession of mathematics, among the faculty the goal and purpose of doctoral education in the field is quite clear. To borrow from the principles of the current CID, the goal is "generation, conservation, and transformation" of the knowledge of the discipline. To quote Lee S. Shulman, president of The Carnegie Foundation for the Advancement of Teaching: "The Ph.D. recipient is expected to serve as a steward of her discipline or profession: dedicated to the integrity of its work in the generation, critique, transformation, transmission and use of its knowledge" (The Carnegie Foundation for the Advancement of Teaching, 2002). I very much agree with this statement. Certainly, the future health of the discipline cannot be guaranteed if we cannot generate its human resources and train its next generation of leaders.

Yet we have to keep in mind that the federal government, the universities, and the doctoral students have different perspectives on the goals of doctoral education in mathematics. From the perspective of the federal government, funding for doctoral students is justified primarily by societal needs: at one time, that was for national defense during the Cold War; now it is for a workforce that is trained well in science and is therefore capable of supporting industry and the government in order to ensure a robust economy and international leadership in science and technology. The federal government is interested in the workforce issue, not the specific research output generated by doctoral students.

For their part, universities support mathematics primarily for its role in providing service teaching to a large number of students from other disciplines. They pay for teaching assistantships and want qualified students—

those with content knowledge, as well as communication and teaching skills—to staff them.

For the doctoral students, the purpose of the doctorate is usually more than the stewardship of an academic discipline. They care about their future careers and hence the job prospects of the discipline. Those who enter our doctoral programs expect career preparation, as well as the skills and content knowledge of the discipline necessary to become a scholar and researcher. These goals and perspectives, although quite different, need not be conflicting. And, to be realistic, U.S. doctoral programs must take all of them into account.

Ensuring Our Source of Quality Doctoral Students

A key issue in any discussion on the doctorate in mathematics is our "pipeline." How do we increase the number of students in the field, and how do we ensure that we attract the best-qualified students to join the field?

Much of the problem is our own fault. Traditionally, we have expected that undergraduate students choose to enter a doctoral program in mathematics purely out of intellectual interest in the subject. Perhaps the student has been "good in math" from elementary school into college classes. Perhaps she was inspired by a teacher in an upper-division class. Our basic assumption has been that if you are good at it, then surely you will want to do it. However, if the data in the many national reports are correct (that U.S. students have a declining interest in entering doctoral programs in mathematics), then our assumptions are not well founded.

Perhaps this decline is not felt as much in the handful of top mathematics departments in the country, as they continue to attract the "cream" on the top of the student pool, even as the size of the pool shrinks. But many departments, including my own (which by all measures is among the top research departments: 11th in the 1995 NRC [National Research Council] ranking [Goldberger, Maher, and others, 1995] and 10th in the most recent *U.S. News and World Report* survey) acutely feel the decline. And some suggest that we might briefly see a silver lining over the dark clouds of the recent dot-com collapse, which has led to increased applications to and enrollments in doctoral programs in all the physical sciences. The good news notwithstanding, what this says to me is that, clearly, the talent pool is there but career choice is a critical factor for potential students.

Entering a doctoral program in mathematics is usually one of many choices for a talented undergraduate student. The virtue we often preach about—the versatility of an undergraduate degree in mathematics—is true; students qualified to enter mathematics doctoral programs have many choices: mathematics, other scientific disciplines, and industries that require a good mathematics background. Some of these choices are as intellectually interesting or financially rewarding (or both) as mathematics, and many students choose other fields for a postbaccalaureate degree. Are we missing an opportunity?

One opportunity occurs as undergraduates choose majors. We should try to increase those numbers. Mathematics would seem to have an advantage over other fields, as most undergraduates are required to take at least one course in mathematics; many take more. But many freshmen and sophomores have told me something like this: "I was really interested in math in high school, but after the calculus sequence I lost my interest and chose another major." I have told students that mathematics is not just calculus and that there is a whole new world waiting for them to explore. Nonetheless, we lose many potential majors and potential doctoral students.

I have often wondered if mathematics departments could offer an undergraduate "Math 101" course to give students a panoramic view of the field. Perhaps this course could be offered at the sophomore level, in order to present the scope and the excitement of the field to potential majors. (I proposed such a course when I was department chair but was advised by the faculty that it would never work because it would not be a required course for any other majors.)

As I mentioned, aside from purely intellectual reasons, career prospects are a critical factor in a student's decision. In my opinion, mathematics faculty members could do a much better job of presenting employment prospects for those with undergraduate and graduate degrees. For example, the career paths most obvious to undergraduate math majors are high school teacher and perhaps actuary—respectable professions, certainly, but not commonly viewed as the center of excitement in either science or the business world.

Similarly, students often assume that with a doctorate in mathematics their career choices will be limited. The career path most obvious to them is becoming a professor, preferably one in a department that values and allows time for research. However, in reality only a small percentage will become faculty members in a research-oriented department. Simple arithmetic confirms this: consider the small number of research universities in relation to teaching-focused colleges and universities, and the mode of nonexpansion in most universities. The number of new Ph.D.'s produced each year far exceeds the number of current research faculty who retire. Available data in "2001 Annual Survey of the Mathematical Sciences, Second Report" (Loftsgaarden, Maxwell, and others, 2002) show that only about 25 percent of mathematics Ph.D.'s are finding jobs in doctorate-granting academic departments; most others who find jobs in academia are at colleges with heavy teaching duties. The doctoral degree often takes six to seven years, and the opportunity cost, as well as lost potential earnings, constitutes a high barrier for entry. Moreover, the *apparent* noncentral role of mathematics in the frontiers of science and technology, as well as the necessary specialization inherent in a doctoral program, would seem to limit employment options outside academia. Against this background and considering the other career choices that do profitably leverage a good mathematics undergraduate training, it is not surprising to find that only a small percentage of our math majors choose to pursue a doctorate in mathematics.

Such is the case with U.S. students. Many of our doctoral programs have a high percentage of foreign students who are often the most talented students in their countries of origin. When these students enter our doctoral programs, they are focused on mathematics as a career. However, as time passes, they begin to appreciate the array of career choices available to them. Some choose to switch to other fields with better prospects, such as computer science and finance. This can be quite frustrating for the mathematics departments that gave them the initial financial support.

My point is that to ensure a good source of quality students for our doctoral programs, we have to consider the potential candidates' perspective and address their concerns. We have to make the doctorate itself as attractive as—or more attractive than—other fields. The doctorate must take less time to complete than it takes currently. We must recognize the fact that most of our "products" will not become professors in research universities, so we must train them in a way that better prepares them for a broad range of career options.

To ensure a steady talent pool for the doctorate, mathematics departments should start by improving the undergraduate math major, making it more attractive, and providing research opportunities to students well before they graduate. Departments should also get more involved with K–12 mathematics curricula and teacher-training programs. The whole pipeline need not feed into the doctorate. In fact, it is beneficial to have students branching off to other math-related careers. But if we do not pay attention to increasing the source of good students, then we risk turning our doctorate into a kind of esoteric priesthood for the few.

Ensuring That Mathematics Is Part of Science

Another critical issue is the role of mathematics in the overall science enterprise. Despite good formal relationships with other science communities, often for political expedience in arguing for increased funding for science in general, mathematics generally has not been seen by other scientists to be at the frontiers of science. This may come as a surprise to some in our community; historically, mathematics has always been at the core of science as both its language and its method of analysis. Giants of the past, such as Newton, Gauss, and Poincaré, were all great mathematicians with enormous impact in other sciences. But how often do we see articles on mathematics in *Science* or *Nature* these days? And even in the few articles that do appear, the mathematics is usually not immediately relevant to the other sciences. Many scientists I have talked to view mathematicians as bright people who "prove theorems" but who are not relevant to the frontiers of their particular field of science. The notable exception is perhaps theoretical physics: historically, its interaction with mathematics has been extremely beneficial for both. But even the most heralded of the recent interactions (such as string theory) have quite a few skeptics in physics. In any case, the influence of deep mathematics is felt at only a portion of the frontier of modern physics.

Why should mathematics concern itself with being at the frontiers of science? One can argue that mathematics can do quite well on its own. History has shown that many purely internally driven developments in mathematics have ultimately proven to be essential for science. However, I see at least two reasons for getting our community more directly involved in science and working at its frontiers. One is lost opportunities; the other is our doctorate.

Let us consider the first: lost opportunities. Many problems at the frontiers of science are fundamentally mathematical in nature. By being inward-looking and not getting involved, mathematicians are missing out on the chance to make a real impact on science. Take two recent examples I have come across. The 2002 Nobel Prize in Chemistry was given for work that involved a mathematical framework for determining the 3D geometry of large bio-molecules by using nuclear magnetic resonance (NMR) techniques. Similarly, a recent issue of *Science* (January 24, 2003) includes an article on a breakthrough by two chemists: a fast mathematical algorithm for doing NMR analysis that is based on Fourier analysis (Service, 2003). These contributions are mathematical and are of immediate relevance to science, yet our community has not been involved.

Science is not only fertile ground for the application of mathematics; it can also give inspiration for mathematics itself in the form of new problems and new ideas. The opportunities for interaction with science are plentiful and well documented. See, for example, the NSF report *Mathematics and Science* (Wright and Chorin, 1999) and the NSF report *Opportunities for the Mathematical Sciences* (Division of Mathematical Sciences, 2000). Others in our community have also called for a closer integration of mathematics within science (E, 2002).

Working to place mathematics at the frontiers of science can also be beneficial to our doctoral programs. If we make mathematics more explicitly central to the science enterprise, our doctorate will be more attractive to students who are intellectually interested in the interaction between math and other sciences. It will also provide a means to broaden the perspective of our doctoral students. If backed up by appropriate changes in doctoral training, our students will be more versatile and more attractive in the job market.

I would even go as far as advocating that we require some formal interaction with at least one other science during doctoral training. This is probably common practice for "applied" mathematics students, but it should not be limited to them. This interaction could take several forms: a course or a seminar series in another department, a joint research project with someone from another discipline, or in-depth reading on the scientific background of a mathematical problem.

Our doctoral students should be encouraged to explore all areas of science, especially the current frontiers. They should not limit themselves only to the "classical" areas, such as classical theoretical physics. New opportunities for mathematicians are present in many exciting new frontiers in nanoscience, biomedical research, the Internet, and computational science, to name just a few examples.

Ensuring Societal Support for Mathematics Doctoral Education

Finally, mathematics must consider the issue of support for doctoral-level education in the discipline. Few would argue that the health of mathematics doctoral programs, at least in their current forms, depends critically on governmental support. Unlike the other sciences, we can, in theory, carry on most research and train graduate students without federal support. But this would make mathematics much less attractive than other fields to potential students. To ensure continued governmental support, we need to convince society at large that mathematics is worth supporting. We must ensure that outsiders—from other scientists to the public at large—understand the purpose of our field without needing a detailed understanding of its inner workings. It is not intrinsically obvious to the public that research in mathematics at the doctoral level is worth supporting, any more than the humanities or the arts.

Society expects a return on its investment. Government support for academic research has always been tied to short-term national needs and benefits to society. My experience from serving on NSF advisory committees suggests that societal support for science is based on three kinds of expected returns: (1) long-term investment (fundamental research and human knowledge), (2) impact on the economy and furthering national goals (for example, national defense), and (3) education and development of human resources. The history of U.S. governmental support for science bears this out. Vannevar Bush proposed our current system of national support for academic scientific research after World War II to prepare the nation for national defense. Sputnik led to a further strengthening of support for science as a response to the Soviet challenge. Will September 11, 2001, be the new Sputnik? The current rationale for structuring support at the NSF is "Ideas, People and Tools"—the "People" are as important as "Ideas."

What does this mean for the mathematics doctorate? The first two returns I described call for a balance between fundamental (including curiosity-driven) and targeted research, even though some of us would prefer more of the former. The third return emphasizes the importance of ensuring a stable pipeline of talented students, trained in a broad way to meet a variety of societal needs. Most of our recent success in garnering more funding from Congress for the mathematical sciences is, in fact, based on our discipline's promise to deliver a combination of all three returns. It is certainly not an act of benevolence from Congress to correct past "injustice" in funding level. Our promise requires the mathematics community to pay more than lip service to the important role of mathematics in society, the economy, and the private sector, as well as to the impact of mathematics on other disciplines. Our promise should be reflected in how we train our students, including our graduate students. After all, if our products do not satisfy societal needs, then society will stop supporting us and will hire students from other disciplines.

Ensuring That Mathematics Doctoral Education Meets Its Goals

After laying out the different perspectives and goals of the stakeholders in mathematics doctoral education, pointing out the obvious importance of ensuring a stable and talented pipeline of doctoral students by making our doctorate more attractive and more relevant to a variety of career choices, and arguing for a stronger integration of mathematics in science in our doctoral programs, I hope I have provided a context to begin a discussion of concrete steps that we can take to improve our doctorate. Actually, if we can agree on the context and the goals, then the steps are quite natural. In fact, the plethora of reports published by national organizations contain a wealth of specific ideas and suggestions.[1]

I cannot add many new ideas to the many already suggested, but I can offer four practical steps in light of the goals and perspectives of the stakeholders in mathematics doctoral education and the critical issues of the discipline. I hope these steps and accompanying examples will prompt discussions within individual departments so that they arrive at their own plans, based on local strengths and constraints, for improving their doctoral programs.

Step One

We should make doctoral education in mathematics more attractive to students and more competitive with other fields. We might do the following:

EXPOSE STUDENTS TO THE FULL RANGE OF MATHEMATICS. We should emphasize the intellectual challenges as well as the usefulness and applications of mathematics.

SHORTEN THE TIME-TO-DEGREE. For example, departments could streamline qualifying examinations without lowering academic standards. We could offer summer courses to better prepare the students for their examinations. We could also bring students into research groups as early as possible rather than after several years spent preparing for these examinations.

ENSURE AMPLE RESEARCH SUPPORT FOR DOCTORAL STUDENTS. At present, many doctoral students are supported by non-research-related jobs, such as being T.A.'s and tutoring, which take time away from their research and increase time-to-degree. Faculty should explore all sources of funding and consider various strategies for supporting students. It might be better, for example, to have a smaller doctoral program and provide better funding for the students.

Step Two

We should prepare our doctoral students for a broad range of future careers by doing the following:

EXPAND STUDENTS' AWARENESS OF REWARDING CAREER POSSIBILITIES IN MATHEMATICS. We could take a big step in this direction by changing departmental culture so that nonacademic careers are as respectable as academic careers. One step in this direction would be to invite a wide variety of outside speakers to talk with the students. A department could invite, for example, former graduates who have successful careers both inside and outside academia, leaders from the mathematics community who can provide a national perspective and a broad science perspective, and potential employers.

MAKE TEACHING AN INTEGRAL PART OF DOCTORAL TRAINING. Many of the graduates who do go into academic settings will have jobs with heavy emphasis on teaching. We could, for example, offer formal T.A. training courses, assign senior T.A.'s to mentor junior ones (with faculty supervision), select a few T.A.'s to be in charge of a small number of classes, and offer teaching awards to recognize the best T.A.'s and motivate the others.

BROADEN THE TRAINING OF DOCTORAL STUDENTS. Students should learn about different subfields within mathematics and interact with disciplines outside mathematics. Students should be encouraged to keep abreast of the latest developments, not just in their own research area but in mathematics as a whole and in science in general. We should require this broad understanding of the field, and of science itself, of all students, not just those in applied mathematics.

DEVELOP PROFESSIONAL SKILLS. We must make sure our students leave our programs with essential professional skills. For example, we could provide training in mathematical writing and presentations, proposal writing, and mentoring of junior graduate students and undergraduates.

Step Three

We should improve mentoring during doctoral training by doing some or all of the following:

MENTOR FOR THE STUDENT'S CAREER. Early in the mentoring relationship, doctoral mentors must have their students' careers in mind. We should recognize that we train both the researcher and the scholar.

HELP STUDENTS DEVELOP INDEPENDENT RESEARCH APPROACHES. We should encourage our students to learn the history and the broader literature of a research problem. We can encourage students to formulate their own problems rather than to solve the next problem in the mentor's research program. We can assign broadly defined research areas that have a potential for postdoctoral investigations rather than niche areas that are potential dead-ends.

HELP STUDENTS FIND THE RIGHT MENTOR. Departments should have a formal mechanism for exposing the full portfolio of faculty research programs to doctoral students early on. For example, faculty could give lectures on their research programs; these lectures would be intended for doctoral students looking for thesis advisers. Faculty could offer research area seminars and encourage new students to join. We should encourage our students to attend department colloquia; we should invite good expository speakers and ask them to use part of their lectures to reach out to graduate students.

ENCOURAGE STUDENTS TO MENTOR ONE ANOTHER. We should encourage graduate students to form their own organizations and have senior students mentor junior ones. The senior students can also be involved in organizing the faculty research lectures.

IMPROVE CAREER COUNSELING. We could formalize career counseling and introduce it early in a doctoral student's career. We should encourage students to attend national and regional conferences and workshops (and, to the extent possible, provide funding for them to attend).

Step Four

We should adopt some effective practices from other sciences, such as:

WORK IN GROUPS. Working in groups is a prevalent feature of almost all areas of science and engineering research. The benefits are peer support and a gentler introduction to a research area.

INCLUDE BEGINNING STUDENTS IN RESEARCH GROUPS. This should be done before they advance to candidacy, to reinforce the idea that the main emphasis of a doctoral education is the research experience, not courses and examinations.

DROP THE BARRIERS BETWEEN "PURE" AND "APPLIED." Most sciences are not organized according to a "pure" versus "applied" dichotomy. Each subdiscipline within a department usually has faculty with interests ranging from foundational to applied. For example, chemistry departments are not organized into "pure chemistry" and "applied chemistry" units. In physical chemistry—one of the common subfields—one often finds theoreticians who solve Schrödinger's equations, experimentalists who look for new molecules and their properties, computational chemists who do numerical simulations, and material chemists who design new materials. Doctoral students in chemistry are thus in a better position than are their mathematics counterparts to be aware of the whole range of problems in their subfield beyond their own research problems. Is there something worth emulating here?

———————— o ————————

In the final analysis, perhaps the most critical questions facing doctoral education in mathematics are not those about how to improve it. The critical questions are these: (1) Do we have the will to make serious improvement? and (2) Is now the time to do so? Specific ideas such as those I offer here have been pointed out for more than two decades, yet until very recently, very few of them have been widely adopted. What is different now? What suggests that change is possible now?

For one, money speaks. And it is speaking now. The NSF has been quite proactive recently in using its funding programs to effect changes in the mathematical sciences doctoral programs. The most notable is the VIGRE program, which specifically calls for an overhauling of doctoral programs. The funding varies from several hundred thousand dollars to close to a million dollars for each department—a sum most departments would consider substantial. The NSF's rationale for VIGRE is that not only is it good for the discipline but it also appeals to Congress: it is the mechanism that allowed NSF to obtain funding for mathematical sciences from Congress. The NSF made a successful case, arguing for the importance of maintaining a pool of well-trained U.S. doctoral students in the mathematical sciences and thus obtained extra funding for implementing the program.

As the VIGRE program currently goes through its first review after an initial three years, it has generated its share of controversy (Durrett, 2002a, 2002b; Mackenzie, 2002). Some leading departments, including some that have not been funded by VIGRE or recently lost the funding, are complaining that the NSF is attempting a form of social engineering of the doctorate and is thus interfering with the long traditions in many top departments. The restriction of VIGRE to U.S. students has also created problems at some departments. Of course, the matter worsened after September 11th, 2001, with tightened issuance of visas to students from "sensitive" countries. Despite the controversies, however, it is generally agreed that VIGRE has had a healthy influence on the mathematics doctorate, but its full long-term effects still remain to be assessed.

But there is another reason that this might be the moment for important change in the mathematics doctorate: the explosion of new, exciting opportunities in—and competition from—other areas of science and technology in which mathematics has the potential to play a big role. Many have pointed out that several decades ago the mathematics community relinquished the enormous opportunity offered by the advent of computer science (Landau, 2000). Are we going to repeat the blunder by letting the current revolutions in nano- and biomedical sciences pass us by?

The question of whether or not we make the improvements we need remains, fundamentally, a cultural issue. Our action cannot be dictated from any one source of authority. Change must be instigated by faculty, yet faculty are often the most resistant to change. It is human nature to base decisions on one's own experience, and when some of us were graduate students, things were quite different. Real change, however, requires real leadership from individuals and institutions. The NSF, at least, is trying to effect change. But real change in mathematics doctoral education must be initiated from within our own community.

Do we have the will to make significant changes to our doctoral programs now? Do we want real changes, or do we simply want the national reports to say the right things only for the expedience of the political process of bringing in more resources to the community? I suggest we look forward and that we do so for the long-term interest of our discipline and for the next generation of doctoral students.

NOTE

1. A useful and comprehensive list is provided in Appendix C of *Strengthening the Linkages Between the Sciences and the Mathematical Sciences* (National

Research Council, 2000), based on the work of a committee chaired by
Thomas Budinger.

REFERENCES

Board on Mathematical Sciences. *Renewing U.S. Mathematics: A Plan for the
1990s.* Washington, D.C.: National Academy Press, 1990.

Division of Mathematical Sciences. *Opportunities for the Mathematical Sciences.*
Arlington, Va.: National Science Foundation, 2000.

The Carnegie Foundation for the Advancement of Teaching. Carnegie Initiative
on the Doctorate. Invitation for Participation. Available at www.carnegie-
foundation.org/CID/CID_IFP2.pdf. 2002.

Durrett, R. "VIGRE Turns Three." *Notices of the AMS,* 2002a, *49*(10), 1237–1243.

Durrett, R. "Whither VIGRE?" *Notices of the AMS,* 2002b, *49*(10), 1221.

E, W. "Mathematics and Sciences." *Beijing Intelligencer,* Aug. 2002. Available
at www.math.princeton.edu/~weinan/papers/beijing.ps.

Ewing, J. (ed.). *Towards Excellence: Leading a Doctoral Mathematics Department in the 21st Century.* Providence, R.I.: American Mathematical Society, 1999.

Goldberger, M., Maher, B. A., and others (eds.). *Research-Doctorate Programs
in the United States. Continuity and Change.* Washington, D.C.: National
Academy Press, 1995.

Landau, S. "Internet Time." *Notices of the AMS,* 2000, *47*(3), 325.

Loftsgaarden, D., Maxwell, J., and others. "2001 Annual Survey of the Mathematical Sciences: Second Report." *Notices of the AMS,* 2002, *49*(7), 803–816.

Mackenzie, D. "NSF Moves with VIGRE to Force Changes in Academia."
Science, 2002, *296,* 1389–1390.

National Research Council. *Renewing U.S. Mathematics: Critical Resource for
the Future.* Washington, D.C.: National Academy Press, 1984.

National Research Council. *Strengthening the Linkages Between the Sciences
and the Mathematical Sciences.* Washington, D.C.: National Academy
Press, 2000.

National Science Foundation. "Announcement of VIGRE." Available at
www.nsf.gov/pubs/1997/nsf97170/nsf97170.htm. 1997.

Odom, W. *Report of the Senior Assessment Panel of the International Assessment of the U.S. Mathematical Sciences.* Arlington, Va.: National Science
Foundation, 1998.

Service, R. F. "Propelled by Recent Advances, NMR Moves into the Fast Lane."
Science, 2003, *299,* 503.

Wright, M., and Chorin, A. *Mathematics and Science.* Washington, D.C.:
National Science Foundation, 1999.

DOCTORAL EDUCATION IN CHEMISTRY

CHEMISTRY, OFTEN CALLED THE "CENTRAL SCIENCE," is the atom-level view of matter. The work of chemists is sometimes described as "the three m's"—making molecules, measuring their properties, and modeling. The discipline of chemistry has a strongly practical dimension and is, at all levels of postsecondary education, strongly linked to the chemical sciences industry. This strong linkage has been the case for at least the last century and is likely to be the case well into the future. Disciplinary boundaries are blurring, as chemical knowledge finds application in many other fields: geology, anthropology, and particularly biology and medical research.

Of the approximately 100,000 working chemists in the United States, 60 percent hold doctorates. Chemistry remains a male-dominated field, even though the proportion of women earning degrees in chemistry has risen steadily in recent decades. The proportion of Ph.D.'s in chemistry now granted to women is nearly 30 percent, and so about 18 percent of working chemists with the Ph.D. are women.

About half of new Ph.D. recipients in chemistry move into postdoctoral positions, which is a relatively low number for a bench science. Ultimately, two-thirds of Ph.D. chemists work in industry and government labs, and about one-third work in academia. These strong connections with industry mandate that doctoral training prepare students for academic jobs and for industrial careers, which demand a somewhat different skill set. One criticism leveled regularly at doctoral programs in chemistry is that Ph.D. students are not taught the kinds of skills necessary to succeed in the workplace. Other than technical and scientific competency, the attributes most prized by chemical employers include communication (both written and oral), information management, team work, product stewardship, understanding of principles of responsible care, independent thinking, creativity, flexibility, vision, and maturity.

Currently, about two thousand Ph.D.'s in chemistry are granted per year—a number that has held steady for the last decade. Although 190 departments in the United States offer doctoral degrees in chemistry, doctoral education is concentrated in large departments; the thirty largest schools enroll almost 50 percent of all doctoral students in chemistry. The average size of chemistry departments is eighty-four students and twenty-two faculty; the average number of doctoral recipients per year per program is twelve. Despite a movement to reduce the number of programs by closing marginal or low-ranked programs, an American Chemical Society study (1995) determined that those programs serve very different markets (regional industry versus national research universities), and the movement did not take hold.

Most chemists enter graduate school directly (or within a year) after receiving their bachelor's degree, and time-to-degree is currently six years of registered enrollment. Thus chemists enter the workforce relatively quickly; the median age for receiving the doctorate is slightly under thirty. Efforts to redefine the doctoral curriculum must face concerns that any changes will increase time-to-degree, which most chemists resist.

Students begin their graduate programs by taking a year or two of course work; the average student takes twenty-two semester hours of courses. Most doctoral programs use placement exams to judge a student's breadth of knowledge and determine any gaps, expecting that students acquired a solid foundation of knowledge about chemistry during the undergraduate years. This expectation is possible because three-quarters of doctoral candidates majored in chemistry as undergraduates. Course work is used to begin specializing: doctoral students report taking only one-third of their chemistry courses outside their area of specialization.

Graduate study in chemistry follows traditional subdivisions in the field. The largest is organic chemistry (a quarter of all doctorates granted), followed by general chemistry, physical chemistry, analytical chemistry, biochemistry-biotechnology, and inorganic chemistry. The different subfields are often organizationally quite distinct from one another within the department, and they typically have different requirements in the doctoral program.

In general, chemistry doctoral students are admitted into a graduate program with the express expectation of joining a particular chemist's lab. One strategy to improve the match and fit between student and adviser is to allow (or require) students to try various research labs through a series of rotations before selecting an adviser; about a quarter of programs report using this process. Twenty percent of students have matched with an adviser within two months and 75 percent within six months. Students then spend the majority of their doctoral program in a laboratory under the direction of their research adviser.

Often the student's own research and the research he or she conducts as a research assistant are indistinguishable. This practice raises a number of important issues, including (1) the ability of students to develop and perform original, independent research, (2) the potential subordination of the student's interests (including time-to-degree) to the lab's interests, (3) the quality of advising, and (4) the problems of overspecialization. Oversight committees, which meet regularly with students and jointly determine student progress and readiness to graduate, are a commonly proposed solution to several of these problems. Although most programs require a thesis committee, it is unclear (and doubtless highly variable) whether these committees provide meaningful opportunities for advising and mentorship or act as advocates for students' interests. In a recent survey, only about one-third of students said that they were annually reviewed—one of the lowest rates of the eleven arts and sciences fields in this study.

Typically, admission to a doctoral program carries with it the commitment of financial support of the student. Overall, about 50 percent of doctoral students are supported on teaching assistantships; about 40 percent are on research assistants as part of research grants, and about 11 percent are on fellowships of various kinds. It is not known how this differs among institutions, but it is likely that larger research university programs support (and rely on) a higher number of research assistants. One interesting feature of chemistry doctoral programs is that the vast majority require the creation and defense of one or more original research proposals.

The essays that follow provide a converging view of the challenges now facing doctoral studies in chemistry and suggest many provocative solutions. In "Time for Reform?" Alvin L. Kwiram emphasizes curriculum change. As his title suggests, Kwiram visits the structure and sequence of the requirements so as not to extend time-to-degree or time-to-career. Even so, he has a long list of elements that ought to become part of the training for doctoral students who wish to become faculty members. He also advocates changes in postdoctoral positions to increase pedagogical preparation.

Ronald Breslow orients the reader to coming problems facing chemistry that a new generation of chemists must be prepared to tackle. He proposes that faculty creatively redeploy existing features of doctoral programs to be more efficient and effective. In "Developing Breadth and Depth of Knowledge: The Doctorate in Chemistry," he urges programs to reduce students' overspecialization and increase their breadth of knowledge. In the third essay, Angelica M. Stacy challenges the reader to consider who studies chemistry and whether programs are truly preparing the leaders the field needs. "Training Future Leaders" calls many assumptions into question, posing questions that pertain to many fields.

———— o ————

BIBLIOGRAPHY

Information and specific data were derived from the following sources:

American Chemical Society. *Employment Patterns of Recent Doctorates in Chemistry.* Washington, D.C.: American Chemical Society, 1995.

American Chemical Society Committee on Professional Training. *Survey of Ph.D. Programs in Chemistry.* Washington, D.C.: American Chemical Society, 1997.

American Chemical Society. *Current Trends in Chemical Technology, Business and Employment.* Washington, D.C.: American Chemical Society, 1998.

American Chemical Society Committee on Professional Training. *Survey of Ph.D. Recipients in Chemistry: Part 1. Statistical Analysis.* Washington, D.C.: American Chemical Society, 1999.

American Chemical Society Committee on Professional Training. *Survey of Ph.D. Recipients in Chemistry: Part 2. Analysis of Written Comments.* Washington, D.C.: American Chemical Society, 2000.

American Chemical Society. *Academic Chemists 2000, A Decade of Change: 1990–2000.* Washington, D.C.: American Chemical Society, 2001.

American Chemical Society. *ChemCensus 2000.* Washington, D.C.: American Chemical Society, 2001.

Brennan, M. "Graduate School: Smoothing the Passage." *Chemical and Engineering News,* 1999, 77(4), 11–19.

Chemical Sciences Roundtable. *Graduate Education in the Chemical Sciences— Issues for the 21st Century: Report of a Workshop.* Washington, D.C.: National Academy Press, 2000.

English, B. "Grad-Student Suicides Spur Big Changes at Harvard Chem Labs." *The Boston Globe,* Jan. 2, 2001, p. D01.

Goldberger, M., Maher, B. A., and Flattau, P. E. (eds.). *Research-Doctorate Programs in the United States. Continuity and Change.* Washington, D.C.: National Academy Press, 1995.

Golde, C. M., and Dore, T. M. *At Cross Purposes: What the Experiences of Doctoral Students Reveal About Doctoral Education.* Philadelphia: The Pew Charitable Trusts, 2001. Available at www.phd-survey.org.

Heylin, M. "Employment and Salary Survey." *Chemical and Engineering News,* 2004, *82*(33), 26–34.

Heylin, M. "2003 Starting Salary Survey." *Chemical and Engineering News,* 2004, *82*(16), 51–55.

Hoffer, T., and others. *Doctorate Recipients from United States Universities: Summary Report 2003.* Chicago: National Opinion Research Center, 2004.

8

TIME FOR REFORM?

Alvin L. Kwiram, University of Washington

U.S. DOCTORAL EDUCATION is respected around the world and is increasingly being seen as one of the factors in the success of the United States in research. Despite this enviable record, a number of studies in recent years have questioned whether or not elements are missing in the Ph.D. program and what should be done to correct any deficiencies.[1] Many of the issues that have been widely discussed in such initiatives as "Re-envisioning the Ph.D." will be explored further in this essay.

To begin, let us examine the essence of the doctoral program, regardless of discipline, shorn of all its trappings.

The Nature of Doctoral Education

Education at any level works best when there is strong motivation on the part of the student—a natural curiosity, an insatiable desire to understand, a question that just has to be answered. When this quest is coupled with an informed and inspiring mentor who can guide the intellectual exploration with the appropriate resources, one has an optimum learning environment: Aristotle at one end of the log and Alexander at the other! One might aspire to achieve this goal at all levels of education, but the demands of mass education on the one hand and the complexity and vastness of contemporary knowledge on the other militate against such a lofty ideal. That ideal has, nonetheless, been reserved formally for those who engage in doctoral education. Indeed, graduate education is first and foremost an apprenticeship—an apprenticeship in the art of discovery.

Arguably, the essence of the Ph.D. degree is scholarly development that demonstrates creativity, independence of critical thought, and the ability to frame incisive questions about an issue. The purpose of Ph.D. training is to help a student develop certain "habits of the mind," acquire an appropriate array of associated skills, and become the unquestioned expert on some specific topic. This process was spelled out nicely (though perhaps a bit too grandly) a century ago by von Sybel, as reported by Paulsen:

> But it is essential that the student should become distinctly conscious of the problems of science and the methods by which they are solved; it is necessary that he should employ these methods in a few directions to their ultimate consequences, to a point at which he can say that there is now no one in the world who can teach him anything about it, where he can stand firmly and securely upon his own feet, and can decide according to his own judgment. Such a consciousness of independence achieved through one's own efforts is of inestimable value. It is practically immaterial what the subject of the investigation was which led to this: it is enough that, in one field, no matter how unimportant, dependence upon the school was done away with; the powers and methods have been tested with which henceforth every new problem can be attacked and carried to a like conclusion (1906, pp. 307–308).

There is a remarkable consensus that this general concept constitutes the essence or core of the doctoral experience. To be sure, there are significant differences in expectations, quality, and performance within any given department and between different Ph.D. candidates. That variability becomes even more pronounced as one expands the comparison to different departments, different institutions, and different countries. Standards vary, the quality of the faculty varies, and the cultures of the disciplines vary. Despite this, there seems to be a tacit understanding of what constitutes a well-prepared Ph.D. student. Indeed, it is remarkable that the Ph.D. program, administered by hundreds of thousands of different individuals in a thousand institutions and in the complete absence of any central repository of rules or a cosmic accrediting agency, remains universally recognizable and extraordinarily stable.

This core concept of the Ph.D. characterizes doctoral training in chemistry. It is an abstraction that is never realized in practice, just as the idea of a perfect single crystal is an everyday working model for a chemist, even though such an entity is never encountered in the real world. The robust nature of the doctoral model in chemistry suggests a tacit under-standing of this concept and the importance of the model. We might tread cautiously before recommending any drastic changes in that model. Indeed, the maxim "if it ain't broke, don't fix it" might well be applied to doctoral education in chemistry in this country. By and large, it has been a highly successful enterprise and if left largely intact would not seriously hamper research advances in the field.

However, much has changed in the research enterprise over the last fifty to one hundred years. A short list of relevant changes might include the introduction of computers, information technologies, and the Internet; glob-alization of the economy and research; intellectual property as a central focus in academic settings; the changing role of women in society; the growing importance of a diverse workforce; the need for interdisciplinary approaches; the decline of hierarchical structures and growing emphasis on human rights; the nature of funding for research; the changing demographics of the student pool; transformation of many disciplines to a molecular focus—chemistry's traditional arena; changing workforce needs in industry, and sim-ulation as a third arm of research (in addition to theory and experiment).

These changes, however profound, do not alter either the essence or the purpose of the Ph.D. In other words, the core remains unaffected by the changes. Nonetheless, a number of practices common in doctoral educa-tion in chemistry are less than optimal, and some are evolving in directions that may be counterproductive. Of these, three are most important to attend to: (1) we need to integrate more professional skills and knowledge into the doctoral program, (2) serious efforts must be made to reduce the time-to-degree, and (3) we must address the biggest shortcoming of the field: our failure to prepare the next generation of mentors for the academy.

The strategies proposed in this essay are intended, not as rigid pre-scriptions but as initial ideas designed to stimulate further discussion and refinement of these key issues.

Integration of Professional Skills and Knowledge

Most of the recent discussions of reform for doctoral education in chem-istry have focused on functional improvements that would give new Ph.D.'s a more complete repertoire of professional skills. Although pro-fessional skills are not the core or essence of the Ph.D., these skills are considered important for all graduates of chemistry doctoral programs, especially those planning to work in industry and government—nearly two-thirds of all Ph.D.'s in the field (Heylin, 2004).

Let's examine a list of possible "missing elements" in our graduate students' training:

- Need for more training in patent law
- Improved communications skills, both written and oral
- Early introduction to the nature of a career in industry
- Instruction in how to work in teams
- Effort to counteract the tendency toward increasingly narrow training
- Development of an appreciation for economic factors in an industry setting
- Greater emphasis on safety training
- Instruction on human behavior and personal interactions
- Emphasis on strategies for research planning
- Greater attention by faculty to their mentoring role

The list was compiled from a 1947 study published by the American Chemical Society (ACS), based on the Committee on Professional Relations' surveys of chemistry department chairs, recent graduates who had taken jobs in industry, and directors of research in industry (*Chemical and Engineering News*, 1947a, 1947b, 1947c, 1948). The concerns identified more than fifty years ago have a striking similarity to those identified in the most recent discussions of problems in the chemistry Ph.D. (Nyquist and Woodford, 2000; Roberts, 2002; Caserio, 2002).[2] Indeed, a current list of desirable experiences and background includes

- Better training in interpersonal communication
- Better skills in writing and public presentations
- More emphasis on how to work in teams
- Development of skills in technology use
- Focused training in ethics and conflict-of-interest issues
- Instruction in understanding entrepreneurial strategies and technology transfer
- More breadth of exposure to other fields
- Better understanding of the need for an international outlook
- Better understanding of opportunities in industry
- Exposure to the economic drivers essential for success in the private sector

Since all these skills continue to be of significant concern to industry—the primary employer of Ph.D. graduates in chemistry—we should consider what improvements might be made and how we might make them.

Some will argue that these are skills and topics that the student should have been exposed to prior to entering the doctoral program. Graduate schools might demand that students be deliberately and systematically introduced to these skills and topics in their baccalaureate chemistry programs, perhaps through new, stand-alone courses and the incorporation of these issues into existing courses. However, even if undergraduate programs included exposure to professional skills and knowledge (which will surely be some time in coming), the doctoral students need to address these skills and topics at a deeper, more sophisticated level. Therefore, if we believe that professionals should be more informed on these topics than they currently are, it is necessary to develop learning activities on these topics at the graduate level.

Unfortunately, adding to the existing doctoral program can exacerbate one of the field's serious problems: the time-to-degree. Taking an additional course in a related field to improve breadth or spending time in another lab (on the same campus, in industry, or in an international setting) requires a commitment of time. However, there are ways to expand training by using time wisely.

For example, training in ethics, conflict of interest, and technology transfer might be accomplished with intense short courses, even a weekend followed by one- to two-hour sessions each quarter, involving formal presentations and group discussion. Likewise, developing skills in the newer and emerging technologies may be an area where self-paced or "distance learning" modules could be very effective.[3] Learning more about the work environment in industry, opportunities in entrepreneurship, and the importance of economic factors in all industry programs may well be handled best by a full quarter or semester course in which faculty and visitors from industry provide a series of lectures to inform the students about these issues (Shulman, 2002). Examples of such enhancements already exist at various institutions, and these could serve as models.[4] A major effort under way in the United Kingdom adds new dimensions to doctoral programs to develop professional skills and knowledge.[5] (At the end of this essay, Table 8.1 suggests a curriculum to develop professional skills and knowledge.)

A key issue is whether a department would require student participation or whether it would be voluntary. That, in turn, would depend on how seriously members of the faculty view the need for improvement in these areas or how much pressure they feel from outside stakeholders. As stated at the outset, there is a strong underlying view among chemistry faculty that doctoral education in chemistry is working quite well in the United States. That automatically will weaken any resolve by a department to introduce enhancements, even if the additional time required on the part of the student is kept to a minimum. The task is made even more difficult if one seeks to reduce the time-to-degree. By and large, chemistry departments have been relatively conservative in keeping the time-to-degree from getting too far out of hand. Nevertheless, as argued next, it needs to be shortened. Although we might agree in a global sense that professional skills need more emphasis, this area will probably not receive serious attention until industry, as the major employer of chemistry Ph.D.'s, demonstrates its seriousness by preferentially hiring graduates who have such training.

Time-to-Degree

One of two major structural problems for U.S. doctoral programs in chemistry is the time-to-degree. Like the weather, everyone complains about it, but no one does anything about it, even though in this case we could more readily effect change. Recent data show that the average time to the chemistry Ph.D. is 6.9 years; for biochemistry it is 7.3. By comparison, the average for engineering is 8.6 years, and in the humanities, the time stretches over a decade (Hoffer, 2004, Table A3-a).[6] Despite chemistry's good record next to other fields, the trend for the past three decades shows a gradual lengthening.

This situation has several negative features. First, it tends to discourage some bright students from entering the program because of the long delay in achieving earning status. Second, it reduces the "window of creativity" because students often do not become independent scientists until their mid-thirties. Third, it is sometimes an exploitation of the student for the benefit of the program. Fourth, it reduces opportunity for other students, both in terms of access to those programs and in terms of access to financial resources. Fifth, other avenues will develop to train individuals for the workforce, as evidenced by the growth in certification programs and the renewed interest in the professional master's degree.

At a time in history when we are experiencing a systematic and long-term decline in the number of U.S. citizens entering doctoral programs in the sciences, it is imperative that we re-examine our programs. We are less and less competitive for the best and brightest, who perceive that the time-to-degree (and even time-to-career) in medicine, law, and business is much more predictable, shorter, and more financially rewarding.

What is an appropriate time-to-degree? Whatever satisfies the essential training program for the student. In other words, if the student could gain the appropriate experience in three years, then that would be the appropriate length of time for the program, not five years or seven years. Those extra years of apprenticeship are serving purposes other than the basic education of the student. Obviously, the skills of the advanced student are a huge advantage in meeting the demands of the sponsored research program. But such extended engagement could be subject to a charge of exploitation. Space does not allow for an exploration of mitigating circumstances (those that might require extended doctoral studies), such as an entering student with inadequate preparation, the student who has to engage in non-dissertation work for much of the period of doctoral studies because there is inadequate funding,[7] or the student who has begun to unravel an exciting mystery and it would not be sporting to interrupt the chase in midstream. However, even if we accept that there are always exceptions to every rule, most observers acknowledge that the time-to-degree in chemistry is too long.

Some contrarians might argue that in today's complex knowledge environment it takes five to seven years for a student to be able to make an original contribution to the storehouse of knowledge. The counterargument is that one can set the dial to any chosen degree of accomplishment from zero to infinity. We do not require a graduate student in chemistry to build a synchrotron and solve the crystal structure of the major histocompatibility complex in order to establish that she has the necessary talent to be awarded the doctoral degree. A thoughtful mentor can design problems with various degrees of complexity, each of which can serve as a training ground to develop creativity, independence, and the ability to "frame questions." We seem to be able to define bite-sized projects routinely for undergraduate research, for master's theses, and for postdoctoral training. Likewise, we should be able to titrate the assigned problem to the appropriate timeframe for graduate students. Unfortunately, too often the mentor does not think carefully enough about the scope of the problem assigned to the student and whether it is realistic for a three-year effort. Of course, even in a well-designed program, a problem may turn out to be intractably difficult. An essential part of the research is often to establish precisely how difficult the problem really is. However, such projects in particular need to be monitored with special care.

Despite the endless debate one could have about how long the dissertation research should really take, there are models from Europe that can be considered. For example, students in the United Kingdom are expected to complete their Ph.D. studies in three years (Higher Education Funding

Council for England, 2004). Exceptions, though possible, are usually discouraged. To be sure, there are differences in the level of predoctoral preparation, but the fact remains that the majority of the students finish in three years. Few would argue that the British Ph.D. is a woefully inadequate preparation for the workplace. The system in Germany is similar. Most students are expected to complete their Ph.D. research within three years of the Diplom (roughly equivalent to the U.S. master's degree).

Why, then, is the U.S. time-to-degree almost twice as long as in these examples? There are a number of factors; a few are fairly obvious. First (in contrast to the U.S. model), the entire undergraduate experience in the United Kingdom and Germany is essentially focused on the discipline being studied. Second, the United States has arguably made a greater effort to open college and Ph.D. programs to a broader cross-section of its citizens than has traditionally been the case in Europe and elsewhere; this means that the range of preparation of those entering Ph.D. programs in the United States is more variable. There is probably also much greater variability in the level of preparation of students in high schools in the United States than in Europe. These factors combined mean that the students enter graduate school with very different levels of preparation. Consequently, many U.S. students will need remedial work and coaching to bring them to roughly the same starting point as their better-prepared peers.

Another factor is the nature of research funding in the United States. Grants are made to the faculty member who, in turn, pays the graduate students who work in the lab. To succeed in getting the grant renewed, the faculty member has to demonstrate significant progress each year. The degree of progress, of course, depends directly on the quality and experience of the graduate students working on the problems. Clearly, the more experienced the student, the more productive he can be. Therefore, keeping the student for an additional year or two is highly advantageous. It can also benefit the student, because as the student becomes more productive, he produces more quality work and publications and enhances his chances for recognition and career advancement. In addition, because job opportunities are episodic, the student expands his chances of finding just the right position by expanding the timeframe in which to seek a position. However, the extra two or three years of "service" are not an essential feature of the doctoral program; it is often simply a matter of convenience or a response to funding pressures.

Changing the duration of the doctorate is intimately connected to the duration and nature of the postdoctoral training period. (I turn to the content of postdoctoral positions later in this essay.) One could arbitrarily divide up today's common ten-year training period into seven-year doctoral and three-year postdoctoral periods, or one could have five-year doctoral and five-year postdoctoral periods. The economics will be different, but other issues are more important than the cost to the research program. These funding issues should be revisited with an eye to a more balanced, effective, and shorter program.[8]

Shorten Time-to-Degree

Should we shorten the time-to-degree in the United States? Yes. Is that likely to happen in the absence of a crisis? No. It would require fundamental structural changes in the way graduate students are funded, in the culture of the peer-review system, and in the attitudes at funding agencies and among the faculty supervisors.

Should we organize ourselves to achieve such change? Yes. If the universities, together with the professional societies (for example, the ACS, the American Physical Society, Federation of American Societies for Experimental Biology, the American Association for the Advancement of Science), higher education organizations (American Association of Universities, National Association of State Universities and Land-Grant Colleges), the National Academies of Science, foundations, and the federal agencies agreed that this was important for the nation, they could, in short order, set in motion the necessary actions in order to accomplish this goal. This is not a difficult problem to solve; it is a matter of summoning up the will to solve it.

Clearly, such changes would have ramifications that would need to be addressed, including the serious matter of sustaining adequate productivity. But those secondary consequences could be handled by a more deliberate postdoctoral program, combined with more realistic policies to support technicians and staff for an individual research group, as well as for groups of researchers. Employing such a strategy, when combined with additional means of providing teaching support (now handled almost exclusively by teaching assistants), could also help rationalize the size of graduate programs. The size of graduate programs (in departments with large service-teaching loads) under the present paradigm is often strongly influenced by the need for teaching assistants to cover large lower-division teaching loads.

Address Tension over Teaching Versus Research

It may be appropriate at this point to address another serious underlying issue in graduate education: the confusion about the proper role of the faculty member in a research university setting. There is often an ambiguous attitude on the part of new, as well as more established, faculty about the primary purpose of their professional academic activities. Indeed, one can get into animated discussions about whether "teaching" or "research" is the more important element. Often this discussion merely serves to confuse the mission with the reward structure. In a research university, research is invariably rewarded more explicitly than undergraduate teaching, but this misses the central point. Although research and graduate teaching are complementary, like the two halves of a pair of scissors, the primary mission of the faculty member is education, not the production of research results. Fortunately, in many cases the intense pursuit of a research project serves many of the needs of the student (by default) by helping her develop creative thinking skills and other scholarly attitudes.

However, if a faculty member does not understand that his primary role is to educate students, then it is easy to fall into the trap of using the student as a pair of hands to ensure that results will flow to justify the next grant proposal. Rather than thinking carefully about how to design a series of increasingly challenging tasks and projects tailored for the aptitudes and background of the student, and how to lead the student to adopt increasingly more sophisticated analysis and problem-solving strategies, the mentor may inadvertently simply offer a series of different projects essential to the success of the research program and largely neglect the task of considering how this course of study will help the student develop into a productive and accomplished investigator. The fundamental philosophical distinction just described is misunderstood by far too many. (Fortunately, the intrinsic nature of the research program often channels the student's development along a trajectory that approximates conscious mentoring.) Both the importance of this fundamental responsibility and strategies for achieving it can be communicated and inculcated.

Preparation for a Faculty Career

The second critical structural problem in chemistry doctoral education lies in the failure to provide an integrated and comprehensive training program—graduate study plus postdoctoral work—for those planning an academic career. There is today a serious mismatch between the nature and purpose of the doctoral degree and the demands and expectations of the academy—a significant employer of those with the Ph.D. degree. Imagine spending years training an athlete to learn the intricacies of playing football, and then once he finishes playing college ball, assuming that because he is a well-trained athlete he can immediately be appointed head coach. This is essentially what we do in the academy. Although the responsibility of faculty members goes far beyond mere research prowess, there is no systematic effort to prepare them for the critically important role of being faculty members.

This failure is one of long standing, but it is becoming increasingly unacceptable. In essence, most institutions encourage their new graduate students in the sciences and engineering to get busy on their research topics, in many cases even dispensing with much in the way of formal course work at the graduate level, except for any needed remedial work. The reasonably prepared student often immediately begins to identify a research topic and then spends the next four to six years devoted to an intense pursuit of that research program.

Once her research is completed, the newly minted Ph.D. will probably elect to spend a year or two as a postdoctoral fellow in another institution, either expanding her repertoire of skills in the same field or in a closely related field of endeavor. Again, this can be an intense period of focused research activity, sometimes writing papers and maybe even writing some initial proposals to seek research funding.

Once that coveted academic job offer is nailed down, the pressure to produce results begins in earnest. Without much time for reflection or preparation, the next stage typically finds the new faculty member developing her first lectures for an undergraduate course, writing more proposals, setting up a lab, recruiting graduate students and postdocs to the research group, and getting oriented to the new career demands. Since, in many cases, the new faculty member will soon no longer be doing hands-on research at the bench, it is fair to say that all the tasks the individual now faces are ones for which she has had no formal preparation. This approach is not optimized to ensure success. Indeed, the mismatch between training and task is glaring.

Preparing Future Faculty

The need for some training beyond the Ph.D. to prepare the individual for the profession of teaching has been recognized for a long time. The best-known example is the German *habilitation* program. This program was typically a five- to seven-year (or longer) post-Ph.D. apprenticeship in the academic vineyard before the formal "Dr. Hab." was conferred and the candidate was considered qualified to hold a professorial position in the university.[9] The *habilitation* concept was excellent; the execution left much to be desired. Indeed, somewhere in the distant past a serious commitment to a systematic preparation for the academic role seems to have atrophied, and the *habilitation* process simply became another formal hurdle to surmount on the way to the coveted professorship. Both the gradual lengthening of the period for the *habilitation* process and its increasing divergence from its original purpose have recently been addressed by the German government. Beginning in 2002, institutions began to phase out the *habilitation* process, in keeping with the Dienstrechtsreform Act,[10] in favor of something akin to the U.S. research assistant professor position but without the direct tenure path or its equivalent (Schiermeier, 2002). I would argue that the baby is being thrown out with the bathwater. In particular, might it not have been better to reform the *habilitation* process by shortening the process from the roughly ten-year post-Ph.D. sojourn to two to three years of "internship" (inclusive of postdoctoral work)?

Ironically, while Germany consigns its venerable *habilitation* process to the historical archives, I am suggesting that the *habilitation* concept, but not its structure, should be implemented in the United States. The fact that there is a problem is recognized on both sides of the Atlantic. As noted earlier, in the United Kingdom a dramatic change is currently being introduced, in part, to address a number of the issues through the "The New Route Ph.D." Although its primary focus is on "functional enhancements," it implicitly contains some elements that could benefit a new faculty member.

A more direct attack on the problem has been gestating for more than a decade in the United States, spearheaded originally by the Association of American Colleges and Universities and the Council of Graduate Schools, and funded by The Pew Charitable Trusts (and more recently by The Atlantic Philanthropies and NSF). This program, called Preparing Future Faculty (PFF), seeks to provide graduate students with some orientation regarding academic careers.[11] (The more recent PFF initiative in chemistry has been led by the ACS, the Council of Graduate Schools, and the NSF.) This is an excellent start. However, it is far too limited, both in the time devoted to the task and in the scope of the effort, to serve as an adequate preparation for the academic career. Much more needs to be done, and it needs to be done formally and systematically.

To justify this statement, we need to examine the goals one might identify to properly prepare future faculty. In what follows, I suggest a program during the postdoctoral period, when those planning on an academic career are trained in some of the essential skills for such a career—skills that are now either missing or addressed only in a rather rudimentary fashion.

Elements of a Program for Future Faculty

The process of developing a strategy to address this problem has several parts. First, one must begin by identifying what is missing: in other words, one needs to start with an analysis of what one expects new faculty members to know when they begin their academic career and take on the awesome role of being stewards of the discipline.[12] Second, one has to decide on the content and how much time should be devoted to the training program. Third, one has to devise a strategy for providing those learning experiences. And, fourth, one needs to consider other changes in the prevailing culture and funding paradigms that would be required to enable the changes to be realized.

What are some of the topics that a new faculty member should have been exposed to before taking on the weighty role of supervising the development of the next generation of educators? A thoughtful and informed group of experienced educators should be able to construct a list of experiences that would benefit the prospective faculty member. The topics outlined next represent my suggestions, by way of illustration. The twelve topics included are intended to be suggestive and to stimulate discussion rather than to serve as a recipe.

EDUCATION AS A PROFESSION. As a result of increasing pressure in recent years, many institutions now have brief "orientation" sessions for new faculty in which they are encouraged to participate in "instructional development" tasks. At least this rudimentary effort is an acknowledgment that there is a problem, but the effort is hardly commensurate with the magnitude of the challenges faced by a new faculty member. The entire scope of the orientation needs to be changed and a broader array of elements included. The orientation needs to begin with a focused discussion of the underlying philosophy that should inform the professional educator. We also need to be explicit about the responsibilities implicit in the role of educator. Maybe we even need to develop something like a Hippocratic Oath for educators.

APPRENTICESHIP IN TEACHING. We need to provide some effective training on the practical issues associated with developing and presenting a course in an effective manner. To illustrate, let me recount my own experience. I had the good fortune of benefiting from an experience that provided some of the latter "orientation." I was awarded the Alfred A. Noyes Fellowship at Caltech upon completion of my Ph.D. This unique award allowed me to carry on any research project of interest, but it also required me to serve as an assistant to one of the senior faculty members. I teamed up with Professor Wilse Robinson, who was teaching the course in physical chemistry. This experience of working directly with a seasoned educator, giving lectures from time to time (reviewed in advance by Professor Robinson), preparing problem sets and exams, mentoring students, and preparing explanatory and background material provided a solid foundation for my later teaching responsibilities as a new faculty member at Harvard. I cannot overemphasize how constructive and important that experience was to my future role as a faculty member.

There are other important elements (all too often ignored or taken for granted) that are essential to working effectively in the classroom. These include an understanding of the psychology of students, the role of the mentor, and the utility and fairness of assignments, grading, and expectations. Most of the insights that graduate students develop on these topics are currently gleaned in classes they take, resulting in serious variability. When the new faculty member then first applies that experience in the classroom, the result often leads to considerable confusion and consternation on the part of the students. In short, the typical two-day orientation needs to be replaced with a full year of apprenticeship as an instructor, including a short course that puts the professional role of a faculty member into context.

HISTORY OF THE DISCIPLINE. Most students in the sciences gain virtually no background in the history of their discipline throughout the course of their doctoral work and precious little as undergraduates. Although the individuals may know a great deal about the trajectory of the particular topic of their dissertation, the broad sweep of the history of the discipline may never have crossed their field of view. Students who are going to be mentors of the next generation of practitioners should be required to spend at least a modest amount of time reading key works that provide an overview of the major events that shaped the development of the discipline. This would take various forms for different disciplines, but some introduction to the topic should be required. For example, in my view, every prospective chemistry teacher should be required to read Lavoisier's *Elements of Chemistry* (1789/1965).

EXPOSURE TO OTHER DISCIPLINES. The focus and intensity of the graduate experience usually limits the student's exposure to the major intellectual challenges of contiguous fields. Especially in this era when nearly all the sciences (and engineering) have shifted their focus to include the molecular level, it is imperative that chemists, of all those trained in technical disciplines, should have a broad perspective of the frontiers of the scientific enterprise. This can be done in several ways, any one of which could be selected as a means of ensuring greater breadth. For example, a postdoctoral student could spend a quarter in another laboratory not directly related to his Ph.D. He could take a formal course in another discipline. There could be organized reading clubs that would systematically explore a range of related topics. I have argued that such broadening of the educational experience should happen during the Ph.D. program as well; the issue of "breadth" is also of great concern to industry employers (Kaldor, 2000). But it is so critical for effective mentoring that additional breadth could and should be added for those preparing to be stewards of the discipline.[13]

MANAGEMENT AND PERSONNEL SKILLS. The newly appointed faculty member immediately becomes the head of a "small business," with responsibility for hiring and supervising "employees," meeting payroll, engaging in advertising and promotion, managing budgets, and so on. Some of these activities will be somewhat familiar to the individual; some of the necessary skills will have been developed informally, in a well-run research group, during the doctoral program. But there is generally no systematic approach to preparing prospective faculty members to function in this arena, even though it will be critical to their long-range success. This omission needs to be corrected before they join the faculty. Indeed, one can argue that having such training is much more important for the beginning faculty member than it is for a new employee in industry or a government lab. Why? The reason is that in the latter two contexts, the employee normally starts at an apprentice level or as part of a group and receives appropriate mentoring (and often management training) in the early years. By contrast, the new faculty member becomes a "manager" the moment she is appointed and is expected to have acquired all the necessary management skills magically.[14]

INSTITUTIONAL STRUCTURE AND GOVERNANCE. Most faculty members are relatively uninformed about how the institution functions, what the expectations are, and what the opportunities for affecting the direction of the institution are. Even an elementary overview of the broader institutional machinery (including grievance procedures and dispute resolution strategies) could go a long way toward simplifying the life of the new faculty member. There is often an unfortunate and insidious culture of antagonism between faculty and administration. This is as old as humanity and will not disappear. But it is counterproductive, and often the worst excesses arise from simple ignorance and misunderstanding. An introduction that provides a basic orientation to the strategic goals of the institution, together with an overview of the challenges an institution faces, can create a much more harmonious environment of cooperation and constructive dialogue. Well-designed role-playing sessions on selected topics that an administrator has to deal with can be very instructive for new faculty. For example, a simple introduction to indirect costs and how they are used in the institution could prevent a great deal of unhappiness and misunderstanding on the part of the faculty member, both new and established (Kwiram, 2004).[15]

TENURE AND THE TENURE CLOCK. This issue receives much more attention today than it once did, but it is still often neglected, to the chagrin of faculty and institution alike. Especially in the case of women faculty, issues such as granting pregnancy leave and extending the tenure clock are important considerations and need to be clearly addressed and understood at the outset.

ETHICS, CONFLICT OF INTEREST, AND SENSITIVITY TRAINING. Increasingly, the varied cultural backgrounds of our new faculty create significant unevenness in both the understanding and application of key practices in the academy. Issues of sexual harassment, conflict of interest, sensitivity to those of different cultures, and ethical behavior in relationships with coworkers and students are increasingly a source of conflict and even legal action. Ensuring that new faculty members are sensitized early on to these issues and the rules that govern them can prevent grief later.

IMPORTANCE OF DIVERSITY. This topic is obviously on everyone's mind these days. But that does not mean that individual faculty have a well-developed sense of the critical role they can play as role models, as recruiters of minority and female candidates, and as members of a community with an obligation to further the cause of diversity. A well-crafted training session on this topic could have very salutary effects.

LEADERSHIP SKILLS. Some faculty members are born leaders, and others have to learn to lead. Those in the latter category should not be left to struggle on their own for years before they develop some basic skills in this area. Unfortunately, that is the norm. It is ironic that universities, whose business is education, provide virtually no training for their faculty. This failure is most glaring when it comes to appointing a hapless faculty member to the position of chair of the department, or associate dean, or dean, or other administrative position. This behavior is in sharp contrast to the practice at many major companies where ongoing training opportunities are often provided for staff.[16]

There are tried-and-tested techniques that can help develop leaders, and such training would be beneficial, especially since each new faculty member is expected to become a leader of a team immediately. In a broader context, each institution expects the individual to become a leader in some sector of the discipline, however limited. Despite this expectation, there is no provision in general to help a faculty member develop such skills.

GRANT WRITING. One of the major challenges for any new faculty member is the need to win funding for her research through competitively won grants. It is distressing to see how many faculty members do not have the skills to write a clear and compelling proposal and how much valuable time faculty lose by not knowing about sources of funding, how to work with program managers, and how to stay informed of nontraditional sources of funding. Doesn't it make sense to try to provide some basic training for such an essential activity?

REGULATORY AND COMPLIANCE ISSUES. These have grown in complexity and numbers in recent years, to the point of numbing the senses. However, since in some cases there are now criminal penalties for violations, it is imperative that some introduction to these issues be presented early and forcefully. Managing budgets and working with the institutional accounting system could form part of this topic. Again, the situation in the academy is not the same as in industry: for all intents and purposes, as noted, the new faculty member is a CEO the minute he assumes the position of assistant professor, whereas the new industry employee typically has time to learn the ropes as an apprentice in a group. In the academy, there is neither mechanism nor time for learning all the needed skills on the job and no leeway to make serious mistakes.

A Suggested Implementation Strategy

These dozen topics are intended to provide an example, and are not intended in any way to be definitive or to suggest that these are of equal priority. Obviously, some of the relevant skills are picked up in an informal way in the course of the doctoral and postdoctoral work; in some cases particularly conscientious mentors (and, fortunately, there are many of these) will do more than discuss the matter casually in group meetings. But there is no systematic program to provide the new faculty member with the general context of the professorial role, the cultural expectations of the academy or, not least, an adequate sense of the importance of this role.

The topics might also vary somewhat, depending on the eventual career choice, whether in a top-ranked research university or in a four-year college or at the community college level. But regardless of the institution, it would be hard to argue that the kinds of skills outlined are not essential to a successful career. (At the end of this essay, Table 8.2 provides a sample course of study.)

If one were to accept the argument that some topics, like those outlined, merit greater formal attention than they currently receive, how much time should be devoted to such matters? What would some of the elements in such a program be? Following are a few examples of how this might work during an ideal postdoctoral appointment:

- At a minimum, the prospective faculty member should spend one academic year as a teaching apprentice, working with a senior faculty member who has a demonstrated track record as an excellent teacher. This activity should involve a regular undergraduate course (not a lab course or seminar course). The senior faculty member, chosen from among those known to be effective teachers, would be expected to serve deliberately and systematically as a mentor to provide a series of teaching experiences with increasing responsibility and independence. The elements to be included in that process should be determined by the collective judgment of the department, which would set general guidelines. These responsibilities of the new Ph.D. would probably require about ten to twenty hours per week.

- During the summer before the first academic year, the postdoc could take an intensive four-week course on educational philosophy, general concepts of pedagogy, the balance between research and teaching, teaching via lecture versus teaching via inquiry methods, the profound responsibility of mentoring the next generation of students, the use of technology in teaching, and so on.

- A one-term course on the history of the discipline could include readings from closely related fields, together with case studies of major advances in the field, including selected Nobel Prize achievements. What strategies led to success for one scientist and failure for another? Are there common themes that characterize notable achievements? What constitutes a significant strategy in pursuing new understanding? Can one learn from the work of those who have been successful in defining the right question? What are the relative merits of a strategy that focuses on a major problem and tries to solve it by whatever means and the strategy of developing a new experimental method and then seeking to apply the method to important problems?

- A one-term exposure to increase breadth could be a course, work in another lab, or an intensive and formal "journal club" activity.
- A one-semester course on management skills and leadership training should not just be handed off to the business school but could be done productively in partnership with the business school, and it could be done for candidates in all technical disciplines (at least those with significant emphasis on sponsored research programs). The major focus of such a course should be on leadership training, time management, interpersonal communication, dealing with difficult colleagues, and so on. It could also include elementary accounting and budgeting principles, as well as an overview of regulatory and compliance issues.
- An intensive summer program (two weeks) could be devoted to issues of diversity, ethics, conflict of interest, cultural sensitivity, and related topics.
- A year-long seminar (one hour-long meeting a week with "homework") on grant writing could include the preparation of proposals and the development of writing skills, as well as information about the funding environment and strategies. The seminar could also include an introduction to strategies for dealing with the media, fostering the public understanding of science, and communicating across disciplinary boundaries.

The time commitment for the activities described would be roughly half the available time or the equivalent of a one-year internship spread out over a two-year (minimum) time period. (An individual could spend additional time as a postdoctoral student, but only the first two-year stint would have the special "internship" character.) The rest of the time would be available for research activities.

Some will argue that this represents a lot of make-work that the bright student does not need and would pick up automatically. Reality suggests otherwise, as many department chairs (as well as many new faculty members) will testify. And although the bright student may pick up some of this over time, it can be argued that the actual time spent in the self-taught mode may actually be greater than if done in a more organized and systematic manner. That is, after all, the essence of formal education. Further, it should be kept in mind that this is not an activity carried out during the doctoral period. And it is not done after the individual becomes a member of the faculty. It is part of the postdoctoral training period and only for those who plan an academic career. The total time from bachelor's degree to first academic appointment (time-to-career) would be six to seven years (four for the shortened Ph.D. and two to three for the postdoctoral period), which is roughly the period now consumed for the Ph.D. alone.

How would such a program be implemented? One way to approach this task is to consider that most prospective faculty members, at least in the sciences, engage in postdoctoral work before beginning their academic careers. Could one devise a program that would be part of such postdoctoral training for those planning to go into the academic profession? One could imagine generic courses for all (or most all) disciplines within an institution (which could even be taken by those not in postdoctoral positions, that is, by those doctoral students in the humanities who plan to go into teaching). A course on the history of the discipline would have to be more discipline-specific, although it would not hurt to have such a course cover several related fields (for example, physics, chemistry, and materials science), with the reading selections modified accordingly. Alternatively, one could have intensive summer programs at selected institutions on a cooperative basis.

If prospective faculty members took two or three courses during the period of their postdoctoral experience (or before assuming their professorial role) and, in addition, spent some internship time with a seasoned administrator or a teacher in a course, it would have a significant impact on their understanding of their role and responsibilities in mentoring the next generation of professionals.

What other changes would be required? One of the key questions is how this would be paid for. At the present time, 40 to 50 percent of all Ph.D.'s in chemistry go on to a postdoctoral position (Hoffer, 2004). Most of these positions are paid for by the federal government. However, less than half of the postdocs will go on to regular faculty positions. Therefore, the increased "cost" to the government of supporting this educational internship would be roughly 15 to 25 percent above what the government is paying now for postdocs, which is only a fraction of the total research support. Hence, the impact on the total research budget would be less than 5 to 10 percent. This expenditure would be entirely appropriate for the federal government, first because it would be the easiest way to manage the program and, second, because graduate education has largely become a federal enterprise. In the context of the proposed NSF goal of increasing the salary levels for postdocs, what better investment than to build into that increase a dramatic improvement in the training of the next generation of stewards of the disciplines?

There would, of course, be an added cost to the Ph.D.-granting universities in mounting the courses and training programs just outlined. That could be considered the institutional "match" for the federal investment. In reality, the added cost would not amount to more than the teaching load of one faculty member, as many of the programs can be distributed across multiple departments.

Is this too high a price to pay? And would such a program just degenerate into make-work and become sterile and oppressive? Of course it could, but it need not. Its vitality would depend entirely on the attitude of the departments, on the one hand, and the commitment of the students on the other.

In this connection, consider the educational process in medicine. After four years, the medical student is considered to have mastered the basics of medicine. Traditionally, this has been followed by a one-year internship designed to facilitate the transition to a formal medical practice. But for those who are going to become serious practitioners in a specialty, an extended residency program is required. (Usually, we prefer to be treated by a specialist who has had such training.) Alternatively, the proposed program for future faculty could be compared to the M.D.-Ph.D. program, which, though very demanding, is not wanting for applicants.

Table 8.1. Suggested "Enhancement Curriculum" for Ph.D. in Chemistry.

Topic	Year 1	Year 2	Year 3	Year 4
Ethics		Q1		
Intellectual property and technology transfer	Q3			Q4
Interpersonal communication	Q4			
Proposal writing			Q3	Q1, Q3
Team work	Q1			
Interdisciplinary breadth			Q1–Q3	
"Propositions"		Q2	Q2	Q2
Careers in industry		Q4		Q3
Technology and tools	Q2	Q3		

Notes: Q = *academic quarter*

The first three topics would be generic training programs (applicable for all departments) handled by the central administration (for example, Graduate School, Office of Research, Technology Transfer Office). The next three would be handled jointly by the central administration and an individual department. The last three would be a departmental responsibility.

"Propositions" refers to a program requiring the student to present an original proposal for research and defend it to the faculty and students; the students should do this in each of three years, with proposals at increasing levels of sophistication and expectation. Except for activities represented under "Interdisciplinary breadth," most of these topics would be covered as short courses or monthly seminars, not regular three-credit courses.

Table 8.2. Suggested Curriculum for a Postdoctoral Future Faculty Program in Chemistry.

Topic	Summer 1	Year 2	Summer 2	Year 2
Philosophy and pedagogy	1 month			
Teaching apprenticeship		2 to 3 terms		
History of the discipline				1 term
Increased breadth				1 term
Management skills	1 month			
Diversity and ethics			2 weeks	
Grant writing	2 weeks	monthly		monthly

Note: *A term could be either a quarter or a semester, as appropriate. The two-to three-term teaching apprenticeship thus represents one academic year.*

Is the preparation of our future faculty who will teach the next generation any less important than what we expect of our medical caregivers? Are we not prepared to specify merely a one-year "internship" for future faculty as the minimum investment on behalf of our students? Given that the success of our future faculty—and our discipline—depends on the degree to which they do these tasks well, this is where our institutions should invest the greatest energy. Such a formal program of preparation could become one of the most effective means for reforming the Ph.D. for those who plan to become educators and stewards of the discipline. The continued neglect of this task should be deemed unacceptable.

NOTES

1. An extensive bibliography is provided by the project on "Re-envisioning the Ph.D.," located at the University of Washington (University of Washington, 2000). An excellent introduction to the study can be found in "Reenvisioning the Ph.D.: What Concerns Do We Have?" by Jody Nyquist and Bettina J. Woodford (2000). Most of the contemporary concerns regarding doctoral education in this country are reflected in the material available from these sources.

2. One of the arenas in which an active discussion of the need for reform of the chemistry Ph.D. program is being carried on is the Graduate Education Advisory Board of the ACS.

3. For example, the recently established NSF Science and Technology Center for Materials and Devices in Information Technology Research (stc-mditr.org)

plans a series of self-paced learning modules on a range of topics in opto-electronics. Distance learning modules are increasingly available on the Internet.

4. An example of a program designed to foster more teamwork is provided by the NSF-funded Integrative Graduate Education and Research Traineeship (IGERT) program on Urban Ecology at the University of Washington. They have outlined a novel program that provides graduate students with experience working as teams.

5. "The New Route Ph.D." is being introduced in many disciplines across many institutions in the United Kingdom (www.newroutephd.ac.uk). This new program incorporates many of the elements included in our list of functional enhancements.

6. It should be noted that these figures refer to the median time from bachelor's degree to Ph.D. "Registered time-to-degree" is less by roughly a year in the sciences and two years in the humanities, largely because of the delay between completion of the B.A. and start of the Ph.D.

7. Some recognition must obviously be given to factors such as financial support. A student who is unsupported for the entire time (an exception in chemistry) or one who has to serve as a teaching assistant during the entire duration of the doctoral work clearly requires more time than students supported either as research associates or on fellowships.

8. At the NSF's workshop "The Future of Graduate Education," held in Washington D.C. in March 2003, Harvard economist Richard Freeman pointed out that many Ph.D. scientists earn 25 to 30 percent of their lifetime income through graduate and postdoc stipends. This is based on his analysis that the average time-to-degree in all science fields is seven years, plus five years in a postdoc position. When future earnings are discounted at 5 percent, it becomes apparent that nearly 33 percent of the scientist's lifetime income was obtained before he or she got a job.

9. Note that the individual could not enter the *habilitation* program directly upon receiving the Ph.D. but had to have independent employment for two years first. For information on the new German training programs, see www.bmbf.de.

10. Legal action by German states have made the future of the Habilitation Reform Act uncertain.

11. See the description at The Preparing Future Faculty (PFF) program description at www.preparing-faculty.org. The PFF program is pointed in the right direction and represents an important effort in addressing a serious problem. It needs to be expanded.

12. The term *steward* is an excellent expression for those who serve in the professorial ranks. In practice it may be even more applicable to those mentoring Ph.D. students than to those teaching in community colleges, but it has meaning in both contexts. In my usage of the phrase, I limit it to those in the teaching profession.

13. Indeed, it is surprising that we have not instituted general courses at the graduate level designed for the nonspecialist that provide a broad overview of the major intellectual challenges in various disciplines. Maybe this could be considered the tragedy of the intellectual commons: it is everyone's responsibility to do this, so no one does it. One of the most difficult tasks in organizing sessions for AAAS meetings, for example, is to get speakers to present their material in a way that is accessible to the informed layperson. We seem to suffer from a Tower of Babel syndrome that prevents us from conveying the essential ideas in jargon-free language to our colleagues in other disciplines (to say nothing of the public).

14. In July 2002 the Burroughs Wellcome Fund and the Howard Hughes Medical Institute debuted a four-day summer "Course in Scientific Management" (Yarnell, 2002; Burroughs Wellcome Fund and the Howard Hughes Medical Institute, 2004). See also *At the Helm: A Laboratory Navigator* (Barker, 2002).

15. This publication provided first-hand experience in the importance of effective communication between the faculty and administration.

16. For example, many academic institutions do not even have a list of resources they can refer their administrators to for training programs in management, leadership, and related topics. This became very clear in a special workshop for new vice provosts and vice chancellors for research, sponsored by the Council on Research Policy and Graduate Education. For more information see www.nasulgc.org/councils_research.htm, where the 2002 CRPGE Workshop on Research Administration outlines discussion topics that included training opportunities in management and leadership.

REFERENCES

American Chemical Society. "Graduate Training at the Doctoral Level: Condensed Summary of the Main Report of the Committee on Professional Training." *Chemical and Engineering News*, 1947a, 25, 1934–1936.
American Chemical Society. "Graduate Training at the Doctoral Level, Cont'd: Condensed Summary of the Main Report of the Committee on Professional Training, Summary of Part II, Information from Ph.D.'s in Industry." *Chemical and Engineering News*, 1947b, 25, 2010–2013.

American Chemical Society. "Graduate Training at the Doctoral Level, Cont'd: Condensed Summary of the Main Report of the Committee on Professional Training. Summary of Part III, Information from Chemical Industrial Research Directors and Executives." *Chemical and Engineering News*, 1947c, 25, 2076–2081.

American Chemical Society Committee on Professional Training. "Philosophy of Graduate Training at the Ph.D. Level." *Chemical and Engineering News*, 1948, 26, 166–167.

Barker, K. *At the Helm: A Laboratory Navigator.* Cold Spring Harbor, N.Y.: Cold Spring Harbor Laboratory Press, 2002.

Burroughs Wellcome Fund and Howard Hughes Medical Institute. *Making the Right Moves: A Practical Guide to Scientific Management for Postdocs and New Faculty.* Research Triangle Park, N.C.: Burroughs Wellcome Fund and Howard Hughes Medical Institute, 2004. Available at www.hhmi.org/labmanagement.

Caserio, M. "Reflections on Graduate Education." *Newsletter of the ACS Younger Chemists Committee*, Fall 2002.

Heylin, M. "Employment and Salary Survey." *Chemical and Engineering News*, 2004, Aug. 16, 26–34.

Higher Education Funding Council for England. "Higher Education in the United Kingdom." Jan. 2004. Available at www.hefce.ac.uk/pubs/hefce/2004/HEinUK.

Hoffer, T., and others. *Doctorate Recipients from United States Universities: Summary Report 2003.* Chicago: National Opinion Research Center, 2004.

Kaldor, A. "Reengineering Graduate Education in Science and Engineering." Presentation given at Associated Western Universities (AWU) Science Education and Research Conference. Dec. 1, 2000. Available at www.grad.washington.edu/envision/PPT/kaldor.ppt.

Kwiram, A. L. "An Overview of Indirect Costs." *Journal for Higher Education Strategists*, 2004, 1(4), 387–436.

Lavoisier, A. L. *Elements of Chemistry, in a New Systematic Order, Containing All the Modern Discoveries.* (R. Kerr, trans.). New York: Dover Publications, 1965.

Nyquist, J. D., and Woodford, B. J. "Re-envisioning the Ph.D.: What Concerns Do We Have?" 2000. Available at www.grad.washington.edu/envision/resources/ConcernsBrief.pdf.

Paulsen, F. *The German Universities and University Study.* (F. Thilly and W. W. Elwang, trans.). New York: Scribner, 1906.

Roberts, J. D. "How Long Should It Take for a Graduate Student to Get a PhD in Chemistry?" *Newsletter of the ACS Office of Graduate Education*, 2002, 1(1), 3.

Schiermeier, Q. "Breaking the Habilitation Habit." *Nature*, 2002, *415*, 257–258.

Shulman, J. "Teaching Doctoral Students About Industrial Careers." *Science's Next Wave*. July 16, 2002. Available at nextwave.sciencemag.org/cgi/content/full/2002/07/16/6.

University of Washington. "Selected Bibliography on Doctoral Education." Re-envisioning the Ph.D. Project. Apr. 2000. Available at www.grad.washington.edu/envision.

Yarnell, A. "Crash Course in Lab Management." *Chemical and Engineering News*, 2002, *80*, 64, 66.

9

DEVELOPING BREADTH AND DEPTH OF KNOWLEDGE

THE DOCTORATE IN CHEMISTRY

Ronald Breslow, Columbia University

IN MARCH 2003, the National Research Council (NRC) released one of its periodic surveys of the fields of chemistry and chemical engineering: *Beyond the Molecular Frontier: Challenges for Chemistry and Chemical Engineering.* The survey was created by a committee headed by Ronald Breslow, representing chemistry, and Matthew Tirrell, representing chemical engineering.

In this volume, chemists in industry and academia will find many, many pages describing research that needs to be done immediately and well into the future. Each chapter lists challenges in specific areas. A list of "Grand Challenges" for chemists and chemical engineers, reproduced next, covers the entire broad field:

• *Learn how to synthesize and manufacture any new substance that can have scientific or practical interest, using compact synthetic schemes and processes with high selectivity for the desired product, and with low energy consumption and benign environmental effects in the process.* This goal will require continuing progress in the development of new methods for synthesis and manufacturing. Human welfare will continue to benefit from new substances, including medicines and specialized materials.

• *Develop new materials and measurement devices that will protect citizens against terrorism, accident, crime, and disease, in part by detecting and identifying dangerous substances and organisms using methods with high sensitivity and selectivity.* Rapid and reliable detection of dangerous disease organisms, highly toxic chemicals, and concealed explosives (including those in land mines) is the first important step in responding to threats. The next important step for chemists and chemical engineers will be to devise methods to deal with such threats, including those involved in terrorist or military attacks.

• *Understand and control how molecules react—over all time scales and the full range of molecular size.* This fundamental understanding will let us design new reactions and manufacturing processes and will provide fundamental insights into the science of chemistry. Major advances that will contribute to this goal over the next decades include the predictive computational modeling of molecular motions using large-scale parallel processing arrays; the ability to investigate and manipulate individual molecules, not just collections of molecules; and the generation of ultrafast electron pulses and optical pulses down to X-ray wavelengths, to observe molecular structures during chemical reactions. This is but one area in which increased understanding will lead to a greater ability to improve the practical applications of the chemical sciences.

• *Learn how to design and produce new substances, materials, and molecular devices with properties that can be predicted, tailored, and tuned before production.* This ability would greatly streamline the search for new useful substances, avoiding considerable trial and error. Recent and projected advances in chemical theory and computation should make this possible.

• *Understand the chemistry of living systems in detail.* Understand how various different proteins and nucleic acids and small biological molecules assemble into chemically defined functional complexes, and indeed, understand all the complex chemical interactions among the various components of living cells. Explaining the processes of life in chemical terms is one of the great challenges continuing into the future, and the chemistry behind thought and memory is an especially exciting challenge. This is an area in which great progress has been made, as biology increasingly becomes a chemical science (and chemistry increasingly becomes a life science).

• *Develop medicines and therapies that can cure currently untreatable diseases.* In spite of the great progress that has been made in the invention of new medicines by chemists, and new materials and delivery vehicles by engineers, the challenges in these directions are vast. New medicines to deal with cancer, viral diseases, and many other maladies will enormously improve human welfare.

• *Develop self-assembly as a useful approach to the synthesis and manufacturing of complex systems and materials.* Mixtures of properly designed chemical components can organize themselves into complex assemblies with structures from the nanoscale to the macroscale, in a fashion similar to biological assembly. Taking this methodology from the laboratory experimentation to the practical manufacturing arena could revolutionize chemical processing.

• *Understand the complex chemistry of the earth, including land, sea, atmosphere, and biosphere, so we can maintain its livability.* This is a fundamental challenge to the natural science of our field, and it is key to helping design policies that will prevent environmental degradation. In addition, chemical scientists will use this understanding to create new methods to deal with pollution and other threats to our earth.

• *Develop unlimited and inexpensive energy (with new ways of energy generation, storage, and transportation) to pave the way to a truly sustainable future.* Our current ways of generating and using energy consume limited resources and produce environmental problems. There are very exciting prospects for fuel cells to permit an economy based on hydrogen rather than fossil fuels, ways to harness the energy of sunlight for our use, and superconductors that will permit efficient energy distribution.

• *Design and develop self-optimizing chemical systems.* Building on the approach that allows optimization of biological systems through evolution, this would let a system produce the optimal new substance and produce it as a single product rather than as a mixture from which the desired component must be isolated and identified. Self-optimizing systems would allow visionary chemical scientists to use this approach to make new medicines, catalysts, and other important chemical products— in part by combining new approaches to informatics with rapid experimental screening methods.

• *Revolutionize the design of chemical processes to make them safe, compact, flexible, energy efficient, environmentally benign, and conducive to the rapid commercialization of new products.* This points to the major goal of modern chemical engineering, in which many new factors are important for an optimal manufacturing process. Great progress has been made in developing Green Chemistry, but more is needed as we continue to meet human needs with the production of important chemical products using processes that are completely harmless to the earth and its inhabitants.

• *Communicate effectively to the general public the contributions that chemistry and chemical engineering make to society.* Chemists and chemical engineers need to learn how to communicate effectively to the general public—both through the media and directly—to explain what chemists and chemical engineers do and to convey the goals and achievements of the chemical sciences in pursuit of a better world.

• *Attract the best and the brightest young students into the chemical sciences, to help meet these challenges.* They can contribute to critical human needs while following exciting careers, working on and beyond the molecular frontier.

Of course, these challenges are not exclusive, and no one will be surprised if chemists and chemical engineers come up with exciting discoveries that are not presaged in the survey report. But the survey challenge lists form the current "to-do" list for the field.

The NRC challenge lists also give us a window on the profession: in looking at the work ahead, one can imagine the sort of chemists who could actually carry it out. These chemists must have knowledge that is sufficiently broad and deep that they can cross boundaries within the field of chemistry and among the fields of science. As the list of challenges indicates, chemists and chemical engineers of the future must be able to work at the interfaces of their fields with other areas such as biology, medicine, solid-state physics, and environmental science.

If these are the chemists we need now, and if we will need even more of them in the future, how must doctoral education in chemistry be structured? What is the right mix of time and experience that would produce chemists, whether they are in industry or academia (or both), who can easily cross boundaries to work in and develop new fields?

These questions are not new to the profession. For example, in November 1995, representatives from industry and graduate chemistry programs met to discuss the future of U.S. doctoral education in chemistry. They were, as I later reported in *Chemical and Engineering News*, in remarkable agreement about what a doctoral education in chemistry should accomplish: mastery of a specific area within chemistry, as well as a broad knowledge of chemistry and related fields; strong communication skills; and a sound understanding of the ethics and good practice of the profession.

Are our current doctoral programs organized to produce such chemists? In 1996, the American Chemical Society's Committee on Professional Training conducted a survey of doctoral programs. The findings pinpoint the areas in most need of change to meet this goal and suggest that we can make much better use of existing practices. In this essay, I review current practice in doctoral education and offer recommendations for structural and procedural changes in our programs that would yield chemists with the substantive knowledge and professional skills that the future demands.

None of my recommendations would extend the time to a Ph.D. degree in chemistry, which should not exceed five years. They are designed to make better use of those five years.

The Range of Chemistry

To appreciate the need for chemists with the breadth and depth necessary to cross boundaries within chemistry itself and also among fields of science (as well as other fields), we need first to consider the range of chemistry and the way academic departments are organized.

Typically, academic chemistry departments are made up of subfields: organic chemistry, physical chemistry, theoretical chemistry, inorganic chemistry, and, in some departments, biological chemistry and analytical chemistry (although the last two are not represented in all departments). Within these subfields there are further divisions. For example, organic chemistry includes synthetic methodology development, physical organic chemistry that is focused on understanding how reactions occur and on structure-reactivity relationships, bio-organic chemistry, natural compound isolation and identification, and many other areas. Some organic chemists also work in the field of medicinal chemistry. The other subfields of chemistry also have their own subdivisions, such as physical chemistry concerned with gas-phase reactions, physical chemistry focused on spectroscopy, and biophysical chemistry.

Furthermore, many fields are so close that they may well be considered part of chemistry. For example, some fundamental chemical research is done in chemical engineering departments, as well as in chemistry departments. Similarly, the field of biochemistry is really part of chemistry, although it is often taught in a separate department. In the same way, medicinal chemistry is often taught in special departments in medical schools or pharmacy schools. The *ACS Directory of Graduate Research* lists all these departments, and also departments of clinical chemistry, polymer science, food science, toxicology, marine science, forensic science, materials science, and environmental science as places where graduate work in some aspects of chemistry is undertaken.

The Basics of Chemistry

The two fundamental aspects of our work in chemistry—substances and transformations—also have bearing on how we educate future chemists.

Substances

Chemists want to understand the structures and properties of every substance that already exists in nature. In the earliest days there was a strong focus on separating pure chemical substances from natural mixtures and on determining the exact chemical structure of each of the substances so isolated. This led to the identification of all the natural amino acids, for instance, as well as vitamins and sugars. Such work is still under way to some extent. For example, the structures of many proteins have been determined, usually by X-ray crystallography, but many more are yet undetermined. The sequencing of the genomes of various species, including humans, involves the determination of their chemical structures; increasingly, chemists are determining the chemical structures of multi-molecular systems such as the photosynthetic reaction center or the ribosome. The question is not just what molecules make up these systems but also how those molecules are arranged.

Chemists want to create new, unnatural molecules as well, not just explore nature. In fact, well over 90 percent of all known chemical substances have been created by chemists, not found in nature. The purpose of this work is partly to explore what is possible, but many of these created substances are also very useful. Most modern medicines, for instance, as well as pesticides, herbicides, plastics, and synthetic fibers, are the product of the creativity of chemists. After they are made, their properties are examined, including biological properties, to see if they can be useful. The modern pharmaceutical and chemical industries are the result of such explorations into the unknown.

Transformations

The other fundamental aspect of chemistry is transformations—what chemists call reactions. These are processes in which chemical substances are transformed into other substances, and they also have both a natural and a created aspect. Natural transformations include all the biochemical reactions in which food is transformed into proteins and fats, for instance, as well as those that produce the molecules whose energy can be used to drive muscle contraction and other vital processes. Another example is the conversion of carbon dioxide and water into carbohydrates in green plants, using light energy in photosynthesis.

Again, the new transformations invented by chemists greatly outnumber the natural biological processes, and the invented transformations are what make the creation of novel molecules possible.

Some significant part of chemistry involves the continued creation of new molecules and new transformations in a field generally called synthetic chemistry. To put this in perspective, it has been estimated that at least 10^{40} molecules can exist, made up of the common elements found in most medicines and with about the size of a typical medicine. Some estimates are even larger. Since only a million or so molecules are now made and registered with *Chemical Abstracts* in a typical year, there is still plenty to do in the synthesis of new molecules. Many chemists are engaged in such synthetic efforts and in devising the novel transformations that will make synthesis possible.

Chemistry also involves understanding. How are the structures of molecules related to their properties? How, in detail, do chemical reactions occur? Which atoms move where, and when do they move? How is chemical energy used to achieve a transformation? How do other substances catalyze the reactions? Chemists working in this area can be divided into two classes: (1) those who perform experiments to determine structure and property relationships, or reaction pathways, and (2) those who use theoretical methods to predict properties and pathways.

Advances in techniques have made many things possible that could not be done previously. For one, advances in X-ray crystallographic methods and in other spectroscopic methods such as NMR (nuclear magnetic resonance) have made it possible to determine the chemical structures of increasingly large molecules and organized systems. For another, advances in computer power and better computational programs have made it possible to predict chemical properties and reaction pathways with much better accuracy. Furthermore, new spectroscopic techniques using lasers have made it possible to measure reactions so rapidly that intermediate structures can be detected that were only matters of speculation previously.

As the "Grand Challenges" suggest, the scope of chemistry has also widened enormously. Chemists are engaged in exciting research on the borders of classical chemistry with other fields, and we see much less concern with working simply within the classical subdisciplines of chemistry. Chemistry and the environment, chemistry and nanoscience, chemistry and molecular genetics—these are areas in which many of the most promising young research chemists are now making their mark.

Implications for Doctoral Education

What do the scope of the discipline and the nature of work in chemistry suggest about how we might improve doctoral education? Our Ph.D. students must learn that narrowness in education or interest is not an asset. Departments must be open to the new directions in which chemistry is moving, and they must reassess where the classical division of chemistry departments causes a problem. (Are there barriers to hiring faculty whose interests do not fit within one of the classical divisions? Are the courses, as taught, sufficiently refocused on the new areas in which modern chemistry is moving? Are the texts and other teaching materials suitable for chemistry as it is developing?) The negative effects of divisional structure within departments can be minimized. For example, departments can regularly hold departmental colloquia with visiting speakers who are told that they will be speaking to a general chemical audience, not just to specialists in their subfields.

Our students may well find that their future careers bring them into close contact with chemistry's sister fields. Therefore, members of regular chemistry departments should forge connections with these departments, in particular, medicinal chemistry, chemical engineering, polymer chemistry, materials science, and environmental science.

Developing Breadth of Knowledge

Ph.D.'s in chemistry should have educational breadth that covers chemistry and related fields. What does this mean? It means that students should have a sense of the ways knowledge can be applied in other areas and should be familiar with experts and literature outside their own subdiscipline. As they extend their thinking about science, they will continue to grow intellectually.

How can we develop this sort of breadth in graduate students and prepare them for careers that may take them in many directions?

First, let us consider our graduate students' starting point as they enter our programs. Typically, students are admitted into graduate programs in chemistry only if they have a strong undergraduate education in chemistry. This would include at least three years of chemistry, as well as courses in physics and mathematics. The ACS Committee on Professional Training certifies the undergraduate programs of all U.S. chemistry departments on a regular basis; it also tracks the practices of graduate programs. In particular, the committee examines whether training and education have sufficient breadth among areas of chemistry, so that students do not end up narrowly educated in one of the subfields, or even in one aspect of one of the subfields. Recently, the committee has listed some undergraduate education in biochemistry as a necessary component of an undergraduate major in chemistry, in addition to organic, inorganic, physical, and some analytical chemistry. Thus graduate students who have attended U.S. undergraduate institutions should arrive with a reasonable breadth of chemical education.

A significant fraction of Ph.D. students in U.S. graduate schools come from other countries, with different educational systems. In general, they will have had even more intensive education in chemistry, with undergraduate degrees almost entirely focused on science in general and chemistry in particular. These students are usually even better prepared for our Ph.D. programs, especially if their English language skills are sufficient.

Usually, students take placement exams at the start of their programs so that their departments can identify any deficiencies in preparation. Some institutions ask students to audit courses or complete a set of readings and then test them to assure mastery of elementary material. We must not produce Ph.D. chemists unskilled in the basics of our field.

Courses

How we organize the students' course work affects the breadth of their understanding of the field. Given our students' general level of preparation, the graduate program should start with a full year of advanced course work. In most chemistry departments this would include advanced courses in the subspecialty of the student (for example, quantum mechanics or synthetic chemistry methodology), along with one or two courses outside the student's specialty, for breadth. The 1996 survey indicated that, surprisingly, some departments with otherwise excellent reputations have minimal course requirements and make no demand that students do some work outside their subdiscipline. Many chemists believe, however, that such a lack of requirements produces students with an undesirably narrow education. Requiring even one-third of the advanced course work to be outside the student's general area of research (for example, physical chemists taking courses outside that area) would lead to more breadth.

Advanced courses need not occupy an entire semester or quarter. As revealed in the 1996 survey, several departments are experimenting with modular courses, each module extending over half a term or less. The goal of educational breadth might be well served if early modules deal with the basics that are suitable for nonspecialists, and later modules focus on the knowledge needed to develop experts.

As an improvement in Ph.D. programs, I would urge that every department have some requirements about courses that broaden students' understanding of chemistry. In particular, departments should offer a course in quantum mechanics that is designed for students whose major interest is not physical chemistry and who are, therefore, less comfortable with heavy mathematics than are the physical and theoretical chemists. Similarly, departments should offer a course beyond elementary organic and inorganic chemistry, including related biochemistry, for students whose major interests are physical or theoretical chemistry. Students in organic chemistry and inorganic chemistry should also take a course in chemically sophisticated biochemistry, with some medicinal aspects. They can learn much from such courses, and, indeed, many of them will end up pursuing careers in medicinal chemistry or biochemistry.

Generally, after their first year, students are immersed in research. However, there is still room in their lives for advanced specialized material or courses outside the chemistry department, perhaps at a rate of one course at a time. Students should be able to audit these courses. By allowing students to audit courses outside their special area, the department would be encouraging breadth yet would keep the students' load manageable so that they can meet their research obligations.

I also recommend making minicourses or seminars available for students to attend, if not to enroll for credit, after their first year. Auditing courses can broaden education without taking too much time from research.

Seminars, Lectures, and Colloquia

The chemistry department's seminars, lectures, and colloquia with outside speakers afford another opportunity to broaden and deepen students' knowledge. Of course, the department must offer a regular series of these events. Students should attend as many of these department seminars, lectures, and colloquia as possible, not just those in their special area. The students should be made aware that attending these programs will help them understand the range of the field; as I discuss next, attending these events will also help them deal with exams and research proposals.

In many chemistry departments, the graduate students themselves have the right and responsibility to invite one or more of the outside lecturers. This stimulates them to follow the scientific literature to see who and what is exciting, and student interaction with the visiting speaker helps them mature as scientists. Even with outside lecturers invited by faculty, not students, it is important that Ph.D. students have a real opportunity to speak with the visitors and discuss their own work.

Departments should invite some of their speakers from industry so that their students learn about nonacademic research. Close connections between university departments and industry can also help students plan and launch industrial careers. In any case, the outside speakers should be told that they will be speaking to an audience with broad interests and asked to introduce the topic, not just plunge right in.

Most important, the chemistry faculty should attend these seminars and colloquia, including those outside their immediate field of interest. They should attend the presentations by outside speakers, departmental colleagues, current students, and postdocs. Their presence makes clear to students the value of these events and that narrowness of interest is not a virtue in the field of chemistry.

Exams

The exams we use to measure our students' progress offer an opportunity to help them acquire the breadth they need. The one-time qualifying, or candidacy, exam that is used to test the advanced knowledge of the students a year or so after they enter does not stimulate students to pursue further knowledge (for example, by attending lectures or taking minicourses) after they pass. However, the practice used by some departments—giving cumulative exams six or so times a year in the various fields of chemistry—does encourage further study. These exams could include topics and material described in recent lectures (students can be notified ahead of time that a cumulative exam will be based on one of the next three outside lectures). A cumulative exam system is one way to encourage students to continue their broad education after their formal course work is done.

Interdisciplinary Research

Many of the most exciting research opportunities in chemistry can be found on the borders with biology, physics, material science, medicine, and chemical engineering. Ph.D.'s who will work in industry (two-thirds of the 160,000 members of the American Chemical Society are, in fact, employed in chemical-related industry) will find it necessary to work in teams with other scientists. They will have a great advantage if they have already done so as part of their graduate work. Thus in the ideal Ph.D. program in chemistry, some of the research would be interdisciplinary and would involve collaboration with scientists outside the special field of the principal research sponsor. Students would learn to appreciate the expertise of scientists in other fields, while developing self-confidence as they see how their own expertise is valued by others.

I encourage all chemistry departments to emphasize the idea that Ph.D. research should be done, if possible, on an interdisciplinary project with more than one supervisor. This will add much to the education of the students, while preparing them for a future in which they are likely to need to work on an interdisciplinary basis.

Developing Depth of Knowledge

Students should leave our doctoral programs with mastery of a specific area of chemistry so that they can perform successfully as true professionals. Their extensive involvement in research, leading to a thesis, is the means to this mastery.

Doctoral Research

In chemistry, as in other fields, the core of the Ph.D. program is research. Generally, a student joins the research group of a faculty member and pursues a research problem that is suggested by the mentor. Also the mentor monitors progress and makes suggestions throughout the course of the program. The intensity of such monitoring varies, from "What did you do yesterday, and what are you going to do today?" to "Please let me know if you run into any problems or make any important observations." Some students, especially at the beginning, benefit from close supervision, while others learn more if they are left, to some extent, on their own.

It is quite unusual for students to propose and carry out their own research ideas, unrelated to the interests of the faculty mentor. Generally, it is a goal of the Ph.D. program to bring students to the point at which they could, indeed, propose a sensible research problem. However, it is expected that students will read the background and current progress in their field and make useful suggestions that can alter the course of the research project. As the project progresses, supervision usually becomes looser and looser.

A successful Ph.D. research project normally leads to scientific publication, and students are usually asked to write at least the first draft of a paper reporting the work. As a rule, the faculty mentor would be a coauthor, recognizing his role in initiating the project and in guiding it. Thus the final draft of a paper is the responsibility of the faculty mentor.

Research in chemistry generally receives financial support from funding agencies, with grants to the faculty mentor. The Ph.D. students are supported financially from the funds that support the project in which they are engaged. In addition, some students can win independent fellowships or become part of a general training grant awarded to the department.

Stimulating Creativity

One of the marks of an educated Ph.D. chemist is the ability to propose good research projects. The projects should have the following characteristics: (1) they should be novel, not just trivial extensions of previous work; (2) they should have a reasonable chance of being successful, either achieving a predetermined goal or likely to produce new information in an interesting area; (3) they should be important enough that the student would be proud to publish the work, if successful, in a leading journal; (4) ideally, they should have a reasonable chance of opening up a new field or area of research. In proposing such a project, students should be able to indicate not just the goals of the work but also how they will be approached. Students should be able to describe possible problems that can arise in the course of the work and how those problems will be solved.

As I noted earlier, one of the goals of a Ph.D. program in chemistry is to enable students to reach a maturity that will let them propose good research ideas and programs. Students who hope to obtain an academic position in chemistry will be expected to propose three to five research ideas that they will pursue if they are hired, while even students who will not be entering an independent research career will benefit from having learned how to propose research ideas. For example, those Ph.D.'s working in a pharmaceutical company are expected to be able to propose new goals and procedures if they are to progress in the company.

How might departments make better use of the students' research experience so that they have sufficiently deep mastery of their areas and are also encouraged to think creatively about research?

Research Proposals

Original research proposals, defended orally, play an important role in both deepening students' mastery and extending their broad knowledge. They also prepare students for the future in practical ways. Preparing a research proposal involves reading the chemical literature—a habit that is the hallmark of a professional. Students who hope to win postdoctoral fellowships will need to make such proposals part of their applications. Students who hope to obtain academic positions will need to have a group of such proposals ready as part of their job applications. Those seeking positions in industry will find that research proposals are used as an indicator of the candidate's creativity.

All chemistry departments should require students to propose one or more research ideas as part of their education. One proposal might be closely related to the thesis research; it could, for example, elaborate on the ways the research can be extended. Another research proposal could be on a topic different from the one the student is researching. The students should be required to submit a written version of each proposal, with adequate references, and to defend their proposal before a faculty committee. To preserve the intellectual property of the students, these proposals would not normally be presented in an open public meeting.

Many chemistry departments already require that students submit and defend one or more research proposals as part of their program. For practical reasons, it is expected that these proposals will not be very close to the research project that the student, or another student in the department, is pursuing. In a few departments, students actually fill out dummy NIH research proposals to be graded; in this exercise, they learn not only how to present an idea but also how to estimate and justify the cost of pursuing it.

Lectures, Journals, and Exams

When students know they are expected to propose research ideas of their own, they will listen to lectures by departmental and outside speakers and read papers in the major journals with this question in mind: Is there something here that can stimulate a research idea of my own? A system of regular cumulative exams, based on recent important advances reported in the research literature, will also keep students thinking about possible research projects related to recent advances in research.

The Thesis

Every Ph.D. student is required to submit a final thesis. Normally, this is an extensive written document that contains a history of the problem, a description of the results obtained, and an experimental section describing how the work was performed. It usually describes not just the positive findings that led to publishable work but also the other efforts that did not (or would not) make it into a scientific publication. It is thus a more valuable document than a mere collection of published papers, as those who follow the work need to see the downs as well as the ups in the field. Also, a thesis is normally the product of the candidate him- or herself, whereas papers have many authors. Thus I urge departments to consider the value of a written thesis over a collection of reprints or preprints.

The faculty should carefully mentor their students through the thesis process. For example, early in the process, each student should have a thesis committee. The committee members should hear and critique the student's presentations (for example, in public seminars), read and respond to research proposals, monitor research progress, and participate in any special examinations. The members should be part of the final dissertation committee, and they should be prepared to serve as important references in the student's job search.

Thesis directors have special responsibilities. They must follow the progress of the student's research and give sound advice. They should coach the students as they develop their speaking and writing skills. They should preview and critique the talk that students will give during job interviews. Finally, all faculty mentors should recognize the variety of rewarding and meaningful career paths that Ph.D. chemists can follow, and should support and encourage the student's career decisions, whether traditional or nontraditional.

Typically, an exam is part of the thesis defense. That is, the thesis committee will ask the student questions, not only about the details of the thesis but also about advanced-level material in the general field. For example, a student with a thesis on nuclear magnetic resonance spectroscopy will be expected to be able to explain electron paramagnetic resonance spectroscopy. A student with a thesis on various synthetic reactions will be expected to know how those reactions occur in molecular detail or perhaps to know how the same transformations are performed biochemically.

Requiring an examination with the thesis defense offers another opportunity for departments to encourage deep mastery of an area. Departments should institute this requirement as a way to confirm the quality of the Ph.D. students, as well as their theses, and to signal expectations about deep knowledge.

Further, in departments where students are required to propose new research ideas, the examination will uncover not only how good the proposal is but also how much the student knows about the field in which the proposal is centered.

Developing Professional Skills

In addition to broad and deep knowledge, Ph.D.'s in chemistry need professional skills: speaking and writing well, making information and ideas clear to different audiences, teaching effectively, understanding good scientific practices and ethics, and providing service to the discipline. As I suggested in describing ways to help Ph.D. students achieve breadth and depth of knowledge, graduate programs can make good use of existing structures and requirements to give their students solid skills for their professional lives.

Strong Communication Skills

Readers will note that among the "Grand Challenges" is a call for effective communication. Scientists need strong skills for communicating with their colleagues in science and a variety of other audiences: for example, non-science professionals, policymakers, students, and the public. The graduate years offer several opportunities for students to develop strong communication skills.

Oral and Written Skills

Scientists need to speak and write well. Graduate programs should make efforts to help their students develop these skills. For example, students should deliver several public seminars, both on their research and on topics from the research literature. The exercise of planning and delivering a public seminar or lecture—even an informal one—gives the student practice describing research and conveying both the relevance and the details of the work.

Students should regularly report orally on their research progress, usually in meetings of their research group with their sponsor. These reports, although informal, are important occasions to practice speaking skills. In addition, students should give at least one talk before all the students, postdocs, and faculty in their area of interest, for example, in front of all the physical chemists or organic chemists. In preparing this talk, the student should give great attention to organization of the material and the use of visuals (overheads, slides, or, increasingly, PowerPoint).

Although students should have many opportunities to speak about their own research achievements, there is much to be said as well for giving a talk on some topic from the chemical literature that is not very close to the research of the student. These "literature" talks teach the student how to do a good literature search and how to select a topic with good general interest. The result of the talk is that the student will have gained expertise in an area other than his or her thesis topic, and this expertise can be the basis for creative research proposals. For many students, a talk based on the work of a scientist from a different university leads to an interest in doing postdoctoral work with that scientist.

Speaking at a national or regional chemistry meeting can be a particularly maturing experience. The student should have a good deal of support from the department, with detailed and helpful feedback on draft proposals and presentations, as well as opportunities to rehearse in front of students and faculty, including practice fielding questions from the audience.

I urge that all departments give their Ph.D. students the opportunity to give at least one or two formal talks before the department or one of its subdivisions, with a written abstract and references and with visual aids. The quality should be comparable to what the student might use later in job interviews. The faculty should make every effort to attend these talks and give students helpful critiques.

The few departments where presentations are not required (often quite distinguished departments) explain their position by arguing that listening to such talks consumes faculty time and preparing them consumes student time that is better spent on research. As a result, both students and faculty miss an important opportunity for learning and teaching.

Preparing for the kind of oral presentations described here is one way to hone writing skills. Likewise, preparing research reports and research proposals offers students an opportunity to develop and sharpen writing skills. These tasks can also lay the groundwork for a well-written thesis and for scientific papers. But the students can only develop and improve these skills if they receive thoughtful and timely critiques from the faculty and peers.

Another important communication skill for any scientist is the ability to summarize research in ordinary language for the public. Those who are our students now will spend much of their careers trying to make their achievements comprehensible to intelligent nonscientists, such as government officials. Some will also have the responsibility of speaking about the field to the public. And some will teach. To develop this skill and emphasize its importance, a few departments now require that the thesis contain an additional section, sometimes at the end, summarizing, in laymen's terms, what has been accomplished in the student's research and how it is important. The section is written so that a nonexpert could get a reasonable grasp of the main point of the thesis. This requirement gives students practice in explaining their work to nonchemists, indeed to nonscientists. This requirement is unusual but should not be.

Language Skills

Some ability to read foreign languages is extremely valuable. At one time, all Ph.D. students in chemistry were expected to pass one or two examinations in foreign languages, usually German and French. This requirement has largely faded away, as the scientific literature is increasingly published in English, regardless of the country of origin. Now there is no language requirement in most departments, although foreign students are expected to be able to read and speak English. However, organic chemists still need to be able to read the old chemical literature, especially that written in German. For example, articles in *Chemische Berichte* and in Liebig's *Annalen* are still relevant. Procedures are described for the synthesis of compounds that can be needed in modern research. The compendium known as *Beilstein* is still a source for the properties and preparative procedures of organic compounds. Thus it is by no means true that chemists have no need for some proficiency in foreign languages, even if the formal requirements are disappearing.

I urge all chemistry students planning to work in organic chemistry to attain at least the skill in reading German that lets them understand the experimental sections of papers in the leading German chemical journals of the 1930s or so, when English translations were not routinely produced.

Teaching

As the saying goes, "If you want to learn a subject, teach it." For this reason, teaching in labs and classrooms is a valuable part of graduate education. Teaching helps solidify knowledge, and teaching elementary material helps call attention to significant intellectual gaps in the field that can be subjects for future research. Teaching experience is also helpful for those who will later take up academic careers, and for those in industry it will be helpful in learning to deal with technicians, for instance. It also affords practice in explaining scientific material to nonexperts.

Chemistry Ph.D. students usually do at least some undergraduate teaching as a component of their programs. In part, this is a source of financial support; teaching assistantships support many students in their first year or so of graduate study, although it is common for them to be supported from research grants or training grants or fellowships in the later years of their program. However, when other sources of support are not available, students often do part-time teaching through all the graduate years.

Graduate students report that the teaching they do is extremely valuable to their education. Thus even when students arrive in graduate school funded by personal fellowships, such as those given by the NSF, it is not unusual for them to do some teaching for its educational value to them, not for financial support.

For graduate students in chemistry, teaching normally involves acting as teaching assistants (T.A.'s) in laboratory courses. In addition, the T.A.'s will give some laboratory lectures and may also do some subsidiary teaching of material covered in the lecture courses. It is quite unusual for graduate students themselves to have full responsibility for chemistry lecture courses, however. At most, the graduate students might run some recitation sections or exam review sessions, while the regular faculty members deliver the lectures in the courses.

I urge that some teaching experience be part of the requirements for all Ph.D. students, even those with adequate financial support from fellowships or grants. The teaching should involve some lecturing, for instance in supplementary or review sections, not just policing the lab. Laboratory supervision is useful, but the students learn more by giving laboratory lectures or running recitation and review sections. Of course, departments should make sure that their students are adequately prepared for their teaching assignments and are supervised in carrying them out.

Good Scientific Practice and Ethics

As professionals, chemistry Ph.D.'s will be expected to follow good scientific practice and act with integrity. They also need to know how to decide whether research results are correct. Many chemistry departments now offer short lecture programs devoted to discussing scientific responsibility, validating research, and learning the techniques that can be used to avoid serious mistakes. I urge that all beginning Ph.D. students receive at least a few lectures on scientific responsibility and integrity. The lectures can also discuss intellectual property, patenting, and other nonscientific matters, such as proper record keeping.

Professional Service

Active membership in the professional society of the discipline is an important service to the field—a habit that students can develop long before graduation. The activities of the ACS are directly concerned with carrying forward the best practices in chemistry and improving on them. For example, the publications include many of the leading journals in the field, at prices well below those of commercial competitors. There are dozens of committees concerned with every aspect of chemistry, including best practices in education. Of course, most of the members of those committees are established professionals, but great efforts are made to involve young people, even below the level of graduate students. Most colleges and universities have an ACS student chapter for undergraduates, and there are ACS publications specifically directed to them. The ACS has a Younger Chemists Committee that meets regularly and reports to the Council of the ACS at every national ACS meeting.

Chemistry Programs Must Keep Pace with the Field

There is much interest among U.S. chemists in the topic of improving and changing doctoral education. For example, the ACS recently established an Office of Graduate Education to promote useful change and to monitor progress. The new head of the Chemistry Division of NSF is very concerned with education in chemistry, including graduate education, and he recently participated in a symposium devoted to graduate education at a national ACS meeting. I hope this chapter will contribute to this ongoing discussion.

Chemistry is undergoing great changes in its research areas, both fundamental and applied, and our graduate programs must keep up with these changes. As I hope the preceding discussion makes clear, graduate chemistry programs could considerably strengthen the way new Ph.D.'s are prepared to work in this changing field by making better use of existing structures and adopting effective practices already used in some departments.

REFERENCES

American Chemical Society Committee on Professional Training. "Survey of Ph.D. Programs in Chemistry." 1997. Available at www.chemistry.org/portal/Chemistry?PID=acsdisplay.html&DOC=education\cpt\cptsr01.html.

Breslow, R. "The Education of Ph.D.'s in Chemistry." *Chemical and Engineering News*, 1995, 73, 65–66.

Breslow, R. "Best Practices in Chemistry Ph.D. Education." *Chemical and Engineering News*, 1996, 74, 43.

Committee on Challenges for the Chemical Sciences in the 21st Century. *Beyond the Molecular Frontier: Challenges for Chemistry and Chemical Engineering*. Washington, D.C.: National Research Council, 2003.

IO

TRAINING FUTURE LEADERS

Angelica M. Stacy, University of California, Berkeley

OVER THE PAST DOZEN YEARS or so, I have encountered a number of students who have wanted to leave our doctoral program in chemistry. When I learned that they were considering leaving, I tried to find opportunities for them that might make remaining in the program a more attractive option.

Many readers are probably thinking, "Well, if these students want to leave, it is probably because they can't cut it. They just are not good enough." What I have found is quite the opposite: these students are among the best and brightest, most talented and promising, with the very kinds of skills and interests that the field needs. Yet they are saying, "This is not for me." They are creative people with wide-ranging interests, and they feel constrained in our doctoral program.

One graduate student, for example, did superbly on her second-year oral exam. She was clearly at the top of her class; she held a prestigious fellowship, and yet she wanted to drop out. When I asked her why she didn't want a Ph.D. in chemistry, she explained that although she really liked chemistry, her passion was for teaching. But, of course, she needs a Ph.D. to teach chemistry at the college or university level. Ultimately, she did remain in the program because we were able to tailor it to her interests. She wrote half of her thesis on research in physical chemistry and the other half on research in chemistry education. Both halves were substantive pieces of work, showing an amazing breadth of achievement. This student has gone on to teach at the college level and continues to do research in chemistry education in order to determine how best to assist students in learning the subject matter. She is an excellent contributor to the discipline.

I have known other students with interests in biology, materials, environmental sciences, engineering, education, diversity, management, and public policy. They all identify themselves primarily as chemists, and this is where their main training lies. Yet they seek projects and experiences outside the normal boundaries of the chemistry doctorate. One took an internship at a local company and worked on a project at the interface between process engineering and chemistry. Several others have worked with engineers on applied projects in which new materials are required to enhance device performance.

What sets these students apart is that they have shown the independence of thought and the tenacity required to seek the resources they need to pursue projects that are outside the norm. They all have a strong background in chemistry and have done "traditional" research, but they have chosen to contribute in nontraditional ways. Moreover, rather than apologize for taking a nontraditional path, they are passionate about what they do.

Chemistry: At the Interface of Many Disciplines

Now readers may be wondering, Why do we want to support students who pursue new projects that lie at the interface between chemistry and a variety of other disciplines? Certainly, it can be argued that some of the frontiers of research in chemistry lie at interfaces with other science and engineering disciplines. But why should we support students whose interests lie at other interfaces such as education, policy, and business? My belief is that a diversity of perspectives enriches and strengthens the discipline of chemistry; moreover, a diversity of talents provides a necessary foundation, as chemistry moves into a new era of multidisciplinary research.

There is much more to being a chemist these days than each of us knowing our own area of specialty. No longer is the chemist in a white coat, working alone in a lab by himself. The frontiers of research are multidisciplinary, and it is difficult, if not impossible, to do the work alone. Increasingly, "doing chemistry" involves a team of individuals with a variety of expertise working together on problems, issues, and research. For example, research in nanoscience involves preparation of nanoparticles and nanowires, characterization by electron microscopy, property measurement, and device design. It is difficult to imagine that a single individual could master all these areas alone. Multidisciplinary teams in the pharmaceutical industry include chemists, biologists, medical doctors, marketing experts, engineers, and lawyers working together to bring new drugs to market. Similarly, joint efforts among scientists and policymakers are essential in setting water- and air-quality standards, and in figuring out how to clean up nuclear-waste-disposal sites. Chemists could also collaborate with educational researchers, sociologists, and cognitive psychologists to raise the level of science literacy for all students.

Because cutting-edge research requires cooperation—a team of people pooling their extensive knowledge of many disciplines—it also calls for new ways of negotiating, working with others, and communicating. And because our work now involves educating other experts, educating the public, and advocating for certain directions to be taken by a team, chemists must be able to consider the implications of their work well beyond the lab and understand psychology, sociology, education, communication, policy, and politics. This is why I believe the students described earlier are a critical part of the mix of desirable chemistry doctoral students: they are creative, energetic, and interested in thinking across all sorts of boundaries.

In short, enormous changes in both chemistry and society demand that we think differently about how chemists work and teach, and even about who becomes a chemist. Chemistry needs diverse people with diverse skills and interests who will help shape the directions of chemistry education, research, and development.

Need for a New Kind of Leadership

I believe that the key to producing the kind of chemists we need lies in our understanding of leadership: what leadership means for a faculty member working with undergraduate students, graduate students, and postdoctoral fellows; what leadership means for managers and researchers working in teams in industry; and what leadership means for those working at establishing new initiatives in such areas as pharmaceuticals, semiconductor devices, science education, and environmental policy.

To be a Ph.D.-level chemist today is to be a new type of leader, colleague, researcher, and teacher. Evidence elsewhere in society and in the academy suggests that leadership has been shifting away from an authoritarian model to a more collaborative model. Rather than just saying, "This is my way; go do it," the person at the top instead understands how to accumulate the knowledge he or she needs, how to bring the right people together, how to listen, and how to make things happen.

This kind of leader is what we might call an "expert learner." Expert learners know how to learn the important things in the field and how to connect with other fields. They are interested in learning new things and are excited about spending an entire career taking on the challenge of being a beginner at something as they work alongside experts in other areas and learn from them. They also have tenacity. That does not mean they stick to one research idea and one way of operating. Instead, they have the courage and humility to learn new things, even if it means starting very low on the learning curve, again and again.

Using Ph.D. Programs for Developing Leaders

If our Ph.D. programs in chemistry are going to develop the expert learners who can become such leaders, we need to attract and keep in our doctoral programs people who can—and want to—think and work in these new ways. Our programs must develop students with independence, creativity, and facility in working across disciplines.

But how? If we want our new Ph.D.'s in chemistry to be expert learners who can take on leadership roles and think at high levels, then what kinds of experiences must they have in their doctoral programs? What kind of flexibility should the programs have? What kind of guidance can the faculty provide?

I see many possibilities for our graduate programs, and much that is already in place and on which we can build. So I am not suggesting that we dynamite our programs and start over. Nor am I suggesting that we relax standards. I am suggesting instead that we raise our expectations for both students and ourselves. I am suggesting that we examine what we do in our graduate programs, including whom we attract and keep as students, why we do what we do, and how we might make it better. I am also suggesting that we examine the reward structure to understand how it creates barriers to important, exciting, and necessary change for students and faculty alike.

It is not so much *what* we do in our programs as *how* we do it; small changes could have an enormous and positive effect. For example, being more intentional about how we prepare graduate student teaching assistants and also new faculty, as well as about how courses, exams, advising, and the thesis are structured, could make a significant difference in who enters, stays, and flourishes in our chemistry Ph.D. programs. By carefully designing experiences and projects, we can ensure that our students are prepared for the roles and work they will need to do to be successful over the course of their careers.

As an additional benefit, designing our graduate programs more deliberately would help to break an unfortunate, unnamed pattern in chemistry: we expect students to become competent at something by virtue of having received it, not by learning how to do it. For example, none of us are prepared to teach. (When I started as a faculty member, I was simply assigned to teach a certain course. I was allowed to decide what to teach, how to teach, and how to grade, despite the fact that I had little prior experience with teaching a course.) Nor are we prepared to be mentors for research students. (I became a faculty member because I did well in courses and in my research, but being a successful faculty member requires so much more.) Yet year after year, we expect our brand-new assistant professors—the people who were our students not that long ago—to take on graduate students, initiate their research, write papers and grant proposals, teach courses, and succeed. And they are desperately wondering how to do these things—how to manage it all. With some effort, we could change this.

To begin the task of improving our practices, we should ask some hard questions about what we are doing to meet the needs in our field and the needs of society:

- Who enters and completes our programs?
- What might we do differently in the programs?
- What stands in the way of the changes we need to make?

The next sections of this essay are intended to launch a discussion of possible responses to these three questions.

Who Enters and Completes Our Programs

We should first ask ourselves questions about our students: Who enrolls? Who leaves graduate school without a degree? Who earns the Ph.D.? When our students complete our programs, where are they getting jobs and of what sort? Who is going on to what are considered the best positions? (And why do we consider these to be the "best" positions?) With answers to these questions, we can then think about how to attract and retain the kind of students our field needs.

For most programs, the answer to "Who completes our program and goes on to the 'best' positions?" is white men who are about twenty-eight years old. Compared to many other fields, chemistry has far to go in achieving gender and racial diversity or in including students of various ages.

The available pools of potential new graduate students that are increasing are women, minorities, and older students. The young-white-male population is shrinking, relatively, among bachelor's degree recipients. For example, the population of those receiving a bachelor's degree in chemistry is nearly half women (46 percent), but not even a third (31 percent) of doctoral recipients are women (National Center for Education Statistics, 2002, Table 259). Indeed, we often complain about how many foreign students we need to admit to fill our programs, yet we are not looking at pools here in the United States that we could tap into if we were more creative. For example, biology, engineering, and other science majors could thrive in a chemistry or biochemistry Ph.D. program. In order to maintain excellence, we need to tap *all* the top domestic talent, not just a limited pool. Otherwise, we lose a lot of valuable ideas and perspectives, as well as a lot of brain power.

Achieving Excellence Through Diversity in Gender, Ethnicity, and Age

We could expand our pool of potential Ph.D. candidates by being more flexible in the structure of our programs and accommodating people at different stages of life. At present, we discourage women, minorities, and older students from our programs by expecting that students follow a certain track from undergraduate through graduate school. For example, at the University of California at Berkeley, like most other doctoral programs in chemistry, we have a very narrow age distribution, between twenty-two and twenty-eight. These students started as undergraduate chemistry majors and have just kept going right through. That is the typical pattern. Is it serving all students well? Even though they have been "on track," some of these young students struggle in the program and would have benefited from working a few years; they would have gained perspective and focus. And if it is difficult for students in their late twenties to enter chemistry doctoral programs after a break from undergraduate school, it is almost impossible for older, mid-career students to do so. Yet consider, for example, the valuable contributions to the field that people who have had careers in industry, policy, or business might make. One of the strengths of the social sciences is the diversity of age among the students and, consequently, the depth of experiences that these students bring into graduate school.

Expanding the pool of applicants might mean changing our vision of "potential." Now, we simply wait for students to apply to our programs. I suspect that many students with potential do not know about the opportunities that graduate school opens to them. We need to be more aggressive in recruiting students, particularly from undergraduate institutions that have not traditionally sent students to top university programs.

Some doctoral programs are happy to accept students who don't fit traditional admissions criteria, but I believe that *all* programs should consider how to include these students. Of course, we must figure out how to evaluate and bridge the gaps in each prospective student's knowledge and experience. However, we might adapt models from the health fields, such as the postbaccalaureate programs in which the students bring their skills and knowledge up to date before entering medical or veterinary school. We should be able to design something comparable in chemistry. Such strategies would bring us more students and a new, important quality to our programs: quality that is consistent with the direction of the field and the needs of society.

Not only could we admit a more diverse group of students but if we would encourage them to structure their programs differently, they might be more successful or move through more smoothly. We also could accommodate younger women who would like to take time to have children while in graduate school. At the top institutions, like the University of California at Berkeley, there are very few graduate students with children. (We should think about that—what loss is there to a field that demands a choice between career and family?)[1]

One thing we do very well in chemistry is to graduate students in a reasonable time. That should make us an attractive field to those eager to get into careers. Compared to other sciences and the social sciences and humanities, we are efficient factories. The students spend, on average, six years in our programs.[2] Then, if they are headed to academic positions, they spend about two years as a postdoctoral fellow and go on to their positions. Students going into industry can be in their positions right out of graduate school. Because the time-to-degree is reasonable, we are in a position to better accommodate students who need to take time off before or during the program and to attract mid-career students.

Empowering Students in Chemistry Doctoral Programs

As my opening anecdotes suggest, we also lose enrolled students. Unfortunately, in chemistry we turn off some talented students, especially creative students with the kind of wide-ranging interests that the field needs. Too often, the students in our programs are left with the impression that success is equivalent to turning yourself into a copy of your adviser. These perceptions often are not far from the truth. In chemistry, the thinking has been that the faculty adviser has nearly complete control, designs all tasks and assignments, and expects that his or her graduate student advisees should do little else but help produce as many papers as possible. At many institutions, the professor and his or her students are working in isolation from the rest of the university. Yet working in isolation is not how many talented individuals—students and faculty members alike—want to be spending their time. Many want to be part of a group that is working collaboratively on important ideas, issues, and tasks.

A few years ago, I was invited by a group of chemistry graduate students to visit the University of Michigan.[3] This group of very talented students (students we would gladly have accepted to UC Berkeley) are involved in research in chemistry education, as well as in more traditional research in chemistry. They are doing extremely well in chemistry research; they are also thinking at very high levels about chemistry education. They are knowledgeable in both areas and bring a degree of energy and enthusiasm to their work that many of us do not see in the students in our programs.

The difference is not in the students themselves or in the training they received as undergraduates. The difference is in the program—the structure and the attitudes that inform it. These graduate students are empowered by the opportunity to construct their own projects in an effort to improve instruction and laboratory work for undergraduate students. They are afforded the opportunity to work with faculty as colleagues, and they benefit enormously from working with each other. We, in our programs, can ensure that all of our students experience the same sort of deep engagement that these students do by providing them opportunities that build on their interests. In this way, we can prepare them to think independently and work collaboratively.

Finally, we would encourage more potential and enrolled students to enter and complete our programs if we changed our assumptions about their career interests and options. Our students go on to teach at a wide range of institutions, accept positions in diverse industries, and do all sorts of work that builds on their chemistry Ph.D. Few remain working as bench chemists, which is how they spend the vast majority of their time as Ph.D. students. If we are to expand the talent pool to include more women, minorities, and older students, if we are to retain students who are looking for a broader range of options, and if we are to support our current students in meeting the demands of working on multidisciplinary research projects, we need to consider how to augment our programs and make them less faculty-centered and more student-centered. The challenge we face is how to orient our programs to build on strengths that individual students bring rather than constraining them to meet *our* needs.

What We Could Do Differently in Our Programs

As I noted earlier, we move students through our programs in a timely way. How well we use that time, however, is a different issue. If we believe, as I said at the outset, that our students should leave us ready to think and communicate at very high levels—to be expert learners—we must focus on this goal in designing our programs.

So the next step is to ask hard questions about our practices. What are our goals for our students? Do we teach our courses toward these goals? Do we organize the elements of our programs to yield the results we want? Do we devote enough thinking to questions about how people learn? Can we adapt effective approaches to graduate education from other fields?

Encourage Good Questions and Creativity

At present, our students' experience is rather narrow. The student comes in and chooses a research adviser. The adviser assigns a problem to the student (because research is expensive, and the advisers have research grants and agendas). The student works on that problem; in fact, the student often is expected to work on that problem to the exclusion of everything else, to get as much done as possible. By the time the student finishes the thesis, he or she is very narrowly focused, highly trained in that area. In this environment, many students do not learn how to ask good questions because the adviser has posed most of the questions. Many students do not learn to make connections to other areas, to synthesize and integrate ideas and information. They have had little or no opportunity to learn about communicating, negotiating, and working with people in other areas.

Consider, for a moment, our approach in contrast to that of other disciplines. Students in the humanities and social sciences choose the topics of their dissertations. Consequently, they spend a lot of time trying to figure out what constitutes a good question. (Indeed, many say that students in these fields spend too much time stalled at this stage of their training.) However, there is something to be learned here. For as frustrating and time-consuming as this process might be, it teaches the students to think at much higher levels. They must, for example, compare and contrast to figure out what is a good question to ask, and they learn a lot about how to design research projects.

In the sciences, we could give our students more independence. Indeed, the irony is that the scientific method is predicated on asking good questions, conducting an investigation, and building evidence. However, observe an undergraduate general chemistry class: three hundred students sit quietly and take notes. Observe a graduate course in chemistry: the professor is at the board, and the ten students sit quietly and take notes. Is our assumption correct that students cannot really *do* anything until they have memorized a great deal of information; they cannot think until they have been filled with facts? Are we sure that sitting and listening for three hours a week, over fifteen weeks, for six or more years is the most likely route to becoming a good researcher? Is there a critical mass of information that, when mastered, spontaneously erupts into hard-hitting questions?

As undergraduates, our students learned that there is a "right" answer. (At this stage, in the undergraduate courses, we probably lose many students who enjoy thinking and wrestling with open-ended problems.) Through their graduate courses, right up to the oral exam, they continue be told that there are right answers. But then, suddenly, for the oral exam, the students are supposed to think, integrate, and apply ideas, even though to this point they have mainly sat in class, taking notes. As faculty, we generally do a good job on these oral exams: we ask good questions. But we are dismayed when our students cannot answer them. We don't stop to consider that they have never encountered anything quite like this before. And then, when the students get into research, suddenly they are expected to ask good questions—questions that do not have "right" answers. So we need to give our students opportunities, from the outset, to pose questions and struggle with them, to think at higher levels about what a good question might be.

Many students are not given the chance to work on something they are passionate about. Yet as my opening anecdotes suggest, when we allow chemistry graduate students to do what students in the humanities and social sciences do—find their own topics, develop their own ideas—they stay in the program and they flourish. Each student chooses a problem, struggles with it, and becomes quite passionate about it. The students figure out what they need to know from a variety of places so that they can become as expert as possible in that timeframe. Perhaps our chemistry students cannot do this for the entire thesis. But surely we can find ways of providing such opportunities for those who want to develop their own ideas for at least part of their thesis work. It seems odd—and sad—that in our pursuit of the highest levels of thinking, we stifle the creativity of our students.

Develop Breadth, Depth, and Skills

A few changes in our programs could have an enormous impact. Among these, the one change that could have the most far-reaching effect is our expectation about the thesis. The thesis is an important experience for students. It requires very hard work, and the students learn a great deal. Producing a thesis requires that students organize a large number of their ideas into one document and communicate successfully in writing. Those are all good things. But, as I explain next, we could improve the process in two ways: (1) we could improve the experiences leading to the thesis, and (2) we could add a breadth component to the thesis. These changes would, I believe, result in more students completing our programs and more students being prepared for the work ahead after they complete the Ph.D.—the work they will be expected to do as expert learners.

We could prepare students differently for the work they will do as Ph.D. chemists by identifying and developing the kinds of experiences that would efficiently and effectively lead students to become good researchers. The way we go about things currently, we leave much to chance. For example, advisers who were never trained in writing theses are advising students how to write their theses. If there were a set of experiences that a faculty member could provide for his or her first-, second-, and third-year graduate students—nicely scaffolded, really well-thought-out activities combined with careful mentoring—we would see an enormous improvement in the quality of our students' experiences and in the number of students who complete our programs. Imagine if each new faculty member would receive a guide on mentoring students at various stages of research, helping plan what experiences they should be given and in what sequence.

If we could begin to be more strategic about developing students as researchers, we would probably rethink the way we teach our courses. We might start by asking more of the integrative questions—the sort we ask in oral exams—in the graduate (and undergraduate) courses. We might make it a point to send students to the board to think through problems on their feet and to question the assumptions behind the problems. We might also organize the oral exams differently. Rather than ask students to take one oral exam, we might develop a series of oral exams.

We would also move away from the lecture-based course and make more use of the kind of seminar course used in the social sciences at the graduate level. In that model, the students are given information that is important in carrying out research, and then they are given opportunities to practice using that information. I've seen wonderful things happen when faculty members use this approach in education courses. For example, for a course in quantitative methods in education, the students must first design their own assessment, administer this assessment, and do a statistical analysis of the data they collect. That is the point of the course: they are actually doing the work, not merely hearing about it. They present their ideas and get feedback. By trying to figure out how to set up a research project, they really understand the material being taught in the course.

I can imagine something similar for graduate-level chemistry. Of course, we are a bit limited because laboratory courses are more time-consuming and more difficult to run. (It is notable that we rarely offer graduate laboratory courses. The one exception is perhaps X-ray crystallography.) However, students could be generating and discussing proposals for synthesis of new compounds and then perhaps testing out their ideas. Or they could be interpreting spectra or solving theoretical problems related to areas that interest them. Some courses of this type already exist, but there is a clear need for the development, documentation, and dissemination of courses that engage students in pilot research projects that apply the core materials being taught in the course.

I realize that what I am suggesting is difficult. For each day that I would walk into such a classroom, I would need many days of thinking. And few of us have seen or participated in what I am suggesting. And it would be easy to do this badly: the discussions can become loose or disjointed or take a lot of time; the students and faculty member might feel that they are not getting anywhere or are not covering content thoroughly. What I am suggesting is not a free-form discussion but something quite guided. Perhaps we might think of it as something more like coaching than the teaching we are used to doing. Rather than doing most of the talking, the faculty member constructs engaging tasks for groups of students to work on. The faculty member guides and mentors them as they think and work out solutions. (These tasks could be developed collaboratively and disseminated so others could use them. Then there would be minimal burden on creating such tasks on any individual faculty member.) The point is to challenge the students to go beyond copying notes from the board and to use ideas in ways that help them begin to understand how to do research.

To be perfectly honest, there is a certain safety in the lecture method we know so well. When we lecture, we are in control of the material and the situation. It is hard to imagine teaching differently. However, as expert learners ourselves, faculty should enjoy learning and experimenting with new ideas about teaching. We certainly do so in our fields of chemistry: when we need to master a particular area of the research literature, we simply learn it. It is just the same with learning different approaches to teaching.

If we invest the necessary work in creating the kind of learning experiences that I have described, we can do much more mentoring—and more effective mentoring—about how to frame good questions (a key to excellent research), how to communicate in a variety of settings, how to work with others, how to teach, and how to learn broadly across the field. Then, to build on this strong foundation, we could add a breadth component to the thesis.

Add a Breadth Component to the Thesis

One section of the thesis could be focused on something other than the student's portion of the adviser's research. For example, part of the thesis could contain the hard data and results that we currently expect, based on the student's assignment within the adviser's research program. Another section could then be focused on a research topic reflecting the student's interest within or related to chemistry.

As my opening examples indicate, we have used this approach with a few students at UC Berkeley. The results are remarkable. The students do a large amount of work on both aspects of the thesis. They grow as individuals and attain high levels of achievement. They have managed to track down resources, to find mentors across campus and indeed around the world, and have produced exceptional research that they designed and are thus extremely passionate about.

This expectation could change the way the student approaches the program and participates in courses, exams, lectures, and research proposals. For example, requiring a breadth component to the thesis would create incentives for (and give permission to) students to take courses relating to their interests. At present, of course, it is acceptable for students in materials chemistry to take a course in engineering or physics; likewise, students in biochemistry are free to take courses in biology. What I am suggesting are options to go into more far-reaching areas: public policy, social sciences, education, and business. Many of our students who earn the Ph.D. end up doing all kinds of things in careers that involve the areas I just mentioned. We need to develop a mechanism by which we can encourage students to pursue the broader interests they have without getting side-tracked from the research work that gives them necessary depth. As I see it, an efficient solution is a thesis project that requires them to cross areas, connect them, and ask meaningful research questions in both.

So far, I have recommended that we find ways to make our programs more attractive to a broader group of potential students. I have also recommended that we improve the way we approach teaching and learning so that we accomplish two important things: (1) attract and retain the kind of creative students we need in the field and (2) do a much better job of preparing people who can have deep and broad knowledge and who can ask good questions. Ultimately, I am advocating for more support of the graduate students: more support for them to develop who they want to be. We all could put more effort into finding ways to attract and develop very talented students who have clear ideas about who they are and what the field can be, who are already on the path to being professionals, expert learners—leaders in the field.

What Stands in the Way of These Important Changes

As I have noted, there are several ways in which we can expand the experiences we offer graduate students. However, implementing these suggestions may require some important changes in the culture of academe, both in the funding structure and the advising system it leads to.

The Advising Relationship

If we are going to attract and retain the talented students we need, we need to address the very awkward subject of the funding and the adviser system and the seemingly unbreakable link between the two. The subject is awkward because it is about people, relationships, and money. And so it is really about power.

Let's start with the adviser. Being a good Ph.D. adviser is more than having legions of students help do the things that will make you famous, or even just get a lot of research done. A good Ph.D. adviser is deeply invested in mentoring each student as an individual who, in turn, will someday be a great researcher and adviser, and so on.

For students, the choice of adviser—and thus the research that choice will lead to—is critical. Yet it is also problematic. Because of the financial structure of research in the field, students have to take what they can get, not necessarily what they want or might be good at. Some faculty members have a lot of funding and can take on a lot of graduate students. The money might be specifically targeted for some aspect of the larger research project, so that is what the students must work on. All too often, this is a less-than-optimal situation for the graduate students. An excellent researcher is not necessarily an excellent mentor. Or the faculty member might be overloaded with students and just unable to give each student an appropriate amount of attention, or even enough attention to know what is appropriate for that particular student. In the meantime, other faculty members might be doing work that interests students, or they might be excellent mentors but do not command the resources to support students.

Many worrisome strings are attached to the adviser-student relationship. Yes, usually the relationships work out; fortunately, faculty members are generally good, well-meaning people. But many of the options that students might have—taking courses in other areas, developing research questions—really depend on the attitude or interest of the adviser. Students can tell you, "If you have the right adviser, you can put effort into teaching or taking courses for breadth; if you don't, you can't." Indeed, whether we realize it or not, we really do have a great deal of control over the lives of our graduate students. And the students have few alternatives. If the match is wrong, the worst that happens is indeed bad: the student might never launch his or her career and might even leave the field altogether.

But even if the relationship is good, the student may not have adequate room to grow as an individual, may be stuck on a project, and may have few or no opportunities to develop his or her own questions. There is a great difference between working *for* and working *with* someone. We only need to talk to graduate students to find out that their enthusiasm for research and the work they have done diminishes with time because they do not feel as though they are collaborating on the creative part of the work. The very thing that had attracted them to the field has been dampened.

There is a solution, and it lies in the way funding is allocated. We could give the stipends directly to the graduate students and let them decide with whom to work. Doing so would balance the power. Imagine if the graduate students could choose an adviser to work with and did not have to work for someone because he or she has the funding. It would push those who truly care about the next generation of chemists to do terrific research and become great advisers. But would we ever be so bold as to do this?

Would we also be so bold as to allow students more than one adviser? If we expect a breadth component in the thesis, we might need a team of advisers for the project. But if, from the start, a student could work with two people whose research interests and skill in mentoring were complementary, our students would benefit greatly.

There are a number of ways in which we might reduce the tremendous power imbalances in the adviser-student relationship. Some universities have had positive experiences offering students a year of rotating research positions in which students spend about three months at a time in three or four different labs before matching with a research adviser. This allows time for both students and faculty to assess (before making a commitment to working together) the working style, lab climate and culture, and other intangible factors that contribute to a positive mentoring relationship.

Students have also done joint theses, with two advisers assisting with the same research project or two separate projects, one with each of the two advisers. These are among the possibilities that change the relationships between faculty and students and also create an environment in which students are more likely to flourish. But these solutions clearly have financial implications that, with some thought, we can work out to the benefit of our students.

The Reward Structure

The faculty reward structure, which is based largely on research productivity, influences the policies, practices, and even the culture of our chemistry departments. These, in turn, influence the policies, practices, and culture of our graduate and undergraduate programs. To meet the demands of our field, we need to make changes in the reward system that influences the culture and practices of our graduate programs.

First, we should consider whether or not the practices and the reward systems in our universities reflect the enormous changes in research and whether we are keeping pace with the changes. For example, only in recent years have we started to move past the idea of the single investigator. Until relatively recently, if an assistant professor produced a paper with a senior coauthor, the paper was not counted for promotion and tenure to the same extent as papers in which the assistant professor was the sole senior author. Now such work is accepted if the assistant professor's contributions to the work are clearly identifiable. When the NSF first began pushing the idea of collaboration, people complained; now they are starting to get used to submitting grant requests collaboratively. We need to consider whether the reward structure is keeping pace with these changes.

Second, we should consider the degree to which the reward structure influences the climate of our profession. Our students are very aware of that climate. For example, when we ask our entering Ph.D. students what they hope to do when they complete a program at a place like the University of California at Berkeley, ranked one of the top chemistry departments in the world, almost all will tell you that they want to teach at a liberal arts college or research university. Yet when they finish the thesis (and, all too often, before), they walk away from a life in the academy, saying "No way. This is not for me." When, for example, women are coming through our programs in such large numbers, and so often they are at the top of the class but not seeking positions at colleges and universities, it is time for us to stop saying, "Well, if they don't like it, it's their problem." It is not their problem. It is our problem. Clearly, we are not behaving in ways that make it attractive to students we want and need. We need to examine the climate that surrounds our students and colleagues.[4]

Think about what our graduate students see of life as a research chemist: we are working nights and weekends, we are constantly scrambling for grants, we seem perpetually stressed. Consider also what they see about who succeeds. Each year *Chemistry and Engineering News* publishes photographs of winners of ACS awards. Those who receive the fifty or so awards given each year are typically white men. There are years when woman and minorities only receive awards that are specific for women and minorities. There are even some awards that have never gone to a woman and many more that have never gone to a minority.

Consider what our doctoral students see about careers and options. In the last decade, the top fifty chemistry departments (and these hire two to three people each year) have hired no African Americans (Nelson, 2004). Women are not faring much better. Although women are now one-third of the Ph.D. population in chemistry, they are going in large numbers into industry and doing quite well; they are also going into faculty positions at four-year colleges. But at the top research institutions, women make up only about 10 percent of the faculty.

The students can also see that in hiring and promotion, research universities do not take into account how personal and career paths are in conflict with one another. The current model is that a student finishes graduate school at twenty-six, takes a faculty position at twenty-eight, and becomes a star by thirty. We seem to believe that if you can't follow this model, you don't belong in chemistry. Even though, on average, men are a lot more confident when they are younger and their careers take off much earlier, this expectation puts extraordinary pressure on men, and it forces women to make choices between family and career. However, women's careers soar after they have raised their children, and many men would like to participate in family life.

One reason we have not looked hard at our practices or the climate of our departments and the field is that, according to the ways we measure success right now, we have been successful. There is no incentive to change. But what does it mean to be ranked number one? What is the measure of success? The members of the National Academy, editors of journals, reviewers of grants, award committees, and tenure and promotion committees all have a relatively large say in defining success. There are relatively few women and minorities who serve in these groups. This is unfortunate because these groups do not benefit from a greater range of ideas that could be had if they were more diverse.

Consider the university that says, "Our football team is successful, so why should we change our sports program?" What they fail to measure is participation. In the decision to put all the money into the football team, many people—men and women—are excluded from playing sports, and the institution limits itself from achieving success of a different sort by having excellent fencers, lacrosse players, and swimmers on campus.

In our academic programs in chemistry, we have standards about what it means to be successful: a certain number of publications (a self-fulfilling process to some degree: you know the editors of journals, so they carefully choose who reviews your manuscripts) and awards (it took me years to figure out that people write their own letters and nominations and ask others to submit them). However, although our criteria for success may yield a top ranking for the department, our criteria for success may not be the best criteria in the long run. It may not help us produce the colleagues and leaders our field and society need.

In a field that is devoted to results, we are oddly uninterested in the result of our efforts with graduate students. Can we find new ways to measure success that are based on results? For example, what if faculty members were evaluated and rewarded, in part, on the basis of completion rates (how many of the students in your group complete the program?). What if, similarly, departments were ranked, based on where their graduate students were placed and how well they were doing in their careers? What if we regularly gathered and used information and feedback from our graduate students about what works and what doesn't in our programs? What if we were to solicit their ideas about courses, projects, and even the structure and pace of graduate education?

If we really want to enhance our doctoral programs in chemistry by making them more student-centered, then we need to consider how to structure faculty careers so that faculty are rewarded for the efforts they put forth in mentoring and supporting graduate students. This involves thinking carefully about how research funding is allocated and how faculty members are rewarded.

Will We Seize the Opportunity?

Chemistry is the central science—a discipline that is at the nexus of many areas of social science, engineering, business, and professions. But I believe we are at a crossroads, where different paths may lead to different consequences for chemistry as a discipline. We need to choose, strategically, a path that will allow chemists and chemistry to flourish, and we need to find new kinds of leaders to shape this path and guide us along it. Our

Ph.D. programs can produce the leaders that chemistry needs by guiding students to become expert learners.

If we are to reach this goal for our Ph.D. programs—producing the leaders that chemistry needs—then we need to begin to wrestle with questions about who enters and completes our programs, what we could do differently, and what stands in the way of important changes. These questions will cause us to consider excellence through diversity in gender, ethnicity, and age. They will move us to empower students by teaching them how to ask good questions and by offering them a breadth component in addition to the depth we currently offer. And they will show us how to remove barriers imposed by the current funding and reward structures.

As I wrote this essay, my intent was to pose as many questions as possible and offer suggestions that might launch a rich, ongoing discussion about where we should head as a discipline and how we might rethink the chemistry doctorate. I sincerely hope that chemists will seize the opportunity to be leaders in developing doctoral programs aligned with the changing needs of society.

NOTES

1. These choices affect men as well, but women continue to be disproportionately affected. See "Do Babies Matter? The Effect of Family Formation on the Lifelong Careers of Academic Men and Women" (Mason and Goulden, 2002).

2. This is the median registered time in graduate school (Hoffer, Dugoni, and others, 2004).

3. The Chemical Sciences at the Interface of Education (CSIE) program is described at www.umich.edu/~csie.

4. Recent data (Golde and Dore, 2001) show that doctoral students in chemistry are less interested in faculty careers than are their counterparts in other disciplines.

REFERENCES

Golde, C. M., and Dore, T. M. *At Cross Purposes: What the Experiences of Doctoral Students Reveal About Doctoral Education.* Philadelphia: The Pew Charitable Trusts, 2001. Available at www.phd-survey.org.

Hoffer, T. B., Dugoni, B. L., and others. *Doctorate Recipients from United States Universities: Summary Report 2003.* Chicago: National Opinion Research Center, 2004.

Mason, M. A., and Goulden, M. "Do Babies Matter? The Effect of Family Formation on the Lifelong Careers of Academic Men and Women." *Academe*,
2002, Nov.-Dec., 21–27.

National Center for Education Statistics. *Digest of Education Statistics*, 2002.
Available at nces.ed.gov/pubs2002/digest2001/tables/dt259.asp.

Nelson, D. J. "Nelson Diversity Surveys." Norman, Okla.: Diversity in Science
Association, 2004. Available at cheminfo.chem.ou.edu/~djn/diversity/
top50.html.

University of Michigan. "Chemical Sciences at the Interface of Education."
Available at www.umich.edu/~csie.

DOCTORAL EDUCATION
IN NEUROSCIENCE

NEUROSCIENCE—THE STUDY OF BRAIN AND BRAIN FUNCTION—is a relatively new field, although research on the brain and nervous system has been conducted for many years and in many disciplines. As Eric Kandel, Nobel laureate and past president of the Society for Neuroscience, explains, "As currently structured, neuroscience has woven into one cloth these previously independent scientific strands" (Kandel, 1982, p. 299). Today it has developed a distinct disciplinary identity, and neuroscience is without a doubt a scientifically burgeoning and vital field. The Society for Neuroscience (SfN) was founded in 1969 and now has a membership of over 36,000. Moreover, a very high proportion of the members—nearly 30,000 scientists—attend the annual conference.

Although there are now many neuroscience departments, neuroscience researchers continue to come from a wide range of disciplinary backgrounds and make their home in departments that range from pharmacology to psychology. Entering students in neuroscience graduate programs most often come from undergraduate programs in biology, psychology, or chemistry, and a small percentage of students majored in interdisciplinary undergraduate programs in neuroscience, behavioral neuroscience, or psychobiology. This broad range of background, training, and departmental home—on the part of both students and faculty—is a challenge to those who run doctoral programs.

Currently, over 250 programs in the United States offer study at the undergraduate or graduate level in neuroscience. Of these, over 130 are graduate training programs; in a situation unique to neuroscience, a number of institutions are home to more than one graduate training program.

Neuroscience programs are varyingly situated in colleges of arts and sciences and medical schools. The recent trend has been to link neuroscientists in universitywide programs that span both schools of medicine and schools of arts and sciences, and now 40 percent of programs are organized this way—a significant increase from a decade before. This organizational structure means that faculty within the same program are often located in a host of departments. This structure can make program coordination difficult, and the physical distance between labs, offices, and classrooms can hinder interactions among program members. The advantage, of course, is that the integration across campus provides opportunity for a more collegial community.

Graduate programs range in size from fewer than 10 students to more than 80 students; the average program has 33 students. In 2003, 472 neuroscience doctorates were awarded nationwide—double the number from a decade before. In 2003, nearly 43 percent of doctorates were awarded to women. As is the case at the doctoral level in other areas of science, African American, Latino, and Native American students are underrepresented. Neuroscience has seen a steady increase in the number of students who are not U.S. citizens, currently about 20 percent.

Typically, neuroscience doctoral students spend the first year of the program taking courses. Because students come to neuroscience from a wide range of backgrounds, many programs offer one or more core courses that are intended to convey the span of neuroscience—from the molecular to the system level to the behavioral. During the first year, most students also engage in research rotations, spending time (eight to ten weeks per rotation is common) in several labs doing a small project and learning about the science being done in that lab. By the end of the first year of doctoral study, most students have affiliated with a primary lab, and the center of learning moves from the classroom to the lab. In order to maintain a core identity as neuroscientists (rather than the identity of the department in which their lab is located), students participate in journal clubs and other activities deliberately designed to maintain a sense of community. The average time-to-degree in neuroscience is 5.6 years.

Professionally, neuroscientists hold positions in academia, industry, and government. The wide range of disciplinary influences means that there is no single path that neuroscience graduates take; many entering students aspire to academic positions but are increasingly unlikely to attain those jobs. Recent reports on the life and biomedical sciences raise questions about the growth in the number of students in graduate programs and the decreasing number of academic positions available to them—an issue characterized as a problem of supply and demand or a "crisis of expectations." The biological sciences may be heading toward the kind of "job crisis" already seen in the humanities. Marincola and Solomon describe this as a "Malthusian crisis" in the biomedical sciences: "a pyramidal growth in trainees, which is generating demand for jobs and funding that outpaces even the impressive growth in federal funding of biomedical research of recent decades" (1998, p. 3004).

Only a small percentage of neuroscience students find permanent positions upon graduation; the vast majority—70 percent—are likely to take a postdoctoral position. This "second stage" of training is not surprising. As with many life-science fields, preparation and training in neuroscience is generally not considered complete until students have held a postdoctoral position. Increasingly, Ph.D.'s in neuroscience hold several postdoctoral positions; the postdoctoral period now stretches to four or five years. During the 1990s questions about the status of postdocs emerged. Are they independent researchers or employees in someone's lab? To what extent does postdoctoral training have an educational function, and is it incorporated into the overall academic enterprise?

Doctoral education in neuroscience is still relatively new. Despite a long tradition of research, it is only in the last generation that there have been enough formal programs and departments to begin to see common strategies and challenges in graduate-level training. Neuroscience programs face both the opportunity and the challenge of drawing from the wide variety of participants across schools and departments to address gender and racial representation, academic and nonacademic paths for students, and the balance of educational and professional commitments of postdoctoral fellows. As a field, neuroscience appears prepared to look closely at the experiences of students and their contributions to the field. This thriving and dynamic discipline can take advantage of its lack of historically embedded institutional structures to adapt quickly to changing conditions.

Many of these challenges are described in greater detail in the two chapters that follow. Zach Hall, in his essay "Maintaining Vitality Through Change: Graduate Education in Neuroscience," provides a cogent overview of current strategies and configurations of neuroscience graduate programs. Their inclusiveness and flexibility are advantages, he suggests, but present risks. Despite its multidisciplinary character, new opportunities and challenges will face neuroscience in the future, particularly in its relationship with the behavioral sciences and engineering.

Steven Hyman, in "The Challenges of Multidisciplinarity: Neuroscience and the Doctorate," argues that neuroscience is different from the other fields of the CID, precisely because it is new and deliberately multidisciplinary. His essay elaborates on the organizational and intellectual challenges that face neuroscience, arguing for flexibility so that programs do not succumb to bureaucracy and stasis and lose the vitality of inquiry. Those in other multidisciplinary fields—anyone seeking to extend into multidisciplinary collaboration—will find his observations germane.

_____ o _____

BIBLIOGRAPHY

Information and specific data were derived from the following sources:

Association of American Universities Committee on Postdoctoral Education. *Report and Recommendations.* Washington, D.C.: Association of American Universities, 1998.

Association of Neuroscience Departments and Programs. Available at www.andp.org.

Bloom, F. E. "Training Neuroscientists for the 21st Century." *Trends in Neuroscience,* 1992, *15*(10), 383–386.

Davis, G. "Doctors Without Orders." *American Scientist,* May-June 2005, *93*(3) Supplement. Available at www.postdoc.sigmaxi.org/results.

Hoffer, T. B., Selfa, L., and others. *Doctorate Recipients from United States Universities: Summary Report 2003.* Chicago: National Opinion Research Center, 2004.

Kandel, E. "The Origins of Modern Neuroscience." *Annual Review of Neuroscience,* 1982, *5*, 299–303.

Marincola, E., and Solomon, F. "The Career Structure in Biomedical Research: Implications for Training and Trainees." *The American Society for Cell Biology Survey on the State of the Profession.* In *Molecular Biology of the Cell,* 1998, *9*, 3003–3006.

National Research Council. *Trends in the Early Careers of Life Scientists.* Washington, D.C.: National Academy Press, 998.

Society for Neuroscience. Available at http://web.sfn.org.

Stricker, E. M. *The 2000/2001 ANDP Survey of Neuroscience Graduate, Postdoctoral, and Undergraduate Programs.* Association of Neuroscience Departments and Programs, 2002. Available at www.andp.org/surveys/reports/2002/2002survey.pdf.

Stricker, E. M. *The 2003 ANDP Survey of Neuroscience Graduate, Postdoctoral, and Undergraduate Programs.* Association of Neuroscience Departments and Programs, 2003. Available at www.andp.org/surveys/reports/2003/Survey03Report.pdf.

11

MAINTAINING VITALITY THROUGH CHANGE

GRADUATE EDUCATION IN NEUROSCIENCE

Zach W. Hall, California Institute for Regenerative Medicine

NEUROSCIENCE IS A YOUNG FIELD—one that has arisen during the professional lifetimes of many of its practitioners. Scientists, of course, have been pursuing research on the brain for well over a century, but through the first half of the last century they defined themselves by their respective disciplines—as anatomists, physiologists, neurologists—rather than as neuroscientists. In the late 1960s, several scientists, of whom Steven Kuffler at Harvard was perhaps the most influential, saw the advantage of having scientists from different disciplines carry out research on the brain collaboratively. The rationale was that the immense biological complexity of the nervous system could be most effectively addressed if scientists with different skills were brought together in a single group, devoted specifically to study of the nervous system.

As a research strategy, the idea was brilliantly successful, and it soon became the standard model for research groups, departments, and doctoral training programs. In time, the interdisciplinary training offered and espoused by these programs produced a new kind of investigator, fluent in several disciplines and easily able to incorporate them into a single research program organized around a problem rather than a technological approach. Interdisciplinary graduate training in neuroscience has thus been a catalyst that has transformed the way we do brain research.

Currently, neuroscience research and graduate study is a thriving enterprise—intellectually vigorous, confident of its identity, and looking forward to an expanding future. Research on the brain is broadly supported by a number of institutes in the National Institutes of Health, employment opportunities remain relatively good as the field expands, and a mood of optimism prevails. Students stream in from other fields, and each year's cohort seems stronger than the last. This sense of relative health may set neuroscience off from some of the other disciplines included in the Carnegie Initiative on the Doctorate (CID). These disciplines, which have a much longer history, currently experience a sense of crisis over identity and relevance (see, for example, the essays on English, the humanities, chemistry, and mathematics in this volume), as they struggle with the important question of how to find the balance between stewardship of an important academic tradition and adaptation to a changing intellectual landscape.

Graduate training in neuroscience faces a related but different challenge, arising in part from its success. The current vigor of neuroscience is a direct result of its synthetic and inclusive nature and its sense of open boundaries as it operates as a sort of European Economic Community of science, allowing and encouraging students and investigators to roam across disciplinary borders, free of academic tariffs. As the field has grown over the last several decades, it has successfully incorporated other disciplinary approaches (for example, immunology and genetics) from the life, or biomedical, sciences. Their inclusion has been relatively easy, as many different fields within the life sciences share a common language and a common set of scientific standards, based heavily in laboratory research. As neuroscience grows and expands, however, it is beginning to include other fields, for example, the physical sciences and the behavioral or social sciences, which have languages and experimental traditions that may be quite different. How can neuroscience most productively incorporate research on the brain in these important areas? This question will be particularly acute for graduate training in neuroscience, as it faces the issue of how far interdisciplinary bounds can be stretched without producing investigators who are conversant in many fields but expert in none.

As neuroscience extends its reach and increases its interactions with other disciplines, it will continue to redefine itself in new ways. The changing shape of graduate training will both reflect and drive the continuing evolution of neuroscience. To understand some of the opportunities and risks that we face as our field continues to develop, we must first examine the current structure of graduate education in neuroscience and understand the forces that have shaped it.

Current Configurations of Graduate Education in Neuroscience

The administrative forms that accommodate neuroscience graduate education differ from university to university. Some institutions, particularly those with medical schools (for example, Harvard and Duke), have established neuroscience departments that take their place beside traditional departments. Other institutions (for example, Washington University, University of California, San Francisco) have formed interdepartmental graduate programs, with members drawn from many different departments. In many cases, the interdepartmental graduate program has become a more important scientific and intellectual community for its members than are their home departments. In recent years, the model of broad programs has tended to prevail, even at institutions with departments of neuroscience already in place. Thus Harvard now has both a department of neurobiology at the medical school and a neuroscience graduate program that extends across the university.

At some universities, traditional departments (anatomy, physiology, pharmacology) have resisted the move toward integrated graduate programs in neuroscience, as they have been unwilling to share their claim to parts of the scientific and academic turf that they regard as their own. Not surprisingly, departments with strong traditions of excellence in neuroscience research have sometimes proved the most resistant, slowing the development of the new, interdisciplinary field of neuroscience at their institutions. Paradoxically, neuroscience departments and programs have often thrived at institutions where traditional departments were weak.

In general, the process of curriculum development in neuroscience over the last thirty years has been fluid, locally developed, and responsive to comparative and competitive pressures. As graduate programs in neuroscience have been formed, each institution has developed a curriculum that reflects the local structure of the program (department-based or interdepartmental), as well as the interests and judgments of the particular scientists at that institution. Because the considerable mobility of scientists, students, and postdoctoral fellows has allowed a certain level of shared experience, those features of programs that have been the most successful, as judged both by what and how they teach and by their ability to attract students, have gradually become adopted by other programs. Common experiences and "market forces" have thus driven convergence to a more or less standard curriculum.

As in other disciplines, the aims of a graduate curriculum in neuroscience are to give students a broad base of knowledge, as defined by the canonical "core" of the field, and to help them acquire cutting-edge expertise and knowledge in one or more specialized areas. Indeed, the challenge of maintaining the balance between breadth and depth is particularly acute in neuroscience because of its interdisciplinary nature. In general, during the first two years students acquire broad experience in the laboratory and classroom. They then build on this base of knowledge in their thesis work, as they learn to become independent investigators, creating original knowledge.

The formal curriculum typically consists of a basic neuroscience course, required of all students, plus a variety of advanced, more specialized courses, usually elective and often given as seminars. Relevant courses outside the neurosciences program are either required (for example, a course in cell or molecular biology) or elective. The length of the core course varies in different programs, from one quarter or semester to a full academic year. A year-long course enables students to learn a broader range of material in more depth, but many programs offer a short, introductory course, followed by a series of more specialized courses that may be tailored to the needs of a particular student. The shorter course is often more attractive because it permits students from other graduate programs who are curious about neuroscience to easily take a comprehensive introductory course; for neuroscience programs that have close reciprocal relations with other graduate programs, this is often an important consideration.

Although there is a core of classical knowledge, the curriculum has been marked by its adaptability to new developments in the field. As new discoveries have been made, or as new disciplines have become important, the curriculum has been altered to include these. When comprehensive neuroscience courses were first taught in the 1960s, the two fundamental elements were the electrical basis of neuronal signaling (Hodgkin-Huxley; Fatt and Katz) and neuroanatomy, with a little transmitter biochemistry and developmental neurobiology thrown in. With the explosion in molecular biology and the development of new physiological and imaging techniques, the basic core has shifted to include the new knowledge.

In most neuroscience graduate programs, the canonical body of knowledge, as defined by the basic course, includes the electrical and molecular basis of signaling in the nervous system, the cell biology of neurons, developmental neurobiology, and systems neurobiology, including the structure and functional organization of the mammalian nervous system. Other important areas, which in some programs are part of the core and in others offered as electives, include the neurobiology of disease, neurogenetics, computational neuroscience, and the neurobiology of behavior. Thus the original division into disciplines (such as anatomy, physiology, biochemistry) has given way to a more integrated approach that considers the nervous system at various levels of organization: molecular, cellular, and systems.

As noted earlier, the topics that neuroscience faculty members choose to include in the core curriculum offer an important clue to shifts in the research agenda, and in most programs, the content of the course has evolved as knowledge has changed. Electrophysiology, for example, which was the starting point for cellular neuroscience a generation ago, now shares its central role with molecular neuroscience. Indeed, our increased knowledge about the molecular basis of electrical signaling has recast our understanding and teaching of classical electrophysiological principles. The core course has also adapted to the increased neurobiological sophistication of students, most of whom have now had an undergraduate course in neuroscience. Students in neuroscience—more than in most other life sciences—arrive from a variety of backgrounds, including engineering, mathematics, physics, and psychology, as well as biology. The core course, required by all students, should have the aim of bringing all students to a standard level of sophistication, with a common body of knowledge from which they proceed to more advanced work. Having students of different backgrounds in a common core course has the added advantage that they teach each other.

Students develop specialized knowledge through the advanced courses, whose number and variety differ from program to program. Some programs strive to move students into the laboratory to begin thesis work as quickly as possible. Others promote the idea of science as a lifelong learning process and encourage students to continue to take one or two courses a year, even while working on the thesis. Achieving specialized knowledge, however, often requires that students go outside neuroscience to complete their education. Thus, for example, students in neurogenetics need to be well trained in genetics, as well as in neuroscience, and students in computational neurobiology must be adequately trained in mathematics. As I discuss next, larger structures of graduate education, which facilitate and promote these excursions into other fields, play an increasingly important role in broadening the educational experience and in sustaining disciplinary rigor for neuroscientists.

Laboratory rotations, which advance the aim of interdisciplinarity, are now a prominent feature of most graduate programs in neuroscience. Typically, during the first year, students spend a quarter in each of three laboratories, carrying out individual research projects. The purpose of the rotations is twofold: (1) to give students experimental experience in diverse laboratory and scientific settings and (2) to allow students (and advisers) to try out potential laboratories for thesis work. These two aims are related, in that the range of neuroscience work is so broad that most students who enter a graduate program, even those with extensive undergraduate laboratory experience, will have had the opportunity to explore only a narrow sample of the many approaches to neuroscience research. A successful and exciting experience in a previous laboratory may have led them to think that they know what they want to do, but a broader experience often leads to a change in direction. Rotations in different laboratories not only broaden the students' technical repertoire but also allow them to understand how those in the different disciplines of neuroscience think about research: what questions they ask, how they frame a problem, what levels of proof they require. Finally, as students go from lab to lab, they often become important vectors of scientific information within a program; the students are vectors of information, skills, and ideas not only within programs but also across them.

One of the key features of neuroscience graduate programs from the beginning has been the opportunity that they offer students to combine different disciplines for their research. A generation ago, for example, a student might have defined him- or herself as either an electrophysiologist or a molecular biologist, regarding these as separate domains of investigation. Through the curriculum courses and through rotations, many students now master both areas of expertise, allowing them to pursue a broader range of problems without regard to disciplinary borders. A similar marriage is currently taking place between theoretical and experimental systems neuroscience. As they move from rotation to rotation, students often lead the way in bringing information and new approaches from lab to lab, combining disparate disciplines, enhancing their own scientific capabilities, and further contributing to the vigor of the field. The role of graduate programs and graduate students in promoting these fusions between approaches has been crucial to the advancement of the field.

After a period of intensive course work and laboratory rotations, students qualify for the Ph.D. degree by choosing an adviser and taking a preliminary examination, commonly at the end of their second year or the beginning of the third year. The structure of the preliminary exam, which varies in different programs, is a topic of traditional faculty disagreement, as they try to balance the two aims of neuroscience graduate education: breadth and depth. The question is usually framed in terms of whether the preliminary exam is meant to test the student's broad knowledge (looking backward) or to test the student's ability to undertake independent work (looking forward). Although the balance is achieved in different ways, almost all programs now have students describe and defend the problem that they intend to attack in their thesis work, often including the presentation of preliminary data.

After the preliminary examinations, students begin their thesis, working in close conjunction with an adviser and with postdoctoral fellows and other students in the adviser's laboratory. Thus begins a kind of apprenticeship that is the key experience of graduate education. Through the experience of defining and investigating a problem, analyzing the data, assembling the experimental evidence necessary to establish a finding, and writing a paper describing the results, the student learns and internalizes the scientific values that will last him or her throughout a scientific lifetime.

For some students and in some programs, the intense focus on thesis work is accompanied by withdrawal from the larger graduate community. The most successful graduate programs, however, encourage students to maintain their participation in the larger community by joining journal clubs, teaching, and continuing advanced course work. This participation outside their narrow specialties helps students maintain their contact and fluency in broad areas of neuroscience. Through engagement with the larger community, students have the opportunity to learn from a wide range of faculty, as well as from a variety of peers. At its best, the larger scientific community reinforces and extends the development of scientific values that is the most important product of graduate education. Through its various activities and discussions, members of the program express a set of standards for the quality of scientific inquiry, for what constitutes an interesting problem, for scientific rigor, and for ethical scientific behavior that becomes the foundation for a future scientific career.

A student completes graduate education in neuroscience by presenting and defending a thesis, often after presenting the results at a public seminar. As with other scientific disciplines, many of the student's results will already have been published as a series of separate papers before he or she writes the thesis. Many neuroscience programs allow students to collect these papers into a thesis, often with a general and extended introduction and discussion. Additional unpublished data can be included as one or more separate chapters. The number and quality of published papers have now become more important determinants of research success and professional advancement than the thesis, which is generally read only by those directly concerned with the thesis exam. The thesis nevertheless offers an important opportunity for students to expand discussion of experimental results, engage in creative speculation, or express an individual opinion or interpretation that might have been suppressed in a multiauthored journal work.

The Larger Context of Graduate Education in Neuroscience: Relationship to Other Graduate Programs

Neuroscience, both as a research activity and as a discipline for graduate education, has a close reciprocal relation to other life sciences, both drawing from them and contributing to them. Its youth is not unusual in the life sciences, where new fields abound; indeed, over the last half century, the dynamism of graduate education in the life sciences is one of its most characteristic and idiosyncratic features. Because of the importance of the relationship between neuroscience and the other life sciences and because developments in neuroscience have often mirrored those occurring in the larger sphere, it is worth considering briefly some of the recent forces that are changing the overall landscape of graduate education in the life sciences.

Graduate education in the life sciences is distinctive, both because of the multiplicity of related disciplines that it encompasses and because of enormous local variation in their definition and configuration. All universities have graduate programs in mathematics, chemistry, and history, for example, whose structures have remained relatively stable over many decades. Compared with these "standard" disciplines, the life sciences display an astonishing and confusing variety, both among universities and, over time, within the same institution. The variation is particularly striking at universities with medical schools: during the last few decades, most medical schools have redefined their traditional basic science departments, adding, eliminating, or combining departments in a variety of ways.

The remarkable plasticity of graduate education in the life sciences stems in part from the vitality of modern biology, which has been reshaped again and again by powerful new technologies (exemplified by the case of molecular biology); in part from tensions within the life sciences, both historical and contemporary (for example, botany versus zoology or molecular biology versus population biology), and in part from the fragmented status of life sciences within the university curriculum, where graduate degrees may be offered by many schools. The result has been an unusual fluidity in graduate disciplines, as departments at particular universities have fused, divided, redefined themselves, or arisen anew. The most striking effect has been the proliferation of new programs. Neuroscience is but one of a number of new disciplines that have arisen in the life sciences over the last half century (including cell biology, molecular biology, and, more recently, genomics, chemical biology, and systems biology).

One negative effect of these changes has been to fragment graduate education in the life sciences. Indeed, the often bewildering variety of programs has made their comparative evaluation difficult; witness the difficulties that have attended the National Research Council's (NRC) decennial attempt to rank different life science programs.[1] Many universities complained strenuously that the particular categories chosen by the NRC in 1995—biochemistry and molecular biology, physiology, and the like—did not fit the graduate programs offered at their institution, resulting in an unfair evaluation.

In recent years, a second, countervailing trend has dominated, namely the confederation or consolidation of individual graduate programs into large, overarching structures. These broad programs (for example, molecular, cellular, and genetic biology, or biomedical sciences) often have multiple tracks within them or consist of independent programs that are bound together in a confederation defined by common curricular elements and a free exchange of students among the separate programs. The intent—and the result—of these programs is to give students a wider choice of laboratories for rotations and thesis work and to give faculty access to a larger group of potential students. Not surprisingly, a strong motivation for building these large programs has been their attractiveness to prospective students.

A more important driving force behind these confederated programs, however, is a scientific one. One of the major themes of modern biomedical research is the commonality of molecular mechanisms that connect apparently disparate biological fields. Thus investigators in invertebrate development, botany, or immunology may suddenly find themselves studying the same signaling pathways or surface molecules. Finally, the most powerful technologies of modern biology often find application in quite different fields; the fields then become linked by the use of a common "toolkit" and a common technical language. As a result, the relevance of different areas of biomedical research to each other has increased. Because of these linkages, students are able to move more readily between the different areas. Although most of the linkage in life sciences occurs within different fields of laboratory research, molecular methods now find increasing use in ecology, population biology, or even in field research.

The trend to convergence has also affected neuroscience. Ironically, although neuroscience arose, in part, because of the distinctiveness of its techniques such as electrophysiology and neuroanatomical methods, the technological and intellectual barriers that had separated brain scientists from their other biological colleagues began to diminish, just as the new departments and programs were formed. Over the last several decades, neuroscience has increasingly joined the mainstream of biology. Neurofibrils, for example, which are the basis of many neural-specific stains, are now recognized as just one more member of the family of intermediate filaments found in all cells, and the ion channels responsible for electrical signaling in the nervous system are known to be present in many types of non-neural cells as well. The emergence and dominance of molecular biology, in particular, has transformed neuroscience, as well as other fields, giving biologists across many fields a common language and set of technologies.

As a consequence of these centripetal forces, many neuroscience graduate programs are joined with other biomedical graduate programs as part of much larger confederations—"umbrella" programs—in the life sciences. The intent of these programs is to create an open intellectual and scientific environment in which students have access to a broad range of people, technical facilities, and ideas. The neuroscience program at the University of California, San Francisco, for example, is part of the Program in Biological Sciences (PIBS),[2] which includes graduate programs in cell biology, molecular biology and genetics, developmental biology, and structural biology.

These alliances make it easier for students to take courses, do laboratory rotations or, in some cases, to do thesis work under mentors who do not define themselves as neuroscientists but whose work may be related to neuroscience. Through courses, journal clubs, and other activities, the larger structures facilitate formal and informal contact between neuroscience students and students and professors in other programs. The larger programs are not only a resource for neuroscience students but also help promote interest in the nervous system among students and faculty in other fields. The lowering of barriers between fields facilitates the free flow of ideas, personnel, and technology, which is essential to any scientific community. Neuroscience, which has historically profited from its ability to include those from many disciplines, is particularly well situated to benefit from the advantages of these larger programs. Graduate education in neuroscience thus cannot be considered apart from the scientific community in which it is embedded. Indeed, the quality of a particular neuroscience program depends heavily on the surrounding biomedical research community and the strength of its ties to it.

As an interdisciplinary field, one of the challenges of neuroscience has always been to maintain disciplinary standards of excellence: that is, neurogeneticists should be good geneticists as well as good neuroscientists.

By maintaining open channels of communication and collaboration, the umbrella programs play a key role in this regard. Thus neuroscience students are in close contact with students in other fields of biomedical science and also have access to their faculty, courses, and laboratory rotations, where they are expected to meet the same standards as their peers in other fields.

One of the most interesting new developments in graduate education in the life sciences derives from the recent expansion of professional opportunities for Ph.D.'s. A generation ago, almost all students were directed toward full-time academic careers of research and teaching. In my own experience as a student in the 1960s, other possibilities were rare, and consideration of them was a tacit admission of failure. The occasional student who went into industry was generally never heard from again. Now there are multiple opportunities for Ph.D.'s in the biotechnology and pharmaceutical industries, in science writing and journal editorships, in patent law and government agencies, and in patient advocacy groups. As these opportunities have expanded, students at many universities have taken the initiative to organize workshops to inform students about nontraditional career opportunities.

At most universities, these efforts have not penetrated the formal course curriculum, but informal and elective courses are beginning to appear. At the University of California, San Francisco, for example, a course about the biotechnology industry, "Idea to IPO,"[3] given as an elective for credit since 2000, rapidly fills to the limit of forty students, with some eighty in attendance each week, each time it is taught. There are opportunities for other types of courses, such as science journalism, that may be particularly well suited to co-sponsorship with relevant schools or departments. Such courses should not replace courses in the scientific curriculum but can be usefully given as add-on electives. Because of its broad interactions and the broad implications of its research, neuroscience is especially well suited to explore such possibilities.

The Coming Challenge for Graduate Education in Neuroscience

Neuroscience, which was founded as an interdisciplinary field, continues to incorporate new scientific technologies and disciplines as they become relevant to biologically based brain research. Many of the new technologies, such as those of structural biology or genomics, can be accommodated within the broad programs of the life sciences that currently exist on many campuses. Others extend beyond the traditional boundaries of the life sciences. Two of these are of particular importance and pose special opportunities and challenges to neuroscience research and education as they evolve: bioengineering and the behavioral sciences.

Bioengineering, like neuroscience, is in a current phase of rapid growth. Many physical scientists have been attracted to research related to health, both because of the scientific opportunities it offers and because of the change in funding opportunities as the nation's priorities have turned from the Cold War to matters of health and quality of life. Thus at many universities, bioengineering, both at graduate and undergraduate levels, is the most robust of the engineering sciences. As the interests of investigators in engineering and physical science have increasingly turned to biology, many universities have explored academic structures that will facilitate research across traditional boundaries. Stanford University's Bio-X initiative,[4] for example, attempts to bring together in one building researchers and students in engineering, the physical sciences, and biomedical science. QB3[5] (the California Institute for Quantitative Biomedical Research)—a joint program between three University of California campuses (San Francisco, Berkeley, and Santa Cruz)—is another effort to promote interaction between the quantitative and biomedical sciences, in this case across institutional boundaries.

Brain research has a special attraction for bioengineering and physical science students. The complexity of the brain offers fertile ground for quantitative and systems engineering, and engineering technologies, particularly imaging, computation and, more recently, nanotechnology, offer powerful tools for brain research. In addition, there is the exciting prospect of developing neuroprosthetic devices that interface between the brain and microelectronic circuitry to extend and repair brain function. Neuroscience and engineering are thus natural collaborators, with much to explore.

Although both engineers and biomedical scientists recognize the benefits of working at the interface, few training programs have been established to explicitly encourage this connection. How can graduate education foster the growing relationship between neuroscience and engineering? Should bioengineering and neuroscience programs continue to be developed side-by-side? Should they develop new relationships that allow interchange of students? Or should entirely new programs be developed to train students who are equally adept in biology and engineering? Each university will find its own solution to this challenge, depending on its structure, its capabilities, its history, and, most important, on its academic leaders.

The question of how to balance disciplinary and interdisciplinary ties for neuroscience has been solved by its relationship to other life sciences within large umbrella structures. Engineering and the physical sciences are generally outside these structures. Can they be included or will neuroscience find itself part of two larger communities? As with the origins of current neuroscience programs, many solutions will likely be sought, with the most successful attracting emulators. Whatever the particular format, the short history of neuroscience suggests that the guiding principles must be to choose solutions that maximize flexibility and give students the widest opportunity for access to a broad range of ideas, mentors, and technical expertise.

The other area of special opportunity is the intersection of neuroscience and the behavioral sciences. Understanding the biological basis of human and animal behavior is one of the most exciting and far-reaching prospects of neuroscience in the twenty-first century. New tools, particularly those of imaging and genetics, have led to investigations of the neurobiological basis of a variety of behaviors, including language, emotions, and addiction, and social behaviors such as lying or cheating, even religious and ethical feelings. Other experimental approaches examine the biological basis, in animals, of perception, decision making, and intention—topics that were previously the territory of psychologists and philosophers—or use simple organisms, as well as human patients, to explore the genetic basis of behaviors. The powerful alliance of behavioral and biological scientists is thus laying the foundation for a new understanding of how the brain is influenced by experience and how it determines our behavior.

The progress in behavioral neuroscience has reinvigorated the biological approach in departments of psychology and psychiatry and has added behavioral techniques to the repertoire of the modern neuroscientist. Most important, biologically and behaviorally based scientists are collaborating in their investigations as, increasingly, each specialty needs the techniques of the other. For those involved in graduate education, the challenge will be how best to bring these two areas together in the context of training. Graduate programs in neuroscience and in psychology have very different traditions and histories, including some historical antagonism between "hard science" biologists and "soft science" social scientists, so that the problem of incorporating both into a larger structure for graduate education may present unusual challenges. Forward-looking institutions, however, will recognize the importance of this area and will seek to find creative new ways to join the two cultures.

The increasing impact of neuroscience research is being felt in other areas as well. For example, computation, psychiatry, education, law, and economics offer opportunities for rich, reciprocal interactions between neurobiology and other fields. In economics, for example, the new term *neuroeconomics* refers both to understanding the biological basis of how individuals make economic decisions and to using formal theories of decision making developed by economists to understand how large ensembles of neurons make decisions. Indeed, the implications of neurobiological research are so broad and so fundamental that many feel that neurobiology, in its broadest sense, will be one of the dominant themes of intellectual life in the university in the twenty-first century. Such considerations lie behind the formation of Harvard University's Mind/Brain/Behavior Interfaculty Initiative,[6] for example—an institute that goes far beyond the life sciences to include philosophers, theologians, psychologists, and others.

How will these developments affect the future of graduate education in neuroscience? The challenge is to develop a program (or programs) that will capitalize on these new interactions to encourage and facilitate the development of vital, new interdisciplinary fields while, at the same time, maintaining core expertise in neuroscience. Each university will decide, based on existing structures, history, and personalities, how it fashions academic structures to meet these competing demands. As with the life sciences in general, the solutions that particular universities choose are apt to be myriad, with the most successful serving as models that others will follow. Large, inclusive programs give expression to the richness and variety of modern neurobiological research, and, because few are excluded, are politically easier to create and maintain. They run the very real danger, however, of becoming so broad that they lose a strong, shared sense of scientific identity and values. Moreover, as traditional disciplinary moorings are loosened, standards of quality become threatened. Finally, successful and innovative new programs usually thrive best when a small, intellectually congenial and enthusiastic group has a common vision and is convinced that it is blazing a new trail. Their zeal and purity of vision, when communicated to students, is often the cornerstone to successful new programs. As programs grow larger, the qualities that originally made it successful are often difficult to sustain.

Within this context, the theme of stewardship raised by the CID becomes double-edged. On the one hand, it is important that students develop their talents within an intellectual tradition that gives them knowledge of a historically defined corpus of knowledge, that provides continuity and support to their efforts, and that gives them historical examples of rigor and creativity to which they can aspire. On the other hand, excessive loyalty to a historical tradition can inhibit the emergence of new programs. It is precisely the challenge of adapting graduate education to an ever-changing scientific landscape that has been so acute for the life sciences and that will be so for the neurosciences going forward.

NOTES

1. Goldberger, M. L., Maher, B. A., and Flattau, P. E. (eds.). *Research-Doctorate Programs in the United States: Continuity and Change.* Washington, D.C.: National Academy Press, 1995.

2. University of California, San Francisco Program in Biological Sciences (www.ucsf.edu/pibs).

3. University of California, San Francisco "Idea to IPO" course (www.ucsf.edu/cbe/ideatoipo.htm).

4. Stanford University's Bio-X Initiative (biox.stanford.edu/clark).

5. California Institute for Quantitative Biomedical Research (www.qb3.org).

6. Harvard University's Institute for Mind/Brain/Behavior Interfaculty Initiative (see www.mbb.harvard.edu).

12

THE CHALLENGES OF MULTIDISCIPLINARITY

NEUROSCIENCE AND THE DOCTORATE

Steven E. Hyman, Harvard University

NEUROSCIENCE—THE STUDY OF THE NERVOUS SYSTEM but most especially the brain—has all the trappings of a discipline. It has dedicated departments, a large number of self-identified neuroscientists, doctoral and postdoctoral training programs, strong professional societies, numerous textbooks, and both general and specialized neuroscience journals. Despite this, neuroscience is anything but a traditional discipline. In its very nature (and quite self-consciously in its origins), neuroscience is intrinsically multidisciplinary.

Neuroscience is based neither on a core set of scientific approaches nor on a single level of analysis—two factors that help demarcate disciplines within the life sciences. For example, biochemistry is defined as a discipline largely by its intellectual and technical approaches to certain sets of problems. Molecular biology and cell biology define themselves by their level of analysis, which brings with it a set of core technologies that all students will at least learn about, if not employ. In contrast, neuroscience incorporates approaches from multiple disciplines and attempts to gain understandings at multiple levels of analysis, ranging from the molecular to the behavioral. Its central organizing principle is an organ system.

Not surprisingly, many self-identified neuroscientists who publish in neuroscience journals and attend neuroscience meetings work *outside* neuroscience departments, for example, in departments of genetics, biochemistry, pharmacology, cell biology, psychology, engineering, and diverse clinical departments. At universities in which neuroscientists populate both the neuroscience department and departments in allied fields, the graduate program is very often the glue holding together an otherwise highly dispersed community.

As a field, neuroscience is relatively young. Several quantitative measures illustrate its relatively recent and rapid development. The Society for Neuroscience was formed in 1970 with approximately 500 members, all of whom perforce had their doctoral training in other constituent disciplines. Today, it has 31,000 members, and neuroscience organizations outside the United States are also growing, in both numbers and intellectual strength. More directly germane to the topic at hand, there are now more than 200 neuroscience doctoral training programs in the United States.

Neuroscience is a vital, growing, multidisciplinary field. And despite the large number of training programs already in place, the trajectory in neuroscience is still one of growth: the study of the brain is a fascinating and increasingly tractable intellectual frontier, with enormous implications for human self-understanding and human health.

We need to keep careful track of this growth. As all fields mature and change, practitioners have to ask, *What will our core issues be?* As neuroscience matures, its constituents must consider how the field will maintain its vitality. Neuroscience is so young and its overall intellectual focus so challenging that this question has not yet presented itself in the way that it has, for example, in some subdisciplines of physics. Neuroscientists generally have the strong belief that they are not about to run out of interesting and demanding problems that will attract bright young students into their fold. Neuroscience is categorically not like some older areas of science, in which many of the fundamental issues seem to be settled.

Two Challenges to Neuroscience

The main challenges to neuroscience in the coming decades are quite different from those facing older, more settled disciplines. Our challenges derive from the multidisciplinary underpinnings of neuroscience and have enormous implications for graduate training. I believe these main challenges are twofold: (1) managing centrifugal forces that might cause critically important constituent disciplines to opt out and (2) maintaining vibrant two-way connections with the core practitioners of the constituent disciplines in order to maintain quality.

The struggle against centrifugal forces can be illustrated by issues that have occasionally arisen with respect to the annual meeting of the Society for Neuroscience ("the Neuroscience meeting"). The annual Neuroscience meeting has always striven to represent all areas of neuroscience, but the event often feels unmanageably large and intellectually overwhelming to its attendees. Its poster exhibits alone exceed fifteen thousand at each meeting. The occasional suggestion that the event be broken up into smaller meetings of component areas has, fortunately, always been rejected. The intellectual power of the meeting for students and faculty alike lies in the possibility of hearing about the gamut of neuroscience. Beyond sheer size, there is the question of whether every constituent discipline feels equally valued. For some years, a number of behavioral scientists, worried about an excessively reductionist chord being played in mainstream neuroscience (indeed in all of biology), thought that they might be better appreciated if they had their own behavioral neuroscience society and meeting.

With time, neuroscience and the Neuroscience meeting weathered the storm, and this particular issue has receded—I hope forever. It has receded partly because the problems of behavioral and cognitive neuroscience are so intrinsically interesting that they have attracted collaborators from a large number of other subfields, and their papers are being published in the most prestigious general neuroscience journals. (For example, molecular geneticists analyzing transgenic mice have often found the behavioral traits the most interesting.) But also contributing to the resolution of the issue is that the tide of reductionism in the life sciences (which may have reached its apotheosis with the genome project) now appears to be receding.

Reductionism as practiced in the life sciences was not, for those who even think in such meta-analytical terms, a philosophical goal. It was the very sensible art of the possible, taking René Descartes' good advice that we break problems down into manageable bits. There have always been more holistic approaches to brain and behavior, as represented by "systems neuroscience" and some aspects of behavioral science. Given the existing tools, however, such "top-down" approaches to the nervous system were more challenging than "bottom-up" approaches that dealt with molecules, genes, cells, and small circuits. Even cognitive neuroscience made progress by breaking mental and behavioral functions down into components. Throughout biology there is a conviction that we know enough about the component parts of cells to begin thinking more holistically at a variety of levels. At the subcellular level, instead of studying one gene or one protein at a time, there is a movement to study complex networks of interacting molecules. At the level of the brain, improved imaging tools make it possible to think about the interactions of brain regions and the overall functioning of distributed circuits. The inclusion of more mathematical modeling into biology in general and neuroscience in particular should enhance our capacity to address more integrative and systems-level problems.

Although the place of behavioral science in neuroscience is secure for now, other centrifugal challenges to neuroscience are bound to appear. And so the key time to instill a healthy culture in neuroscience, as in other disciplines, is during graduate training. The balance of courses, the tone of the faculty (especially those advising students), and the quality of labs representing different academic perspectives will either strengthen or undercut intellectual connections. Faculty who really believe that we can understand the brain only if we work together from the molecular level to the cognitive will produce students who see promise and value at all levels of analysis and who will strive to connect them. Such respect should not inhibit the capacity of students to ask hard questions about different areas, about tradeoffs between complexity and rigor, or about the values of more basic and more applied research; respect makes such questioning safe and productive.

The second challenge is, to my mind, the canonical problem for all multidisciplinary fields, and it has implications for how these fields train their students: *How does the field maintain quality in its constituent discipline?* As an example, a generation ago, many self-styled neurochemists worked in richer, but less readily analyzable, systems than did their biochemist mentors (for example, in mixed populations of neurons rather than pure cultures of an undifferentiated cell type). By the second generation, some neurochemists might have received all their biochemical training outside an introductory course, within a neuroscience department. There is a clear risk that some of their work will be scientifically weaker than that of disciplinary biochemists—the result of tackling problems prematurely or of applying fundamental discoveries made elsewhere to their experimental system. Who, then, should train neuroscientists who want primarily to use biochemical approaches to the nervous system? How do we mediate between simpler model systems in which new principles are to be learned and less fundamental applications of those principles and methods to the rich and complex systems of neuroscience? (Ironically, the neurochemist who might have seemed reductionist to the behavioral scientist might be perceived by a biochemist to be working on overly complex and very poorly defined problems.) Even today, with the advent of a new "systems" biology that will attempt to understand the interactions of multiple cellular components, the neuron does not seem like the most opportune eukaryotic cell with which to begin; yeast might be a better candidate. Such challenges illustrate the never-ending need to find a balance, and they have profound implications for graduate training, often influencing the choice of thesis problems.

The key ideas of this essay sound very simple, but working out their implications in practice has proved quite difficult. Doctoral training in neuroscience must achieve a balance between breadth as a neuroscientist and depth, part of which will usually entail a strong connection to one or even two constituent disciplines—a connection that must remain vibrant over a long career. No department can expect to launch students on successful careers if it does not find a successful way to address the Scylla and Charybdis of multidisciplinary fields: ensuring that the trainee is as complete a neuroscientist as possible—someone who can read nearly all the articles of our general neuroscience journals with understanding and who would not feel a stranger at any part of the Neuroscience meeting, but, at the same time, someone who will not become isolated from the advances of the nearest neighbor core discipline or disciplines that make up the large world of the life sciences. There is no single right way to address these challenges.

How Has Neuroscience Emerged as a Discipline?

So far in this discussion, I have made the assumption that neuroscience is, in fact, a discipline,[1] but we should look more closely at that assumption. One could argue that neuroscience is not actually a discipline but something that might be better described as an area or field. What is the difference? Many universities have centers that bring disciplines together to study an area of knowledge from different perspectives and to share that knowledge among the members. For example, at Harvard University, we have brought together economists, sociologists, anthropologists, literary scholars, historians, and others into centers that focus on geographic areas such as Japan or on Latin America. We have brought together microbiologists, epidemiologists, physicians, economists, anthropologists, political scientists, and others to think about global health. The participants may spend their entire post-training career immersed in their area and, working shoulder-to-shoulder with colleagues with different disciplinary backgrounds, may incorporate some methods from other disciplines. My observation is that these scholars tend to maintain their original identity as, say, an economist or an anthropologist. Neuroscience has done something different from these centers—something that begins with graduate training: it confers an identity as a neuroscientist.

To this point, I have carefully chosen to use the word *multidisciplinary* to describe the origins of neuroscience, but in more than a few areas of neuroscience, enough integration and blurring of disciplinary bounds has occurred that what has emerged can be fairly described as *interdisciplinary*. This process is not in any sense complete, nor is it ever likely to be. The members of the class of "academic disciplines" are not all tidily alike in their scope, complexity, origins, clarity of boundaries, or trajectory. I think it is fair, indeed, to say that enough specialist knowledge and new ways of thinking have developed in the service of understanding the brain that neuroscience has moved from being a multidisciplinary area or field to being a discipline itself. But it is a discipline with areas of more and less integration. And it is a discipline still dependent on methods, technologies, and understandings from other, more basic disciplines of the life sciences (psychology, applied mathematics, engineering, and others).

One further point is interesting in this regard. Two of the critical components of disciplinary knowledge in neuroscience are neuroanatomy, an understanding of the myriad cell types and intricate structures and circuits of the brain, and neurophysiology, the study, using such techniques as electrical recordings and many forms of imaging, of the excitability of neurons. Although anatomy and physiology are component disciplines, relevant to many other complex fields, it may be fair to say, especially for anatomy, that they are currently most alive within neuroscience. At times there may be a tug-of-war for interesting constituent disciplines between graduate programs, departments, or funding agencies.

Consider an illustrative example from my period as director of the National Institute of Mental Health (NIMH), which was a major funder of neuroscience research and doctoral training programs, along with the National Institute of Neurological Disorders and Stroke (NINDS), the National Institute of General Medical Studies, the National Institute on Aging (NIA), the National Institute on Drug Abuse (NIDA), the National Eye Institute, and several other National Institutes of Health (NIH) institutes. Early in my tenure, a consortium of institutes, led by NIMH and NINDS, reorganized the review of grant applications for neuroscience and for the behavioral sciences. Basic neuroscience applications that came in to NIMH, NINDS, or NIDA, for example, had been considered in separate committees based on the funding institute. At the end of the reorganization, the assignment of applications to review committees was based on the subject matter rather than the potential funding institute. Ultimately, nine NIH institutes that received applications related to neuroscience joined in a review consortium. An interesting problem arose that was most acute with respect to the review of applications for grants in neurodevelopment. Based on the timing of the reforms of the NIH review system, the neuroscience community had completed its work before other large segments of NIH followed suit. The neuroscience community had, logically enough, incorporated neurodevelopment into neuroscience committees.

However, when an examination of review committees was extended to all of NIH, the developmental biologists expressed strong concern that neurodevelopment grants were moving out of their review committees into neuroscience review committees. Their view was that developmental biology study sections were already multidisciplinary and had the right expertise (which in their view was developmental biology rather than neuroscience). They further argued that moving the neurodevelopment grants out would impoverish the discussions in their review committees (by removing some important investigators) and at the same time could initiate a slow drift of neurodevelopment away from mainstream developmental biology, with a consequent risk of a slippage in quality. They argued, as could many from other disciplines, that as review of grants for the NIH moved toward multidisciplinary study sections with organ systems and classes of disease as the organizing principles, there was a risk of diminished rigor in review. Specifically, a multidisciplinary neuroscience review panel might have only a small number of individuals who were developmental biologists.

In contrast, the neuroscience community, which ultimately succeeded in retaining the developmental neurobiology applications, argued that pure developmental biology study sections, divorced from organ systems and diseases, would not be in a strong position to evaluate the significance of lines of research, even if they were in a stronger position to evaluate their technical merit—and even that was questionable because the organ-system-based review would be more familiar with the particular experimental system. This story highlights the fact that there is not single right way to organize science, whether funding or doctoral programs, but that history, personalities, and the advocacy of certain views can have a significant effect on the way in which scientists and students aggregate and the way in which funds flow.

The foregoing does not really tell us how neuroscience—an area of science with an organ system as its organizing principle—emerged as a new "higher-order" discipline, with departments and graduate training programs of such broad scope. One might ask, *Why only the brain and not the heart, the kidneys, or other organ systems?* After all, within academic health centers, postdoctoral training programs exist to address almost every organ system in the body, including the brain, in multidisciplinary fashion. There are, for example, cardiology and nephrology training programs. Labs within those programs may welcome doctoral students doing basic research with the caveat that the doctoral degree will almost always be in some more basic, general discipline such as biochemistry or physiology, with which the lab is also affiliated.

Why did vibrant basic science departments of neuroscience begin to emerge about thirty-five years ago but not basic, university-based (as opposed to health-center-based) departments of cardiology or dermatology, even though the latter may be engaged in much basic science research and may even have doctoral students? Almost certainly, the motivation for creating basic science departments and training programs in neuroscience relates to the relatively unique complexity of understanding brain and behavior, the extraordinary reach across levels of analysis that is necessary to bring to bear (from molecules to behavior), and a less rational but no doubt important factor: the romance of the brain and the quest for human self-understanding. This extraordinarily complex organ is, after all, what underlies our ability to have disciplines at all, write poetry, fall in love, make war, or, at a less exalted level, move, think, and feel.

These considerations notwithstanding, there is a contingent historical dimension to the emergence of neuroscience. The community of scientists interested in the nervous system came to recognize in the 1960s and 1970s that significant intellectual progress on the problems that people ultimately cared about would not only require progress within disciplines and at single levels of analysis but also a robust sharing of information and approaches across levels. Thus if we are ultimately to understand vision, we need information about the cells of the visual system, their chemistry and cell biology, and their mechanisms of cell-cell communication. We need to understand their circuitry, and we need both experimental and theoretical approaches to understanding the relationship of the physiology of those circuits to cognition and behavior (leaving aside for now the important problems of consciousness—the study of which is in its infancy). Important insights have also been brought to bear on the basic understanding of vision, both from the study of normal development and from the genetics and pathophysiology of disease. The important insight was that scientists who, for example, might study a particular ion channel in the retina might want to interact on a regular basis not only with other scientists studying the molecular structure, physiology, or pharmacology of ion channels in diverse experimental systems but also with colleagues interested in other aspects of vision from other vantages. Perhaps this desire to have one's intellectual home in a multidisciplinary setting extends to scientists who study other areas as well, such as developmental biology, but it is a powerful, cohesive force in neuroscience.

Historically, these kinds of considerations led to the establishment of departments of neurobiology or neuroscience and their graduate programs in the 1960s and 1970s. In some cases, as at Harvard University, visionary individuals brought together anatomists, biochemists, physiologists, pharmacologists, and others to form new departments and initiate new training programs. An alternative early model is typified by Washington University, in St. Louis, where a department of anatomy, for which neuroanatomy was the remaining viable research discipline, expanded its purview and was transformed by its leadership into what was essentially a department of neurobiology. Over time, departments that began with a limited number of disciplines, most commonly neuroanatomy, neurophysiology, and perhaps biochemistry (occasionally rechristened as "neurochemistry"), reached out to include additional disciplinary approaches, including behavioral science, computational neuroscience, and, beginning in the 1980s, molecular biology and genetics. In more recent years, studies of the neurobiology of disease, once largely the province of clinical departments, have begun to migrate into basic science departments. Indeed, throughout the life sciences, the boundaries between fundamental and medically relevant biology have been breaking down: problems of disease often cannot be addressed without strong connections to fundamental biology; conversely, fundamental biologists are finding problems of disease compelling and increasingly tractable.

I have been a faculty member with students in my lab; I was the director of a university-wide interdisciplinary initiative in mind, brain, and behavior (that was very broad, including colleagues from the English department and divinity school, as well as psychologists and neuroscientists); now I am a university provost. From my various experiences, I am certain that the key to coalescence of a new discipline is the graduate program. The graduate program draws the faculty together: research collaborations among faculty come and go as projects start or come to fruition, but teaching together creates different kinds of bonds of understanding. Further, the students themselves play an important role. The students themselves force integration. It is most often the graduate students who are in the best position to make new connections as they integrate their course work and laboratory rotations, and find the richest problems for their thesis work. Historically, in the 1960s and 1970s the founders of neuroscience had the wisdom to do more than establish multidisciplinary research centers: they started graduate programs.

What Constitutes Knowledge and Understanding in Neuroscience?

As knowledge expands explosively, and as the approaches of constituent disciplines become more arcane and even linguistically isolated, it becomes increasingly challenging to define what we mean by "adequate knowledge and understanding" in a field such as neuroscience, with multiple constituent disciplines.

For example, consider the enormous challenges of reading the primary literature. For example, reading a paper modeling a neural network might demand a deeper quantitative background than most biologists would possess. The neurogenetics literature might now assume rarified knowledge of cutting-edge approaches to mouse or human genomics. A cognitive neuroscience journal might be replete with paradigms and approaches that the cell biologist would have trouble evaluating.

Indeed, the would-be polymath might ultimately have to choose between keeping up with key developments in every constituent discipline and maintaining real depth in his or her chosen research area. It may be that we must define adequate knowledge and understanding functionally rather than abstractly and that we must define it on two axes—depth and breadth. Clearly, these considerations must weigh on everyone who plans a doctoral curriculum. Moreover, an individual's view of the ideal balance between breadth and depth is often set during the doctoral years. As I noted at the outset, there is no single ideal solution, but it is clear that as we approach the extremes of breadth and depth, we may do our students a disservice.

Let us address depth first. I would argue that every successful doctoral trainee must have mastered at least one constituent discipline or approach from among those that contribute to neuroscience: systems neuroscience, physiology, behavioral neuroscience, computational neuroscience, genetics, or the like. What might we mean by having mastered a constituent discipline? A useful functional test might be derived, based on consideration of those constituent disciplines that are not only a part of neuroscience but also part of a broader scientific community outside of neuroscience. Obvious examples include molecular or cell biology, biochemistry, genetics, or psychology. By the end of training, the scientist should be in a position to contribute, *if he or she so wishes,* not only to neuroscience journals but also to the more general journals of that constituent discipline and to participate effectively in that broader intellectual world. This criterion might be controversial, but it is still far more likely that someone can have a productive and significant scientific career mediated by depth in a narrow constituent discipline than he or she would with a broad understanding of neuroscience and no developed strength in an area of focus.

At the same time, a perusal of the most significant primary data and review journals in neuroscience suggests that an increasing number of problems considered important or interesting by the field involve broader thinking and, often, the interaction of multiple disciplines. Put another way, within the broad multidisciplinary field of neuroscience, subfields have developed that represent not only disciplinary subfields but interdisciplinary subfields. For example, the developing subfield of learning and memory incorporates behavioral, neural systems, physiologic, and molecular approaches and currently makes broad use of such cross-disciplinary approaches as the generation of transgenic mice, which are then put through complex behavioral test batteries while undergoing physiological recording, prior to a molecular analysis of relevant brain regions. Obviously, such experimental approaches require that large collaborative groups be assembled or that networks of collaborating labs form and change with need.

Many other interdisciplinary subfields exist or are coming into being. Thus, for example, analysis of the relationships between structure and function of an ion channel or neurotransmitter receptor requires tools of molecular biology, pharmacology, physiology, and structural biology. Satisfactorily informative genetic manipulation of the mouse might require tools of genetics, neuroanatomy, physiology, and behavioral neuroscience. The effective use of current imaging tools, such as functional magnetic resonance imaging (fMRI) requires, beyond the specialized methodologies of image collection and data analysis, approaches from systems-level neurobiology, cognitive neuroscience, and, depending on the object of study, clinical neuroscience as well.

It is quite clear, therefore, that in addition to depth in a chosen area, those neuroscientists most likely to make significant contributions must also have adequate breadth. Without adequate strength across a range of neuroscience areas, one might be limited in the choice of problems to study, and one could not be an effective collaborator. Effective collaboration extends far beyond selecting the right person or lab to interact with; it demands the ability to talk about experiments together and to understand the analysis of the data, as well as the ability to agree on what is said in the resulting paper. Clearly, this capacity depends, in large part, on the offerings of a training program and, even more, on the habits of mind that permit one to venture beyond the safety of one's most familiar constituent discipline.

What might be the functional tests for adequate breadth? As I suggested earlier, a successful trainee should be able to read and criticize any paper appearing in the field's general journals (not the most highly specialized journals) and should have the working understanding (that is, should be in a position to be a strong and effective collaborator) in those subdisciplines most likely to be necessary to effective work in the person's chosen area.

This level of breadth can be accomplished partly with course work during the doctorate, partly through laboratory rotations (which ideally should be offered by doctoral programs), where appropriate, through collaborations, and certainly through seminars, journal clubs, and opportunities for students to share their work. Programs should develop explicit philosophies of breadth and depth, and student progress should be monitored in this regard, through the doctorate, along with more nuts-and-bolts issues such as achievements in course work and progress on the thesis. It can certainly be a good strategy to carry out one's thesis work and postdoctoral work in complementary constituent disciplines.

Doctoral Education and Beyond: The Balance Between Depth and Breadth

In all multidisciplinary fields, a looming risk begins in the doctoral years and extends throughout one's career: an excessively inward focus within the community can produce relative isolation of the practitioners of the constituent disciplines who carry those traditions (for example, cell biology or genetics) in their full richness and rigor. Neuroscience is no exception.

Isolation from the broader world outside neuroscience could lead to a weakening of the individual components of the multidisciplinary activity; with excessive inwardness, the practitioners of the constituent discipline might slip to the rearguard of their area, such as genetics or cell biology. Instead of being innovators in genetics or cell biology, they might find themselves applying well-worn insights or experimental paradigms to brain-relevant experimental systems or, worse, might be applying outdated or suboptimal tools.

Here an anecdote may explain some of my views. During my period as director of the NIMH, one of the most challenging areas of science that we nurtured was the genetics of behavior, especially of disabling mental illnesses. This area was, and remains, extraordinarily difficult because of the difficulty of defining the phenotypes (that is, of carving nature at the joints before subjecting it to genetic study) and because of the complexity of the genetics. Common behavioral phenotypes, including mental illnesses, result from a complex interaction of multiple genes, environmental factors, and chance. I engaged a blue-ribbon panel of geneticists to advise me how to proceed because success was far from assured. One of the striking findings of their 1998 report was how poor the core disciplinary training in genetics was for a substantial fraction of the neurogeneticists receiving NIMH grants. The body of investigators was relatively weak in the rapidly changing fields of statistical genetics, genomics, and other approaches that seemed absolutely necessary for success. Conversely, the well-trained geneticists whom we welcomed into the study of mental illness were often very accepting, even naïve about the behavioral phenotypes to which they planned to apply their powerful tools. Although an obvious solution would be strong collaborations, in truth, it was often the case that neither the best behavioral scientists nor the best geneticists knew precisely what to look for.

It is, of course, a complex issue to find the right balance in training or in the selection of problems. Important leverage is gained by working out a basic process using a simple model system, and the simplest and most tractable systems will rarely be neurons or brains. However, it is often the more complex model system that eventually holds the greater interest and significance.

To appreciate this point, we might focus on an example that is currently an area of intense activity both outside and inside neuroscience—the investigation of intracellular signaling pathways. For eukaryotes, the simplest directly relevant cell type in which to study signaling would be yeast, and for animal cells it might be a relatively undifferentiated cell such as a fibroblast. Many fundamental insights have come from investigations in such systems. Of course, there are also advantages to studying intracellular signaling in some nerve cell types, precisely because of their greater complexity: they express exactly those signaling proteins that we might be interested in as neuroscientists. The critical point is to be in a position of mastery of the basic constituent discipline so that one can get to the interesting experiments that really make use of neurons rather than simply demonstrating that the same pathway that has already been shown to be present in five undifferentiated cell types is also present in neurons. It is likely that the scientist working on more reduced preparations will make different kinds of discoveries than someone working on neurons. The scientist working on a neuron might discover new neuron-specific family members of a protein kinase or protein phosphatase or find significant differences in the interactions among proteins that do not occur in the simpler cell type. To perform such research effectively and in a timely fashion, however, the neuroscientist who works on intracellular signaling pathways cannot afford to become isolated from the broader signaling community. Without such Janus-like interactions—interactions outside as well as inside the neuroscience community—there is a risk that the person in a multidisciplinary field who is working on a more complex set of problems and experimental systems might end up relegated to less interesting, more obviously applied research.

Goals for Doctoral Programs in Neuroscience

How do we develop and train people with this balance of breadth and depth? As I have already asserted, there is no single best approach to neuroscience training. Both research progress and training opportunities benefit from the existence of programs that take different areas as a focus of intellectual critical mass and that exist within different types of settings. For example, a neuroscience department might share a building or share faculty with strong cell biology, biochemistry, or engineering departments or behavioral science departments or be embedded in academic health centers. Each type of setting, contiguity, and local culture will yield different strengths and weaknesses.

Unfortunately, given the vast areas of inquiry that neuroscience has staked out for itself, no program of manageable size can afford equivalent depth in every subfield. However, because a critical goal of neuroscience training is to gain a strong understanding of the *range* of the field, strong training programs must have at least some representation of most of the major subdivisions of the field. At the coarsest grain size, a program might include molecular and cellular neuroscience, development and plasticity, systems neuroscience, behavioral neuroscience, and neurobiology of disease, or clinical neuroscience.

Ideally, neuroscience departments will also have strong connections with faculty in other departments. Although the interdisciplinary goals of neuroscience must be strongly represented in training, it is important not to lose sight of the need for trainees to be masters of at least some set of disciplinary approaches. For many departments or training programs, this may require collaboration with other departments such as departments of biochemistry, cell biology, genetics, or psychology.

Again, there is no single right way to organize the pursuit of knowledge of the brain that works for all research projects or training programs. Fortunately, there are opportunities in well-designed curricula, journal clubs, lab rotations, and well-chosen meetings to balance breadth and depth. Different programs will approach the balance in different ways, permitting diverse opportunities for students. On the one hand, the neuroscientist must be broadly educated in the diverse approaches and multiple levels of analysis that neuroscience comprises. On the other hand, as the students settle on the particular set of experimental approaches that they will be primarily using in their laboratories, it is important that programs not permit them to become too isolated from other exemplars of that constituent discipline. Finding the right balance will require constant effort on the part of those individuals who are overseeing the doctoral program.

The need for breadth in neuroscience and connections to component disciplines, as practiced outside of neuroscience departments, presents an ongoing set of challenges for graduate students, postdoctoral fellows, and faculty members alike. Given the limited number of hours in the day and the core needs to attend to research and teaching, the neuroscientist can attend only a finite number of seminars and read a finite number of journals. There are also limitations in time and resources for students to attend national or international meetings, often only one per year or, at most, two.

Ideally, training programs will encourage a good mix of course work within neuroscience but with some attention to core disciplines. In many cases an ideal curriculum during the first year will have some course work specific to neuroscience and some general course work shared with students in other areas of the life sciences. Departmental journal clubs should focus on neuroscience but select a few key papers from other fields of biology. Potentially relevant seminars in other departments should be encouraged, and perhaps at least one meeting during the doctoral years should be in the basic discipline closest to the student's thesis work in neuroscience.

To amplify what I am recommending: departments should develop explicit expectations concerning these matters, which are too often left to chance. In some cases it may make sense to make explicit agreements with other departments that will permit rotations in labs of constituent disciplines.

The Organizational Challenges of Multidisciplinary Doctoral Education and Recommendations for Addressing Them

The multidisciplinarity of neuroscience at the intellectual level is mirrored at the organizational level by complexity—complexity in the departmental organization of neuroscience research and training at universities and complexity in the organization of federal funding for both research and training.

At Harvard University, where I serve as provost, there is a department of neurobiology in the medical school; there is no such department within the faculty of arts and sciences. Rather, there are neurobiologists in the two biology departments (molecular and cellular biology, organismal and evolutionary biology), in the division of engineering and applied science, and, increasingly, in psychology. Many of these neurobiologists are about to organize themselves in a center focused on systems-level neurobiology.

In addition, our affiliated hospitals, like those of other universities, are replete with clinical departments that house both basic and clinical neuroscience research and training. For historical reasons that seem less and less compelling, both neurology and psychiatry remain separate (separate clinical residencies, overlapping but different board examinations, different medical school and hospital departments, different journals and societies), even though both focus on diseases of the brain, indeed diseases that often overlap at the level of biology. In addition, neuroscience research and training may go on in departments of neurosurgery, ophthalmology, otolaryngology, and anesthesia.

At Harvard, it has been possible, through an umbrella program in neuroscience, to match thesis students with laboratories throughout this confusing welter of departments. In addition to overseeing the classroom work, the program vets the labs that want to admit students, oversees progress on the thesis, and oversees degree examinations. This is one example of the fragmentation of neuroscience, and varying scenarios exist at many other universities, but the common approach for doctoral training programs, especially those at large, complex institutions, is to place and oversee students in a diversity of departments, maintain connections among students, and ensure a sense of community.

A similar picture of fragmentation exists at the level of funding of both research and training. What I found as NIMH director was a system in which federal training grants for neuroscience were funded by individual institutes with different missions. Thus, for example, the training director of a neuroscience training grant from NIDA had to show the relevance of the training to addiction research; the training director with an NIA grant had to show its relevance to aging or to neurodegenerative disease.

This system is not ideal for the support of early neuroscience training (that is, the period early in doctoral training at which the student cannot be said to be committed yet to an area that could be identified with an institute mission). Indeed, students in their first two years of doctoral training should have a broad intellectual view and should not prematurely commit to an area of research focus. More problematic for the funders:

it was not possible to predict what area of research the student would end up in. At the NIH, we addressed the excessive influence of institute mission by forming a consortium of institutes to provide undifferentiated neuroscience training grants. Institutes also retained mission-specific training grants but often targeted to later, more differentiated stages of training.

The need to form carefully negotiated and often metastable consortia to fund basic disciplinary needs for neuroscience reflects a deep problem with the fragmentation of the NIH structure. This structure frequently distorts the research and training goals of the basic neuroscience community. It may also thwart the goal of funding the best and most timely science or the strongest basic training programs from a large competitive pool. The root cause of this fragmented system reflects the disease advocacy communities who lobby for the NIH budget. They steer their efforts toward the support of late-stage, mission-oriented research and training. Given this political reality and the truly remarkable degree of fragmentation of neuroscience funding, the neuroscience community must be constantly vigilant to protect our "commons"—support for basic research and for the early, undifferentiated years of graduate training. Such difficulties are not unique to neuroscience training or neuroscience research, but no discipline is more affected, given the large number of NIH institutes involved. (I am aware that chronically underfunded colleagues in the humanities might, at this point, be scratching their heads, wondering what I am complaining about.)

Throughout this essay, I have focused on challenges for doctoral education in neuroscience that arise from neuroscience being a discipline that emerges out of many component disciplines. That emergence is not, and perhaps should not ever be, complete. Neuroscience must encourage integration within but must also encourage close connections with component disciplines. For both intellectual and historical reasons, neuroscience faces the challenge of organizational fragmentation in many universities and certainly at the level of federal funding agencies.

Further, I would argue that doctoral programs in neuroscience must work to ensure adequate breadth of course work and laboratory research opportunities. In many cases, this will require forming coalitions across multiple university departments. Such broad coalitions bring richness of intellectual opportunity but also management challenges. Programs need transparent processes to ensure that all labs are strong enough to function as good training sites. The larger and more dispersed the program, the greater the challenge of maintaining community among the students during their thesis years, ensuring a strong advisory committee structure, and ensuring that students do not get lost. Not only should such breadth be made available, but students should be encouraged to engage diverse areas of neuroscience. Programs should have explicit discussions and policies concerning breadth and depth. At the same time, doctoral programs should not become isolated from other component disciplines. Students should be encouraged to develop depth in one or two component areas. Opportunities for interchange will differ, depending on the setting, but neuroscience doctoral students should not be permitted to become isolated from students in other disciplines of the life sciences (here I include psychology), and, where appropriate, engineering, mathematics, chemistry, or physics.

As stewards of the discipline, neuroscientists cannot afford to become isolated on an intellectual island, especially at a time when disciplinary boundaries in the sciences are falling. Finally, neuroscientists must keep pressure on the funding agencies, as they are now constructed in the United States to support fundamental neuroscience and the early, undifferentiated years of doctoral training in the face of powerful pressures for NIH institutes to focus narrowly on their missions.

NOTES

1. This question is not unique to neuroscience. For example, see Virginia Richardson's essay in this volume (Chapter Thirteen) and note the question of whether education is a discipline or a field.

DOCTORAL EDUCATION
IN EDUCATION

EDUCATION IS A SPRAWLING FIELD of study, broad reaching and multi-disciplinary. The study of education ranges from the administration and supervision of educational organizations to the theory of individual learning. Education draws on many disciplines and is organized into many specialties. Practice-oriented areas such as educational administration and leadership, curriculum and instruction, and educational policy form a relatively large portion of the field. Research-oriented areas include educational psychology and social and philosophical foundations. It is a very large field: in the United States, about 10 percent of all bachelor's degrees, 25 percent of all master's degrees, and 15 percent of all doctorates awarded annually are in the field of education.

With these numbers, it is not surprising that education programs are usually housed in their own college or school. But many of these programs do not offer a doctorate. They focus on teacher education and training at the bachelor's and master's level. Currently, about 200 universities in the United States offer the doctoral degree in education. Each year, they award a total of about 7,000 doctorates—approximately 2,100 in educational administration and leadership, 1,000 in the "teaching fields" such as math education, literacy, and physical education, 800 in curriculum and instruction, 400 in the study of higher education, and 300 in educational psychology.

The feminization of the field is an important trend. Although most bachelor's degrees in education have always been awarded to women, the doctorate in education was a male domain. In the last thirty years, this has changed dramatically. By the early 1980s, the number of women exceeded men, and in 2003, two-thirds of education doctorates were awarded to women—a higher proportion than in any field except psychology.

Although two-thirds of education doctoral recipients are white, the field also has the largest number and largest percentage of minority doctoral recipients among all doctorates awarded. Nearly half of all African American Ph.D. recipients are in education. Faculties in schools of education (as in all disciplines) have been slower to change in ethnic and gender composition, which may create obstacles to effective communication and mentoring. Fewer than 10 percent of doctoral students are international, often clustering in programs with which their home country has a formal relationship.

Education doctoral candidates have often worked as teachers before pursuing the doctorate, so doctoral work often comes at the middle, not the start of the student's career. Consequently, doctoral students in schools of education are older than in other fields; the median age at receipt of doctorate is forty-four years. Little data about career paths after the doctorate are available, as no comprehensive study of doctoral education in education has been conducted since the 1960s. It is assumed that most recipients of the doctorate return to or remain in their prior workplace, perhaps with an increase in salary or responsibility, rather than seek an academic position.

Education students differ from their arts-and-sciences colleagues in three other important ways. First, a large number of students self-finance their educations or are funded by their employers. Education does not offer many teaching or research assistantships, nor would these low-paying positions be attractive to students. Instead (and this is the second way education programs differ from arts-and-sciences doctorates), most doctoral students attend graduate school part-time, while continuing to work. In response, schools of education often schedule classes at night or on weekends. As a result, students face a relatively long registered time-to-degree—an average of 8.3 years (which is, however, still shorter than in the humanities).

The last difference is that only one-third of the students starting a doctorate in education have an undergraduate degree in education. Faculty can make no assumptions that students share a common core of knowledge upon entry (as they can in chemistry). The diversity of backgrounds can provide richer experiences but challenge departments to provide a shared core of knowledge. For most students, the return to school is a deliberate move guided by their professional goals. For many, "researcher" is not, nor will it ever be, at the center of their professional identity, which presents another challenge to faculty, for whom research is usually an integral part of their professional identity.

Education has struggled to strike a balance between the *practice* of education and *research* in education. Partly as a reflection of this research-practice dialectic, education (like medicine) has accommodated two terminal degrees—the Ph.D. and Ed.D. The literature is rife with studies comparing the Ph.D. and Ed.D. and arguing for either a sharper distinction between the two degrees or the elimination of one of them. In theory, the two degrees are expected to occupy two overlapping, yet distinct, niches. The Ed.D. aims to prepare managerial and administrative leadership in education. Its focus is on preparing practitioners who can use the existing knowledge about the field to solve complex educational problems. A Ph.D. in education is a traditional academic degree that aims to prepare researchers, college teachers, and scholars in education. The research questions, techniques, and thesis requirements for the Ph.D. are relatively more theoretical and similar to other academic disciplines than the Ed.D. In practice, however, the requirements for the two programs are strikingly similar, and the Ed.D. is often perceived as a "Ph.D.-lite."

Doctoral studies in education primarily take place in the classroom: several years of course work, followed by the dissertation. Although most learning happens in the classroom, there is no shared, core body of knowledge or courses for most doctoral students in education. This may be because there is no single, national disciplinary society for education. It may also be a result of the tensions between theory and practice and is surely, in some measure, because of the fragmentation and division between fields—educational psychology, mathematics education, or educational leadership. Instead of common core courses, each subdiscipline and program within the school of education defines its own curriculum and requirements. Often the only courses that are taught to all doctoral students are methodology or inquiry courses, and even these are subject to dispute, given the wide range of methodologies used in the various specialties.

Typically, students define a research project in consultation with their adviser and carry it out relatively independently, often in their work setting. Research methods are learned in class, not while apprenticed to a research project. Dissertations usually follow a "five chapter model": problem, literature review, methods, findings, and analysis. After the oral defense, few dissertations are ever published. Critics perceive a lack of quality in educational research, especially in dissertations.

In "Stewards of a Field, Stewards of an Enterprise: The Doctorate in Education," Virginia Richardson addresses the unique conundrum of education:

it is both an enterprise and a field of study. She also considers whether or not education is a discipline. She offers a table describing elements of scholarly inquiry that students should master and the associated knowledge, skills, and habits of mind. (A table like this—disaggregating outcomes into specific skills and abilities—is a tool familiar to educators.) This chart is adaptable to other fields, although the form may not be familiar.

In "Toward a Future as Rich as Our Past," David Berliner tackles a case of the particular: the field of educational psychology. His history is illuminating and provides context for five proposed charges for doctoral education. He also analyzes four "things we do, but could do better" (a formulation any field could borrow). Although he speaks to educational psychology, his proposals could be applied to the Ph.D. in any area of education.

———— o ————

BIBLIOGRAPHY

Information and specific data were derived from the following sources:

Anderson, D. G. "Differentiation of the Ed.D. and Ph.D. in Education." *Journal of Teacher Education,* 1983, *34*(3), 55–58.

Brown, L. D., and Slater, J. M. *The Doctorate in Education.* Vol. 1: *The Graduates.* Washington, D.C.: American Association of Colleges for Teacher Education, 1960.

Carpenter, D. S. "On-Going Dialogue: Degrees of Difference: The Ph.D. and the Ed.D." *Review of Higher Education,* 1987, *10*(3), 281–286.

Clifford, G. J., and Guthrie, J. W. *Ed School: A Brief for Professional Education.* Chicago and London: University of Chicago Press, 1988.

Cremin, L. A. *The Education of the Educating Professions.* Washington, D.C.: American Association of Colleges for Teacher Education, 1978.

Deering, T. E. "Eliminating the Doctor of Education Degree: It's the Right Thing to Do." *Educational Forum,* 1998, *62*(3), 243–248.

Dill, D. D., and Morrison, J. L. "Ed.D. and Ph.D. Research Training in the Field of Higher Education: A Survey and a Proposal." *The Review of Higher Education,* 1985, *8*(2), 169–186.

Hoffer, T., and others. *Doctorate Recipients from United States Universities: Summary Report 2003.* Chicago: National Opinion Research Center, 2004.

Holmes Group. *Tomorrow's Schools of Education: A Report of the Holmes Group.* East Lansing, Mich.: Holmes Group Inc., 1995.

Labaree, D. F. *The Trouble with Ed Schools.* New Haven: Yale University Press, 2004.

McClintock, R. *Homeless in the House of Intellect: Formative Justice and Education as an Academic Study.* New York: Laboratory for Liberal Learning, 2005.

Metz, M. H. "Intellectual Border Crossing in Graduate Education: A Report from the Field." *Educational Researcher,* 2001, *30*(5), 12–18.

Neumann, A., Pallas, A., and others. "Preparing Education Practitioners to Practice Education Research." In E. C. Lagemann and L. S. Shulman (eds.), *Issues in Education Research: Problems and Possibilities.* San Francisco: Jossey-Bass, 1999.

Osguthorpe, R. T., and Wong, M. J. "The Ph.D. Versus the Ed.D.: Time for a Decision." *Innovative Higher Education,* 1993, *18*(1), 47–63.

Pallas, A. M. "Preparing Education Doctoral Students for Epistemological Diversity." *Educational Researcher,* 2001, *30*(5), 6–11.

Schoenfeld, A. H. "The Core, the Canon, and the Development of Research Skills." In E. C. Lagemann and L. S. Shulman (eds.), *Issues in Education Research: Problems and Possibilities.* San Francisco: Jossey-Bass, 1999.

Young, L. J. "Border Crossings and Other Journeys: Re-Envisioning the Doctoral Preparation of Education Researchers." *Educational Researcher,* 2001, *30*(5), 3–5.

13

STEWARDS OF A FIELD, STEWARDS OF AN ENTERPRISE

THE DOCTORATE IN EDUCATION

Virginia Richardson, University of Michigan

WHAT ARE THE ESSENTIAL GOALS AND CHARACTERISTICS of a doctorate in education that is designed to develop persons who are stewards of their field? As described by The Carnegie Foundation for the Advancement of Teaching, stewards are able to generate new knowledge, understand the intellectual history of the field, use the best ideas and practices in current work, and represent that knowledge to others, both within and outside the field. Stewards have a respectful sense of the broader intellectual landscape, including paradigms and questions, and they are able to speak about how their field contributes important understanding to these larger questions. They have a strong sense of obligation to their field and to helping preserve the best while promoting change and improvement. This essay discusses the steward of education and the role of doctoral programs in fostering stewards of education.

There are two doctoral degrees in education—the Ph.D. and the Ed.D. Although I focus on the Ph.D. degree, the overarching frame of this analysis applies to both degrees.

Education as an Enterprise and Field of Study

A fundamental characteristic of education differentiates it from other disciplines, thereby suggesting that the Ph.D. degree might also differ. The term *education* stands for both the study of the field and for the formal enterprise (or system) that is being studied. To understand this dual meaning, consider two definitions of *education*. The first is a standard definition from the *American Heritage Dictionary:*

> (1) The act or process of educating or being educated; (2) The knowledge or skill obtained or developed by a learning process; (3) A program of instruction of a specified kind or level; (4) The field of study that is concerned with the pedagogy of teaching and learning; (5) An instructive or enlightening experience (1996, p. 586).

The second is from the essay on "Education" by William Frankena in the four-volume *Dictionary of the History of Ideas:*

> (1) As the activity of the one doing the educating, the act or process of educating or teaching engaged in by the educator; (2) the process or experience of being educated or learning that goes on in the one being educated; (3) as the result produced in the one being educated by the double process of educating and being educated; (4) as the discipline or study of education (1973, p. 72).

From these definitions, it is clear that education can be viewed either as a field of study and, therefore, a contemplative search for theory and science or an enterprise that consists of the various systems of education and, therefore, primarily an activity. Viewed through the functions of stewardship of education, the enterprise and its study are linked. A major purpose of education as a field of study is to help to understand and improve the enterprise. As an activity, the education enterprise is highly complex. Its immediate purposes relate to the intellectual, moral, social, and physical development of our students, and it functions, socially and civically, to maintain and improve a democratic way of life. Such complexity, with competing goals and values, requires strong analytical thinking and understanding so that the system is operated in a thoughtful and effective way. The Ph.D. program should be designed to prepare scholars who can provide normative as well as epistemic theory, research, and analysis in ways that place discussions about the enterprise in frameworks that are both analytical and morally defensible. The Ph.D. degree, then, should denote a steward who is responsible for both the field of educational study and the education enterprise.

Education as a Discipline

There are serious questions as to whether education can be called a discipline, and there are three schools of thought on the subject. The first suggests that since education borrows from and combines with other, more traditional, disciplines and often focuses on practice, it should not be called a discipline but a field of study or a second-level discipline. Using the same rationale (that many areas within education bring together a traditional discipline within an educational frame), the second school of thought calls education an "inter-discipline." And because education has its own set of problems, questions, knowledge bases, and approaches to inquiry, a third school of thought pushes for accepting education as a discipline.

One reason for the lack of consensus around the use of "discipline" for education is that, as a field of study, education may be seen as one of a set of academic program anomalies in which the enterprise itself is primarily an activity. Within universities, this includes schools and colleges that are considered "professional schools": engineering, nursing, medicine, law, social work. We could say that education, as a professional school, is a second-level discipline in that it focuses on a unique activity—education— by borrowing, considerably, from many traditional disciplines.

Looking specifically at areas in education that bring together a traditional discipline and education, we could use the term *inter-discipline* to describe education. Considering education as an inter-discipline suggests that the work of scholarship in education should focus on bringing together disciplines as "a means of solving problems and answering questions that cannot be satisfactorily addressed using single methods or approaches" (Klein, 1990, p. 196). However, there is often confusion (or at least several disparate approaches) within these inter-disciplines as to the purpose of scholarship that goes on within them. A number of years ago, Fenstermacher and I examined these different notions in the case of educational psychology by examining two quite different purposes in the subfield:

1) . . . educational psychology has as its primary mission contributions to the discipline of psychology through the thoughtful and creative study of education.

2) The primary mission of educational psychology is to advance our understanding of education through the application of the discipline to educational problems (Fenstermacher and Richardson, 1994, p. 53).

These differences in purposes of the disciplines and education areas have undoubtedly kept education from being viewed as a discipline. At this point, however, it would be well worth examining education as a discipline. Not only does education have its own set of problems, questions, knowledge bases, and approaches to inquiry but that which is borrowed from other disciplines often becomes transformed within the study of education. If education does become accepted as a discipline, however, it exists because of and in relationship to educational practice; the purposes of maintaining the best and allowing change to lead to improvement must always be kept in mind.

Ph.D.'s as Stewards of Both a Field of Study and an Enterprise

Because education is both a field of study and a set of formal and structured actions, stewards of education have several responsibilities. As stewards of the field of study, Ph.D.'s in education generate new knowledge, understand the intellectual history of the field, use the best ideas and practices in current work, and represent that knowledge to others both within and outside the field. Stewards have a respectful sense of the broader intellectual landscape, including paradigms and questions, and are able to speak about how the field can contribute important understanding to these larger questions. They have a sense of obligation to their field in helping preserve the best while promoting change and improvement.

As they work within the enterprise of education, stewards of education have duties related to communicating and engaging in decisions concerning the practice of education. In particular, they communicate normative as well as epistemic theory, research, and analyses to very different audiences so that decisions about the enterprise are made within strong analytical and morally defensible frameworks.

As I discuss in the following sections, preparing such stewards through Ph.D. programs in education requires attention to the three forms of knowledge and understanding—formal knowledge, practical knowledge, and beliefs and misconceptions—that together define the practice of being a steward. For example, in becoming stewards of the enterprise of education, it is useful for Ph.D. students to develop strong communication skills. But in order to do so, students need both to understand the nature of education policy development and educational practice and to generate policy arguments using formal knowledge, based on research and scholarship. In addition, Ph.D. students should understand how beliefs and misconceptions based on under-examined experience and the general public's various beliefs about education, in combination with current policy imperatives and the structure and requirements of public positions, lead policymakers to define educational problems and focus on solutions in certain ways. Ph.D. students need to develop and present policy analyses within strong analytic and deep normative theories of the educational systems.

Forms of Knowing and Believing in Education

What are the particular forms of knowledge, understanding, and belief that should be of concern, in different ways, to stewards of education and, therefore, significant elements of the Ph.D. degree? I shall provide a frame for the types of knowledge addressed in Ph.D. programs.

The first form of knowing I call *formal knowledge* and understanding. It is this variety of knowledge that we think of almost exclusively when we consider the Ph.D. I call the second form of knowing *practical knowledge;* the third is *beliefs and misconceptions.*

It is important to differentiate between knowledge and understanding. Without getting deeply into definitions of these terms, I will point out that I am using a philosophical rather than psychological definition of knowledge, particularly in my discussion of formal knowledge.

Understanding also means many different things to many different people. Lee Shulman's definition appears to be the one that is quite appropriate to considerations of Ph.D. programs:

> Understanding is the category we spend most of our time as educators worrying about. . . . It includes knowledge, and it includes the ability to restate in one's own words the ideas learned from others. . . . In contrast to knowledge and information, understanding connotes a form of ownership (2002, p. 40).

Formal Knowledge

Formal knowledge requires epistemic warrant that is gained within a discourse community. A discourse community defines the field, conducts the research within it, determines criteria for validity, and helps to mentor and support developing stewards. In considering a doctoral program in education, it is important to understand the organization of formal knowledge within the field.

One way to think about the organization of formal knowledge in the field of education is by considering the organization of departments, units, and programs within universities, and within colleges and schools of education. The journals generally match the way departments and programs are organized, as do the positions that Ph.D.'s hold in institutions. For purposes of considering the Ph.D. degree, formal knowledge fields in education that translate into Ph.D. programs or subprograms may be divided into the three categories I describe next.

1. *Traditional disciplines and education*: This category includes areas that bring education together with a traditional discipline. These areas include mathematics education, science education, history education, English education, and the foundations areas of philosophy, sociology, history, anthropology of education, and educational psychology. I place two additional areas—social studies education and literacy education—in this category, although both include several traditional disciplines within their study. I would also place the research methodology and assessment areas within this category because of their strong relationship to statistics (quantitative) and to anthropology and sociology (qualitative).

2. *Special-interest fields*: This category includes programs that have developed a significant scholarly literature and draw on the disciplinary programs but focus on an area of educational practice or a particular student grouping. These areas include policy studies, teacher education, curriculum, educational administration, higher education, special education, and early childhood education.

3. *Cross-disciplinary programs*: These programs are designed to traverse the traditional foundational disciplines and include such programs as social, cultural, and critical studies in education. Over time, should these programs become well-established fields of study, they will be called special-interest fields or, eventually, traditional disciplines.

Ph.D. students major in one of these areas and often minor in another—or sometimes minor in a traditional discipline across campus. As suggested by the description of the organization of education knowledge, the fields do not stand on their own, are often difficult to differentiate from other fields, and do not stand still. For example, it is possible to focus on teacher education within any of the particular education/discipline areas while still seeing oneself as a member of the larger education/discipline area. It is also possible for a student majoring in teacher education to focus on an education/discipline area such as English education.

It is important, then, for the Ph.D. students to acquire a sense of the whole and develop conceptual understandings of the ways these various pieces might fit together in their programs. In order to be stewards of the discipline (in the sense of the word meaning "the enterprise"), they will require more understanding of the system than their own specialized field of study will provide. Further, having an expansive appreciation of the field will enable the students to understand the place of their field within a broader intellectual context, to work in the future to bring together different fields, and to reconceptualize their own area of the field. Stewards of the field not only participate in shaping formal knowledge and understanding; they also need to have a meta-awareness of the movements, goals, and potential future of the field, so that eventually they can both provide scholarly leadership and help to mentor new Ph.D.'s as stewards of the field.

Practical Knowledge

Much of what goes on in a steward's life during and after obtaining a Ph.D. is enhanced by practical knowledge that is systematically subjected to critical reflection. Practical knowledge is gained through experience in practice and may also be thought of as "knowing how" (Ryle, 1949). Practical knowledge is helpful in many of the activities in which a Ph.D. student will eventually engage, such as teaching, engaging in certain research-related activities such as submitting a proposal for funding and managing a research program, and operating as an academic within a department and college. The development of practical knowledge can and should begin during the time a student is in a Ph.D. program and, undoubtedly, does. However, as many mentors eventually find out, this acquisition often does not happen. In conversations with new Ph.D.'s out in the field, it can be quite shocking to discover how little practical knowledge they have picked up in their four or more years in the program.

Two aspects of this issue need to be considered in developing a Ph.D. program. The first is that students will develop a limited amount of practical knowledge during the time they are in a Ph.D. program. Thus it is necessary to understand the importance of the mentoring process for new faculty members; this mentoring is essential in supporting and adjusting the development of the new Ph.D.'s practical knowledge on the job. The second is that developing students' practical knowledge requires attention within the curriculum, broadly defined. That is, it is not enough for a Ph.D. student simply to spend a number of years within a functioning academic unit; they are students and approach their experience as such. Thus certain learning opportunities that focus on practical knowledge should be consciously structured into the Ph.D. program.

Beliefs and Misconceptions

We have a unique situation in education. Nearly everyone has been a student, and on the basis of that experience, many claim knowledge of the field, perhaps even consider themselves to be experts. They act on unexamined beliefs and understandings that they gained simply through extensive experience as students in the educational system. Their beliefs are deep, strong, and often incorrect, or at least misguided and unworkable. Unfortunately, these beliefs often drive policy and practice in education.

The Ph.D. students likewise enter their programs in education with strong beliefs about the nature of teaching and schooling, often based on their experience in the educational system as students, teachers, and administrators. These experiences are very helpful in the Ph.D. program in bringing constructs and theories together with practice. However, these experiences have often been underexamined, leading to beliefs that have little warrant. For example, consider that educators might enter Ph.D. programs with concerns about the nature of research and its use in education. Although the students might have an interest in engaging in the scholarship of education, because of certain beliefs they might also be ambivalent about the purpose and use of research; they might even consider it worthless. Because of the beliefs and misconceptions that students bring with them, it is important that students have opportunities throughout the time they are involved in the Ph.D. program to explore their beliefs and reflect on alternative conceptions to their sense of both educational scholarship and educational systems.

In exploring their own beliefs, the Ph.D. students should become more cognizant of how unwarranted beliefs and misconceptions develop in others and what it might take for others to change these beliefs. It is this process of examining beliefs, in combination with the formal knowledge they have acquired in the program, that will place stewards in a position to work with educators, policymakers, legislators, and the public to raise the level of analysis and understanding about education. This is a critical element of their role in the stewardship of the enterprise.

Therefore, Ph.D. programs need to help students not only examine their own beliefs but also understand how to help others recognize and, possibly, change theirs. Ph.D. students should also become acquainted with issues of policy, policymaking, and implementation (formal knowledge), and they should learn to communicate (practical knowledge) with those who are passionate about the improvement of education but have little understanding of the complexities of the system and the potential for reform.

Epistemologies and Methodologies

Education shares with other fields in the social sciences and many liberal arts considerable turbulence around questions of research methods and approaches. Postmodernism raises questions that jar the very foundations of our research understandings. These questions concern the nature of knowledge, who owns it, who produces it, and how it may be used. Cognitive science, constructivist learning theories, and sociocultural approaches have strongly affected what we choose to examine, how we examine it, and the very fabric of the education system.

Within education, the tensions between qualitative and quantitative methodology died down for a while, but they are again strongly present. These tensions, however, are playing out in a different arena: Washington, D.C. There has been a strong policy initiative in Washington to bring particular medical research design models to play in education, particularly, randomized experiments. In fact, there is an effort under way to require such models within federal funding for research, for a while, at least. There are also expressed concerns about the quality of qualitative studies, and there is much discussion related to criteria for their assessment. Although there may have been subtle political involvement in educational research methodology in the past, it is now no longer hidden.

The question of how the politicization of research methodology should or will affect Ph.D. programs is critical. In the recent past, students were expected to become bi- (or tri-) methodological, with strong and deep knowledge and skills in at least one approach. The rationale for this approach is that students would leave their Ph.D. programs equipped with a set of methodological skills and understandings that would allow them to immediately participate in quality educational research. However, because the students would also have an understanding and some skills in other approaches, they would understand in some depth research that employs these other methods and be prepared to conduct mixed-methods studies.

I suggest that the goal of developing depth in one methodological approach and breadth in several others is still viable and desired, although certainly there will be more emphasis placed on randomized experimentation. But perhaps more important, an emphasis within the Ph.D. program should be placed on the benefits and limitations of the various methodologies being introduced to the students in terms of the nature and potential use of the knowledge being generated, ethical issues involved in a particular methodology, and the criteria that should be used in judging the quality of the work within the particular methodology. The Ph.D. student should also become aware of the dangers of methodological hegemony, particularly when it emanates from the federal government, and the ways in which academics' efforts often help to exacerbate such situations.

The Ph.D. Program

The steward of the education discipline, then, is someone who has responsibility toward both the field of study and the enterprise of education. Ph.D. students who are to become stewards of the field will need to develop expertise in normative, epistemic, and rhetorical analysis, research, and representation. They will need depth and breadth, as well as thorough involvement in a disciplinary field. As I did earlier, I will use the forms of knowing, understanding, and believing—formal knowledge, practical knowledge, and beliefs and misconceptions—in describing what the Ph.D. program may include.

Formal Knowledge

One way of considering the nature of what needs to be learned in relation to formal knowledge is to examine a model developed by David Cohen and Deborah Ball for a proposal from the School of Education of the University of Michigan to the Spencer Foundation. A table derived from the one they prepared to explain the model appears in Table 13.1.

The "Crucial Elements of Scholarly Inquiry and Student Learning" outlines the outcomes of learning the practice of research, the knowledge and skills students develop in their Ph.D. programs, and the habits of mind that the students need to develop. (Note that some of the habits of mind or kinds of understanding and skill appear in more than one place. For example, "seeking and using criticism" and "connecting one's work to that of others" appears several places.)

It is interesting to note that only one of the outcomes groups relates to substantive knowledge of the field. Very often, substantive knowledge outcomes and research methodology skills (appearing in rows five and six of the table) define a particular Ph.D. program and its courses. The four additional outcomes relate to a quite different sense of the field. "Think theoretically and critically," for example, goes well beyond gaining substantive knowledge of the field. This outcome is a type of meta-awareness of the field in relation to others, and it asks students to understand deeply the nature of different perspectives on the topic. The last group of outcomes—"communicate with various audiences about research"—brings in both roles associated with stewards of education: conducting scholarship in the field and maintaining and improving the enterprise.

Table 13.1. Crucial Elements of Scholarly Inquiry and Student Learning.

Outcomes of Learning the Practice of Research	What Students Need to Know and Be Able to Do	Habits of Mind Students Need to Develop
1. Have substantive knowledge of the field.	• Know theories, analytical frameworks, empirical results, and ideas of the fields central to one's work. • Understand major controversies or theoretical positions. • Have a historical perspective on a field and its evolution. • Understand the nature of particular claims and theories.	• Be curious about how others have thought about an area. • Read partly to get more substance and partly to identify the growth points of a field. • Keep up with developments in the field in and outside one's own area.
2. Think theoretically and critically.	• Distinguish conceptual and analytical from empirical issues. • Understand different theoretical perspectives and what each illuminates and obscures. • Read broadly in other fields, seeking connections that are not at first obvious. • Compare across traditions of research and allied philosophical traditions.	• Have humility to respect prior work, courage to question accumulated wisdom. • Be aware of one's own assumptions and have the disposition to examine those critically. • Discriminate between knowledge and belief. • Be willing to change one's mind based on argument or evidence.
3. Frame fruitful research problems.	• Understand issues in the field (Where are gaps or unexamined issues? Where is controversy? Where is something that needs to be challenged?). • Read literature in related fields. • Articulate researchable questions. • Formulate hypotheses and hunches. • Connect one's work to that of others. • Identify critical elements of a problem.	• Have passion for the ideas but dispassion for scholarship (genuine curiosity or desire to develop a careful, analytical contribution to a problem). • Be willing to take intellectual risks.

Table 13.1. Crucial Elements of Scholarly Inquiry and Student Learning, Cont'd.

Outcomes of Learning the Practice of Research	What Students Need to Know and Be Able to Do	Habits of Mind Students Need to Develop
4. See research as socially situated.	• Be aware of different people or groups who have worked on related issues. • Understand the history of one's research tradition or field. • Connect the purposes of one's work to the work of others (for example, challenging, adding, shifting, refuting). • Keep up with the literature. • Ground questions in practice as well as theory.	• See criticism as contributing to the quality of one's work. • View one's work as a contribution to an ongoing conversation. • Recognize and use local knowledge in the inquiry process. • Be sensitive to different discourses in the design, conduct, and communication of research in different settings and with different audiences. • See research as part of an ongoing conversation.
5. Design research (join researchable problems to appropriate methods of inquiry).	• Look for different sources of data. • Match research questions to kinds of information needed. • Know different methodological traditions and orientations. • Understand central conceptual constructs (for example, dependent and independent variables, change, comparison). • Know and use different methods of data collection. • Conceptually map aspects of the inquiry, developing methods to address particular aspects of the map. • Create frameworks.	• Have intellectual honesty and integrity, respecting settings and participants in research and setting up research to investigate, not merely support, belief. • Seek and use criticism. • Choose methods without partisan loyalties, matched instead to intention and question. • Seek methods, designs, instruments from others' work.

Table 13.1. Crucial Elements of Scholarly Inquiry and Student Learning, Cont'd.

Outcomes of Learning the Practice of Research	What Students Need to Know and Be Able to Do	Habits of Mind Students Need to Develop
6. Collect and analyze data.	• Be proficient in the use of data analysis. • Be familiar with standards of evidence. • Know sources of ideas and uses of literature. • Write. • Use different methods of data analysis.	• Be open to surprise. • Look for disconfirming evidence, considering alternative interpretations or explanations. • Seek and use criticism. • Use the literature to help develop explanations; balance such use, neither directly importing others' ideas nor using unnecessary invention.
7. Communicate with various audiences about research.	• Address different audiences. • Use different genres and forms (for example, essay, empirical article, case study, conceptual analysis). • Know what constitutes "findings" or "products" of particular programs of research. • Understand the kinds of claims being made and what are effective means of presentation and provision of evidence. • Write well, generally and technically. • Persuade and argue. • Structure arguments. • Write precisely and plainly. • Participate in oral presentation and debate. • Examine the ways in which the research activity is a form of dissemination.	• Seek opportunities to present draft analyses or arguments and revise as a result of listeners' reactions. • See writing as part of interpretive and analytical work, not merely "writing up" research. • Seek and use criticism. • Expect the revision that writing and rewriting entail. • Have respect for language; use caution in introducing new terms; take care in creating needed ones. • Be sensitive to different discourses in the design, conduct, and communication of research in different settings and with different audiences. • See research as contributing to an ongoing conversation.

Source: *Derived from a table created by Cohen and Ball (Miskel, 1996).*

The "Crucial Elements" table places a heavy emphasis on knowing theories and understanding the differences between conceptual and analytical frameworks and empirical ones. Although the table does not differentiate between descriptive and normative theories, it is clear that both are acknowledged; understanding descriptive and normative theories and skills in developing both forms are important outcomes. As stewards of the educational enterprise, Ph.D. students will have to develop a sense of "shoulds" and receive the education necessary to analyze and develop such theories. In addition, within their empirical research, they should emphasize theoretical framing and development.

One can also observe in the table a strong call for moral and intellectual virtues to be fostered in the Ph.D. students. These include such virtues as humility, intellectual honesty and integrity, curiosity, and the ability to choose methods without partisan loyalties.

Given the nature of the interdisciplinarity of Ph.D. programs, the "Crucial Elements" table could be used as a guide in developing programs. For example, if programs were to follow this model, the students focusing in the three organizational areas described—traditional disciplines/education, special-interest, and cross-disciplinary—would probably have quite different required courses and experiences. A student in the traditional disciplines/education might be required to take a minor or cognates across campus in the discipline. This would not necessarily be the case in a special-interest field such as teacher education, where the cognates or minors could be taken within the School of Education. However, for those students in a cross-disciplinary field, the number of required cognates or the nature of the minor would be quite different. Nonetheless, the "Crucial Elements" table is useful for all three areas of education because it describes skills, knowledge, and habits of mind that could be acquired within the three corresponding types of Ph.D. programs. This model also allows a faculty to assess needed courses and experiences on the basis of outcomes needs.

The "Crucial Elements" table focuses on the outcomes of learning; it does not make a statement about the process of achieving these goals. Thus these outcomes are not meant to map onto specific courses, although "research design" could, in fact, be a required course taken by all students. Developing a set of outcomes such as this would provide a strong foundation for a new or revised Ph.D. program or for the assessment of an existing one. It would be important for a faculty, as a collective, to develop and agree on the nature of the outcomes of its Ph.D. program. With such a tool, it would be possible to determine what and when students are learning these elements in the program as a whole and to determine what they might be learning in individual classes.

Translating a set of desired outcomes such as those in the "Crucial Elements" table into a Ph.D. program is difficult and requires experiment. An outcomes box on the table does not translate into a course; these outcomes are learned across the curriculum. Therefore, I recommend two approaches to using such a table in developing and assessing learning outcomes:

1. *Working within a faculty on an ongoing basis to develop a sense of the courses and experiences that provide opportunities to master the various learning outcomes.* For example, when faculty develop new courses or consider changes in the curriculum, the learning outcomes table should be a central consideration.

2. *Working with the individual students who engage in self-assessment around the learning outcomes.* For example, Ph.D. students could use the table to assess their learning in a yearly process in which students provide a written assessment of their progress, using the table as one of the measures. These would be reviewed by the adviser and possibly the program faculty to provide some guidance for the next year's opportunities for the student.

The outcomes called for in the "Crucial Elements" table require a number of approaches to learning, including standard seminars, research internships, occasions for tutoring and mentoring, opportunities and support for study groups, educative "hurdles" such as preliminary exams, support for attendance at major conferences, and involvement in research programs. The issues of type, quantity, and timing of these various approaches need to be worked out within a faculty with a strong orientation toward program assessment and improvement.

Practical Knowledge

All practical knowledge that one should learn as an academic cannot be crammed into the Ph.D. program. It is neither realistic nor possible, particularly given that practical knowledge must be acquired through experience. But programs could do a better job of helping students develop some practical knowledge. For example, students' opportunities to learn practical knowledge are often provided on an ad hoc basis; it would be helpful if, instead, a certain number of areas of practical knowledge be explicitly attended to in Ph.D. programs. Several candidates are as follows:

- *Teaching.* Most graduates of Ph.D. programs in education take academic positions that include teaching undergraduate and graduate courses. Recently, more attention is being paid to this role, and Ph.D. students could receive better preparation in teaching and the scholarship of teaching as well. Internships are one way of preparing students, but these should stress critical reflection and not be designed to lead toward imitation. Programs could offer additional courses that inquire into the scholarship of pedagogy in a particular field of study within education.

- *Research proposals and management.* Many Ph.D. students work within research projects. The topics that are addressed within these research projects should be more systematic and begin to provide students with organized experiences in writing proposals and managing projects.

- *Writing for publication.* It is useful for students to understand the nature of the various publications in their field from the standpoint of the written genres that are acceptable. It would also be helpful if students could receive formal support in writing for conferences and publication.

- *Networking.* It is very important for students to begin to get to know academics in their field of interest. This might involve preparing students to attend conferences, meeting well-known figures in their field, and learning norms for communicating with these people.

Beliefs and Misconceptions

Students could have opportunities to explore their beliefs about various aspects of educational systems, teaching, learning, equity, and other topics of significance in the field of study. It is also important to help students who have spent considerable time in the schools as teachers or administrators to learn how to move to a different level of analytic scholarship than the experiential level with which they enter the program.

This exploration could take place in a number of different forums, both formal and informal. For example, within a given program, there could be a professional seminar that helps students examine their beliefs and develop analytic skills to question and examine them. It would also be helpful if the students developed a meta-awareness of the process of examining beliefs so that, in turn, they could learn how to approach others in such an examination. This knowledge would then inform their development of practical knowledge around communication with policymakers, practitioners, and the public about education.

The Task Ahead

It is important to prepare Ph.D. students in education as stewards of the discipline who have the three forms of knowledge and understanding, as represented in skills, knowledge, and habits of mind described in the "Crucial Elements" table. The faculty who develop and manage Ph.D. programs have in front of them a challenging task of socialization and education in preparing stewards. It will require goal setting, analysis, assessment, and constant vigilance on the part of a Ph.D. faculty if we are to develop Ph.D. graduates who are able both to conduct important, high-quality, useful research on educational practice and issues and provide guidance in improving the education enterprise.

REFERENCES

The American Heritage Dictionary of the English Language. (3rd ed.) Boston: Houghton Mifflin, 1996.

Fenstermacher, G., and Richardson, V. "Promoting Confusion in Educational Psychology: How Is It Done?" *Educational Psychology,* 1994, 29(1), 49–55.

Frankena, W. K. "Education." In P. P. Weiner (ed.), *Dictionary of the History of Ideas.* Vol. 2. New York: Scribner, 1973.

Klein, J. T. *Interdisciplinarity: History, Theory and Practice.* Detroit: Wayne State University, 1990.

Miskel, C. G. "Meeting the Challenge of Improving Research Education at the Turn of the 21st Century." Proposal to the Spencer Foundation. Ann Arbor, Mich.: University of Michigan School of Education, 1996.

Ryle, G. *The Concept of Mind.* London: Hutchinson's University Library, 1949.

Shulman, L. "Making Differences: A Table of Learning." *Change,* 2002, 34(6), 36–44.

14

TOWARD A FUTURE
AS RICH AS OUR PAST

David C. Berliner, Arizona State University

FROM WILLIAM JAMES at the end of the nineteenth century and by means of E. L. Thorndike's influence during much of the twentieth century, educational psychologists dominated research in education. We won the battle for "rigorous scientific thinking" in education, over the objections of philosophers and educationists, around 1915 (Berliner, 1993). After that, educational psychologists became the "scientists" in America's schools of education.

But as the twentieth century closed, the influence of educational psychology waned. Educational psychology had trained so many people in other subjects to do rigorous research that scholars in these areas emerged, and thus the special role of educational psychologists was diminished. Further, in the latter part of the twentieth century, scholars in other social science fields turned their attention to educational phenomena. As anthropologists and sociologists produced more and more scholarship on education, educational psychology was no longer the only social science represented in schools of education. In addition, as the twentieth century ended, we saw a need for less research that was "relevant" and more research that was directly useful to the educational community. Yet because educational psychology saw itself more as a discipline than as a profession, it did not always concern itself with issues of practice; such issues, particularly classroom teaching and learning, became the focus of national attention.

It is time to revitalize educational psychology. Although we can easily defend the importance of psychological perspectives on education (it is a discipline with a natural relationship to education), educational psychology's epistemology, methods, domains of interest, and ways of interacting with teachers and other scholars are all in need of an examination, perhaps a modernization. It is time that we explore educational psychology's role as a profession as well. As I explain in this essay, we can start modernizing educational psychology by redesigning our doctoral programs.

The Evolution of Educational Psychology

As with Scrooge, apparitions of educational psychology past and present become the necessary elements for determining possible futures for doctoral training of educational psychologists in the twenty-first century. To be a steward of the field requires understanding of how that field started and what it has become, so that the future of the field is both faithful to its origins and appropriate for its times. It is particularly important to understand the history of educational psychology, because in some ways the field has been so successful that many of the territories that once were its alone to study in a rigorous manner—teaching mathematics, studying reading processes and comprehension, using assessment in classrooms, working in groups in social studies—have been re-colonized by the indigenous peoples of those territories: subject-matter specialists in mathematics, reading, and social studies.

The success of traditional educational psychology, tied closely as it was to scientific psychology, is evident also in the current desire by federal policymakers to promote only "scientific research in education." From its inception, that was the singular goal of educational psychology. Although the goal of the discipline has never been contested, heated arguments about what it means to do "scientific research" continue. Those arguments first appeared among our founders, originally between Dewey and James on one side and Thorndike on the other, and continue unabated today (for example, Barone, 2001; Berliner, 2002; Mayer, 2001; Shavelson and Towne, 2002).

The Past

Broadly speaking, the ghost of educational psychology past is still with us when educational psychology is housed in departments of psychology or when it lives in schools of education but is divorced from the problems of teacher education and the practice of education. In those contexts, educational psychologists often see themselves as linked to and allied with the discipline of psychology. For their professional development, they attend the meetings of the American Psychological Association and conferences on experimental psychology, cognition, and methodology.

The Present

More frequently, and for some time now, educational psychologists have been practicing their profession in schools of education and choosing problems of relevance to teacher education and to classroom teaching and learning. These educational psychologists have allegiance to both the discipline of psychology and the field of education. For professional development, they rely on the American Educational Research Association and conferences in subject-matter areas such as reading, science, and mathematics education, as well as teacher education.

Relevant research, however, is not always the same as *appropriate, generalizable,* or *usable* research. The latter kinds of research more often occur in natural school settings. An example may help. Across decades, it was clear that Piaget had relevance to education. It seemed obvious to educational psychologists that his brilliant ideas had to be shared, so Piaget was taught in every textbook in the field. But Piaget had virtually nothing to say about instruction and little to say about education (Groen, 1978). To be useful, other research had to occur to move from "relevance" to an understanding of Piaget's ideas *in situ.* Unfortunately, educational psychology has a history of remarkably good science in areas such as mnemonics, study skills, map reading, strategy learning, transfer of learning, and motivation, to name only a few. But for many reasons, the impact of these well-crafted and highly relevant studies on classroom teaching and learning has been negligible. The research is not usable, and that state of affairs needs attention.

The Future

For a vision of the future, we might take a look at those who are trying to move the research of educational psychologists from being relevant to issues of practice to being enmeshed in practice; from seeking to simplify complex phenomena by means of studies in simple settings or through experimental design to accepting the complexity of life in schools; from being almost exclusively etic researchers to often being emic researchers; from being handmaidens to those who make policy to being critics of and contributors to policymaking. The ideas about doctoral education that arise from this vision of the future of educational psychology are different from those that emanate from past or present ways of thinking about our field.

Transitions in Thinking

Throughout most of the twentieth century, doctoral education in educational psychology has kept close ties to scientific psychology. This meant a focus on the individual: studying how individuals learn, inquiring about what motivates them, attempting to understand individual differences in both of these domains, and making use of methods for determining causation and correlation. Empirical research—the hallmark of the profession—was frequently done in controlled settings rather than in the contexts of ordinary classrooms or schools. But in the latter third of the twentieth century, many educational psychologists realized that we should have been emphasizing the individual in context. One of the first to give these ideas prominence was Lee Cronbach, who, as an educational psychologist and psychometrician, as well as president of the American Psychological Association, called for the merging of the correlational and the experimental traditions in psychology (Cronbach, 1957). His research into "aptitude-treatment interactions" was a major step in understanding that people bring vastly different aptitudes and in-aptitudes to learning settings. The importance of considering the moderating effects of individual differences (for example, race, class, gender, motivational state, level of anxiety, degree of previous learning) on learning grew exponentially.

An equally important transition in thinking was the understanding that treatments, environments, or contexts were modifiable. With the burgeoning of work on the sociology and anthropology of education, with critical theorists making themselves heard, and with emphasis on the poor performance of particular groups of students in schools, educational psychologists in the latter part of the twentieth century came to understand the power of interpersonal, social, institutional, and economic contexts to shape cognition, volition, and performance. As we saw that contexts moderated aptitudes, context came to the foreground of the research. The boundaries of educational psychology, therefore, had to blur with those of anthropology and sociology (among others) so that the powerful effects of social and cultural contexts could be understood and built into research, neither pushed to the background nor controlled away through experimental designs.

Cronbach (1975) noted that the number and complexity of the interactions between sociocultural influences and individual differences made educational science much harder to do than other sciences. He thought that generalizations in educational psychology would be hard to find and, if found, would swiftly decay. For him, generalizations were much more like working hypotheses, not solid conclusions. He argued, therefore, for an educational psychology that was interested in pinning down the facts of particular classrooms and schools rather than for an educational psychology that was concerned about developing broad scientific generalizations. He argued, as I do, for an educational psychology that attends more to local conditions of practice and uses methodology more appropriate for that task. He cautioned against an educational psychology that seeks only to emulate the physical sciences.

Sociocultural influences on cognition are now well established. Abetted, no doubt, by the enormous increase in diversity in America's schools and the voices of critical theorists raising issues of race, class, and gender, sociocultural thinking in educational psychology has become more prevalent. As we look back, we can see that one noisy shift of paradigms in educational psychology—from behavioral to cognitive psychology—was accompanied by another, much quieter shift in paradigms. The latter shift was from the study of the individual to the study of the individual situated *in,* and bringing a sociocultural history *to,* a context that exerts powerful influences on the thoughts and actions of all those in that context.

Over the last century, the race between E. L. Thorndike and John Dewey for the heart of the discipline was almost won by Thorndike—the experimental psychologist who was not interested in going into schools and who saw individual differences as a bit of an annoyance to the study of learning (Lagemann, 1989; Berliner, 1993). Dewey is now clearly winning the race; this social philosopher's influence has been enhanced by the growth of cognitive psychology and the American discovery of the Russian Lev Vygotsky. Dewey (1899), often prescient but ignored, always saw individual differences as a strength in a democracy (its roots for change) and as the basis of interest—the central concept in his theory of motivation. He also pointed out the potential failure of educational psychology if it did not recognize that the teacher lives in a social sphere.

> [H]e [*sic*] is a member and an organ of a social life. His aims are social aims. . . . Whatever he as a teacher effectively does, he does as a person; and he does with and towards persons. His methods, like his aims. . . . are practical, are social, are ethical, are anything you please—save merely psychical. In comparison with this, the material

and the data, the standpoint and the methods of psychology, are abstract. . . . I do not think there is danger of going too far in asserting the social and the teleological nature of the work of the teacher; or in asserting the abstract and partial character of the mechanism into which the psychologist . . . transmutes the play of vital values (Dewey, 1899, p. 117).

As Dewey and others noted, at least two of the factors associated with the failure of educational research in general, and educational psychology in particular, to affect practice have been the failure to take into account the social lives of teachers and students and the use of "sterile" methods of investigation. Cronbach (1975), Kaestle (1993), Lagemann and Shulman (1999), and Lagemann (2000) have described the many contemporary problems of educational research. But these deficiencies can be remedied.

Doctoral Education for the Twenty-First Century

As I said in opening this essay, to modernize our field we could start by making considerable changes in doctoral education, thus giving educational psychologists the tools, perspective, and experience necessary for the discipline to keep pace with the society we serve. We need to improve the methodological training of educational psychologists, provide stronger training in the big ideas of educational psychology, introduce students to the sites where public school students live and learn, offer research internships in complex environments, and develop our students' understanding of educational policy. We should also give special attention to our doctoral students' training in technology, brain research, multicultural education, and subject-matter knowledge.

In the next sections, I describe my ideas for these changes in detail: what they are, why they are important, and what they would look like in operation. I believe that our field would be much improved if, in our doctoral programs, we would simply take the following important steps.

Rethink the Methods Courses

We must wrest control of the methods courses from those with narrow conceptions of methodology. This is an age of proliferating epistemologies, and it is no longer appropriate for educational psychologists to claim methodological purity and superiority without having a deeper knowledge of other forms of scholarship and their methods of inquiry.

It is tempting to say it this way: "Grab them by their methodology and their hearts and minds will follow!" The ways in which a social scientist conceives of teachers, students, and the environments in which they find themselves are strongly influenced by the methods they ordinarily use (Behrens and Smith, 1996). The primary approach of educational psychology to research has been etic—the outsiders' view of the world. But educational researchers have learned over the years that there is reason to also appreciate the emic view—the insiders' view of what is happening in a learning environment. Lest their findings be forever relevant but never useful, educational psychologists need to give attention to the meaning of the research to both the participants in research and those involved in implementing research.

To paraphrase an old adage, if you give people t tests, they are sure to see the world in terms of main effects. They are likely to see the world as a horse race between treatments A and B. But this is too simple a view of the way the educational world works. Missing in most instances of such research are the subjects' feelings, beliefs, understandings, critiques, and suggestions for improvement of the research. Missing also are the many interactions that surely occur. It is quite likely that educational treatments are appropriate for some students and not others, work better in some kinds of subject matter rather than in others, and have different effects on the achievement of some kinds of outcomes and not others. Measuring myriad interactions may not be possible, but the research can find clues to their existence from interviews with participants in the research.

In addition, traditional methodology courses lead educational psychologists to scrutinize the reliability and construct validity of their measurement instruments but often gloss over the ecological, catalytic, and consequential validity of their research. These courses typically emphasize random assignments of subjects and seek a distancing of the researcher from those subjects, thus discouraging the researcher from becoming a participant-observer in the study itself. Yet there are noteworthy issues involved in the linguistic and behavioral transformation of the subject and object of study in educational psychology to that of participant or co-investigator in the research. These issues are not merely unexamined in traditional methodology courses; they are often actively avoided.

The more recent development of causal modeling and hierarchical statistical designs allows for much more of the complexity of schooling to be analyzed statistically, but in no way has this changed the nature of the relationship between the researcher and the subject of that research. Apparently, too many of the instructors of methodology courses in educational psychology fail to have as a goal that their students discover qualitative and humanistic methods, discuss their underlying epistemologies, and learn to appreciate their place in the study of educational phenomena.

Pallas, an educational sociologist, has noticed and responded to the challenge of proliferating epistemologies for doctoral education. He describes how the various ways of knowing (for example, positivism and post-positivism, postmodernism, feminist and critical theory) and the various methods they use to inform themselves (for example, large data sets, narrative, N = 1 studies, participant-observer, symbolic interactionism) each give rise to important questions that doctoral students in education participating in a liberal program of studies should address:

> Is there a single, absolute truth about educational phenomena, or are there multiple truths? (Or is the concept of truth itself so problematic as to be of no value in understanding the world?) Can we count on our senses, or on reason, to distinguish that which is true about the world from that which is false? Are there methods that can lead us close to understanding, or are there inherent indeterminacies in all methods? Epistemologies are central to the production and consumption of educational research. Since epistemologies undergird all phases of the research process, engaging with epistemology is integral to learning the craft of research. Moreover, epistemologies shape scholars' abilities to apprehend and appreciate the research of others. Such an appreciation is a prerequisite for the scholarly conversations that signify a field's collective learning (Pallas, 2001, p. 6).

Pallas notes further that doctoral training is about entering a community of practice, be it educational psychology, mathematics, or chemistry. And that community is often small—composed of a mentor and some related faculty and doctoral students. However, schools of education are never single communities of practice. Their faculties are rarely from a single discipline. (Of course, even in a single discipline communities of practice vary, and faculty may dispute the scientific claims of others. Consider clinical and experimental psychology or cultural and physical anthropology.) Educational psychologists, therefore, will often spend their professional lives among educators and members of other disciplines who also work on the problems of education.

To integrate well, then, educational psychologists need, as a minimum, course work and experiences that make them appreciate and be discerning consumers of other scholars' work. They need course work and experience in what Metz (2001) calls "border crossings." She and her colleagues have some experience running this kind of "multicultural" education course. The design of such experiences for doctoral students requires the involvement of a broad group of scholars from diverse communities of practice. It would require a schoolwide commitment to develop such a catholic form of methodological training, something rarely seen today.

Behrens and Smith (1996) offer some thoughts about what such course work and experiences should emphasize. They detail what is *common* to data analysis across methods, noting that (1) the act of analysis is a construction of the researcher; (2) what is common to all data analysis are words and numbers, both of which are symbols, and so neither can be said to be hard or soft; (3) the process of analysis is social, with the analyst working from the data back to the transactions with subjects and participants, as well as forward to transactions with colleagues and audiences; (4) the aim in analysis of all kinds is the reduction of large amounts of data to a comprehensible amount while ensuring that the meanings of the data are not lost; and (5) whether one works with numbers or text, the results of analyses are contestable. There are no warrants that are uncontestable, though how one makes an argument from data provides stronger or weaker warrants.

It will be a difficult job for an educational research faculty to design the course work and experiences in a newly conceived methodology sequence so that educational psychologists learn to assume different epistemologies and use different methods in order to formulate and answer questions of psychological importance. That is a much harder task to accomplish than having doctoral students learn to merely appreciate other forms of scholarship. Nevertheless, it is a proper goal of a redesigned methodology sequence because many of the central topics of educational psychology—learning, motivation, individual differences, and teaching—are no longer the sole province of our discipline, and new ways to address the study of these phenomena exist outside the discipline. If educational psychology expects to keep its core areas of study such as learning, individual differences, motivation, development, assessment, and teaching, it will need intimate familiarity with the ways that other scholars address these same areas of study.

Educational psychologists, like other scientists, seek strong warrants. That is why the randomized trial will always be a preferred method in the armamentarium of the educational psychologist and why educational psychologists will continue to have a strong attachment to true experiments, ex-post-facto designs, and survey research methods. But not every important question can be answered with these kinds of research designs. More important is what I noted at the beginning of this section: when we think about educational issues with certain kinds of designs, we may be limiting the kinds of questions that arise about the phenomena that are of interest to educational psychologists. The solutions to these problems are (1) to place a greater emphasis on learning alternative epistemologies and (2) to incorporate greater breadth in our methods courses, not just for educational psychologists but for all students seeking the Ph.D. in education.

Consider the Rationale for Presenting Big Ideas[1]

We must teach the content of the discipline through the use of big ideas, putting less emphasis on adulation or critique of theorists and their positions as a way to organize content.

Much of educational psychology's core field of study—learning—is typically presented through the study of various theoretical approaches. The corpus of various theoreticians is often studied intensively. Once it was Pavlov and Watson, then Hull, Spence, and Tolman. Eventually, it was Thorndike and Skinner, while still later we studied Piaget and Bruner. Now we study Vygotsky. Along the way, we learned the key ideas of behaviorism, classical and operant conditioning, information processing, cognitive theory, situated cognition, social-cognitive theory, and so forth. Learning this material was often from texts such as Hilgard's *Theories of Learning,* or similar ones, featuring theories of learning and theoretical positions. Educational psychology textbooks did some of the same, perhaps because early in psychology's history there was a belief that a single theory would someday be found to account for learning across all contexts. Thorndike and Skinner—giants in educational psychology—believed this. They also believed they had developed such a general theory. But for most educational psychologists, the search for a universal theory of learning is now seen as too simple—a form of antiquated thinking that ignores the remarkable differences in persons and environments and their interactions. Past leaders of the field seemed to deify or demonize theorists, while not focusing enough on the big ideas that the theories made use of.

Historically, the chronological study of theorists and theories made sense, and important insights into aspects of the learning process did come from careful study of theorists and their ideas. But educational psychology often carries out its research in environments that are complex, and the theorists did not. Learning in a T-maze was the domain of interest to the theorists Hull and Spence; an extremely small box containing a hungry rat or pigeon was the basis for Skinner's theories; Piaget had little to say about schooling; and Bruner, when he came into education, was an essayist and curriculum developer who was demonized and rejected when he tried to move his curriculum into the schools. With the exception of

Vygotsky, few of the theorists relied upon by educational psychologists understood schools. The theories of some of the brightest social scientists simply could not stay pure for very long when confronted with the booming, buzzing confusion of ordinary classroom life. The ideas embedded in the various theories remain relevant, but the purity of the theories is almost always sullied.

Schools and classrooms are extremely complex places in which to conduct research. As Cronbach (1975) advised us, theories and other generalizations do not often hold up well in the face of such complexities. Even Skinner was reported to have said that when learning theorists joined the armed forces in World War II, learning *theory* went into the trash bin. The demands of training soldiers were simply nothing like the laboratories from which learning theories had emanated. However, although grand theories have trouble being useful in complex environments, the key ideas that were the focus of the theoretician often do have great utility. Educational psychologists might therefore try to approach the teaching of learning and motivation with somewhat less concern for the theorists and somewhat more concern for the big ideas to which they attended. It is the big ideas contained in theories that have usefulness in schools and classrooms, not the formal theory itself.

Behaviorism and its branches (instrumental learning, connectionism, classical conditioning) are all response-oriented and focused on consequences to responses. Consequences to behavior are important also in attribution theory and control theory, and have a role to play in social-cognitive theory as well as others. An understanding of responses and their consequences would seem to be more important to an educational psychologist and to a teacher than would intimate knowledge about Pavlov, Thorndike, or Skinner.

The power of social models in learning is a crucial part of Bandura's social learning theory, and it is within this framework that the influence of models on learning and motivation is often taught. But learning from models is an equally important part of cognitive apprenticeships and an element in learning through legitimate peripheral participation, as in sociocultural theories. The developing notion of community of practice, from Vygotskian theorists and others, is about the power of models on thinking as well as on overt behavior. The important idea that the psychological starts out first in the social plane is part of this emerging understanding of the power of models to shape thought and action. In other words, there are big ideas that cut across theorists that need to be understood at least as well as the theorists and theories themselves.

As other examples of this point, we see that cognitive and social development is affected by "challenge" in Piaget's theory, Vygotsky's theory, and in Bandura's self-efficacy theory. We see also that while "scaffolding" as a big idea comes in its modern form from David Ausable's cognitive theory, this concept is also integral to Vygotsky's discussions of the zone of proximal development and the related work of Reuven Fuerstein on mediation and cognitive modifiability, as well as a feature in theories of instructional design.

These comments about the big ideas that are found across theories are not meant to downgrade theory development or the intensive study of theoretical positions. My intent here is to redress the overemphasis on theorists and the theories in their purest form. An educational psychology that is embedded in practice may well have more need to use the big ideas contained in theories than to attempt testing to see whether a theory "works" in practice. Moreover, an educational psychology embedded in practice is likely to contribute to theory development by developing principles that "have greater scientific validity than those that have been developed primarily in laboratory work and in disinterested observations of practice, because they will have to address deeper questions of how practices function and develop" (Greeno, Collins, and Resnick, 1996, p. 41). Embedding educational psychology in practice calls for the development of scholars who are as much at home in conducting research in, and analyzing data from, design experiments as they are in conducting and analyzing data from randomized field studies. It seems desirable that the educational psychology of the future give greater emphasis to working in Pasteur's quadrant (Stokes, 1997) and then design its doctoral training accordingly.

Introduce Doctoral Students to the Sites Where Students Live and Learn

We must use doctoral training to help doctoral students become acquainted with the many sites in which K–12 students live and learn; these are also the sites in which doctoral students are likely to do their own research.

A critical deficit in the doctoral training of educational psychologists (and in traditional teacher education as well) is the lack of opportunity for these students to spend time in settings where they will work or need to know about. For example, if educational psychologists are going to be involved in the educational problems of our times, they will almost assuredly work in urban school settings. Even if they do not, they need to understand them, for these are the settings where our nation is having the greatest problems with public education. Understanding these problems also requires exposure to wealthy suburban public schools so that contrasts in how teaching and learning are enacted in both settings can be understood. Also to be compared and contrasted in those two settings are the differences in course offerings (remedial versus advanced-placement courses versus extracurricular), in quality of the teachers, in expectations for student achievement, and so forth.

Although the most identifiable areas of schooling that educational psychologists choose to study are learning, motivation, and assessment, these processes also take place outside of school settings. And the non-school settings for learning, for affecting motivation, and for assessment have an enormous impact on our youth. We need to understand the effects of after-school youth clubs, raves, Little League participation, rock concert attendance, and the media.

There are cultural groups that many doctoral students do not understand, and yet they are likely to work with members of such groups. Our doctoral students need experiences with the local minority community, whether Hispanic, Hmong, Native American, or African American. They also need to understand support agencies and the role they play in youth development, as formal and informal education takes place in settings such as youth courts, detention centers, and hospitals.

How would doctoral students gain knowledge of these various settings? I suggest that we look at the medical training model. Before they begin training in their specialization, physicians-to-be participate in rotations, spending a number of weeks in each area of medicine—geriatrics, oncology, maternity, emergency rooms, and so on. I propose that all doctoral-level educational psychology students have a year-long practicum requirement for work in settings relevant to the community in which their university is situated. The thirty weeks of the school year might include five placements, each for six weeks, in, for example, the Hispanic community and their schools; at a prison youth group; at an African American church youth club; at a preschool, charter, or exclusive private school; and, of course, as a shadow to an administrator or counselor in an urban, as well as a suburban, school. During each rotation, the student would observe and report back on learning, teaching, assessment, teacher and student motivational interests, problem-solving skills used by teachers and students, parental involvement, peer relations, quality of life for students and teachers, bullying, isolation, and so forth.

The focal subjects of educational psychology should be studied in their various manifestations in different real-world environments. Those who would study both teachers and students need to understand their subjects in real-world contexts. Novice researchers should reflect on and discuss their subjects' behavior before they begin their study. Educational science may be the hardest of the social sciences to do (Berliner, 2003), and this kind of experience might help future researchers understand why that might be so.

Design a Research Internship in a Complex Environment

Following a more catholic view of methods and after experience in various contexts, doctoral students should do a research internship in a complex educational setting.

Many doctoral-level educational psychology programs either require a master's degree along the way to the doctorate or a research internship on the way to preparing for the doctoral dissertation. For either the master's or the internship (or both), it might be wise to require students to learn how to conduct research in complex, real-world settings, right from the start of their careers.

Figuring out how to gain reliable knowledge from complex environments is no mean achievement. Thus it is best learned in a doctoral program rather than after university training ends, when an educational psychologist might flounder as reality bites her research protocol. An example of this comes from early in my career. My colleagues and I took a robust laboratory finding about a strategy to enhance prose learning and studied it in a real classroom setting. We not only randomly assigned students to treatments but we embedded the treatment into ordinary classroom reading materials so that students did not even know they were in a research study. This clever design did produce a significant difference between the treated group and the control, but, to our dismay, it was significant in the wrong direction! The control group, with no treatment at all, significantly outperformed the treated group, even though these subjects had learned in ways that laboratory research relevant to education suggested would enhance learning. Our hypothesis to account for this negative finding was that in the foreign environment of the research laboratory, students used the learning strategy we supplied them. But in the real world, students develop their own strategies for learning. The treatment we provided them apparently interfered with the natural and adaptive learning strategies they had acquired on their own. In other words, our treatment messed them up!

Training in complex environments should begin early in the educational psychologist's career. A verbal learning study in a laboratory setting, with reading passages of a few hundred words, can certainly yield insights into learning. But those same insights may be inadequate when brought from the laboratory to a classroom setting and studied over longer periods of time with longer and more natural prose materials. The lack of replication of laboratory findings in real-world settings is part of a bigger problem—that of a paucity of replications of any of our findings at all. As Peterson (2003) recently pointed out, this is one of the major shortcomings of our field.

Building a field where research is replicated in complex real-world environments is a worthy goal, and the research internship and master's thesis offer opportunities to accomplish that. I can also envision some research university sponsoring an electronic journal that would put such research reports online and make them available to all on the Internet. I believe that this would do much to improve the training of doctoral students in our field. It would simultaneously do much to improve the reputation of educational research by demonstrating that we have replicable findings from which we can do more meta-analyses, thereby providing better estimates of the effect sizes associated with certain recommended treatments, thereby providing better evidence for policymaking.

This is not an argument against doing original research for master's theses and in the research internship. But it is an argument for requiring more replications of research findings to be part of doctoral training programs so that more of what is now "relevant" research can be tested in schools and classrooms, and possibly transformed into useful research. Completing a Ph.D. in educational psychology is not ordinarily a lengthy process, so it should not be difficult to accommodate a research practicum of this type in either full-time or part-time degree programs. In fact, many doctoral programs now have such a practicum requirement but do not emphasize using it for replications and real-world research experience, as recommended here.

Develop an Understanding of Educational Policy

Our doctoral students in educational psychology need some experience with and course work in policy analysis. This is desirable if educational psychology is to be viewed as both a profession and a discipline.

This essay is intended for the discipline of educational psychology and addresses the ways the discipline might come to train its novices. But we have an important question to examine: *whether educational psychology is a profession, as well as a discipline.* Members of a profession are involved with the policies that affect its practice in ways that members of a discipline need not be. Physicians, clinical psychologists, and lawyers—professionals who do not think of themselves as members of a discipline—are typically involved with the policies that affect their practice. Educational psychologists rarely identify themselves as professionals, and they generally do not become as involved in policy issues. Yet thinking of ourselves solely as members of a discipline and thus not participating in policy debates has important consequences for our field.[2]

A profession appears to have six characteristics (Shulman, personal communication to the Committee on Teacher Education, July 2001). The first is *service* to society, implying some kind of ethical and moral commitment to clients—say, teachers and other school personnel. Second, a profession has a body of *scholarly knowledge*. Deep familiarity with that body of knowledge forms the basis of the entitlement to practice one's profession. Third, a professional also engages in *practical action*. That is, professionals bring their knowledge to bear on issues of practice. Fourth, the members of a profession work with *uncertainty*—a condition caused by the different needs and the nonroutine nature of the problems faced by those whom the professional serves. The complex world of schools, as opposed to the laboratory, provides this kind of uncertainty, entailing the need for professionals to develop judgment in applying the knowledge they possess. Fifth is the importance of *experience* in a profession: the nonroutine nature of the problems of practice cannot be solved or ameliorated on the basis of packaged, off-the-shelf solutions; thus experience that has been reflected upon becomes the basis for professional actions. Sixth, there is an identifiable *professional community*—one that shares knowledge and develops professional standards.

Given these characteristics, it is clear that educational psychology qualifies as a profession as well as a discipline (the reasons for this are elaborated in Berliner, 2003). Therefore, educational psychologists have obligations to engage in policy debates about which they have some knowledge. For example, consider some of the recent educational policies and those still the subject of debate: what kinds of school settings our youth will be educated in (including charter schools and voucher-supported private schools that are either religious or secular); the nature of the competencies that children must demonstrate on the assessments they must pass to receive high school diplomas or to be allowed into the next grade; the qualifications of teachers and the form of their teacher education programs; the nature of the English, history, science, mathematics, and reading curriculum; appropriate ways to foster English language acquisition; after-school and summer programs, and preschool programs. Educational psychologists have knowledge to share with the different sides in these policy debates and expertise to offer in court cases where some of these policies are decided. Further, the outcomes of each of these debates affect the research funding in our field and the research agendas we develop. In addition, our participation in these debates as social scientists affects both the kind of society in which we will live and the reputation we develop as professionals.

It is important to understand, however, that policymaking is about competing values, *not* competing data. So social scientists often have a hard time convincing those who debate policy that what they have to offer is relevant (Rein, 1976). When social scientists do research that can influence policy, they provide policymakers "*is* data." The policymakers, however, generally use "*ought* data." But there is a huge difference between "is" and "ought." You simply cannot go directly from a statement of fact to a statement of value. Nevertheless, providing reliable data for policy debates is no trivial accomplishment, and the data are almost sure to be used by those whose arguments the data support. In these debates, however, data are frequently distorted, and it is up to the educational psychologist and others who have the technical skills to provide clarification (Smith, 2004; Berliner and Biddle, 1995).

Because professions have moral obligations in ways that disciplines do not, it is hard for any educational psychologists who see themselves as professionals to suppress their opinions about the policies debated in legislatures and courts. Perhaps, then, the values, opinions, and beliefs of educational psychologists should more frequently lead them to pick policy-relevant research topics. This could allow educational psychologists to participate in policy debates more frequently. "Jeffersonian research" is the name given to research done to address the needs of society in order to make it better. Educational psychologists who choose to rely on their values when they choose which research topics to investigate rigorously could do much more Jeffersonian research than they have done to date.

Doctoral training programs that provide course work and experiences that help students understand our nation's public policy debates will almost surely inspire ideas for research. With such experiences, doctoral students are likely to pick research problems that have a better chance to contribute reliable, scientific data to the partisans in the debate, as well as influencing those who hold neutral positions while hoping that persuasive data will be forthcoming. Over time, through experience with the complexity and uncertainty surrounding data collection on research issues relevant to policy, educational psychologists will learn to provide expert testimony to policymakers, as well. This is what professions regularly do. But because educational psychology has never consciously seen itself as a profession, there is no doctoral training for this kind of professional role. Course work on the nature of educational policy analysis is as important for an educational psychologist as it is to an economist of education, a doctoral student of school finance, or a school administrator. Developing more useful research for teachers, along with the moral commitments to our field, requires more sophistication in policy analysis and policy research than we now have.

Four Things We Do in Our Doctoral Training Programs but Could Do Much Better

While we are taking these five important steps to change our doctoral programs, we should also continue doing some of what we ordinarily do as part of doctoral education. But we must be more thoughtful about what we do. Most educational psychology programs address technology, brain research, multicultural education, and subject-matter knowledge. We must consider each of these subjects more explicitly if they are to be useful for educating those who wish to enter our discipline and profession.

Technology

Doctoral programs of educational psychology have usually been closely related to technology programs in schools of education. This is because instructional designers—those who develop learning programs—typically were trained in educational psychology departments. Instructional designers have an understanding of learning theory and motivation; they then apply what they know to the expanding field of learning from and with computers.

Because the importance of the computer in schooling and society grows daily, every educational psychology doctoral training program has obligations to ensure that its students are sophisticated computer users, understand principles of instructional design, and recognize the cognitive, social, and societal consequences of raising a generation of youth that finds learning on the Web as ordinary as previous generations found learning from the television. Although computer use and instructional design are often addressed in our graduate courses, the consequences of technology on learning are not. What is especially interesting is to recognize that an understanding of learning and motivation may be the knowledge base that entitles an educational psychologist to practice in this field, but the medium itself may be transforming what it means to be learning and to be motivated in these environments. That is a much more sophisticated outcome than is usually thought about when children interact with computers and is a proper, though complex, issue for educational psychologists who hold a social-cognitive view to study.

A doctoral program, therefore, is deficient if it does not provide ways for its students to think about these more global issues associated with computers, and the cognitive and social developmental consequences of their frequent use. It is worth studying, as we do often, the use of the computer as a tool in teaching. But an even more worthy goal is to attempt to understand our reciprocal relationship with computers: computers influence the cognition and social relations of our youth, both in and out of school.

Brain Research

Research on the brain is surely of great import to education and thus to educational psychologists. Indeed, I have waited my whole professional life for revelations from this area. Yet they never seem to come. While research advances in studying the brain seem to be made daily, as yet they have led educational psychology nowhere. We still study mind, cognition, learning, and emotions as we have for decades (Bruer, 1997). Nevertheless, a contemporary doctoral training program would be remiss if it did not have some course work on neuropsychology, because some day information that is directly useful for education may actually be forthcoming. Particularly helpful for a contemporary educational psychologist may be knowledge of pharmaceuticals and their effects on learning and motivation; this is increasingly a drug-dependent nation, and more and more children in the schools regularly take behavior-altering drugs. Furthermore, the genetic origins of some problems affecting special education populations are now better understood. Because educational psychologists often work with such populations, they need to understand both the role of genetics on behavior and the role of drug and genetic therapies for changing harmful or inappropriate student behavior. Neuropsychological and psychopharmacological training are important in their own right and also as a safety measure in case the always-imminent breakthroughs in brain research do occur.

Multicultural Issues

Every school of education has addressed the issues of the changing face of America and tries to train teachers and researchers to work with diverse populations. Children of poverty and of color, as well as those who speak other languages, all need special attention from a teaching force that is predominantly white, female, and middle-class. There is room here for educational psychologists to make their contributions. For example, the finest scholars in this field have invested a lot in the idea of culturally relevant pedagogy. This means teaching children with different backgrounds than one's own in such a way that their culture and life experiences are validated, the teaching materials used are intrinsically interesting to their culture, and the teaching methods used capitalize on their strengths. That, of course, is abstract language about a very important new concept. Here we argue that the contemporary study of teaching and learning in schools cannot be undertaken without concern for this concept, but the idea of culturally relevant pedagogy is desperately in need of empirical study. Psychologists, with a rich history of studying cultural influences on teaching, learning, motivation, and assessment, should not cede this important field to others. Doctoral training in educational psychology should, therefore, address the research issues in multicultural education so that our discipline and our profession can contribute to the improvement of our nation's schools. These courses should not be about how wonderful our nation would be if we had more Italian dinner nights and Filipino dancing at assembly, as too many of these courses for teachers seem to be. I am proposing courses that call for deep inquiries into the nature of cognition, motivation, and the meaning of competence across cultures.

Subject-Matter Knowledge

The Handbook of Educational Psychology (Berliner and Calfee, 1996) makes abundantly clear that teaching and learning in, say, mathematics and history are very different enterprises. The structure of knowledge in each field requires a different psychology for understanding each subject matter present in our schools. Teaching, learning, the motivation of students, the developmental stage most appropriate for learning different kinds of concepts, and the nature of assessment—each subject takes a slightly different form in the different subject-matter areas. The generalist in educational psychology has much to contribute, and not all research in our field needs to be done in classrooms. But an educational psychologist with deep knowledge of a subject matter area also has much to contribute. Thus when we find a doctoral student in educational psychology with highly developed knowledge of a subject-matter area and a love of that subject, that student should be encouraged to minor or specialize in that subject. When possible, our doctoral students should become subject-matter specialists, as well as psychologists. It would afford them extra insight into particular domains of knowledge that are taught and learned in our schools.

The Next Step

It would not hurt me at all to have each of the suggestions I have made debated and rejected. What I would find unacceptable, however, is for educational psychology to continue to be unexamined as it declines in influence. It is my hope, therefore, that readers of this essay will engage in the dialogue necessary to ensure that the next generation of educational psychologists becomes a strong and vital part of both the world of educational research and the world of practice and policy.

NOTES

1. My thanks to Jeanne Ormrod and Ali Iran-Nejad for helpful suggestions about this issue.

2. Education is not the only field that faces this issue. For example, Hyman Bass makes a similar point in his essay about doctoral education in mathematics in this volume (Chapter Six).

REFERENCES

Barone, T. "Science, Art, and the Predispositions of Educational Researchers." *Educational Researcher,* 2001, *30,* 24–28.

Behrens, J. T., and Smith, M. L. "Data and Data Analysis." In D. C. Berliner and R. C. Calfee (eds.), *The Handbook of Educational Psychology.* New York: Macmillan, 1996.

Berliner, D. C. "The Science of Psychology and the Practice of Schooling: The One Hundred Year Journey of Educational Psychology from Interest, to Disdain, to Respect for Practice." In T. K. Fagan and G. R. VandenBog (eds.), *Exploring Applied Psychology: Origins and Critical Analysis: Master Lecturers, 1992.* Washington, D.C.: American Psychological Association, 1993.

Berliner, D. C. "Educational Research: The Hardest Science of Them All." *Educational Researcher,* 2002, *31*(8), 18–20.

Berliner, D. C. "Educational Psychology as a Policy Science, Including Some Thoughts on the Distinction Between a Discipline and a Profession." *Canadian Journal of Educational Administration and Policy,* 2003, 26. Available at www.umanitoba.ca/publications/cjeap/articles/miscellaneousArticles/berliner.html.

Berliner, D. C., and Biddle, B. J. *The Manufactured Crisis.* Menlo Park, Calif.: Addison-Wesley, 1995.

Berliner, D. C., and Calfee, R. C. (eds.). *The Handbook of Educational Psychology.* New York: Macmillan, 1996.

Bruer, J. T. "Education and the Brain: A Bridge Too Far?" *Educational Researcher,* 1997, *26*(8), 4–16.

Cronbach, L. J. "The Two Disciplines of Scientific Psychology." *American Psychologist,* 1957, *12,* 671–684.

Cronbach, L. J. "Beyond the Two Disciplines of Scientific Psychology." *American Psychologist,* 1975, *30,* 671–684.

Dewey, J. "Psychology and Social Practice." *The Psychological Review,* 1899, *7,* 105–123.

Greeno, J. G., Collins, A. M., and Resnick, L. "Cognition and Learning." In D. C. Berliner and R. C. Calfee (eds.), *The Handbook of Educational Psychology.* New York: Macmillan, 1996.

Groen, G. J. "The Theoretical Ideas of Piaget and Educational Practice." In P. Suppes (ed.), *Impact of Research on Education: Some Case Studies.* Washington, D.C.: National Academy of Education, 1978.

Kaestle, C. F. "The Awful Reputation of Educational Research." *Educational Researcher,* 1993, *22,* 26–31.

Lagemann, E. C. "The Plural Worlds of Educational Research." *History of Education Quarterly,* 1989, *29,* 185–216.

Lagemann, E. C. *An Elusive Science: The Troubling History of Educational Research.* Chicago: University of Chicago Press, 2000.

Lagemann, E. C., and Shulman, L. *Issues in Educational Research: Problems and Possibilities.* San Francisco: Jossey-Bass, 1999.

Mayer, R. E. "What Is the Place of Science in Educational Research?" *Educational Researcher,* 2001, *29,* 38–39.

Metz, M. H. "Intellectual Border Crossing in Graduate Education: A Report from the Field." *Educational Researcher,* 2001, *30,* 12–18.

Pallas, A. M. "Preparing Educational Doctoral Students for Epistemological Diversity." *Educational Researcher,* 2001, *30,* 6–11.

Peterson, P. L. "Some Thoughts of an AERA Past President." Comments made at symposium no. 45.010 at the meeting of the American Educational Research Association, Chicago, Apr. 2003.

Rein, M. *Social Science and Public Policy.* New York: Penguin, 1976.

Shavelson, R. J., and L. Towne (eds.). (Written for the National Research Council Committee on Scientific Principles for Education Research.) *Scientific Research in Education.* Washington, D.C.: National Academy Press, 2002. Available at www.nap.edu/catalog/10236.html.

Smith, M. L. *Political Spectacle and the Fate of American Schools.* New York: Routledge, 2004.

Stokes, D. E. *Pasteur's Quadrant: Basic Science and Technological Innovation.* Washington, D.C.: Brookings Institution Press, 1997.

DOCTORAL EDUCATION
IN HISTORY

THE DISCIPLINE OF HISTORY AIMS TO, in the words of a recent report on doctoral education, "examine the human experience over time, with a commitment to the explanatory relevance of context, both temporal and geographical" (Bender, Katz, and Palmer, 2004, p. 4). History is a discipline with a clear and cohesive identity, but at the same time it borrows techniques and theories from many other fields (requiring students to develop familiarity with other disciplines). Consequently, historians are difficult to categorize; sometimes they consider themselves part of the humanities and sometimes part of the social sciences. Recently, the study of history has moved from recounting narratives of progress that emphasize the nation-state, with a Eurocentric point of view, to embracing a variety of theoretical analyses and a "global history" perspective. The report continues: "In the last four decades, the intellectual map of the entire discipline has been redrawn by new subjects, new theories, and new approaches" (Bender, Katz, and Palmer, 2004, p. 121).

Like most humanities fields, graduate education in the discipline is largely oriented toward academia. However, history also has a public face. Every nation and people have histories—their collective understandings of their past and their place in the world. People's understandings of their history inevitably affect their actions. Histories are written by professional historians, as well as by those who have not gone through doctoral study in history, and these histories are read by professional historians and average citizens alike. History is represented at museums in nearly every city and town; in the United States, history even has its own television channel.

At doctorate-granting institutions, history departments are generally quite large. The average department has 25 faculty members, about 80 graduate students, and an average entering class of about 19 Ph.D. students. Annually, about 950 Ph.D.'s in history are granted, marking a resurgence from the mid-1980s, when the annual number of new Ph.D.'s dropped to about 500. The current focus of specialties within the discipline reveals a shift from European history to Latin American, African, and Asian history—a trend that is particularly noticeable when comparing the specialties of new Ph.D.'s with those who are nearing retirement. About 40 percent of doctoral recipients are female; most are white, and 10 to 15 percent are not U.S. citizens. Only about half majored in history as undergraduates, which presents challenges to doctoral programs, as students are expected to move from *learning* history to *writing* history.

Doctoral study in history is a time-consuming process; average time-to-degree is 9.3 years. The lengthiness is due, in part, to the need for students to learn another language and travel to other countries to collect data. Because funding for archival research is not readily available, students also spend time writing grant applications to help fund their research efforts. Most students are promised multiple years of funding (typically a combination of fellowships and teaching assistantships), and they receive on average three and one-half years of financial support. This is insufficient, and many still rely on student loans to make ends meet.

As do students in other humanities disciplines, doctoral students in history typically work toward the degree in two stages: first taking courses and then writing a dissertation. Most students take courses for several years; the typical program requires fourteen courses. Small seminars (two to three students and a faculty member) focused on historiographic reading are common, usually centering on a topic in a specialized area. Exams, generally given in the third year of the program, certify the student's readiness to continue to the dissertation stage. These exams are generally comprehensive, typically covering one major field and from one to three minor fields. Minor fields are generally considered the fields for which the student is preparing to teach, and the major field is the student's intended research field. This structure of exams, and perhaps the rationale, has remained unchanged in most departments for many years, although the breadth of content has shifted considerably.

Once the student completes the exams, she or he then begins the research that will lead to the dissertation. A history dissertation presents a coherent narrative argument, usually presented in chronologically organized chapters. In its entirety, the dissertation is a book-length manuscript, which is ideally published in a university press after additional revision.

Students are expected to consult regularly with their adviser and possibly other committee members, but in history (like other humanities), "regularly" means conversations on a monthly basis, not the daily or weekly meetings common in the sciences. Some departments have dissertation writers' seminars, which serve as supportive, yet critical, intellectual communities during a time that can often be lonely and in which students can find themselves adrift.

Both the academic and the public faces of history reveal themselves again in the job market. The American Historical Association's survey found that in the 2000–01 academic year, a quarter of the students found jobs at research universities, half found jobs at teaching-intensive colleges and universities, and the remainder found positions outside academia. Nonacademic employers include archives, museums, historical consulting firms, historical editing projects, and government agencies. Students and faculty alike report that the training priorities of doctoral programs focus on preparing students for faculty positions in research universities. They report insufficient emphasis on teaching or on the skills needed for work in public history. And yet, unlike English, nonacademic public history positions are recognized and form a relatively visible career track. Indeed, at some institutions public history is a formal specialty within the doctoral program.

In 2004, the American Historical Association published a comprehensive report on doctoral education in history. It was the culmination of several years of research, conversations within the field, and careful thought and writing. The book identifies a number of "necessary discussions" in which all doctorate-granting departments ought to engage. These include program size, funding, premature professionalization, undergraduate education, pedagogy, career paths, interdisciplinarity, graduate student unions, new technology, and the role of the American Historical Association. This report is recommended to all historians and has much to offer those who care about doctoral education in any discipline.

The senior author of this report, Thomas Bender, uses the report as the foundation of his essay, "Expanding the Domain of History." He begins his essay by identifying four principles of the discipline—the four cornerstones on which the study of history rests. He concludes by identifying nineteen qualities that a professional historian who is educated to be a steward of the discipline would exhibit. Those in other disciplines might find the exercise of generating similar lists to be both instructive and fruitful.

Joyce Appleby provides a short overview of the evolution of the study of history in the United States in her essay "Historians, the Historical

Forces They Have Fostered, and the Doctorate in History." She thoughtfully examines the intersections between academic history and the public. She also imagines what a history graduate program begun *de novo* would look like.

Finally, in "Getting Ready to Do History," William Cronon describes the shared attributes of historians. His list is similar to but different from Thomas Bender's list. He concludes his essay with an important discussion of the kind of intellectual community that all departments in all disciplines ought to strive to create and support for their faculty and graduate students.

○

BIBLIOGRAPHY

Information and specific data were derived from the following sources:

Bender, T., Katz, P. M., and Palmer, C. *The Education of Historians for the Twenty-First Century.* Urbana: University of Illinois Press/American Historical Association, 2004.

Hoffer, T. B., and others. *Doctorate Recipients from United States Universities: Summary Report 2003.* Chicago: National Opinion Research Center, 2004.

15

EXPANDING THE DOMAIN
OF HISTORY

Thomas Bender, New York University

LIKE OTHER MODERN ACADEMIC DISCIPLINES, history has been professionalized for only a bit more than a century. The making of historical narratives to locate oneself or a people in time and place is a very old social practice, however. Perhaps it is even a generic human activity. Most histories, whether orally communicated or written, are ephemeral, but some—the Old Testament, for example—can remain in working order for a very long time. Even pagan histories, unsupported by religious traditions and institutions, can survive. Take the histories of Herodotus: still in print, they address big events and also consider different modes of everyday life in various times and places. His histories reveal, moreover, a modern historian's concern for the critical use of sources, whether oral, written, or material objects. My own scholarship and teaching does not address ancient history, yet in Herodotus I recognize an indispensable predecessor and continuing colleague.

I emphasize this connection and the duration of history as a practice and an intellectual tradition, first, to send us into the essay with a bit of humility in relation to our predecessors, some as near as a generation before us, others as distant as millennia ago. A respectful awareness of our discipline's history sustains a necessary sense of stewardship on behalf of historical thinking and knowledge. Second, we should keep in mind that our practices, unlike those of some newer disciplines, were figured out well before the invention of the graduate school. I do not say this to encourage pride of place among the disciplines. Rather, I am concerned, perhaps paradoxically so, to embolden us, to loosen the claim of a century's precedent by enlarging the context. We can be as bold as our predecessors a century ago. Finally, I want to put before us at the outset the possibility that the industry-like, highly specialized professionalization of history in its graduate school form may involve losses as well as gains.

The Nature of Historical Knowledge

All humanities disciplines, but especially history, are Janus-faced. They are directed in varying proportions to peers and to a nonprofessional public. History seems to lean more than other disciplines toward a generalized public, while other disciplines within the human sciences seem to be more peer-oriented and less directly engaged with the public as an audience. And the findings of historians are open to debate, both within and beyond the profession.

The common and public product on offer from history is not the *fact* or specific advice or expertise. It is, rather, a narrative that is imaginatively constructed but empirically grounded (Chartier, 1995, p. 154). Although the discipline values archives and is founded on the "primary" or "original" source, its work goes well beyond merely recovering information and bringing it forth. The work of history, whether in the monograph, the grand narrative history, or the op-ed page, is configurational, bringing together recovered elements of past ideas, feelings, things, and acts in a pattern of relations that reveals relative significance. In their public roles, which include teaching, historians provide, among other things, large narratives that give coherence to our experience of social time and, to a lesser extent, the relations of space and time. Historians thus highlight the importance of place and chronology in the interpretation of social life. At their best, these historical narratives both enter into and reveal the subjective meaning understood by the historical actors and a causal explanation of transformations or events.

Moreover, these configurational narratives do not claim to be definitive or final. They change on account of new information or new sources, but they also change on the basis of new ideas brought into what is a conversation with the past in the present about the future. It is thus an inherently dialogic work. History is, then, a hermeneutical discipline, and something of the original interpretation (if grounded in the sources) is sustained, despite the changing dialogue with the past, hence the continuing value of Herodotus.

This points us toward one of the more complex aspects of the *epistemology* of history, if I may use such a formal word. Is history objective? Recent discussion among historians has deepened understanding of this issue and its place in the professional ethos of the discipline.[1] Although a sophisticated notion of objectivity is of vital importance to the discipline, I do not think it is the most fundamental intellectual or professional value. The commitments of history as a discipline (critical examination of the archive) and as a profession (enhancement of historical knowledge and thinking in public life) come together in an affirmation of intellectual *independence,* not objectivity. Archives are foundational to the professional practice of history, but their importance is not wholly captured by the notion of objectivity. The archives establish intellectual independence. Original documents empower the historian to speak truth, as she or he sees it, to power. That is the historical basis for the profession's almost religious embrace of the archives.

The importance of independence was publicly and dramatically displayed in 1917, when Charles A. Beard, who had a few years earlier published his controversial book, *An Economic Interpretation of the Constitution* (1913/1986), resigned from Columbia University. Beard was impelled to act by a series of actions by the president of the university, who fired and otherwise intimidated faculty members who spoke out against the war. Beard supported the war, but he resigned because the president's actions undercut his claim in public to independence. If he was not publicly known to be free to disagree with the university policy, then Beard feared that his defense of the war would be suspect.[2] This incident, involving perhaps the most important historian of the United States in the past century, ought to remind us that in doctoral programs we are educating highly talented people to be independent thinkers, both within the academy and in public.

Four Principles of Disciplinarity

Disciplines consist of a broadly shared fund of subject knowledge and agreed-upon protocols for establishing provisional truths. In most disciplines, including history, not everyone will have the same fund. Yet all will command a substantial body of knowledge, including considerable overlap. However important this disciplinary competence is—and it is very important—it is neither a thing in itself nor an end in itself. The protocols and content of the discipline should be respected, and our stewardship of them should be at the heart of the intergenerational process of education. But we must not thus allow these traditions to intimidate us. It was just that danger inherent in tradition that Ralph Waldo Emerson warned of in his address "The American Scholar" (Emerson, 1837/1965, p. 223). This is the first principle of the discipline: *The discipline's intellectual heritage must be a rich and flexible resource, not a template or container of intellect. Likewise, the institutional structures developed to educate and sustain professional historians should always be subject to revision and adaptation.*

Academic scholarship, especially in history, is supported to generate and disseminate civic knowledge and human understanding of the social world. There is no real or implied contract between society and academe to supply the academically talented with high-level intellectual games, nor is there a commitment to support the advancement of disciplines as an end in themselves. Intellectual play, which is properly valued as a mode of creative thinking, is distinct from and immune to the criticism I am offering here, and it is important to clarify the difference in public in order to make more secure the case for this vital intellectual space for creativity in the academy.

If disciplines are not ends in themselves, the motivating questions for disciplinary inquiry presumably come from our common experience of the natural and social world around us. Although some disciplinary work will focus on technical issues within the discipline, the important questions originate in concerns larger than the discipline. And the discipline is subordinate to them. Fortunately, it is linguistically impossible to say what a colleague in the economics department once declared in a faculty meeting: "I do not want to teach students about the economy; I want to teach them economics." Whether historians can quite say that or not, the sentiment expressed represents a powerful half-century trend across the social science and humanities disciplines, including history. Since World War II, the growth, prosperity, and elaboration of academe and academic professionalism has enabled many academic disciplines to turn inward on themselves, to become worlds of their own. However big and interesting these worlds may be, they are inevitably parochial, and their academic enclosure carries the risk of a new scholasticism. A second basic principle follows from this: *It is important to recover the notion that the disciplines are merely means—powerful instruments surely—but means not ends.*

A Ph.D. in history (or any discipline) should signify more than possession of a specialized methodology and esoteric knowledge. A Ph.D. prepares one to speak or write with authority about esoteric knowledge on the basis of rigorous methods of inquiry. Much of the knowledge brought forth will be directed to peers within the discipline. But a bilingualism is indispensable and, to my mind, obligatory because it enables the historian to bring esoteric knowledge into the public sphere in the common language of that sphere. A third general principle of disciplinarity that I want to emphasize is this: *Graduate education in history must keep in mind this public connection, however difficult it is to keep it in focus and in balance in the seminar room.*

Fixing historical truth within a community of historical inquirers commits the historian to a life of mutual (but constructive) criticism. To be a meaningful contribution to fixing truth, for seeing the various facets of a historical question, the community of inquirers must strive for diversity, even at the cost of conflict. *A consensus achieved through avoidance of difference fatally weakens truth claims.* This principle, grounded in the American pragmatic tradition of truth-fixing, constitutes the fourth basic working principle of the discipline.

Change in the Discipline and the Profession

The discipline, the profession, and the careers in history have all undergone considerable change in the past half-century. In 1945, historians were overwhelmingly white males, and a small number of graduate programs had trained the great majority of them. In 1950, twenty departments produced 75 percent of all history Ph.D.'s. By the 1990s, the proportion trained in those programs had declined to 40 percent. The number of departments offering the Ph.D. doubled in the same years, indicating the nationalization of doctoral training in the field.

Historically, the range of professional careers in history has been much more various than contemporary graduate programs ordinarily recognize and grant. Let us start with demographics. Although it is often assumed that after World War II all Ph.D.'s obtained academic jobs, the assumption holds, at best, for only one decade—1961 to 1971. Of the cohort that received Ph.D.'s in 1959, only 70 percent found employment as college faculty; the figure for 1995 was 65 percent. In fact, roughly the same percentage of the Ph.D.'s in history conferred by Johns Hopkins between 1876 and 1926 entered academic careers (Bender, Katz, and Palmer, 2004). Any vision of doctoral education in the discipline of history must recognize that the profession includes a variety of career paths, with a substantial number of historians pursuing what are often called public history careers, whether in historical societies or in editing, journalism, filmmaking, and other intellectual careers. The education of historians must not lose sight of this range of professional practice. The employment situation for doctoral students also demands that faculty face up to their potential conflict of interest: their desire for doctoral students may be at the expense of the best interest of the students they recruit. Smaller and better doctoral programs may be the order of the day.

The number of women with doctorates in history has increased dramatically in the past generation. In 1970 the ratio of men to women among new Ph.D.'s was 85:15; in 2000 it was 55:45. However, at the professorial rank white men are still vastly overrepresented, even more so at the more prestigious institutions. (Projected retirements indicate a considerable alteration in this situation by 2010.) Although under-represented groups now constitute 15 percent of all new Ph.D.'s in history, this proportion trails American studies, sociology, and political science, while exceeding those in English. Nor are all underrepresented groups having the same experience. African American representation has leveled off or even slightly declined. Increases are coming from the growth in Asian American and Latino(a) historians. In addition, there is some troubling evidence of a decline in the openness of the profession to students from families of lower educational achievement and lower socioeconomic backgrounds (Bender, Katz, and Palmer, 2004).

Most discussion of diversity deals in numbers. Statistics are significant, but the actual experience of students and faculty in the everyday life of departments is at least as important, and the two are obviously related. To what degree are departments accepting and adapting to diversity—and being practically affected by it? If diversity did not produce some complicated social and intellectual relations, the push for diversity would bring little to the institution of higher education. We should anticipate the necessity for greater sensitivity and thought about different intellectual and personal styles. More important and more controversial, faculty must also face up to the risk of falling into forms of intellectual racism that expect less of some students. Students should not be admitted unless they are expected to succeed. Once a student is accepted, he or she deserves equal respect and equal expectations on the part of the faculty and the department community—and should be held to the same rigorous standards. The entire department community should make a self-conscious effort to ensure that the departmental culture is universally supportive of inclusion and achievement (Bender, Katz, and Palmer, 2004, p. 48).

Changing Intellectual Agendas

Professional history in the United States—indeed, most secular history since the eighteenth century—has depended on the idea of human progress. By the second half of the twentieth century, American historians, lagging behind their European counterparts, found it increasingly difficult to assume the progressiveness of history. The dissolution of that nineteenth-century teleology has changed the way historians frame historical questions: histories have become synchronic as often as diachronic; they explore subjective meaning as often as they examine causation or external transformation, and they are less likely to stress the continuity of past and present.

The movement of history closer to the humanities over the past couple of decades has reinforced this trend. History has always straddled the humanities and social sciences, listing from side to side over the decades. The recent tilt toward the humanities has brought significant gains, particularly a new sensitivity to the power of language and theories that provide insight into texts and linguistic issues, but there is a danger that too great a movement away from the social sciences will weaken the capacity of history to address institutional forms of power and social transformation. Graduate education in history needs to find a workable balance between the new methods taken from the humanities and a re-engagement with the theories and methods that address institutions, social structure, and social transformation.

There is every reason to believe that more and more intellectual work will be conducted at the interface of the disciplines. To maintain inherited disciplinary boundaries too firmly and to insist on old, essentially nineteenth-century categories of analysis (such as the nation-state) could marginalize history and discourage the most imaginative and intellectually adventuresome students from entering the field. There is also a danger of a post-disciplinary school of humanities emerging under the rubric of "culture studies." To the extent that the established disciplines fail to address the pressing moral and intellectual issues of our time, culture studies (which does) will be all the more compelling to many of the talented and socially committed students history should want to attract. And to the extent that we encourage interdisciplinary work (as we should), it is essential that we demand and arrange for adequate grounding in the relevant disciplines for our students. That will mean far more interaction and collaboration with neighboring disciplines and departments than occurs at present, and it doubtless means more collaborative teaching and research projects.

With the end of colonial empires and the emergence of new nations in the postwar era, the territory of history has been transformed. The discipline of history has finally incorporated those vast parts of the world earlier relegated to anthropology. This represents a vast extension of history's disciplinary domain, as well as a new and potentially fruitful realignment with anthropology. While the territory of history was being extended geographically, the social space of history was also enlarged to incorporate daily life and the realms of private life into the agenda of historical inquiry.

Within the traditional geographical fields, new topics have thus emerged, and the numbers of students going into the histories of East Asia, Africa, Latin America, and the Middle East have been increasing over the past decade or more.

At the same time the numbers studying Europe have been declining. So stated, it seems that a welcome cosmopolitanism is on the horizon. But if one includes American history in this conversation, one concludes that, quite to the contrary, the discipline is worrisomely parochial. More than 50 percent of all Ph.D.'s in history are in the American field. Even more striking, 60 percent of those are in twentieth-century American history. These data suggest a strong presentism within the discipline but also a divide between those seeking in history only a modest extension of their own present and those seeking to explore different times and places. Less generously, it might be considered a worrisome split between cosmopolitans and parochials. The solution is not necessarily to proscribe or limit entry into modern American history but to demand a larger contextualization in the program requirements, including language skills, which will de-parochialize the study of American history.[3]

Professional history and the modern nation-state grew up in a partnership. History found favor in Europe and the United States because creating a national history would help form national citizens, thus affirming the nation as the primary form of solidarity. Until recently, it has seemed beyond question for history to take the national state as the natural unit of history. But now, that nineteenth-century assumption is coming under challenge by way of globalization and multiculturalism talk. Money, things, people, and knowledge are not confined by national borders, and history has been partially liberated from the nation as container, with more and more transnational history being written and taught. All of this invites or demands rethinking some of the most fundamental concepts in the discipline and the way the curriculum is framed.[4]

The notion of stewardship implies a belief in the progress of the discipline. Yet that version of progressiveness, too, is at risk in contemporary academe. At least in the humanities there has emerged a practice of distinguishing one's work from all other work in the field. Contemporary preoccupation with difference thus returns in a perverse way that individualizes each work of scholarship. Put differently, by differentiating itself from all other works, each new work of scholarship presumes to be its own context. New histories not only ignore the old scholarship, they rhetorically banish it with the rhetoric of newness. Partly, this follows the Tocquevillian imperative of competitive individualism in a putatively egalitarian society. But it is no doubt also the result of the pressure to distinguish oneself in a grim job market, combined with perhaps too much absorption of the values of the market into the professional ethos. The result, as the German critic Winfried Fluck has compellingly argued, is that the explosion of scholarship in American universities is not matched by the growth of knowledge because so much of each new work denies (or seriously obscures) its relation to past and contemporary scholarship. For Fluck, an epidemic of "expressive individualism" is endangering the collective pursuit of knowledge and a sense of stewardship (Fluck, 2002, p. 343).

Rethinking Courses, Curriculum, and Practices

One cannot but be struck by the magnitude of change in the demographics of the profession, the intellectual agenda of the discipline, and the increasingly complex pattern of careers over the course of the past half-century. Equally striking is the relatively small institutional change in the past century, including the categories that organize the curriculum and fields and the forms of determining competence. Surely some rethinking seems appropriate at this time.

If stewardship is at the center of the profession, the shared ethos of historians must be to keep the past available and in working order for the profession and the public. Toward that end, doctoral education will have to respect the intellectual legacy of earlier historians more than it presently does, and it must recognize the public, as well as peers, as a relevant audience for historical research and teaching. This goal points to a greater emphasis on the fund of knowledge, both within and beyond one's specialization, than is currently the case. A larger sense of the discipline points toward an introductory course that includes all students, regardless of their specialized interest. Such a course (and several departments are developing such courses) would introduce students to the discipline, not just their field of special interest. They would discover the different questions and historiographies associated with different eras and parts of the world. Perhaps an additional common course ("Predecessors and Contemporaries") could focus on particularly compelling histories by historians identified with major methodological or interpretive significance. Yet another common course—a dissertation seminar, mixing fields—would come near the end of the student careers, though I see no reason why students might not be brought into it at the prospectus stage.

Departments should be much more committed to preparing students as teachers, both as T.A.'s and for their later careers, and should devote considerable attention to questions of professional ethics and responsibilities. Here are opportunities for new and revised courses.

The curriculum proper should be individualized (a large benefit of the decrease in the size of programs), but it should be structured to make sure that the students develop a variety of contexts for their research fields and that they are prepared for teaching fields.

I would even propose a radical reframing of the categories that usually frame the curriculum and fields, which are essentially the nineteenth-century categories given permanent life by the Library of Congress subject-heading catalogue. To escape the legacy of the founding moment of the modern disciplines, I would establish a division of the disciplinary domain that would undercut the nation-state distortion. Students should define an examination field within each of these categories, plus an interdisciplinary field. For example,

- Nations and empires[5]
- Multisited histories (transnational, comparative, or international)
- Ideas, themes, groups, institutions
- Periods: early (before 500 CE), middle (500–1500), late (1500–)

I would emphasize individual "directed readings" to prepare students for examination. Formal courses would be limited and unrelated to the exams and would address big questions relevant to more than one field or to interdisciplinary issues. I would make a bigger event out of the preparation and defense of a prospectus, and I would urge that the whole dissertation committee be involved and meet regularly, from the beginning. Before they leave the program, students should have some experience in a collaborative project, and there should be explicit recognition of the history of the profession and academic life.

Accepting Responsibility for the Next Generation of Historians

The education of historians is a direct and important responsibility of senior colleagues in whatever academic department or other professional work setting the new historian begins her or his career. These five or six years before tenure is the period when a responsible professional is formed, as a teacher, researcher, educator, as a public voice, and as a potential institutional leader or, at least, a participant in institutional governance and management.

Much more attention needs to be directed to the culture of the department: making it a safe place for all faculty and students; making intellectual and pedagogical discourse part of the department's public culture; making it a place of participatory governance, openness, and recognizably fair in the treatment of all members, with adequate grievance procedures. One might say that the long preceding sentence moves away from the curricular matter of doctoral training, but in fact I am convinced that the hidden curriculum embedded in the department culture is of enormous importance in the intellectual and professional formation of doctoral students.

Educating Historians

The education of historians is a long-term project. Graduate school is the most significant and intensely focused part of that education, but it is not the whole of it. The undergraduate experience and even K–12 schooling are, in a literal sense, foundational, if only for sparking and sustaining interest in the field. For that reason alone (ignoring the civic responsibility of professionals for the moment) graduate faculties must take more interest than they usually do in the whole educational system and the quality of history instruction in it.

The education of historians does not end with the completion of their Ph.D. Of course, all serious learning is life-long, but a more familiar institutional marker of the work of making an academic historian is the achievement of tenure *and* thus the moment of rethinking possibilities for bolder and more ambitious work, whether as a teacher or a scholar. Just as doctoral education should encourage independence, something protected by tenure but not necessarily prompted by it, graduate school mentors should, by precept and example, make their former students aware that with maturity and security comes the possibility of work marked by new levels of boldness and significance.

History and other disciplines must address the persistence of a medieval custom in the modern university: the "master" and "apprentice" concept of doctoral education implies a work of replication. The master must reproduce himself or he fails, while an apprentice who fails to assume the form of the master is also a failure—for both teacher and student. This particular teacher-student bond, with all the perverse forms of power and identification it encourages, as well as the sense of failure that it produces, needs to be opened up. Mentoring of doctoral students on this model needs ventilating (Damrosch, 2000, p. B24). Although a principal adviser is essential in doctoral education, the culture of the department must encourage more open relationships and sustain a plurality of significant advisers at all stages of graduate education.

Doctoral programs see their mandate to be the production of researchers. Most changes in doctoral programs over the past decade have been in the direction of emphasizing research. Only with pressure from university administrations, who are in turn worried about tuition-paying parents and state legislators, have departments recently given focused attention to preparing doctoral students as teachers, both as T.A.'s and as future faculty. Such beginnings are welcome, but more is required. Doctoral students need to be prepared to be colleagues, to be educators who think about curriculum and pedagogy, to be well versed in the ethical issues related to scholarship and teaching, to be knowledgeable about the place of higher education and professional scholarship in American public life and the civic responsibilities of the historian, whether working in an academic setting or as a public historian.

The seminar is a great mechanism for critical inquiry. My experience is that students become extremely adept at criticizing the work of others. In the greater number of their graduate courses, we mostly ask them to write critical essays. We do not spend enough time on synthesis, on putting narratives together, on developing different rhetorics for different audiences. One sees the consequences when talented students perform unexpectedly poorly on their qualifying exams or when we see in their dissertations the great difficulty they have in persuasively linking the detailed analysis of their sources with the larger claims they make. The failure is ours, not theirs. We do not properly prepare them. The balance between critical and synthetic work needs to be changed. Various rhetorical strategies or presentation strategies for different purposes need to be addressed more directly.

The fund of knowledge that the qualifying exams test (usually in quite unimaginative ways, like a timed, sit-down test) is greatly reduced in its coverage. Partly this development occurred because comprehensiveness is impossible, but even more because of a desire not to divert the student from her research project. This practice not only weakens the student's preparation as a teacher or public historian but it makes her a weaker researcher, lacking a capacious sense of context. Such an education, which effectively treats the research project as self-contained, doubtless makes it difficult for the historian in question to make a compelling case for the significance of her work, even to fellow historians, let alone broader audiences. The "So what?" question must be central to the supervision of doctoral research, and the curriculum should prepare the student to understand the importance of the question and to answer it.

In the 1940s and the 1950s, the Ph.D. was understood in history and other disciplines as a "research-based teaching degree." By the 1990s it could fairly be considered a research degree pure and simple, perhaps even a hyper-research degree. Although most students enter history with the ambition of becoming teachers, the successful application for top graduate programs in history looks increasingly like a mid-career research grant proposal. Doctoral curricula and the culture of the department rarely suggest a community of educators; rather, it has the character of an elite researchers' club. It is important to shift the frame. Doctoral students in history, whatever their career objectives, are educators in the making, whether in a classroom, a government agency, or as a documentary filmmaker.

The big change I would propose in doctoral education is to recover and affirm the idea that the work of doctoral programs is to form educators—men and women with powerful research skills, a substantial fund of historical knowledge, skills that would enable them to teach in a variety of settings, and the capacity to think philosophically and in policy terms about the educational issue of enhancing the public significance of historical knowledge in the United States.

Education for Stewardship

In the fashion of historical writing, I have offered a rather discursive approach to the issues at hand. Let me shift from that mode to a denotative one. Drawing on the proposals I have already made, I offer a list of the qualities of the professional historian educated for stewardship. He or she should

1. Be an independent thinker, escaping the traps of both convention and fashion

2. Possess a substantial fund of historical knowledge, not only in a primary field but in the discipline as a whole

3. Have a worldly, expansive, and cosmopolitan sense of the discipline, reaching as far as world history and a readiness to develop and adopt analytic vocabularies and narrative strategies adequate to such a vision

4. Possess a broad knowledge of historiography and the history of the discipline

5. Have knowledge of research methods and archives, including newer electronic resources

6. Be aware of the philosophical foundations of historical knowledge and of current thinking about the grounds for fixing historical truth

7. Have a commitment to a socially and intellectually diverse community of historians

8. Have a capacity to evaluate good historical work in fields outside of one's own special field

9. Be respectful of the various careers in which professional historians are employed

10. Be skilled in both constructive critical analysis and empirically grounded creative synthesis

11. Be aware of relevant developments (empirical or theoretical) in other disciplines of relevance to historical scholarship, especially in relation to one's special field

12. Be comfortable in the role of educator and be engaged with the literature of pedagogy that is relevant to history education

13. Have detailed knowledge of a special field, based on one's own independent research, and be able to relate that research and the field itself to larger historical themes

14. Know how to bring the results of research to relevant audiences, ranging from conference presentations and journal articles to the general public, beginning with clear and compelling literary exposition

15. Have knowledge of the history, missions, and sociology of higher education and other historical agencies

16. Have the ability to work collaboratively, whether in organizational work or in collaborative research and teaching

17. Have the capacity to assume some level of responsibility for the institutional governance and management of professional affairs, whether at one's local institution or in the discipline's professional organizations

18. Have a commitment to mentoring younger historians, whatever the level of the relevant relations, ranging from ambitious high school students to junior colleagues

19. Have a commitment to the professional development of more junior colleagues in their research and teaching but also by involving them in local institutional affairs and in the discipline's major professional organizations

This is a long and ambitious list, but the aim is to promote a fuller notion of the formation of historians. It shifts priorities a bit. It asks for more than the current increasingly intense focus on research, often on very narrow topics that students have difficulty relating to larger historical issues. It also asks for a broader embrace of history as a discipline, a larger fund of historical knowledge to improve both the research and educational obligations of historians. It also gives greater prominence to the historian as educator, whether in the classroom or to the larger public. Finally, it seeks to better fit the education of the historian to the full dimensions of history as a discipline, a profession, and a variety of careers.

NOTES

1. Much of the current academic discussion was prompted by *That Noble Dream: The "Objectivity Question" and the American Historical Profession (*Novick, 1988). See especially, "Objectivity and Historians: A Century of American Historical Writing" (Kloppenberg, 1989); "Objectivity Is Not Neutrality: Explanatory Themes in History" (Haskell, 1998, chap. 6); "The Social Sciences, Objectivity and Pragmatism" (Bender, 1992). I elaborate on the question of diversity and disciplinary knowledge in "From Academic Knowledge to Democratic Knowledge" (Bender, 1999).

2. Beard's explanation of his action is reprinted in *American Higher Education: A Document History* (Hofstadter and Smith (eds.), 1961, pp. 883–884).

3. For arguments and examples, see *The La Pietra Report* (Organization of American Historians, 2000) and *Rethinking American History in a Global Age* (Bender and others, 2002). On the excess of Ph.D.'s in modern American history, see *The Education of Historians for the Twenty-First Century* (Bender and others, 2004, pp. 56–57). There is some reason to believe that the ease of developing a Ph.D. program in American history, as well as the ease of studying the field without language or much cultural reach, may account for this. In general, the higher the rank of the program, the less the overemphasis on American history is evident. In some unranked or low-ranked programs, three of four graduates are Americanists.

4. See *The La Pietra Report* (Organization of American Historians, 2000).

5. These divisions are taken in slightly modified form from *The La Pietra Report* (Organization of American Historians, 2000), where they are used to describe a proposed undergraduate curriculum.

REFERENCES

Beard, C. A. *An Economic Interpretation of the Constitution of the United States.* New York: Free Press, 1986.

Beard, C. A. "Charles A. Beard Notifies Nicholas Murray Butler of His Resignation from Columbia, 1917." In R. Hofstadter and W. Smith (eds.), *American Higher Education: A Documentary History.* Vol. 2. Chicago: University of Chicago Press, 1961.

Bender, T. "The Social Sciences, Objectivity, and Pragmatism." *Annals of Scholarship,* 1992, *9,* 183–197.

Bender, T. "From Academic Knowledge to Democratic Knowledge." Lecture presented at the College Board and the Woodrow Wilson National Fellowship Foundation Conference on Democracy, Diversity, and the Disciplines, Princeton, N.J., May 19, 1999. Republished in *Values in Higher Education* (Robinson and Katulishi, 2005).

Bender, T. *Rethinking American History in a Global Age.* Berkeley: University of California Press, 2002.

Bender, T., Katz, P. M., and Palmer, C. *The Education of Historians for the Twenty-First Century.* Urbana: University of Illinois Press/American Historical Association, 2004.

Chartier, R. *Actes/Proceedings.* Montreal: 18th International Congress of Historical Sciences, 1995.

Damrosch, D. "Mentors and Tormenters in Graduate Education." *The Chronicle of Higher Education,* Nov. 17, 2000, p. B24.

Emerson, R. W. *Selected Writings of Ralph Waldo Emerson.* New York: New American Library, 1965.

Fluck, W. "The Modernity of America and the Practice of Scholarship." In T. Bender (ed.), *Rethinking American History in a Global Age.* Berkeley: University of California Press, 2002, 343–366.

Haskell, T. L. *Objectivity Is Not Neutrality: Explanatory Themes in History.* Baltimore: The Johns Hopkins University Press, 1998.

Hofstadter, R., and Smith, W. (eds.). *American Higher Education: A Documentary History.* Vol. 2. Chicago: University of Chicago Press, 1961.

Kloppenberg, J. T. "Objectivity and Historians: A Century of American Historical Writing." *The American Historical Review,* 1989, *94,* 1011–1030.

Novick, P. *That Noble Dream: The "Objectivity Question" and the American Historical Profession.* New York: Cambridge University Press, 1988.

Organization of American Historians. *The La Pietra Report.* Bloomington, Ind.: Organization of American Historians, 2000.

Robinson, S., and Katulushi, C. *Values in Higher Education.* Cardiff: Aureus Publishing, 2005.

16

HISTORIANS, THE HISTORICAL FORCES THEY HAVE FOSTERED, AND THE DOCTORATE IN HISTORY

Joyce Appleby, University of California, Los Angeles

CURIOSITY AND INTERPRETATION ACT AS BRIDGES between the present and the past. Questions become searchlights for those doing history. Because someone asks a question, a patch of the unknown past will be investigated. Hunches about a likely answer to that question guide the researcher to the traces left behind, the inquiry itself turning the traces into evidence. The records either confirm or disconfirm hunches and sometimes point the researcher to other sources. Without a question and a hunch, the remains of the past are just that—remains.

Everything that we know and teach in the university is the result of a question that someone has posed. If no one has inquired about a past event or development, histories of the period ignore it. Knowledge of that event will be latent, becoming manifest only with some later historian's question. This explains why new discoveries about the past are always being made and why some events wait centuries to come to light. It also hints at why some subjects are dropped and why whole topics might be neglected for a few decades, as have military and diplomatic history in recent times. Without curiosity, there are no inquiries.

Most historians are aware that curiosity drives historical research, but we are less clear about what drives curiosity. Or whose curiosity is most important. Often overlooked is the fact that the major part of historical research being done at any one time is undertaken by those writing doctoral dissertations. Because history is not a discipline in which doctoral research is organized around a professor's projects, graduate students play a key, if unrecognized, role in steering the whole profession. So a critical question presents itself: *What shapes the curiosity of graduate students?* The future of American history depends, to a large extent, on how the curiosity of the new cohort of scholars is structured. Leaving aside personal experiences that may enter into a choice of topics, the two determinants of curiosity are the attitudes and predilections of their peers and the previous developments in historical scholarship. The first brings in the influence of the here-and-now: the critical events in a generation's biography and the compelling interests that distinguish them from those of their parents and grandparents. The second springs from history's own history. Still exerting an influence, for instance, is the striking break with past scholarship that took place in the 1960s. Rather quickly, historians began to ask questions about society and culture. This richness of fresh inquiries still steers researchers in new directions and will continue to do so for the foreseeable future. And behind their emergence are other historiographical chapters that hold clues about the principal tendencies within the discipline.

In his classic study, *The Liberal Tradition in America* (1955/1990, p. 299), Louis Hartz asserted that American historians represented "an erudite reflection of the limited social perspectives of the average American himself." Hartz was pointing to the fact that earlier historians had quite unselfconsciously celebrated American values, giving their attention mainly to politics. All this changed in the 1960s with the arrival of newcomers to higher education. The curiosity of this new generation of graduate students—always the agents of change—sent the profession into uncharted terrain.

These young people sought and entered graduate school in response to the expansion of higher education following World War II. They were often funded by the G.I. Bill of Rights. Then the nation's colleges and universities put out a welcome mat to women, African Americans, and the grandchildren of immigrants from Southern and Eastern Europe, people once called hyphenated Americans, as in "Italian-American" or "Greek-Americans." These graduate students wanted to know about their forebears: immigrant laborers, sharecroppers, slaves, housewives, and working women. The computer gave them a mechanism for analyzing the long-range data sets that recorded the vital statistics of ordinary people. Soon we had an amazing outpouring of findings about life expectancy, family patterns, employment trends, and social and geographic mobility. These young Turks with their new social history dragged the history establishment into a scholarly zone of the cultural wars; its embers are still smoking today.

This quantitative history, as it was often called, involved a profound reordering of ideas, approaches, and methods. The material lent itself more to analysis than narrative. For the first time, historians drew heavily on sociology, economics, and political science for research strategies that enabled them to tackle vast public records. Their studies began with clearly stated hypotheses and culminated in findings about the past, laced with correlations and statistics and displayed in tables and graphs. The material was so fresh that few could resist pushing to the back of the bookshelf the older, sedate accounts of presidencies, treaty negotiations, and military campaigns.

The emphasis of social history on empirical data, explicit argumentation, and models of social behavior has left an enduring legacy. So, too, has social historians' practice of borrowing topics from the social scientists, such as the sociologists' demography, the political scientists' analysis of voting patterns, and the economists' modeling of the economy. In matters of content, social history opened up vast new areas for investigation.

Before 1960, there were no more than a dozen histories devoted to women or minorities. Today, such studies number in the tens of thousands. The new inquiries about women, slaves, workers, members of minorities, and immigrants gave substance to subjects that had once been treated as abstractions—subjects like slavery, immigration, and labor. Because of the amount of time needed to achieve the exactitude that social history demanded, the scope of studies became smaller and smaller, pulling the professional away from grand narratives that had been constructed with more of a novelist's sweep than the social scientist's precision.

Critics of social history focused on this penchant for concentrating on details, and worse, from the critics' point of view, the details were about unimportant people. They spoke derisively of interest in the Age of Monarchy yielding to the age at menarche. Social historians fought back by dismissing as mere "literary evidence" the memoirs, diaries, legislative journals, and correspondences that had long been the mainstay of reconstructions of the past.

The new scholarship produced what had never existed in American historical writing before: information about how groups, rather than individuals, had fared in the United States. Without express intention, the study of immigrants, African Americans, women, and laborers seriously challenged the national conviction that America was a land of success where outcomes reflected individual efforts uninfluenced by membership in an ethnic group of social class. Soon, too, as the once-unknown became fully examined, the profession's appetite for calculations of patterns, rates, and correlations waned.

The very externality of social research created a demand for more introspective studies that could speak of people's beliefs and motives, reasoning and meaning. Literary evidence recovered its legitimacy, for only it contained the voices from the past. Yet the revelations of social history had lasting power in the transformation of intellectual history into the study of ideology. Instead of examining the ideas of individual men and women, historians turned to ideology, defined as a structure of values and belief that each society carefully passes on to its members. Here, anthropologists who had long investigated various worldviews became influential. Historians began talking about the social construction of reality—a concept that emphasized how people living together elaborated ways of understanding that covered the totality of human experience with nature, other human beings, and their built environment. Again, it is only familiarity that reduces, for us, the shock value of the idea that society constructs reality.

The reigning view in the first half of the twentieth century and earlier had been that individuals, using their senses, searched for the truth about their world, both natural and social. *Culture* was still a word applied to the arts, as in *high culture,* or to exotic peoples. But the idea of socially constructed reality was an elixir to graduate students searching for dissertation topics. Soon we had studies of the social construction of disease, deviance, science, the sacred, sex and gender, and, most dramatically, the subject—the human subject—that had once been accorded the status of an autonomous individual, not a receptacle for social cues. The concept of culture promised to highlight the juncture of ideas and social production—what came to be called *material culture.*

In recent years, what seems to engage graduate students is the exercise of power—a particular kind of diffuse power that a society generates through its cultural products. More specifically, those working in the modern era have explored the mechanisms through which power has been exercised, swooping up the scientific revolution, the market, participatory politics, humanitarian reform, and print communication into one conglomerate of social authority. In its soft form, curiosity about modern social power has moved toward questions associated with the elaboration of an urban middle class—Norbert Elias's "civilizing process" and Richard Bushman's "refinement." Consumers and their consumption, the formation of identities and hybridities, the shaping of attitudes through exhibitions, and the structuring of public memory have been prominently investigated. In its harder form, following Michel Foucault, inquiries about social power have taken on the contradictions, equivocations, and persecutions of the past—the cultural work done to preserve white supremacy, misogynistic regimes, or imperialistic conquests.

Whereas in an earlier age the accomplishments of the West might have been celebrated, today the price that was paid for the "rise of the West" intrigues young scholars. The imperialistic adventures that spawned colonial mentalities and the exoticizing of non-Western people, as in Edward Said's "orientalism," have inspired whole new fields, such as subaltern and postcolonial studies. Here the curiosity of current graduate students converges with public efforts to recover the stories of past wrongs and to use that recovered knowledge as a springboard for restitution campaigns.

Not since the early nineteenth century has history played such a central role in the public sphere. At its beginning as a discipline, history owed much to the fervent nationalism provoked by the American and French Revolutions; today, the power of history comes from the sustained interest in recovering those troubled parts of the past that have been neglected, ignored, or denied. For over forty years, scholars in the United States and elsewhere have worked on the underside of historic events. One of the unintended consequences of their work has redounded to the benefit of participants in worldwide movements directed to securing reconciliation and reparation of past wrongs.

In moving away from the "high history" of diplomacy, politics, and wars, historians, particularly in the United States, began investigating the lives of ordinary people. That first wave of research came under the rubric of "the new social history," followed by the "linguistic turn" that led historians away from causation to a concern with meaning. Instead of playing the omniscient author explaining events in the past, scholars became absorbed with the meaning that people in the past invested in their mores and institutions. And this took historians to the study of culture.

The potent idea of culture referred to the myriad ways that society creates and distributes its facts, truths, institutions, artifacts, and preferences, unhampered by precise definition. As the interest in culture waxed, the theoretical writings of French social theorists Jacques Derrida and Foucault began to stir interest among historians. The postmodernism that had begun in architecture and swept into literary studies now penetrated the walls of history departments. Whereas anthropologists had studied cultures of distant peoples with respect, postmodern thinkers addressed the culture of the modern West with doubt and disparagement.

Critical to this new inquiry was language, dealt with as a closed, cultural system cut off from the objects it strives to represent. Immured in particular cultures, words and symbols were seen as vibrant parts of overlapping communicative systems rather than being tools for giving access to the world of things. Although more influential among literature scholars than historians, postmodernist ideas had an impact on history students in the 1980s and 1990s. They nurtured radical critiques of truths taken for granted and undermined belief in the stability of words.

Although an interest in postmodern themes has faded, culture in all its various manifestations now dominates public discourse, including contemporary issues and historical reasoning. Looking to the future—always a risky venture for a historian—we can see that the cumulative effect of historians' recent changes in topics, methods, and theories will continue to give the profession prominence in the public realm, often accompanied by controversy. Never before has it been so important for those entering graduate school to have a clear sense of what developments have pushed history into the spotlight and how best to manage the differing demands of the public and the profession.

The legitimacy of most movements to secure recognition and restitution for past wrongs depends on credible historical research, making historians central to these efforts, even if the historians themselves are not involved. In many cases, the findings of social and cultural research made possible the recovery of historical wrongs. More generally, giving historical attention to those previously ignored—women, members of minorities, people marginalized by unconventional behavior, laborers, immigrants—has created the sense of self-respect that often precedes demands for redress, though in some cases the movements themselves, like the civil rights movement of the 1960s and the women's movement the next decade, acted as a stimulus to new work in history.

Before we can gauge what this means for the history doctorate, we'll have to look at the changes themselves. For example, the popularity of commemorations, memorials, and exhibitions, evident since the 1970s, has strengthened continuing efforts to use history for purposes of recovery and redress. Although one effort is overtly political and the other academic, their unplanned convergence has made history the most powerful discipline in the humanities and social sciences. Plans for the doctorate need to take into account the challenges and drawbacks of this close encounter with aggrieved activists and the reading public.

History fulfills a fundamental human need by reconstituting memory. Our sense of worth, of well-being, even our sanity, depends on our remembering. But our sense of worth, our well-being, and our sanity also depend on our forgetting. Remembering and forgetting often determine the history that is told. Because history has been so closely attached to nationalism, to telling the story of what nations have done and what they stand for, governments are rarely indifferent to what is remembered and forgotten. The anthropologist Mary Douglas explains it well:

> Any institution that is going to keep its shape needs to control the memory of its members; it causes them to forget experiences incompatible with its righteous image and brings to their minds events which sustain the view that is complementary to itself (1986, p. 112).

It is against this governmental imperative that victims of abuse or their descendents struggle in recovering those patches of the past long suppressed.

The public and those who actually write history have a different conception of the relation between the past and historical research. There's a pervasive notion abroad in the land that somehow the past lingers on to force the hand of historians or exists in a kind of limbo to be examined from time to time. Historians know that once a moment in time is over, the past has vanished. They are acutely aware that what we recover from the past depends on a different calibration of importance than the one that engaged the participants. In this inexorable situation, the here-and-now triumphs over the gone-and-over because the questions that guide historical research are asked in the present.

It is hard to deal with the disappearance of the past because we know that things happened and that their consequences will affect subsequent events. The fact that only through further study can those consequences be determined is also disquieting. Public opinion favors a view of the past as controlling historians, overwhelming them with incontrovertible evidence, but the reverse is actually the case. Even the memories, material traces, and written records that linger on after an event only become evidence when someone asks a pointed question about the past.

When I say something like this in public, someone in the audience will usually ask, insistently, "But aren't there historical facts?" "Yes, there are historical facts," I reply, "but they aren't very interesting, and they rarely tell us what we want to know about the past." Let's take Caesar crossing the Rubicon. That's a fact. He did cross it, but thousands of Romans walked through the stream called the Rubicon every day. Caesar's crossing only becomes interesting when it is connected with Roman politics. His crossing was more important symbolically than actually. Assessing its significance requires an interpretation—another concept the public finds troubling (Becker, 1955). Facts consist of established statements about the past: George Washington was born on February 22nd (actually he was born on February 11th, but the calendar was pushed ahead eleven days in 1756 as part of the Gregorian reform of the calendar). What we want to know about Caesar and Washington has to do with their actions, their motives, their self-understanding, and their responses to the flow of events swirling around them, all information that comes laced with the scholar's interpretations and analyses.

The remains of past living never speak for themselves. Others—historians, museum directors, or op-ed writers—must talk for them, sorting them out as they link them to causes and influences while judging their importance and relevance. This essential interpretive function, which has become salient recently, undermines historians' credibility among many members of the public because they see interpretations as clearly involving "mere" opinions. Scholars cannot deliver the neutral, objective account of the past that the public yearns for, though they once wrote as though they could. A neutral account would be a chronicle that merely listed established events.

Large segments of the public are peculiarly resistant to the idea of historical revisions, even if based on new research. Turned into the pejorative "ism" of revisionism, new scholarship is often considered the result of arbitrary interpretive decisions rather than the normal follow-up to fresh findings. We never hear laments about revisionism in chemistry or economics. We expect those learned fields to be transformed over time with new investigations or new models of reality, while changes in a familiar historic narrative based on new research are often met with dismay.

Some American parents become angry when they discover the addition of women, free blacks, or immigrants to their children's textbooks. The 1994 publication of the National History Standards, developed by professional historians in cooperation with history teachers in the lower grades, caused an outburst from many public figures because they felt that the inclusion of research on slaves, immigrants, and laborers in the standards diminished the glory of the nation's historical record. These differing responses indicate that stability in historical knowledge has a psychological, even political, dimension that other subjects do not have.

Writing history is a peculiar enterprise in which researchers strive for comprehensive and accurate accounts of their findings within the intellectual caldron of their own minds, filled as it is with memories, biases, affinities, and values. Graduate students need to ponder such vexed topics throughout their education to avoid the naivety of the unreflective writer. Without thinking through the epistemological implications of writing about something that everyone knows once existed but has vanished, leaving behind only a pile of detritus, tyros risk fooling themselves about the objectivity of their own work.

The next generation of historians needs to meet the new moral and intellectual demands that have come with the discipline's public prominence. In addition to the transmission of knowledge and preparation for doing research—the two keystones of the profession—the discipline's educational goals should include consideration of the tangled connection of memory, the traces left from the past, and the role of the person who reconstructs past events after memories have long faded.

The Doctorate in History

Graduate education needs to begin with these kinds of ruminations, for it takes time to work through the vertigo of seeking the truth while recognizing the impossibility of rendering an order of events into an ordering of words. Because history impinges on the sensibilities and convictions of the public more than any other field of knowledge, avoiding the tough questions about how historical knowledge is conceived renders the scholar unprepared to answer the public's insistent questioning about the relation of research to interpretation and the tension between objectivity and the historian's subjectivity.

The history doctorate should be configured for the future against this background of history's new prominence in the public realm, its relation to political movements agitating for the recovery of suppressed episodes, and the dramatic rejection of the Enlightenment's concept of knowledge, truth, and objectivity. The divergence between the production of historical knowledge and the public's understanding of the choosing, researching, and reconstructing of topics about the past represents a slightly different challenge, which should also be addressed. It is hard to determine in advance what qualities a historian should possess outside the obvious ones of intelligence, curiosity, and the capacity to hold large amounts of interpreted information in the mind at one time. Students are drawn to history because of their love of studying the past comprehensively rather than examining selected slices of the past found in work done in historical geography, sociology, or political science. They tend to be more appreciative than analytical, more drawn to general assessments of complex situations than the isolation of cause-and-effect generalizations.

The shift of emphasis from learning history to analyzing how it is created is hard for some students to make, but they tend to sort themselves out, largely in response to the demands that are made on them. Departments want men and women who are prepared to think critically, synthesize knowledge, and write gracefully about what they have learned. Hence admissions committees look for these capacities in prospective students.

Graduate education can and should aim at introducing scholarly apprentices to the broad intellectual universe that gave rise to history as an academic discipline. One goal of every doctoral program should be to examine the unexamined assumptions that become embedded in our own, early acculturation. Graduate education should also hone the curiosity that students bring with them as they turn themselves into professionals by giving them the skills to identity sources of evidence and work with them intensely and comprehensively. Intellectual self-awareness, breadth of knowledge of one's own cultural traditions, and acquisition of sophisticated research techniques prepare students to pursue their own research questions within the forms of their chosen profession.

Historians in recent decades have not been very good stewards of historical knowledge, in part, because the idea of a canon to learn is tainted as Eurocentric and, in part, because of the proliferation of topics and approaches. What scholars have recently acquired is a much more sophisticated grasp of how historical knowledge is constructed. An ideal graduate program involves the cultivation of learning and appreciation well tested by a sustained critical and analytical attitude.

If I could start *de novo* and build a graduate history program, it would focus initially on mastering the history of our civilization and the history of historical scholarship itself. I would prescribe two years of course work, followed by the writing of a dissertation, preferably in three years. The ideal trajectory for work toward the doctorate requires levels of financial support that public universities rarely give. It would probably be a good idea to limit the number of entrants to the funds available to sustain them during a five- or six-year period. No more than two years of a student's program should involve work as a teaching assistant, if the goal is steady progress toward the degree.

Year One

Graduate work represents a distinct break from undergraduate work, where the emphasis is on learning historical knowledge and thinking about past societies through this knowledge. With the move to becoming a professional historian, the student becomes conscious of historical scholarship as an intellectual production containing the conspicuous results of research and interpretation and the less visible residue of unexamined assumptions, cultural imperatives, and historians' own personal traditions. A decided ratcheting up of the demands to be critical, as well as analytical, takes place.

The first year should aim to give students the intellectual and practical tools to make this shift. For example, language preparation, if needed, would start at the beginning of each student's program. The first course of the first year would cover the Western intellectual tradition, including the origins and development of the principal disciplines that history draws upon. The second half of the first year would comprise two courses: an introduction to the different methods and approaches used in research on economic, scientific, social, cultural, literary, diplomatic, and political aspects of the past and a seminar examining how historical knowledge is created. The first course, on the modern Western intellectual tradition, would cover, from the historian's point of view, the classic texts from Bacon, Hobbes, Locke, Montesquieu, Wollstonecraft, Rousseau, Smith, Hume, Marx, Darwin, Durkheim, Weber, and Foucault. This tradition, politicized and abandoned as the Western canon (in its classic form, without Wollstonecraft, Marx, and Foucault), needs to be reinstituted because history is a Western discipline, with its own peculiar intellectual footings. Indeed, in some graduate programs the students themselves have become aware of their own ignorance of such classic works and initiated seminars on them.

Against the tendency to see such courses as merely enriching, it is important to stress their epistemological impact. They would provide a shared background across the geographical areas that historians cover and would make clearer the sources of the students' own curiosity, rendering them freer of their own, unconscious prejudices and less susceptible to political pressures. Within this trajectory, students could examine the intellectual origins of the disciplines of literature and the social sciences that they will be drawing on. Such currently resonating concepts as rational choice in political science, utility maximization in economics, feminist theory in literature, and ethnomethodology in anthropology all have histories that deserve to be studied in the context of the larger movements of thought of the past five centuries.

Unlike the social sciences, which take an aspect of social existence for a separate examination, historians look at past societies as a whole. However small the chosen topic, it must be set within the context of the culture, physical setting, and historic events that impinge on it. Looking at the past comprehensively forces the scholar to limit the scope of his or her investigations: historians insist on presenting their findings within a detailed reconstruction of their original setting because history is, above all, about the interconnectedness of social existence, for example, the way child rearing influences and reflects political values or how demographic patterns shape social values.

To give history graduates the widest possible selection of topics, graduate programs should introduce students to the methods and sources across the wide sweep of research fields, from work in economic history to cultural studies, the history of science, and social history. In our age of specialization and microhistorical work, each division of the whole has developed a repertoire of techniques for doing research. These should be shared, for they reveal, as nothing else can, the level of sophistication historians have attained in their broadening of inquiries. For this reason, the second half-year course for the first year would include grounding in the principal sources that serve historians. Here the emphasis would be practical and pertinent to the task of choosing and researching a historical topic. By focusing on how historians in various subfields approach their subjects, students would learn about a large array of possible topics. It would also be important for students to understand how the historians' approach to literature, economics, and politics differs from that of literary scholars, economists, and political scientists. This persistent focus on how historians think and do research would not only heighten the self-knowledge of the student but would introduce substantive knowledge within a professional framework.

The additional seminar during the second half of the first year should help students explore theoretically, but informally, how historical knowledge is created. Here, through exemplars and practical reasoning about the matter, students could explore the tensions between research and interpretation, selective questions and comprehensive answers. Whereas graduate programs once routinely mandated courses in historiography, they rarely do now. These courses lost out to the increasing specialization within the profession and suffered as well from their terminal dullness. There is more enthusiasm today for learning about historical research by doing it, but yielding to the temptation to abandon courses dealing with historical prescriptions and precedents has left students peculiarly vulnerable to chic ideas and passing persuasions.

Whether they realize it or not, students who intend to become historians are entering into a scholarly conversation that goes back several generations. They need to be able to attach the fragments they know a great deal about to early discourses in order to understand why they are asking their questions. Even historians can be unduly present-minded. A common understanding of the historical trajectory of historical intelligence itself gives contemporary students a shared background while it connects them to their predecessors. Historians do best and enjoy most guiding graduate students in research projects in their own fields. Here the student taps into the energizing enthusiasm of a mentor. Teaching students the techniques of research is important but is unlikely to be neglected.

Reforms that will be difficult to effect are those that call for learning about their own society's, hence their own discipline's, intellectual history and structure. Critics will say that it privileges the West, which is true, but it is the contemporary West's collection of unexamined assumptions and half-known traditions that is lodged inside the heads of Western historians. The surest way to reduce the bias from the subjectivity of doing history is to bring to light the nature and origins of the assumptions and traditions in the thought of the investigator. For many faculties, a team approach would work best in presenting courses with broad intellectual sweep. To cover these many approaches, faculty members will have to participate in developing comprehensive courses. Any serious effort to reform doctoral programs will have to involve a department's corporate effort, with a comparable commitment from its members to move beyond the easy job of replicating oneself to the more difficult one of preparing new and demanding instructional programs.

The first-year courses I have described would require a consensus among history faculty members that a shared intellectual framework is critically important to all students entering their program. Such a consensus is not likely to develop, which accounts for the rather random assortment of courses that make up most programs. Since the 1960s, the number of options given students has increased while the requirements have decreased, with an inevitable decline in coherence, if not conviction. Graduate instructors prefer to guide the research of students who are working broadly in their field. It is far more difficult to get commitments of time and thought to a comprehensive preparation for apprentice historians. And the lack of research on doctoral education makes it possible for anecdotal evidence to serve for the real thing.

Year Two

The second year of course work would help the students choose their subjects. The department would offer seminars in the substantive scholarship in specific fields, along with a semester or two-quarter seminar devoted to doing an introductory research project. This year would also include a seminar specifically devoted to writing a dissertation proposal, as well as how to prepare a research grant application. Here the faculty would address the specific challenge of writing and organizing historical material. Students would examine exemplars of lucid scholarship and compelling prose.

As the enhanced importance of historical scholarship in the public realm suggests, historians have career horizons wider than college teaching. The 1980s witnessed the founding of an amazing number of new museums along with the expansions of existing ones. Almost all of these museums have a historical dimension requiring historians as curators. Historians now serve on a variety of commissions serving the public or political groups that require research. The entertainment and information industries are turning to historians as researchers and scriptwriters. New institutes and centers promoting the study of history and improvement in instruction, such as the Gilder-Lehrman Institute and the Bradley Foundation, need historians. The National Park Service employs historians to direct the interpretation of its park sites. Although teaching will likely remain the goal of most Ph.D.'s, the broader scope of opportunities should be presented to all graduate students. It seems preferable to do this through informal sessions geared to the professional needs of graduate students rather than through course work.

Most students who aim for an academic career or teaching and writing learn about teaching through their experience as teaching assistants. It is absolutely essential that this apprentice teaching be accompanied by a seminar that addresses pedagogical problems and offers specific guidance in planning courses, including the development of reading lists and syllabi. Supervising instructors should make classroom visits for all teaching assistants, giving them the benefit of their greater experience in written evaluations. This requirement seems stunningly obvious, but it is the rare department that fills this obligation for all of its teaching assistants.

Year Three and Beyond: The Dissertation

I believe that two years of preparatory work is sufficient, with three or four years subsequently being devoted to writing the dissertation. Although the boundaries of dissertations might be changed in the future, there can be no substitute for this introduction to historical research and interpretation. Writing history is what constitutes a professional historian, whether that person continues to work in an academic institution or not.

Historians serving on prize committees for books or articles often comment on the convergence of the members on a few candidates for prizes, usually representing 3 or 4 percent of the whole. Yet they have difficulty explaining why they chose the same candidates, and even more in specifying the qualities that spoke to them, except in the broadest, even banal, terms. Completing a piece of historical scholarship, under guidance, is an experience. As an experience, it has epistemological consequences. At the end, the graduate student knows something that he or she did not know or understand before. Before finishing, the student has been forced to think and rethink how one imposes an order of words on an order of things.

Unfortunately, students often become stalled or, worse, lost in such a process. The result is that many students do not complete the dissertation or they spend many, many years in graduate school doing so. There are some practical ways to address this problem at the dissertation stage. For example, graduate programs can organize dissertation-writing groups to mitigate the isolation of doing solitary, creative work. The excruciating pressure of creating a first piece of scholarship can be relieved through regular exchanges in a dissertation-writing group in which participants alternate as presenters and critics. Within the supportive environment of such a group, participants, all of whom are writing dissertations, help each other with their assessments, suggestions, and criticisms.

As participants meet fortnightly or monthly, one group member presents a piece of work. Participants work out a set of standards valuable to all. Students do not need to be working in the same field to help each other as readers and critics. Indeed, the very lack of familiarity with a topic alerts each writer to the importance of clarity in the structure and writing of history. As group members comment on the work of others, they become acutely aware of how their observations impinge on their own work. Mentors can and should help students set parameters around their research projects, showing them how to limit their scope as much as possible so they can complete the project in a few years, with plenty of time devoted to studying the context of the event or development being explored. Students should be encouraged to recognize that the transition from a dissertation to a published work will take several more years of thought and work.

Beyond the Doctoral Program: The Historian in Society

The potential for history to disturb the peace is always latent, manifesting itself when some new scholarship upsets conventional thinking on a subject or scratches across some group's prejudices like chalk on blackboard. This has long been the case. What is new today and what will continue to place the discipline in a confrontational posture vis-à-vis the public (or at least public officials) is the turn-about in the profession's thinking about the nature of society and its relation to the individual.

Americans sometimes seem all too human in their desire to have their cake and eat it, too. Inordinately proud of their traditions of free speech, they nonetheless wish fervently that they could suppress unpleasant chapters in American history. John Dower, a historian of Japan caught up in the furor caused by the exhibition of the Superfortress Enola Gay at the National Air and Space Museum in 1995, reminded his fellow Americans that "the lifeblood of democracy itself lies in tolerance of principled criticism, a constant willingness to entertain serious challenges to entrenched and orthodox views." But tolerance is a virtue just because it is so hard to extend it to ideas and people that we find objectionable. The freer the society, the more contested becomes historical research at the cutting edge of new inquiries.

If history, as a discipline, helps a citizenry understand and appreciate its past, as well as cultivate the analytical capacities so necessary to intelligent civic discourse, why is it causing so much unhappiness in the land today? This is difficult to explain, but it probably has something to do with the fact that our country's adults are divided between large numbers who are looking for absolute answers in the face of troubling changes and another group that has accepted the varieties of cultural expression and the limits of objectivity in scholarship. As successive cohorts of children pass through public schools, which by now have incorporated the new social and cultural historical scholarship, it will abrade their sensibilities less. An acceptance of the status quo and a taste for critical thought also divide members of the public. Academic historians, by and large, belong in the latter group. Their education forces them to confront the ambiguities and uncertainties of interpretation from the outset of their careers. They are ideal mediators of the tensions between the public and the profession, and they should be encouraged to take on this work.

REFERENCES

Becker, C. "What Are Historical Facts?" *The Western Political Quarterly*, 1955, 8, 327–340.
Douglas, M. *How Institutions Think*. Syracuse, N.Y.: Syracuse University Press, 1986.
Hartz, L. *The Liberal Tradition in America: An Interpretation of American Political Thought Since the Revolution*. New York: Harcourt, Brace, 1955/1990.

17

GETTING READY
TO DO HISTORY

William Cronon, University of Wisconsin–Madison

BEFORE SPECULATING ABOUT how historians should be trained, we might ask what they actually *do*. Neither question is as easy to answer as one might imagine.

The simplest response, of course, is that historians study the past. But it takes only a moment's reflection to realize that this in no way distinguishes the formal discipline called "history" from its neighbors in the academy. Most disciplines in the humanities, after all, devote much of their energy to studying the past. Literature departments study past human writing and discourse; philosophy departments study past ideas and systems of thought; art history departments study, well, the history of art. None of the social sciences could pursue their policy interests or their concern for human cultures, social systems, or political economies without studying the histories of these things. Indeed, many subdivisions of the discipline called history are heavily parasitic on the social sciences, from which they borrow questions and methodologies. Although sociologists and political scientists do not always recognize each other's work as such, they practice social and political history as much as their colleagues in history do, and there's not much question that economic history and legal history are more often written by economists and law professors than by members of history departments (though how much history, law, and economics have actually benefited from this division of labor remains an open question). As for archaeology, the only thing that would seem to separate it from history is an arbitrary boundary between history and "prehistory" on the one hand, and a rather arcane dispute over what counts as a historical document on the other.

Even the natural sciences are far more historical than we typically admit. Once one gets past the dream of timeless scientific laws that traditionally made physics the envy of its peers, it is quite striking how many of the sciences put the past at the center of their intellectual enterprise. Geology is arguably the most historical of the sciences, and despite the seeming difference between written archival sources on the one hand, and sediments and strata on the other, the underlying epistemological similarities between the ways geologists and historians go about their work are impressive. The revolution that plate tectonics represented for earth science in the twentieth century has been as profound in its impact as the revolution represented by Darwinian evolution for biology in the nineteenth— and both are nothing if not theories of historical change that now permeate every corner of their disciplines. Although astronomy may seem to the uninitiated to study mainly the vast distances of space, in fact those distances are almost always articulated in terms of time, so that the light of every star represents a different historical moment—and thus, if you will, a different historical document. Push astronomy to the outer limits of its vision, and one eventually reaches the earliest moments of creation, where even particle physics suddenly seems to become a study in historical change. Although the relevant time scales differ enormously, it is not too much of a stretch to say that virtually every academic discipline treats the past as one of its most important objects of study—not just as an interesting sidelight on more fundamental questions but as the very heart of its intellectual project.

Finally, one of the nearest neighbors of academic history in studying and writing about the human past is not really a discipline at all: journalism. Although historians sometimes speak pejoratively about journalistic reporting, arguing that it is not yet remote enough from the present to have achieved dispassionate distance, or that adequate historical documents are not yet available for recent periods, or that reporters overemphasize biographies and personalities in their historical explanations, in fact it's pretty difficult to draw a precise boundary between journalism and history. Philip Graham of the *Washington Post* famously referred to journalism as "the rough draft of history," and certainly historians depend on journalistic sources to a remarkable degree. Moreover, the best history written by professional journalists can hold its own with the best history written by academic historians (and often has greater impact) because it is written more accessibly and is usually addressed toward an audience far beyond the academy. Journalists like Allan Nevins or Robert Caro or Frances Fitzgerald or even Winston Churchill had little formal training in history, but this seems not to have diminished the influence of their books on public understanding of the past. Quite the contrary. Academic historians may be jealous of this fact, but it is difficult to argue that such works cannot properly be described as "histories." Dismissing them as "popular" seems a rather odd criticism, since more than a few academic historians would secretly love to apply that adjective to their own writings as well.

So if one of the goals of an academic discipline is to carve out a special intellectual territory to be exclusively its own and to promote its trained experts as high priests who are uniquely qualified to serve as guides (and gatekeepers) for that territory, then one might conclude from all this that academic history has been singularly unsuccessful in monopolizing its subject—the past—for itself. If everyone studies the past and everyone has useful, intelligent things to say about it, then why does one need a doctorate in history to study and hold forth on the subject? The quick answer is that one does not. Good history can and has been written by many, many people who lack a history Ph.D. or any other degrees in the subject. It is worth declaring this fact right up front, lest we forget that there is nothing magic about a doctorate in history. It provides real training for very real skills and also serves as a crucial professional credential without which certain forms of employment (for instance, in the history departments of major research universities and many teaching institutions) are virtually unattainable. These are indisputable practical benefits of the degree. But many other disciplines and professional communities offer equally valuable perspectives if our goal is to understand the past in all its richness and complexity. Historians forget this truth at their peril. For this reason, a key goal in training future historians must be the constant reminder that they share their expertise with many other scholars and scientists. Learning from these colleagues in other fields is an indispensable antidote to the hubris that flows from too exclusive, inward-turned, and narrow-minded a definition of disciplinary boundaries and professional authority.

Shared Values of Historians

Having declared these caveats, though, I still have little doubt that members of the guild called "historians" do share certain normative assumptions, intellectual commitments, methodological approaches, and theoretical inclinations that separate them even from colleagues in other guilds who study the very same subjects. Put historians in a room together with representatives from other fields to discuss a topic of common concern, and they will recognize each other pretty quickly just from the ways they ask and answer questions. A chief goal of doctoral training is presumably to inculcate new members of the guild in precisely these shared ways of asking questions, interacting with each other, and making sense of the world.

So what values and intellectual leanings do we historians generally share? Let me list what I regard as some of the most important ones and then consider their implications for doctoral training.

• Historians study the past mainly to discover how human beings lived back then, putting people at the center of our work. Although this may seem so obvious that it scarcely needs stating, it in fact defines the discipline of history far more than its practitioners typically realize. For one thing, it draws a stark boundary between us and most of our colleagues who study the past in the natural sciences, since for them a default focus on human beings can seem quite surprising and even counterintuitive.

• No matter what the initial question historians may ask about something in the past, our *second* question is always, *"But . . . what are the documents?"* Trivial though it seems, this may be the single most crucial methodological commitment that all historians share. Few scholars who are not themselves historians appreciate just how deep this discipline-defining question goes. Historians know in their very bones that questions about the past are useless unless they point toward documents we can use to answer them. Among our greatest skills is the ability to identify new sources and squeeze new meanings from the extraordinary hodgepodge of fragmentary evidence that the past has bequeathed us. Unlike most of our colleagues in the sciences, we rarely get to query our subject directly and create new evidence by running new experiments; instead, we have to be very clever about extracting answers from documents that were usually created for purposes quite different from our own.

• For us, the past is a single vast experiment that can never be run a second time, and this has enormous implications for why our epistemologies differ so fundamentally from those of the experimental sciences.[1]

• Historians are relatively uninterested in discovering broad generalizations that can be applied more or less universally without regard to time or place. This separates us from many (but not all) of our colleagues in the natural and social sciences. For us, all phenomena exist in time and are uniquely shaped by their peculiar historical moment so must always be placed in that context.

- We are drawn to analyses in which a given event or phenomenon is explained mainly by appealing to prior causes and contexts.

- We typically construct explanations by the narrative device of periodizing, that is, dividing the seamless continuum of past time into a sequence of discrete periods that perform roughly the same storytelling function as the chapters of a book. We periodize in this way regardless of the time scale on which we operate.

- In general, historians tend to concentrate their research within chronological and geographical boundaries that are quite constrained compared with other disciplines, often spending our entire professional careers immersing ourselves in the documents of just one time and place: "the Ancien Regime," say, or "Antebellum America," or "Tokugawa Japan." Our conviction is that only by so doing will we gain a richly textured, almost intuitive understanding of the period we study. We often criticize other disciplines for failing to examine enough evidence to gain this kind of immersive holistic understanding—and for failing to produce the carefully nuanced and contextualized interpretations that go with it.

- Unlike many scientists, historians have little trouble believing that this kind of richly contextualized, thick description of past events and phenomena is genuine analytical work, even if it yields no obvious causal explanations. For us, the unique particularities that define a given historical moment are as interesting as any broader generalizations that might transcend that time and place. Like many other scholars in the humanities, we are as eager to understand the *meanings* of past times and lives as we are to determine their *causes*, so interpretation is as important to us as explanation.

- Although we would not typically use these words to describe what we do, we strongly prefer multicausal explanations of what we regard as overdetermined systems in the past. Tell us that a past event had only one cause, and we will invariably reach for our guns. We are often content (much to the frustration of our colleagues in more scientific disciplines) simply to list causal forces operating at a given moment without making much of an effort to rank them or to offer a rigorously argued assessment of their relative importance.

- Consistent with our preference for descriptive nuance, causal complexity, and immersion in sources, historians resist what we regard as overgeneralization and reductionism in other disciplines.

- As a corollary, historians generally shun the social scientific impulse to offer predictions about the future based on our professional knowledge of the past. Perhaps because the future has not yet generated any documents, we do not feel especially competent—*qua* historians—to talk about it.

- Recognizing a key danger in our own immersive approach, historians are hostile to what we sometimes pejoratively label "mere antiquarianism." By this we mean excessive devotion to the facts and minutiae of the past without enough effort to put those facts in the service of larger questions. We believe that the way to avoid antiquarianism is to ask and answer "significant" questions about the past. We of course argue with each other all the time about what exactly this means. The major intellectual movements of the discipline—and its shorter-lived fads—almost always hinge on struggles over what counts as significant.

- Historians have long believed—many decades before the intellectual movement called postmodernism was a gleam in anyone's deconstructionist eye—that history is always a dialogue between past and present, so that the questions we care about in the present can't help but shape, quite profoundly, what we think we know and care about in the past. We also believe that understanding past human beings requires us to try to see the world at least in part through their eyes—even though we also know we can never fully succeed in that effort.

- "Relativism" thus comes quite easily to most historians in ways that can look to outsiders very much like postmodern skepticism about the limits of factual knowledge. But historians usually couple their relativism with a basic realist epistemology (sometimes loosely labeled "historicism") in which the relational nature of all historical knowledge becomes our best tool for gaining real understanding of the past—rather than serving as a skeptic's proof that the past cannot be known at all.

- Most historians long ago abandoned the conviction that history can ever be "objective" in an absolute sense. We understand not only that different people in the past had different points of view that need to be understood, but that different scholars writing in the present will likewise have different points of view that will necessarily lead them to see different things and draw different conclusions that reflect their own perspectives and assumptions. You can call this bias if you will, but it means that any given scholar inevitably pays more attention to certain features of the past than to others, placing that scholar in disagreement with others whose questions and passions point in different directions. Far from casting doubt on the whole enterprise, these divergent perspectives among historians actually broaden our collective understanding by perennially generating new evidence, new arguments, new insights, even new *facts*. The goal of our professional practice is thus not to eliminate bias—we do not believe that it is possible or even desirable—but rather to recognize, critique, and understand its consequences. The ease with which we embrace this bias-tolerant approach can be genuinely bewildering to colleagues in other fields.

• Because we assume that all history is inevitably written from a particular point of view, we also assume that history is closely tied to present politics. Far from worrying that this will taint our scholarship (as some of our colleagues in the sciences might fear), we usually embrace the chance to explore history's relevance to issues unfolding in our own day.

• That said, despite our belief that history is always political and never "objective," historians quickly become suspicious of scholars who are so committed to particular ideological beliefs that they ignore or dismiss evidence that might refute or complicate those beliefs. Our disciplinary preference for complexity means that we value scholarship that acknowledges contrary perspectives in order to construct more complicated and comprehensive arguments.

• We have what amounts to an aesthetic preference for ambiguity and irony: our work usually favors pastels and shades of gray over bright primary colors. And although we may not believe in objectivity, we embrace values that nonetheless point in its general direction: tolerance, open-mindedness, fairness, and a willingness to engage and acknowledge the worth of contrary points of view.

• Although historians are like any other guild in developing special meanings for words that become heavily used or contested in our professional debates, for the most part we have maintained a deep commitment to ordinary vocabulary and accessible language. We do not like jargon. It is no accident that academic history books find many more readers outside the academy than do those of most other disciplines.

• Finally, historians have never abandoned our commitment to narrative storytelling as an essential rhetorical and analytical tool for conveying historical knowledge. This is consistent with our preferred styles of causal explanation, our periodizing impulses, and our commitment to thick description and contextualization. But it also reflects the sense many of us share that history at its very best remains a form of literature, as much an art as a science. Historians have not forgotten that Clio was among the nine Muses of Greek mythology, and we are proud that her patronage of history sets our discipline apart from most others in the modern academy.

I am sure my colleagues in history will dispute at least some claims on this list and will find much to criticize in the interpretive approach that has led me to emphasize certain aspects of our professional practice at the expense of others. I would happily join them in identifying many exceptions to the broad generalizations I have just offered and the many important features of the discipline that I have ignored altogether. Arguing with each other about such things is, after all, what we historians do. But if even a sizable fraction of the items on this list do in fact describe central tendencies of the academic discipline called "history," setting it apart from its neighbors in the academy, then the obvious next question is what these characteristics imply about the goals and practices of doctoral education for this peculiar intellectual guild.

Mistrusting the Ph.D. Octopus

First, though, I want to reflect briefly on the benefits and costs of creating and reproducing a guild called "history" in the first place. As a historian, I am personally and professionally committed to the values and intellectual tendencies I have just listed. I firmly believe that, on balance, they yield valuable insights about the human past that are often richer, subtler—and more pleasurable to read—than those of many other disciplines. I happily pass these values on to my students and work hard to make sure that their commitment to history's foundational premises is as strong as my own.

At a most basic level, this is the central task of doctoral education. This is how the Ph.D. defines and reproduces a discipline.

But this disciplining process is not without costs. I have already gestured at the many other approaches to studying the past that are embraced just as passionately by colleagues in other fields. A good many of these other approaches are in direct conflict with those of historians, emphasizing universality over particularity, hypothesis testing over thick description, targeted data analysis over broad source immersion, theory over narrative, model building over storytelling, technical vocabulary over the common tongue, science over literature. Suspicious though historians may be of the limitations of these alternative approaches, we should never imagine that our own preferences don't carry comparable liabilities. Every discipline has particular ways of looking at the world that offer profound insights even as they obscure other truths. Given what I have already said about the many different approaches to the past that characterize the modern academy, it would be foolish indeed to claim that any one discipline should ever have a monopoly in interpreting the human past—and this includes the discipline called history that defines the human past as its sole object of study.

A crucial function of the Ph.D. is to draw a boundary around an intellectual community, privileging the "expert knowledge" of those inside the boundary at the expense of those outside it and also defining the social circles within which disciplinary communication takes place. This is another way of saying that the Ph.D. (like the M.D. and the J.D.) has as one of its primary goals the creation of a professional guild. Such degrees and guilds have arguably become indispensable in the modern world, and they serve many valuable purposes. But it is worth remembering that there was a time when it was possible to argue quite vehemently against their pernicious influence.

More than a century ago, William James wrote a famous attack on "The Ph.D. Octopus" in which he argued that the recently imported German Ph.D. was already having baleful effects on American colleges and universities. Although some of his ideas may now seem quaint and his language sexist, his critique is still well worth considering. The doctorate, he said, could distort the meaning of scholarship by encouraging narrow research agendas at the expense of humane learning. It could train young scholars to place greater value on technical gymnastics and inward-turned scholarly debates than on the play of ideas in broader intellectual and public realms. Worst of all, it could undermine good teaching. No mean dilettante himself, James's greatest fear was that the Ph.D. might destroy what might be called the amateur tradition in scholarship and science: the pursuit of knowledge not for formal professional rewards but for the sheer love of learning—a quality all great teachers share.

James wrote:

> To interfere with the free development of talent, to obstruct the natural play of supply and demand in the teaching profession, to foster academic snobbery by the *prestige* of certain privileged institutions, to transfer accredited value from essential manhood to an outward badge, to blight hopes and promote invidious sentiments, to divert the attention of aspiring youth from direct dealings with truth to the passing of examinations—such consequences, if they exist, ought surely to be regarded as drawbacks to the system. . . . The truth is that the Doctor-monopoly in teaching, which is becoming so rooted an American custom, can show no serious grounds whatsoever for itself in reason. . . . In reality it is but a sham, a bauble, a dodge, whereby to decorate the catalogues of schools and colleges (1903, pp. 152–153).

A hundred years later, these criticisms may seem laughably overheated and wrongheaded. Any of us who now do doctoral training in history can come up with lots of ways to rebut James's critique. To the extent that the values I listed in the previous section are indeed essential to good history, then the transmission of those values to the next generation of historians is presumably the chief justification for doctoral training in the first place. If the job of a discipline is to define what constitutes rigorous argument and compelling proof in a given domain of knowledge, then surely the requirement that a doctoral dissertation display disciplined arguments and proofs to make an original contribution to scholarship has yielded enormous benefits to the profession of history. What could be more basic than the doctorate's certification that its holder has mastered core techniques and acquired qualities of mind without which good history cannot be written? Moreover, the public presentation of doctoral research—first in conference papers, then in articles, and finally in a book-length monograph—is the key process whereby professional historians declare their membership in the guild, become known to their peers, and join the circle of critical conversation that is the very heart of the discipline. Surely the doctorate at its best has done an admirable job of delivering all these professional goods.

And yet I think we should still heed James's misgivings as we consider how to provide the best possible doctoral training for individuals seeking to become professional historians. The doctorate is a means to an end, nothing more. Leaving aside its guild-defining and gatekeeping functions, the success of doctoral training should be measured by the profundity of the scholarship it encourages, the habits of mind it cultivates, the excellence of the teaching it fosters, and the quality of public intellectual engagement it promotes. As James warned, the doctorate at its worst can fall short on every one of these measures.

By concentrating students' attention on tightly focused strands of historiography in the service of narrowly defined monographic research pursued first and foremost in the name of rigor, the Ph.D. can discourage the breadth of learning—not just about history but about life and the world—that is essential to creative scholarship, teaching, and public dialogue. To the extent that the Ph.D. encourages historians to read mainly the work of other historians—or worse, mainly the work of historians in tiny subfields—it diminishes the discipline. Although historians employed in academic institutions spend most of their careers providing undergraduates with broad overviews of large historical topics, this is precisely the wide-ranging, synthesizing approach to the past that the doctorate too often discourages as insufficiently rigorous. Perhaps the weirdest feature of the Ph.D., as James noticed with real bitterness, is the way it has become the gateway to teaching jobs—even though most doctoral programs in history do precious little to help their students learn the teacher's craft. I am enough inculcated with the values of the doctorate that I gladly embrace the proposition that great teaching and great scholarship can and should go together—but I cannot honestly say that typical doctoral training gives remotely equal emphasis to these equally honorable goals.

The tendency of all guilds is to turn inward upon themselves, generating specialized vocabularies and methodologies that eventually demarcate the professional community. At their best, these guild-defining tendencies can be a real source of intellectual insight, and the rites of passage that admit new members into the circle of specialized knowledge can be a legitimate source of professional authority. But they can also encourage self-referential work, in which new scholars become ever more knowledgeable about the writings of other scholars, sometimes at the expense of asking broader historical questions or considering how nonscholarly audiences (including undergraduates) might best engage those larger questions.

Self-referentiality has many perils. It can encourage the intellectual faddishness that leads scholars to trot off in pursuit of newness for newness' sake, tempting them to ignore as passé older work that in fact retains great value. It can isolate scholars by placing them in dialogue far more with each other than with members of other disciplines or the wider public, rendering them mutually incomprehensible. The proliferation of subfields can so divide the intellectual landscape of the past that critical interconnections among highly related phenomena become completely obscured. (Nowhere is this more evident than in the marginal status of economic history in the modern academy.) Perhaps most perniciously, these self-referential tendencies can privilege some topics over others so thoroughly that enormously important questions don't even get asked, let alone researched or explored.

These dangers of professional guilds are hardly peculiar to history. But because the historical project of studying and interpreting the past is so widely shared with other disciplines and because the potential sources of historical insight are therefore so scattered and disparate, the costs of succumbing to professional insularity are greater for historians than for other guilds. If I am right that we pride ourselves on the openness and accessibility of our discipline, we should explicitly design our professional training to resist the negative tendencies of professionalization. This is where it can be helpful to remember James's warnings against the Ph.D. Octopus even if our goal is to design the best possible education for history Ph.D.'s.

Because history will never (and should never) successfully monopolize its own discipline the way doctors and lawyers monopolize theirs, the training of historians should always be more open-ended than other guilds, more porous to outside influences, more tolerant of eclecticism. History departments are often criticized by deans and by colleagues in other disciplines for the seeming structurelessness of the history curriculum, the lack of clear progression from course to course and level to level that seems so transparently obvious for subjects like chemistry or mathematics. This apparent structurelessness no doubt reflects the vastness of our subject and its balkanization into so many periods and geographical subfields. But I also think it reflects our collective recognition that the path to good history must always involve a fair amount of wandering and serendipity. I might even go so far as to declare that history remains the great amateur discipline of the academy, in the original etymological sense applied to someone who pursues a subject more for the love of its intrinsic fascination than for money or professional prestige. If this is so, then we might echo William James by saying that the best doctoral training for historians should be training for professional amateurs.

Training Professional Generalists

If the word *amateur* has lost so much of its original meaning that we can no longer use it without implying that historians do shoddy, unprofessional work, then perhaps a less threatening description of the scholars we wish to train and certify with the history doctorate is that they should be *professional generalists*. For that is the ultimate goal of immersing oneself in as many sources as possible relating to a given period or problem: to gain an intricately intuitive understanding of all features of life in a past time and place, in all their interconnections and complexities and contradictions. If we aspire to this kind of holism in the histories we write, then the price we pay is that historians will rarely be as expert in any particular aspect of past life as their colleagues who study just one thing. Our conviction is that this is a price worth paying for the breadth and depth that come from holistic immersion.

So how do we train Ph.D. students to do this? How do we encourage them to become rigorous scholars and thinkers while guarding against excessive insularity and specialization? How do we help them become equally committed as much to teaching and public engagement as to scholarly research and analysis? How do we keep them humble about the limits of their disciplinary knowledge so they remain perennially open to insights from beyond those limits? How can we encourage them never to lose the amateur spirit that William James feared the doctorate was designed to destroy? How do we train professional generalists?

One obvious and crucial answer is that we should always proceed with these questions and the values they imply foremost in our minds. If we accept the premise that historical knowledge grows by accretion, with ever-elaborating networks of lateral associations among bodies of information that are rarely organized in a tidy or hierarchical way, then we will be better able to resist the illusion that any particular technical reform of the doctoral curriculum can somehow supply the magic key that will reliably produce first-rate historians. If wandering and serendipity are essential to the practice of good history, then we should be careful to design curricula that provide adequate opportunities for rambling—even for occasionally getting lost—along with the pedagogical guidance to help students understand how to make this seemingly inefficient activity both creative and productive. A rigid curriculum with too many required courses is likely to achieve the opposite of its intended goals.

This is why, incidentally, the best undergraduate training for historians is a broad liberal education, exposing the future historian to a wide range of disciplines from the natural sciences through the social sciences to the humanities, with strong emphasis on basic analytical skills and as much practice as possible in analyzing, synthesizing, speaking, and writing. Although an undergraduate history major with a capstone research experience in the junior and senior years is undoubtedly valuable for students intending to go on to doctoral work in history, it is not a sine qua non. Excellent students have entered history doctoral programs with undergraduate majors in many different disciplines. Students who were not history majors may need to do catch-up work during their master's training, but if they bring with them broad general knowledge and a wide-ranging curiosity, they should be on a par with history majors by the time they are admitted to candidacy for the doctorate. Lack of specific historical knowledge can always be rectified by hard work. Nothing can cure a sustained lack of curiosity.

As for the doctorate itself, we might as well begin by declaring that the Ph.D. is likely to remain a research degree. In my view, this is as it should be. It was invented for that purpose and seems unlikely ever to shed original scholarship as a core agenda. Its assumption is that even historians who intend to devote most of their time to interpreting and translating historical knowledge in the classroom or in public history settings will benefit from having a deep personal encounter with the process whereby such knowledge is discovered and created. For this reason, the reform of doctoral training should focus on improving rather than replacing its research component. This is likely to be achieved by broadening its intellectual agendas to include greater swaths of time and space on the one hand, and more far-reaching, cross-disciplinary questions on the other. At the same time, the research emphasis of the doctorate should be substantially supplemented with training that explicitly addresses the different venues and audiences in which historical knowledge is conveyed, especially in the undergraduate classroom and in the public realm. Synthesis and communication skills deserve much more emphasis in doctoral training than they typically receive. We should strongly encourage doctoral students to ask bigger questions, to be more generally curious and knowledgeable about fields of history beyond their own monographic research specialties, and to regard effective communication and pedagogy—good writing and speaking and teaching—as indispensable professional skills.

From its beginnings at Johns Hopkins in the late nineteenth century, the research component of doctoral training in American history departments has depended on the seminar, the research paper, and the dissertation as the chief vehicles for introducing students to original scholarship using primary documents. Although there are minor variations among institutions, the typical practice is to require master's-level students to produce one or more research papers—either in the form of multiple journal articles or a single master's thesis—before taking the comprehensive examinations that admit them to candidacy for the doctorate itself. A key feature of the prelim exams and the goal toward which the earlier research papers should be directed is the production of a prospectus that sketches the dissertation itself, complete with a well-bounded topic, well-formulated questions, a survey of primary documents containing the evidence for addressing those questions, a review of relevant secondary literature, a sketch of likely arguments, and, perhaps most important of all, a table of contents that serves the twin purposes of giving shape to the ultimate monograph and dividing the research process into manageable components.

A peculiarity of history, in comparison with many other academic disciplines, is its very strong emphasis on the book-length monograph as the culminating product of doctoral education. The history dissertation does triple duty: not only is it the final requirement of the doctorate itself but it is indispensable for getting a job in most academic institutions and, when published as a book, is the main basis on which tenure is awarded. This puts enormous pressure on graduate students who are all too aware that they are making a high-stakes gamble on which their entire future career may depend. But it has subtler consequences as well. Unlike the sciences, there is virtually no tradition of joint authorship in history, so that graduate mentors very rarely coauthor articles or books with their students. Indeed, good graduate mentors need to make sure that their students' work is sufficiently different from their own that the mentor won't be given undue credit for the most original features of the student's scholar-ship. Probably because the scale of the dissertation is so large and so much depends on it, historians want no confusion about who is responsible for its authorship. For good and for ill, this has the consequence of reinforc-ing the extreme individualism that usually characterizes the production of historical knowledge in the academy, and gives historians very little expe-rience with the forms of collaborative work that are such ordinary and powerful features of intellectual work in many other fields. It also rein-forces the many subtle biases that point doctoral students toward the aca-demic career paths that expect and reward this kind of individualism, as opposed to public history career paths for which collaboration is essential.

Should we move away from the book-length monograph as the default product of doctoral training? Certainly a case can be made that neither the length nor the form nor the content of the dissertation does an espe-cially good job of serving individuals who seek mainly to work as teach-ers, or those who want employment in public history settings where the typical product is a museum installation, say, or a documentary film. In many cases, a well-tailored master's program that is targeted on practic-ing the skills associated with such work might be a more efficient and practical means to the desired end. Furthermore, it may make eminent sense, especially in public history programs, to emphasize capstone pro-jects that differ from traditional research monographs by being presented in different media or by coupling nontraditional media with analyses of the interpretive possibilities and consequences of those media. Even if his-torians intend mainly to work in the academy, they should all be exposed to the special challenges of communicating in nonacademic settings and media, from the op-ed to the documentary film to the museum display. Given the continuing ferment in electronic communication, I am increas-ingly persuaded that even academic historians should learn basic skills in using HTML and designing Web sites as part of their standard profes-sional toolkit. There's not much doubt that these are becoming ever more indispensable to classroom teaching and are likely to be increasingly important adjuncts of the research monograph as well.

That said, although there are good arguments for modifying the form and content of the dissertation in some circumstances, it still makes sense for doctoral training to culminate in what would once have been called a "masterpiece": work displaying mastery of a professional skill to demon-strate that its author is ready to be admitted to the guild. As the econom-ics of publishing continue to change and as new media, especially the Internet and the Web, continue to create new venues for the publication of scholarly research and interpretation, it is quite possible that at least some fields of history that cannot attract wide public readerships will migrate to electronic publication, if only for reasons of cost. As long as these new outlets can be "branded" to certify their rigor and excellence, as happened long ago in the print media, it seems foolish to resist them. But for those subfields that still attract significant readerships, the publication of books as a core professional activity of historians brings benefits we should explicitly recognize and train our students to understand.

Unlike professional journals, most books do not have prepackaged audiences. Each new book must, in effect, gather its own collection of readers. The academic disciplines that depend mainly on journals to publish their findings—which is to say, most of them—enjoy the luxury that their members can write with great rigor and technical precision for precisely the readership that can best understand what is at stake in a given argument or scientific finding. Such journal articles can be wonderfully efficient in conveying new knowledge. But this efficiency is purchased at the high price of rendering the article impenetrable and utterly uninteresting to all but its narrow technical audience. Because books must earn back the cost of their production in the open marketplace, persuading would-be readers to invest both money and time to explore their contents, they must generally be more accessible and inviting to nontechnical readers. The aspect of writing, pedagogy, and rhetoric that creates a sense of intrigue in the mind of readers or listeners, encouraging them to want to learn more, is essential to writing a good book. Furthermore, the vastness and diversity of historical scholarship mean that even most historians count as "nontechnical readers" for most of the writings of most of their peers. Even if we care not at all about writing for the public, we have an interest in writing books that can be understood by colleagues outside our own specialties, which includes most members of our own departments. Books help us do this. For all these reasons, teaching students how to write really good books remains an invaluable feature of doctoral training that I would be loathe to abandon.

To prepare to write good books, students must read books both good and bad, considering not just the ideas and arguments of those books but their rhetoric and literary qualities as well. This is why graduate training at the master's level relies so heavily on reading seminars to expose students to a given body of historiography and orient them to possible ways they might work in the field themselves. Seminars should include readings drawn from classic works, as well as the newer, cutting-edge texts with which students' own research efforts are likely to be in dialogue. In discussing such texts with each other, students should be shown the many ways in which historians use primary documents as evidence to support and elaborate a set of claims about significant historical problems. Learning to read as a professional historian means paying as much attention to footnotes and bibliographies as to the main body of the text. At the same time, the interplay of logic and rhetoric in the construction of the text proper should be fully on display in seminar discussions.

A criticism one often hears of the book-length monograph as a requirement for the history doctorate is that it takes too long to complete and hence renders graduate education in history needlessly time-consuming and expensive. Certainly, it is true that many history graduate students take longer to complete their degrees than their peers in, say, the natural sciences (though if one recognizes the large number of science Ph.D.'s who spend several years on postdoctoral fellowships after completing their Ph.D.'s, the differences may not be quite as large as they appear). In some ways, the extended duration of the history Ph.D. simply reflects the way history graduate students are funded, which is primarily through teaching, with only limited support for research travel and writing. But it is also true that many history graduate students take quite a long time even to identify their major research projects, let alone complete them. For this reason, a well-designed doctoral program should help students focus on possible dissertation topics from the moment they matriculate. The goal should *not* be for entering students to arrive with their dissertation topics already defined—that would almost surely be pernicious—but rather that they should be *seeking* those topics, and consciously gathering ideas and techniques for pursuing them, all along the way in their intellectual journey. If reading and research seminars have as their goal the discovery and pursuit of possible dissertation topics, and if the master's thesis is directed toward the same end, possibly yielding one or more chapters of the eventual dissertation, then in many cases entire years can be shaved off time-to-degree for the doctorate. But this requires students to be much more intentional and directed about their programs of study and requires faculty mentors to help them do this from the start.

In what substantive fields should future historians be trained? There can be no single answer to this question. If I'm right that eclectic wandering is essential to the historical imagination, then the best one can hope to do is to lay out a basic intellectual geography within which such wandering can occur, provide a few formal and wide-ranging opportunities to experience that geography, and then let students embark on their own unique journey. One could make an argument that all graduate students should at least audit—and ideally teach—undergraduate survey courses, both in their own field and in world history, as part of their basic orientation to the challenge of historical synthesis. They should unquestionably be required to take historiographical reading seminars in subjects far afield from their research specialties—the more remote in space and time, the better. Broadly defined preliminary examinations and required exposure to radically distant fields and disciplines: all of these plant the seeds for the kind of creative rambling we should promote. We cannot guarantee that a given student will finally attain the eclectic interests and broad curiosity that characterize the best historical scholarship, but we can certainly create the opportunities and model the intellectual engagements that produce such scholarship.

Perhaps the greatest goal of the reading seminar—too rarely met and often not even explicitly recognized—is to teach and practice constructive criticism. Too often, the students and faculty in graduate seminars spend much more time on criticism that is far more destructive than constructive, systematically demolishing works of scholarship without sufficiently recognizing their achievements or asking how they might genuinely be improved (as opposed to merely destroyed). Demolishing an argument is so easy that many graduate students quickly excel at it. Actually *improving* an argument is much, much harder. Yet this is precisely what graduate reading seminars most need to teach and model for their members. Few of them do a good job of it.

But reading seminars can serve another set of purposes as well, if only their teachers are willing to widen their scope. Because the goal of a reading seminar is to survey a broad domain of historical knowledge, it should ideally prepare students not just to research that field, but to teach it and discuss it in public. If seminars focus solely on scholarly debates and the formal construction of historical arguments, they squander the opportunity to provoke conversation and train graduate students in domains of professional practice that often get much less attention than they deserve. In my own graduate seminars, I regularly devote half of my class time to what I call "professional development," using the specific historiography under review to talk about what it's like to work not just as a scholarly researcher, but as a teacher and writer and public intellectual as well. In one course, we ask each week what it would be like to teach undergraduates the texts we're reading, and how one might design lectures and assignments and discussions revolving around those readings. In another seminar, we practice writing not just professional genres like review essays—the typical products of a reading seminar—but also popular magazine articles, documentary film sequences, museum labels, even television sound bites. One can easily use documentary films, museum installations, and historical Web sites to talk as much about the presentational rhetoric of history as about scholarly research and analysis. The reading seminar can and should train students about all such matters. If the goal is to train historical professionals, then such seminars should address the full range of professional practice, not just archival research and analysis.

The other domain in which graduate students gain professional skills at the same time they strengthen their command of large domains of historical knowledge is of course the undergraduate classroom. Too often, the work of teaching assistants is viewed by faculty members either as a means for providing financial support to graduate students or as a way to relieve professors of the time-consuming duties associated with leading discussion sections and grading assignments. These are indispensable aspects of the labor that graduate students contribute to the academic enterprise, and I in no way minimize their importance. But from the point of view of graduate education itself, working directly with undergraduates is among the most precious opportunities that a graduate program can provide its students.

The old proverb that one never truly understands a subject until one tries to teach it is profoundly true, so undergraduate teaching beautifully complements the reading seminar as an intellectual domain in which graduate students gain real mastery of their subject. But the craft skills they gain as teachers are no less important. Certainly this is true for any historians aspiring to work in the academy, the bulk of whose employment will focus on classroom instruction. But it is equally valuable as training for public historians, who will find college sophomores a plausible approximation for a large portion of the public audiences with whom they will eventually work. Teaching even provides excellent training for the literary skills of historians, since the ability to explain complicated ideas in clear, accessible language readily translates from the classroom to the printed page. For all these reasons, programs that "protect" their best graduate students from teaching—and fellowship programs that create perverse financial inducements to keep such students out of the classroom— do those students no favor whatsoever. They send entirely the wrong signal about what it means to be a professional historian.

The trouble, of course, is that few doctoral programs give remotely adequate emphasis to undergraduate teaching. Formal training programs are often rudimentary if they exist at all, and questions about teaching rarely surface in the regular seminar curriculum. Worse, faculty members working with teaching assistants are wildly uneven in the training and mentoring they give these beginning teachers. Some, astonishingly, never even meet with their teaching assistants except at the start of a semester. Working with teaching assistants should ideally be akin to offering a regular weekly seminar on pedagogical strategies for synthesizing and conveying a given body of historical knowledge. A properly structured graduate curriculum should include formal training for teaching assistants, discussions in reading seminars about teaching strategies, prelim fields that explicitly address pedagogical questions, strong mentoring relationships between faculty members and the teaching assistants with whom they work, and, if at all possible, the opportunity for qualified graduate students to teach their own lecture course as a capstone experience before entering the job market. How many professors and graduate programs actually live up to this ideal? Alas, precious few.

A Closing Word on Professional Relationships, Communities, and Values

I have chosen in this essay not to focus overmuch on formal requirements of the doctoral degree. I have made few recommendations about required courses, methods seminars, prelim fields, theses, and all the other technical features of a curriculum. It is not that such things are unimportant; they are the meat and potatoes of any doctoral program. But I have high confidence that the faculty of any good graduate department will come up with good and creative solutions to these formal challenges, and I also value the diverse intellectual approaches that naturally emerge when different faculties tackle these shared questions from different directions to yield different solutions. The immense variety of American higher education has always been among its greatest strengths. Especially given my emphasis on the rambling and serendipity that I regard as essential to the training of historians, I think we all benefit from the eclectic differences that characterize our graduate programs. To argue for a more unitary approach would be to undermine this virtue.

So I will close by returning to the core values I have defended throughout this essay and end with a couple of very old-fashioned admonishments. Although we rarely describe it as such, I think the history doctorate retains many aspects of the ancient educational practice known as apprenticeship. Under that system, novices seeking entry into a guild or profession attach themselves to a master to learn the mysteries of a craft. Although this relationship can often go wrong—we all know horror stories about faculty members who have exploited and abused students in their care—this master-apprentice relationship remains utterly central to doctoral education at its best. Good mentoring involves teaching, advising, criticizing, coaching, cheerleading, challenging, hand-holding, questioning, advocating, nurturing, and, not least, learning and inspiring in both directions. When it works, it produces intensely personal relationships that can last a lifetime. Those of us lucky enough to have had generous and inspiring graduate mentors know how essential they were to our success. We owe a debt to them that can never be repaid, save by working as hard as we can to pass along the same kind of gifts to our own students.

If the faculty members in a doctoral program are unwilling to make the enormously demanding and time-consuming commitment to being the best possible mentors they can be, then they have no business teaching graduate students. If there is not a critical mass of committed graduate mentors in a department, then that department has no business awarding the doctorate. If a department tolerates the abuse or exploitation of graduate students in the name of a professor's "academic freedom" or by easygoing acceptance of a colleague's "foibles," then that department is betraying the very values it should be striving to defend. Mentoring should of course be a shared endeavor, so that every graduate student should ideally have several faculty members to whom she or he can turn for advice and inspiration, to say nothing of support and advocacy on the job market. But every student should also have at least one faculty member who is present for every step of the doctoral journey, a constant companion on one of the most challenging experiences of their lives. No doctoral program is worth continuing if its faculty is unable or unwilling to devote immense energy to providing this kind of mentoring, which is the hardest and most demanding teaching I know.

How does one foster a departmental culture in which such mentoring becomes possible? There is no simple answer to this difficult question, but the obvious place to start is with the word *respect*. The best doctoral programs foster a deep mutual respect among all their members as the bedrock of their intellectual community. Graduate students respect the talents and achievements of their professors, but professors respect no less the talents and achievements and promise of their students. Indeed, faculty members recognize that at least some of their students will in all likelihood go well beyond what they themselves have accomplished, and they understand what a privilege it is to work with such people. Learning and teaching in such an environment is a two-way street. When professors and graduate students are truly working together as they should, the relationship of student to mentor is more collegial than subordinate. Hierarchy remains, of course, but as time goes on it should gradually diminish, until finally student and mentor become genuine intellectual companions, even friends. This last word is suggestive because of the other qualities it implies: committed scholars who share intellectual passions, who take pleasure in each other's company, who enjoy learned conversation for its own sake, who understand how privileged they are to have found others

who revel in the life of the mind as much as they do. Any doctoral program that can reliably build a culture that transmits these values to its
newest members will almost certainly produce superb historians.

But there is another feature of all first-rate doctoral programs that is
equally important and often insufficiently acknowledged: the relationships
among graduate students themselves. The friendships one forms with
other students who pursue this training together are usually among the
closest and most intense of one's entire professional life. The companionship they provide mirrors, and in many domains goes far beyond, what
the faculty can offer. It is among the most precious things one acquires in
earning a degree from a truly excellent doctoral program. Although they
often fail to do this, departments should give great care and attention to
building and sustaining strong graduate communities. Students should be
helped to get to know and care about each other from the moment they
arrive. Seminars should be designed to model, not just competition and
destructive criticism, but mutual support and constructive engagement
with the intellectual projects of other students. Support groups should be
the norm for all the major benchmarks: matriculation, serving as a teaching assistant, prelim exams, thesis research, and the dissertation itself.
Opportunities for formal and informal gatherings both with and without
the faculty should recur at frequent intervals. Students should eat and
drink together often, and faculty members should join them in doing so
on a regular basis. Students should be given the chance throughout their
graduate careers to exercise genuine intellectual and institutional leadership, both as a source of empowerment and as a way to gain early experience in the citizenship and service that are such important features of
the academic life. Especially given the excessive individualism of history
as a discipline, an intentional commitment to building a lively graduate
community should be an absolutely indispensable feature of every doctoral program. If a department refuses to do the hard work of building
such a community, or if it lacks the resources to admit and support the
critical mass of graduate students needed to sustain that community, then
it should stop pretending that it has any right to award the Ph.D.

History is among the oldest and most profound of human activities.
Pondering the past to make sense of ourselves and our world, passing that
knowledge on from one generation to the next, striving always to understand its relevance for the present and for the future that fills both our
nightmares and our dreams—all these lie pretty near the core of our humanity. If we are to escape the tentacles of William James's Ph.D. Octopus, we must never forget how deeply all human beings share and
participate in this subject that our professional guild claims as its special

domain but can never monopolize or own. History is always about values and community and what it means to be human. The same must be equally true of our guild and of the professional rites of passage we define to sustain it.

NOTES

1. It is worth noting that we share these nonexperimental, essentially narrative epistemologies with the historical sciences, which is a key reason why, though often unnoticed, we actually have more in common than we realize with historical geologists and evolutionary biologists.

REFERENCES

James, W. "The Ph.D. Octopus," *Harvard Monthly,* March 1903, 149–157. Reprinted in *William James, Writings 1902–1910.* New York: Library of America, 1987, 1111–1118.

DOCTORAL EDUCATION IN ENGLISH

THE DISCIPLINE OF ENGLISH traditionally encompassed the study of the English language and American and English literature, and was conventionally divided by century (eighteenth, nineteenth, twentieth) and genre (poetry, the novel). Recently, the discipline has expanded its borders to include all literature created in English, regardless of national origin, and to include genres such as film and multimedia. Postmodern and critical theories have also taken firm hold in the field. These changes have been accompanied by contentious disciplinary debates about how to define the field in the future, as well as the implications for the organization of departments, the undergraduate major, and the doctoral program. Although recommendations for a new graduate curriculum that responds to changes in the field are neither numerous nor well accepted, it is clear that this issue commands considerable attention.

In general, the field of English studies sees itself solely in relation to academia. The often-used term *the profession* refers to the academic profession, obscuring to near invisibility the significant contributions of English doctorate holders to the publishing industry, writing and editing professions, government and nonprofit agencies, and secondary teaching.

English departments are generally large. A 1990 survey by the Modern Language Association (MLA) of the 146 Ph.D.-granting departments of English found an average of 35 faculty, 49 master's students, and 51 doctoral students per department. Two-thirds of doctoral programs are at public universities. Admission to graduate programs in English remains very competitive; often students complete an M.A. at one institution before applying for doctoral work at another. The number of doctorates granted in English studies in the latter part of the 1990s has ranged between 900 and 1,100 per year.

English is becoming feminized. The percentage of women graduate students in English has increased from about 40 percent in 1977 to about 60 percent today. In terms of racial composition, white students constitute about 85 percent of the student population, and the overall pool of doctorate holders in English is about 95 percent white. English attracts only a few international students; the proportions vary by subfield but are under 10 percent. Nearly all doctoral students majored in English as undergraduates, and about 80 percent also hold a master's degree in English.

The life of a doctoral student in English, as in many humanities fields, is characterized by slow progress toward uncertain job prospects. The time-to-degree in English is currently 9.0 years of registered enrollment. Thus most new Ph.D.'s are in their early thirties and faced with heavy student loans. It is little wonder that, as in most humanities fields, the rates of doctoral student attrition are very high in English.

Nonetheless, English doctoral study continues to recruit promising scholars attracted to the romance of the "life of the mind." Long hours of solitary reading, thinking, and writing are punctuated by lively seminars and intense teaching responsibilities. The graduate program typically includes two to three years of course work; in addition to mastery of a specialty, students are expected to command a wide range of knowledge in preparation for teaching. Field coverage is assessed on several written and oral exams completed in the first two to three years.

Doctoral study culminates in a book-length dissertation; the topic is developed by the student in consultation with his or her committee. The dissertation proposal often involves defining "the list"—the fifty to one hundred works the student has command of and that form the intellectual foundation of the particular area of the discipline. Each chapter of the dissertation follows a particular line of thought; taken together, it forms a coherent whole, and the dissertation is, ideally, ultimately published as a book by a university press. The competitiveness of the job market has pressured students to publish during graduate school, leading to concerns that students are professionalizing prematurely, before their ideas have had time to ripen.

A defining feature of doctoral life in English is undergraduate teaching. Most students are funded by teaching assistantships; it is not uncommon for students to teach a 2–2 load (most students teach introductory and undergraduate writing courses) for most of their time in graduate school.

English departments are noteworthy for spending a great deal of effort preparing their students to teach. The students often have available to them courses and workshops on how to teach writing, and students frequently start as section leaders and gradually move into positions of increasing responsibility. It is not unusual, however, for them to have total responsibility for a course from the start. Teaching is often observed and evaluated, and students have opportunities to discuss pedagogical challenges with peers and mentors.

Career paths and the job market for English Ph.D.'s are the most important issues facing doctoral programs. The doctorate in English is focused on preparing students to assume academic positions, as English is a core subject taught at nearly every college in the country. Nevertheless, there is a wide gap between the number of Ph.D.'s granted and the number of tenure-track positions advertised each year. Making matters worse, there has been a steady erosion in the number of tenure-track faculty positions available, as permanent positions are replaced by adjunct positions. However, most undergraduates are required to take writing courses, creating high teaching loads for English departments; doctoral students are an affordable solution to this teaching demand. Graduate student teaching assistants and part-time faculty make up the single largest category of instructors of undergraduates in English master's and doctoral departments. This situation makes it hard to shrink doctoral programs, particularly when the pool of prospective students remains strong.

Ultimately, the majority of doctoral recipients are able to secure positions within the academy. According to the "Ph.D.'s Ten Years Later" study, of those receiving Ph.D.'s from 1982 to 1985, about three-quarters were working in the academy, and over half had secured tenure by 1995. The MLA's survey of new Ph.D. recipients showed that 40 percent secure tenure-track positions in the first year; most others take temporary positions and seem to secure tenure-track positions within one to three years. In part because of the lack of visibility of nonacademic careers and resistance from some in the discipline to actively promoting (or tracking students' progress in) these careers, there remains a group of Ph.D. holders trained to perform and teach literary research and criticism and unable to find positions to pursue those interests in the way they had imagined; they are unwilling to think about the profession more broadly. But another large group of Ph.D. holders have made the transition to nonacademic positions, and they are as satisfied with their work as their colleagues in academia. They lament that they are not recognized as members of the profession and that these career paths remain invisible to graduate students.

Perhaps because the job market, department size, and the organization of academic labor are system-level problems that may require systemic solutions, the essayists focused their attention on the process of doctoral education. Both essayists take a personal approach, using their own biographies as a springboard to discuss the curriculum, as well as the non-curricular elements, of doctoral education.

In "Rethinking the Ph.D. in English," Andrea Lunsford emphasizes the changing face of doctoral study, arguing that the discipline is obligated to be considerably more inclusive than it has been to date. She also makes suggestions for change in the nature of faculty-student relationships, including faculty and students engaging together in large-scale research projects and allowing students to complete collaborative dissertations. Her ideas may seem obvious to those in the lab sciences, but transferring these practices to a discipline like English is a radical notion.

In "Toward a New Consensus: The Ph.D. in English," Gerald Graff repeats his call to "teach the conflicts" and then offers seven other concrete suggestions, many of which might be portable to other disciplines.

○

BIBLIOGRAPHY

Information and specific data were derived from the following sources:

Clarke, E. "Cultural Studies, the English Major, and Doctoral Education." *ADE Bulletin,* 2004, *136,* 37–39.

Coalition on the Academic Workforce. *Summary of Data from Surveys by the Coalition on the Academic Workforce.* Washington, D.C.: American Historical Association, 2000.

Conference on the Future of Doctoral Education. University of Wisconsin, Madison, Apr. 15–18, 1999. *PMLA,* 2000, *115*(5), 1136–1276.

Damrosch, D. *We Scholars: Changing the Culture of the University.* Cambridge, Mass.: Harvard University Press, 1995.

Gallagher, C. "Review: Re-modeling English Studies." *College English,* 2001, *63*(6), 780–789.

Gilbert, S. M. *Final Report of the MLA Committee on Professional Employment.* New York: Modern Language Association, 1997.

Golde, C. M., and Dore, T. M. "The Survey of Doctoral Education and Career Preparation: Results for Future Faculty in English and Chemistry." In A. Austin and D. Wulff (eds.), *Enriching Graduate Education to Prepare the Next Generation of Faculty: Challenges, Research and Practice.* San Francisco: Jossey-Bass, 2004.

Graff, G. *Professing Literature*. Chicago and London: University of Chicago Press, 1987.

"Highlights of the MLA's Survey of PhD-Granting Modern Language Departments: Changes in Faculty Size from 1990 to 1994." *ADE Bulletin*, 1994, *109*, 46–47.

Hoffer, T., and others. *Doctorate Recipients from United States Universities: Summary Report 2003*. Chicago: National Opinion Research Center, 2004.

Huber, B. "Incorporating Minorities into English Programs: The Challenge of the Nineties." *ADE Bulletin*, 1990, *95*, 38–44.

Huber, B. "Recent and Anticipated Growth in English Doctoral Programs: Findings from the MLA's 1990 Survey." *ADE Bulletin*, 1993, *106*, 45–60.

Ingram, L., and Brown, P. *Humanities Doctorates in the United States: 1995 Profile*. Washington, D.C.: National Academy Press, 1997.

Laurence, D. "The 1999 MLA Survey of Staffing in English and Foreign Language Departments." *Profession 2001*, 2001, 211–224.

Leatherman, C., and Wilson, R. "Embittered by a Bleak Job Market, Graduate Students Take on the MLA." *The Chronicle of Higher Education*, Dec. 18, 1998, p. B4.

Lunsford, A., Moglen, H., and Slevin, J. (eds.). *The Future of Doctoral Studies in English*. New York: Modern Language Association, 1989.

MLA Committee on the Status of Women in the Profession. "Women in the Profession, 2000." *Profession 2000*, 2000, 191–217.

Modern Language Association. "Initial Employment Placements of 2000–01 Doctorate Recipients from US Universities." Unpublished data. New York: Modern Language Association, 2003.

Nerad, M., and Cerny, J. "From Rumors to Facts: Career Outcomes of English PhD's: Results from the 'PhD's Ten Years Later' Study." *ADE Bulletin*, 2000, *124*, 43–55.

North, S., and others (eds.). *Refiguring the Ph.D. in English Studies. Writing, Doctoral Education, and the Fusion-Based Curriculum*. Urbana, Ill.: National Council of Teachers of English, 2000.

Pratt, L. R. "In a Dark Wood: Finding a New Path to the Future of English." *ADE Bulletin*, 2002, *131*(Spring), 27–33.

Scholes, R. *The Rise and Fall of English: Reconstructing English as a Discipline*. New Haven and London: Yale University Press, 1998.

18

RETHINKING THE PH.D. IN ENGLISH

Andrea Abernethy Lunsford, Stanford University

IT'S NO EXAGGERATION TO SAY that I marvel almost every day at the fact that I am a professor of English, that I have tenure, that I have enjoyed over twenty-five years of teaching and research in a field I love. It's also safe to say that no one among my teachers, or even my family, would have predicted this eventuality. After all, when I won the typing medal (!) in ninth grade, my father was certain that I had a great career as a secretary ahead of me and assumed I would take such a position after high school. Only after I won a small teaching scholarship to my state university (the University of Florida) did I secure permission to "go off to college." Once there, I learned to live down to expectations: girls shouldn't be too smart. But my intense experience with reading (in elementary school, I was regularly punished for reading books when I was supposed to be doing other things) paid off, and I not only did pretty well in my courses; I also came to understand that I really liked to learn and that I was besotted with reading and writing. And I was increasingly sure I wanted to teach. So one day I ventured into my adviser's office to ask about advanced graduate study. I could remember talking with him only once before, when he had signed some forms for me. He listened to me for a few minutes and then dismissed the idea out of hand, saying that I wasn't cut out for a Ph.D., that I should go home and have a family. I didn't even consider objecting; I just left the office, left the university, and got a teaching job. It took seven years for me to gain the confidence to try again.

I completed my Ph.D. in 1977, and by then some of that patronizing "it's not for you" attitude was gone from our departments. But not all. For all the change we have seen (the National Center for Educational Statistics reports that the number of women entering advanced degree programs increased almost 60 percent between 1989 and 1999), much in our departmental culture needs to change. I want to open this chapter, then, by talking briefly about access to the Ph.D. and about entry—and persistence—in the profession and then go on to describe changes I would make—changes in admissions policies, in curriculum, and in the hurdles students must leap in pursuing the degree—were I actually given the mandate The Carnegie Foundation for the Advancement of Teaching suggested when it asked, "If you could start *de novo,* what would the features of a Ph.D. program in your field be?"

To begin, I would ask that we look honestly and carefully at the culture of English studies, to determine how much of the paternalism and patronizing is still with us. For the last six or seven years, I've traveled extensively to other campuses, visiting dozens of departments each year. At every stop, I meet with graduate students and ask them about the atmosphere in their own departments. Too often, I hear stories that echo my own; often I receive e-mail or mail after a visit, from students who didn't feel able to speak in public about harmful attitudes in their own departments.

One student wrote to send a letter she had written but never mailed to its recipient. Addressed "Dear Dr. Professor," this letter described in detail how overcome with awe the new Ph.D. students were in his class: "We hung on every word and marveled at your vast store of knowledge, your provocative interpretations, even your digressions and comical drawings." But the magic soon wears off and students realize that they are no closer to engaging the challenges of some very difficult material than they were when the course began. Still, no one objects; instead they sit and take notes and wait for an opening to speak. Sometimes, a male class member ventures something, but seldom a female. The class wears on, and this student writer leaves it thinking hard about withdrawing from graduate school: "Too bad," she says, "that I'm leaving this course feeling just as separate from, intimidated by, in awe of, and ultimately uninterested in [the great texts we were being introduced to] as I was when I entered. Sometimes I wonder if that's what you actually want—to keep us from joining some charmed inner circle of knowledge."[1]

I received the "Dear Dr. Professor" letter a couple of years ago. Much more recently—in fact, just a few months ago—I got another letter from a white woman who had just managed to complete a dissertation in one of our most distinguished and elite departments. In the letter, she recounts her struggles and concludes that she would never have had the strength to continue toward the degree, given the virulent arguments among members of her committee and the opposing mandates she was being given by them, except for the support of one senior woman, not even a member of the committee, who worked extensively with her, providing encouragement and support. She concludes her letter, "What I learned in my Ph.D. is that I do not want to be part of such a profession. But I am enormously grateful to one lone woman who, at the end of my ordeal, showed me what graduate school could—and should—be like."

Over the years, I have also heard frequently from students of color who voice frustration and disenchantment with English studies in general and with their departments in particular. At best, they feel patronized; at worst, shunned. A number of students share a similar story of a faculty member saying to them outright that they were admitted only because they were Latino, African American, Chicana, and so on. One graduate student put it this way: "Early on, then, I knew that my presence was a tokenized one, unlike other grad students in the department—though as I thought about it later, I wondered whether or not all the other graduate students were in some way tokens too."

As I write, I can almost hear the protestations: it's not like that here . . . or here . . . or here. Indeed, I think most departments now take pride in their recruitment of women and people of color. But if you look beyond the surface in almost any department, you can find stories like the ones I have told here; most of us just aren't comfortable hearing them, much less looking for them. But if these stories didn't have salience, then why is our profession, especially at the top of the academic ladder, still overwhelmingly white and male?

For over thirty years, the MLA Committee on the Status of Women in the Profession has tracked answers to this question. In its most recent report, the committee reports that a larger percentage of women and students of color are entering graduate school, though the committee notes that this change is occurring at a time when employment opportunities are drying up and when fewer white men are entering the field. "Are the employment opportunities in literary study declining (even relative to those in other disciplines) in relation to the declining presence of white men, that is, to the degree to which white women and women of color have begun to take up positions that reflect their contribution to the profession?" (2000, pp. 192–193).

In spite of the growing numbers, white women and colleagues of color are not finding the success that the increasing numbers should indicate;

white men continue to hold tenured positions and professorial rank far in excess of the percentage of the profession they represent. The recent MLA Committee on the Status of Women report provides national data that indicate that, in English, "the largest group of white men were full professors; the largest group of men of color were associate professors; the largest group of women of color were assistant professors; and the largest group of white women were instructors, adjuncts, or of similar rank" (2000, p. 201). A closer look at the survey reveals that the actual numbers of men and women of color are pitiably small.

In short, although women and people of color are coming into our graduate programs in larger numbers than ever before, they are not faring nearly as well in persevering and in moving up through the ranks of the profession. And part of this problem must surely relate to departmental culture, to the kind of patronizing attitudes that I've described, and also to our continued reliance on agonism, on competition, on individually derived and held authority, and on hierarchy as the currency with which we gain admittance to and advance in our profession. Surely, it is time that we heeded Linda Hutcheon's eloquent MLA presidential address (2001) and recognized that the wolf-like atmosphere she described so well is helpful, at most, to a very small number of our students and colleagues and that it is especially limiting to faculty members and graduate students who are women and people of color.

Recently, members of our profession urged that we at least begin to name such exclusionary practices. In its latest report, the MLA Ad Hoc Committee on the Professionalization of Ph.D.'s stated, for example:

> The committee feels strongly that equity and diversity demand that we not ignore this responsibility [to let students know what the reality is in terms of seeking jobs and advancing in the profession]. As Robert A. Gross has articulated the problem, "It was one thing for female and minority Ph.D.'s to enter an arena from which they had previously been excluded, quite another to find their way through a maze of informal practices that was often impenetrable even to white males. The absence of female and minority role models on the faculty made that progress all the more difficult" (2002, p. 203).

Those role models on the faculty have stories of their own about such difficulties and hierarchies. Listen to Victor Villanueva, now professor of English at Washington State University, look back on a rejection that still troubles him:

I have . . . had a fellow worker bleed in green and red over a paper I had wished to submit for publication, have gotten the maybe-you-could-consider-submitting-this-essay-somewhere-else letter from journal editors. That's just part of the job. But I have [also] felt insulted. Some years have passed, and I have forgotten the editor who had written this rejection letter; I've even forgotten the journal, I realize as I write this. But I still bear a grudge. The essay challenged the idea of a postcolonialism, invoking Frantz Fanon. The Rejecter said he saw no reason to resurrect Fanon. The essay also cited Aristotle and Cicero. Their resurrection went unquestioned. Rejecter also said he feared that in bringing in Fanon, I risked essentializing. . . . In the years that have followed that infuriating letter, I have seen my concerns in that essay echoed, seen a rekindled interest in Fanon grow and grow, and have heard how others of color have been insulted by a particular use of the word "essentializing" (1999, p. 655).

In another piece, Beverly Moss, currently associate professor of English and director of Ohio State's Center for the Study and Teaching of English and a tenured member of the English department, says,

One of my most disturbing moments in graduate school occurred when my professor in a critical theory course wrote on my final paper that my "language was not sophisticated enough to handle the sophisticated ideas of critical theory." As a twenty-two-year-old graduate student, I understood that he was trying to tell me that I did not belong in graduate school, that people like me were not smart enough. I understood that I was the only person of color in his class (and in the entire graduate program) and that he never spoke to me the entire semester. I understood that I was not an acceptable audience in his class. And because I had imagined my audience for the paper I wrote in his class to be people like me, I was an unacceptable audience for this academic exercise. As I went further in the profession, I began to understand that this professor was appalled by my attempt to discuss Hegel and Heidegger in a language other than [the most current jargon]. And finally, I understood that in my own naïve way, I was trying to cross a line or blur a boundary; some would consider it a class line, some a color line, some even a gender line, perhaps all three. I am no longer naïve about my attempts to cross those lines (1998, pp. 167–168).

Beverly Moss is certainly not naïve, and she continues as a role model and exemplary mentor. She is also—by my last count—the last person of color to be promoted up through the ranks at her university, and that tenure was granted a decade ago.

I have taken time to give voice to graduate students and colleagues because I am convinced that their stories are not anomalous. I am also convinced that their stories would be different if we would examine our admission practices and, especially, our retention practices, in graduate school and through the ranks. Attitudes like the ones that kept me out of a Ph.D. program may have lessened, but these stories suggest that they are not altogether gone. In addition, the intense culture of competition that our graduate programs foster is guaranteed to discourage those who do not prefer that mode of discursive behavior, effectively shutting them out of our Ph.D. programs and our profession.

What would admission policies[2] that were inclusive, that did not favor intense competition, look like? For one thing, such policies would abjure the GRE, admitting once and for all that these scores always favor white students. In addition, admissions committees could (and, I think, should) look for signs of multiple intelligences by asking for more than an academic writing sample. Why not consider, for example, evidence of excellence in forms of public service or teaching, or other work-related talents? And why not recognize once and for all that an amazing student can easily emerge from a low-prestige school, and look upon the chance to open historical, literary, and theoretical doors for that student rather than think of having to "remediate." Finally, admissions committees could look at statements of teaching goals, giving applicants an opportunity to connect what they have learned about literature and language with how they wish to develop as teachers who are serious about "professing." Taking teaching into consideration in our admissions deliberations would be one way of strengthening that challenge and changing the mixed messages we have been giving graduate students for a very long time about the relationship between scholarship and teaching.

In the 2002 issue of *Profession,* John Guillory comments on our profession's long-time antipathy to "the very idea of pedagogy," an antipathy he interrogates and begins to challenge (2002, p. 169). Elaine Showalter also takes up the question of teaching in a recent *Chronicle of Higher Education* piece, saying that the new conversations on teaching "are both welcome and long overdue" (2003, p. B7). Showalter turns to the example of drama, where a focus on teaching as performance offers a possible disciplinary model, and she reports on the approach taken in the United Kingdom, where pedagogy has been more seriously engaged than it has been here. Showalter might also have pointed to the extensive research on teaching carried out by scholars of rhetoric and writing studies; indeed, the literature in that field about teaching both reading and writing is extensive, and *College English,* an old and distinguished journal with a very wide circulation, regularly publishes articles on the teaching of literature, language, and writing. We thus have no shortage of models for rethinking our relationship to pedagogy, and a natural place to begin this rethinking is in our graduate programs, by bringing our student colleagues into serious engagement with the issues of how best to teach (and to learn) language, literature, and writing.

Changing the exclusionary culture of our departments through such things as admissions policies or more rigorous attention to teaching is one way to rethink the Ph.D. Another is to consider carefully what students actually do during their years of graduate study, in terms of courses they take, the classes they T.A. for and teach, and the series of hoops all students must pass through in securing the degree.[3] In "The Ph.D. in English: Toward a New Consensus," written for this volume, Gerald Graff notes that the English doctoral program has moved from "a relatively stable institution with pre-established rules and conventions to which students conformed to a do-it-yourself kit that depends for its shape on each student's particular interests and creative initiative." Graff argues that these changes have, taken as a whole, been beneficial, and I agree, since they can admit of a very wide interpretation of English studies and make room for new and often breathtakingly imaginative projects.

These de facto changes, however, carry with them an implicit and very important redefinition of the subjects or Bakhtinian heroes of the field—reading and writing. In other words, such changes reflect changes in what our students are doing as well as in how they are defining (or redefining) our subjects of study. Look around at the projects graduate students are working on now, and you will find a very broad definition of "literature" and of reading—a definition that clearly includes film, video, multimedia, and hypertext, and discourses not traditionally thought of as "literature" (such as Deaf and Spoken Word poetry, cookbooks, tombstone inscriptions) right alongside studies of canonical writers and their print texts. In terms of "writing," an expanded definition is also clearly emerging, as what counts as writing now often includes sound, video, and images of all kinds, as well as a wide and growing range of genre and discourses, from African American vernacular English to Spanglish to American sign language. Rather than seeing such discourses and forms as marginal or as something "extra" added to the curriculum, I favor curricula that embrace these forms as their purview. Of course, learning to teach new forms, new discourses, new genres, even new formats presents a challenge, but many in English studies have already gained such expertise and stand ready to teach others.

What I have said thus far argues implicitly for thinking of English studies—of what we and our students do—as encompassing literature, language, and writing. I am well aware that many departments do not now define themselves in this way; indeed, the last dozen years have seen the rise of new departments (or sometimes programs) of writing or rhetoric and of creative writing that stand distinct from departments that focus narrowly on the reading of American and British literature. And many departments have reduced their teaching of language courses, from Old and Middle English to applied linguistics, discourse analysis, and so on. Some would argue that this trend toward division and separation is of long standing: some thirty-five years ago, William Riley Parker (1966-67) tracked the break-up of English Studies through the withdrawal from the Modern Language Association of several groups, including those that founded the National Council of Teachers of English (in 1911), the Speech Communication Association (in 1914), and the Linguistics Society of America (in 1924).

In spite of such break-ups, as Graff and others have demonstrated, a rough consensus has held in English studies that often allowed for the study of literature, writing, and language to coexist and even (sometimes) profit mutually. The trend toward separation into narrowly defined departments of literature, writing and rhetoric, and creative writing may continue, but if it does, it will be in stark contradiction to the new and expansive definitions of reading and writing just described. Separating reading and writing (and, in fact, subdividing writing) seems especially counterproductive, given the ways in which these communicative acts are merging in electronic communication and in the media and the ways in which new and developing genres make it increasingly difficult to categorize writing into the old, familiar modes.

If graduate study in English can be described as a more open-ended and wide-ranging "do-it-yourself kit," and if it can encompass the broad definitions of reading and writing I have offered, what will hold English together? What will serve as the glue that the old standard curriculum and rules used to provide? First, a clear and detailed articulation of what constitutes the purview of English studies—no matter how far-ranging— would help to accomplish this goal. More important, however, would be rethinking the work students do in our graduate programs.[4]

In regard to introductory course work for the Ph.D., I am in partial agreement with Graff, who has been admonishing us for many years to "teach the conflicts" and who proposes in his Carnegie essay (Chapter Nineteen) that we "organize introductory [graduate] courses around contested issues." I would, however, modify Graff's suggestion in at least two ways. First, I would think of the introductory work of the Ph.D. not primarily in terms of individual courses; rather, students entering the Ph.D. should grapple with large questions and projects, which they would undertake with at least several other students. These projects should, in my view, focus on major issues in much the way Graff describes: What *is* American Literature? What counts as "the best" writing? Are there better and worse ways of reading texts? What is the relationship between literature, broadly conceived, and its media? Taking on a major issue and working with others to explore its many nuances would introduce students not only to important ideas and information in our field but also and importantly introduce them to the powerful effects of collaboration. I have written at length (some would say *ad nauseam*) on the benefits of collaboration for the humanities. Here I will just say that a growing body of evidence suggests that advanced work in the humanities increasingly calls for the kind of research that one solitary scholar is unlikely to be able to do. David Winter, who collaborated with other historians, editors, directors, and artists to produce *The Great War* (1998), argues that this project, which has the potential to shape a generation's understanding, would have been utterly impossible to do alone. By introducing our graduate students to the possibilities and potential of collaborative research, and offering them a means of engaging in it productively, we can begin training a generation of students who can take up Winters' challenge.

Making such a change to the introductory year (or first two years) of Ph.D. work would bring with it other changes as well. It would almost certainly militate against any kind of general coverage exam of the kind I took at the end of my M.A. degree (a two-hour ordeal, as I recall, during which I was to answer questions on a list of texts, from Beowulf to Virginia Woolf), and which still caps the first year or so of Ph.D. work in some programs. Rather, the kind of collaborative research projects I have been describing would call for performative exams, with students preparing written documents, both individually and collaboratively written, and presenting the results of their research to the larger departmental and university community. In some ways, such a system would echo the qualifying papers some departments now call for, though broadening them to include collaboratively written work. In other ways, it would echo the system used in many Canadian and some European universities, where Ph.D. candidates make formal presentations of their doctoral research to "all comers." In any event, such a change in the examination or qualifying framework would be commensurate with the new definitions of reading and writing I have offered here; it would connect the student candidate's research and teaching; and it would focus in beneficial ways on the growing prominence of what Walter Ong calls "secondary orality," that is, spoken presentation that is already very much inflected by writing (1982).

Readers still with me have no doubt guessed where I'm going, and that is squarely toward the notion of Ph.D. students engaging in large-scale research projects, including dissertations, during their tenure. While students should always have the choice of taking a narrow and highly defined topic (gambling in eighteenth-century writing, early modern women's prefaces to translations, a reading of two 1930s women poets), they should also have an opportunity to engage the kind of project that calls for more than one researcher (one that, for example, requires complete fluency in several languages, one that requires expertise in digital media, one that combines two or more disciplines). Allowing for collaborative dissertations will present a great challenge to our imaginations and our organizational abilities: such projects would have to be carefully delimited and described; they would need to require the work of more than one person, and they would have to demonstrate equal contributions on the part of all parties. But they are not impossible to conceive. Indeed, I am aware of two collaboratively written dissertations that have been accepted by their departments, and at the last Conference on the Future of Doctoral Education ("Conference on the Future of Doctoral Education," 2000), an entire working group entertained this issue, with at least some members arguing forcefully for such opportunities for our students. Here we might be wisest to let our students lead us; they are the ones who are conceiving such projects, and they have solid and imaginative ways of going about this work. We have much to learn from listening to them.

A Ph.D. program with any of the features I have described would necessarily be one in which graduate students are colleagues rather than acolytes—our partners in exploring major issues, in constructing new knowledge, and in sharing the wealth of our experiences, our learning, and our teaching. In such an atmosphere, a focus on pedagogy would be right and necessary, though rather than students taking pedagogy seminars or "training workshops" aimed at instructing them in how to be good T.A.'s for large classes or how to conduct first-year writing classes, they would become members of ongoing teaching-pedagogy circles that would include faculty, staff, and graduate students, again working collaboratively on major questions facing all teachers of English: What do our pedagogical practices suggest about the theories we hold? How do we best engage all students in productive and cooperative intellectual debate?

How can we create assignments that call forth the best and most diverse thinking, writing, and speaking of which our students are capable? How can we create an effective classroom ethos? How do we respond to and evaluate student work in ways that are rigorous and honest but not appropriative? How can we establish and share authority among participants? How do we develop and share knowledge both in and out of the classroom?

Ideally, these teaching or pedagogy circles would be small, with faculty and student co-coordinators who would work together to present an agenda to be considered by all. In addition, these groups would offer multiple opportunities for teaching and team-teaching, with time for careful response and follow-up and time for students to make explicit and lasting connections between their research and their teaching. Team teaching could serve as a compelling replacement for the system of using graduate students as teaching assistants who lead discussion sections, meet with the students, and grade written work while the faculty member is engaged primarily with lecturing. Working with a graduate student or students to plan and develop materials for a course, prepare and deliver the lectures, meet with and counsel the students, and respond to class assignments would do much more to prepare graduate students for taking on courses of their own than the present T.A. system, which all too often assigns sole responsibility for a writing class from the moment a graduate student enters the program; indeed, some programs rely on beginning graduate students to teach two, and sometimes even three, such courses. Some universities already have such a team-teaching plan in place, though all too often it is instituted as a way to teach more students at lower costs (a faculty lecturer and three teaching assistants, for example, "teaching" 100+ students) rather than as a way to focus the department's attention on pedagogy and to mentor and prepare new members of our profession. In my view, graduate students should have an opportunity to design and teach (or team teach) several courses during their Ph.D. programs, including introductory courses in writing, in language, and in at least one field of literature.

Rethinking the Ph.D. along the rough lines I have presented here would go a long way toward opening up our discipline to new and exciting voices and toward resisting the hierarchy that still informs most of our departmental structures and practices. Such a rethinking also has the potential to bring the work we do more directly into the public eye, offering us an opportunity to demonstrate the importance of our work to the public good. Toward that end, Ph.D. programs might well follow the example of several departments in engaging faculty and students in community outreach projects. One well-developed and very effective program is in place at Carnegie Mellon, where members of the department have worked for years to establish and maintain a vibrant community literacy center and where graduate students work with members of the center to bring about change and work for social justice in their community. Moving in such a direction would offer opportunities for engaging literacy—reading, writing, speaking—in a variety of settings; such contact would almost certainly double back around to inform the research that graduate students undertake during the Ph.D. It would also bring faculty and students more directly in contact with the work of the public schools. And that contact, in turn, could lead the way toward focusing more directly on the job of preparing teachers for our nation's schools. Finally, working within the community reinforces the practice of collaboration, of shared knowledge production, of responsibility (and what Bakhtin calls response-ability), and of merging literacy practices advocated in earlier parts of this essay.

Can we rethink the Ph.D. in ways that will make our programs more open and inclusive, more truly diverse, more responsive to the dreams and desires of our students, more connected to emerging definitions of reading and writing, more collaborative, more engaged with issues close to the hearts of our communities? *Of course we can.*

NOTES

1. The students I quote have given me permission to report their words but not their names.

2. As it stands now, most admissions committees typically consider the stature of the program from which an applicant comes, along with that person's GRE scores (some departments set a minimum that must be met for consideration), statement of purpose, letters of reference, and a writing sample. As a whole, this set of requirements invites and indeed demands high competition, and it privileges those who have been able to attend the most prestigious schools, as well as those who have begun to "talk the talk" of the profession.

3. In most English Ph.D. programs, students take a specified number of courses, after which an examination of some sort qualifies them for candidacy to the Ph.D. Such exams may include everything from an oral exam aimed at establishing "coverage" to written exams on a student's major and minor fields of study or dissertation project. Thereafter, students present dissertation prospectuses (which may or may not be accompanied by another exam), write a dissertation under the supervision of a faculty director and

several committee members, and then participate in a dissertation defense before graduating.

4. Although it is quite difficult to generalize, I think it is safe to say that most Ph.D. programs require some form of introduction to theories and methods in the field, as well as demonstrated reading mastery of one or more languages and a minimum number of individual courses in English and American literature.

REFERENCES

"Conference on the Future of Doctoral Education. University of Wisconsin, Madison, April 15–18, 1999." *PMLA*, 2000, *115*, 1136–1276.

Gross, R. A. "From 'Old Boys' to Mentors." *Chronicle of Higher Education, Career Network*, Feb. 28, 2002. Available at chronicle.com/jobs/2002/02/2002022801c.htm.

Guillory, J. "The Very Idea of Pedagogy." *Profession 2002*, 2002, 164–171.

Hutcheon, L. "Presidential Address 2000: She Do the President in Different Voices." *PMLA*, 2001, 518–530.

MLA Ad Hoc Committee on the Professionalization of PhDs. "Professionalization in Perspective." *Profession 2002*, 2002, 187–210.

MLA Committee on the Status of Women in the Profession. "Women in the Profession, 2000." *Profession 2000*, 2000, 191–217.

Moss, B. "Intersections of Race and Class in the Academy." In A. Shepard, J. McMillan, and G. Tate (eds.), *Coming to Class: Pedagogy and the Social Class of Teachers*. Portsmouth, N.H: Boynton/Cook, 1998.

National Center for Education Statistics. "Participation in Education: Trends in Graduate/First Professional Enrollments." Dec. 19, 2002. Available at nces.ed.gov//programs/coe/2002/section1/tables/t06_2.asp.

Ong, W. *Orality and Literacy: The Technologizing of the Word*. London: Methuen, 1982.

Parker, W. R. "Where Do English Departments Come From?" *College English*, 1966–1967, *28*, 339–351.

Showalter, E. "What Teaching Literature Should Really Mean." *The Chronicle of Higher Education*. Jan. 17, 2003, *49*(19), B7.

Villanueva, V. "On the Rhetoric and Precedents of Racism. *College Composition and Communication*, 1999, *50*, 645–661.

Winter, D. "Doing Public History: Producing 'The Great War' for PBS and BBC." Paper presented at the MLA Convention, San Francisco, Dec. 1998.

19

TOWARD A NEW CONSENSUS

THE PH.D. IN ENGLISH

Gerald Graff, University of Illinois at Chicago

IN THIS ESSAY, I echo an analysis of the institution of English studies that I have developed in many places before—one that highlights the way these studies have obscured rather than acknowledged and confronted their conflicts. I now also go on to argue, however, that in obscuring their conflicts, English and humanities studies have also obscured important areas of *consensus*. I argue that by obscuring the areas of conflict and of consensus in their discipline, English doctoral programs have made it unusually difficult for those wishing to enter the field to gain the socialization they need.

As my title reflects, I suggest here that, despite the deepening of ideological and methodological conflicts in English over the last half-century, at least two important areas remain where there exists a broad latent consensus that can and should be tapped. These two areas are *teaching* and *writing*. Whether we are traditional scholars or postmodern theorists, partisans of teaching the traditional canon or a de-centered canon of popular culture and minority texts, few of us would disagree on the proposition that undergraduate teaching is a crucial aspect of our profession and that writing, especially the writing of argument or, in this case, literary criticism, is in some sense central both to the teaching of undergraduates and the advancement of scholarship. To be sure, this agreement would end once we asked what should be done, whether the advancement of teaching and writing justify institutional changes and shifts of priorities, as I will suggest they do. Nevertheless, I believe there is more consensus in English (and the humanities) on certain fundamental values than we are used to acknowledging and thus are a basis for concerted action to enhance the clarity, accessibility, and transparency of English doctoral programs.

———— o ————

I got my Ph.D. in English and American literature in 1963 at Stanford University, where I had begun doctoral studies in 1959. Though I was a successful graduate student, it was only after many years as a professor that I started to feel comfortable in "the profession," as it was—and is—called by insiders. In fact, phrases like "the profession," "research," and "the field," always left me feeling confused and inadequate when tossed off by my professors and fellow graduate students. The meanings of these terms had not been explained to me as an undergraduate (though I had majored in English at a leading college, the University of Chicago), and once I got to graduate school, the fear of looking like the greenhorn I was prevented me from asking for clarification. That's how I remember graduate school—as a place where, if you were any good, you supposedly *already knew* what the game was and why it was being played. If you didn't, why were you there?

Though the mental landscape of graduate study has changed utterly in the forty years since I left Stanford, students tell me they still experience the kind of confusion and intimidation I felt in the face of "the profession" and the pressure to appear knowledgeable (or knowing) about its mysteries. If anything, the new theories, texts, and subjects that have opened the field and exploded the once narrowly constricted boundaries of "English" have made the field (the very word now sounds vaguely quaint) even harder to get one's mind around and to locate oneself in with any security. The crises and upheavals English studies have been through now force graduate students to become (or appear) professionally savvy more quickly than my graduate generation had to do, even as the pressures have been vastly intensified by anxieties I never had to feel about whether any job security would lie at the end of the arduous process.

Both my research and my personal experience have led me to think and write about how English studies can better meet the unprecedented challenge of an academic and social world far more diverse and openly conflicted than the world in which those studies originated but which many of their practices still anachronistically assume. The paradigm-shattering and boundary-crossing that have come to typify literary studies (one of the many collections that attempt to chart the new situation is titled *Redrawing the Boundaries*) have changed the English doctoral program from a relatively stable institution with pre-established rules and conventions to which students conformed to a do-it-yourself kit that depended for its shape on each student's particular interests and creative initiative. The old apprenticeship system, in which you attached yourself to a senior professor who assigned you a topic and pretty much told you what to do with it, has broken down, but it has not been replaced by any comparable guidance apparatus. This new open-endedness makes doctoral study more free-ranging and exciting but more stressful and anxiety-producing—or stressful and anxiety-producing in new ways, like moving from a white-collar job to a high-wire act at the circus. Contrary to some critics, I believe that, on balance, this change has been for the better, but I also believe that the English doctorate needs to be rethought from the ground up.

In her memoir, *A Life in School: What the Teacher Learned,* Jane Tompkins, who was in the English Ph.D. program at Yale about the same time I was at Stanford, writes as follows about the absence of genuine intellectual community in the program:

> At Yale, though there was much else, there was no intellectual debate to speak of, in the sense of ongoing discussion of contested issues. Scholars had vendettas against other scholars but there were no critical debates that cut across the periods and specialties to rouse our spirits (1996, p. 81).

My experience at Stanford was very much like what Tompkins describes at Yale. Though "contested issues" abounded in the Stanford English Department and the field at large, these issues were never debated in public. As in Tompkins' case at Yale, the disagreements expressed themselves as "vendettas" that students caught glimpses of through gossip or the ironic asides by which one professor adverted to another in class references that were usually decodable only by the few among us who (wink, wink, nudge, nudge) were in the know.

At Stanford, a frequent target of these coded references was my eventual dissertation director, the poet-critic Yvor Winters—one of the most embattled figures in American letters at the time. Winters had published a series of stringently (his detractors said stridently) polemical books and essays in which he called into question the reputations of many of the most revered names, living and dead, of the literary and critical canon: Wordsworth, Shelley, Keats, and virtually the entire British romantic movement; Emerson, Whitman, T. S. Eliot, Robert Frost, John Crowe Ransom, and most of twentieth century modernism.[1] Not surprisingly, Winters' ideas split the department into pro-Yvor and anti-Yvor factions.

I became a committed Wintersian and more or less remained one for the first ten years of my career. I found myself constantly arguing about Winters' ideas with fellow graduate students and sometimes other professors— arguments that I look back on as the most intense, intellectually exciting, and educationally valuable moments of my graduate education. But because these debates took place only occasionally and in private, they did not satisfy my hunger for intellectual engagement and community. Nor did they help me as much as they might have to make sense of the intellectual territory and thereby mature more quickly as an academic.

In fact, the most intense intellectual community I experienced came from the campus protests and teach-ins that erupted during the mid-sixties in response to the Vietnam War, by which time I had become a junior faculty member. The upheavals of the sixties were one of the major forces that would democratize English studies and thereby explode its traditional coherence. Looking back, I think my experience of the debates of the sixties helped me far more to mature as an academic intellectual than anything I studied in graduate school.

I experienced graduate school not as an intellectual community that sharpened my thinking about important issues, but as a set of disconnected courses and mixed messages. I coped with these mixed messages by giving each professor what he or she seemed to want, even when it contradicted what the professor the previous hour had wanted. In my courses in the romantic period, for example, I suppressed or soft-pedaled the Wintersian hostility to the romantics that I freely vented in Winters' courses and in those taught by sympathetic colleagues. This experience of going along with the premises of each course in order to please (or appease) the instructor was not without value. It forced me to try on provisionally different intellectual universes and see what it felt like to live inside them, and it made me work to create my own overviews, connecting the dots myself instead of waiting for someone to hand me an authorized map. Often, however, my exposure to views that never came together left me suspended with respect to their relationship. The points of disagreement were easy to identify when it came to Winters and his romanticist and modernist colleagues, but in other cases where the alliances or oppositions were harder to project, I could only guess whether views were compatible or incompatible. In the end, I internalized the compartmentalizations of the curriculum instead of wrestling with its conflicts, either resolving the conflicts too easily on one side (usually that of Winters, who did claim to provide an authoritative map) or ignoring them. After all, if the department itself did not care enough about its contested issues to face up to them in public, then why should I?

I came to understand later, when I studied the institutional history of academic literary studies, that the curricular mixed messages to which I was exposed were the result of a system of negotiated compromises that modern educators had evolved to avoid having to confront and (heaven forbid!) debate their disagreements in public. Under this system, which had grown up in the climate of expansion and affluence that universities had enjoyed for most of the twentieth century, intellectual turf wars were neutralized by the simple device of adding a new component in order to appease the feuding parties and preserve peaceful coexistence. Whenever a threatening innovation arose—interpretive criticism, creative writing, feminist criticism, ethnic studies, deconstructionism, queer theory, and so forth—the new challengers could be absorbed by adding a new position, course, program, department, or suite of offices. This tactic pacified both the young Turks, who could now do their allegedly subversive work in their corner of the curriculum, and the old fogeys, who could go on doing what they had always done in theirs. All factions were kept moderately satisfied, as their various agendas were being "covered," or at least represented, and rivals were safely sealed off from each other so that they could tune one another out most of the time rather than bicker.[2]

Yet both students and faculty paid an intellectual price for such arrangements, not only in being deprived of the climate of debate that scholars need to avoid going brain dead (the deprivation Tompkins complains of in her doctoral years at Yale), but in the confusion and disorientation about "the profession" that results from curricular mixed messages. And the degree of confusion and disorientation I experienced forty years ago from the mixed-message curriculum at Stanford can be multiplied several times over for students in the wake of the diversification and dissensus of the post-sixties. My graduate students today are exposed to a far more intimidating clash of mixed messages, along with a heightened degree of anger and frustration over the disagreements, than I was in those relatively quieter times.

As a graduate student you generally occupy a position of double insecurity, as you no longer belong to the undergraduate culture but you aren't yet accepted into the faculty culture. As an apprentice faculty member, you are more dependent on the judgment of your professors than you were as an undergraduate, when you could shrug off a bad grade or a severe evaluation by reminding yourself that you were not, after all, trying to become the kind of professional type that your mentor was. These inevitable insecurities are further deepened when what it means to be part of "the profession" is left unexplained and up to the graduate student to puzzle out on his or her own. These insecurities, as well as the lack of guidance and opportunities for discussion that make them worse, often come to a head when the graduate student first begins to teach. In my case the first experience of teaching was one of deep excitement tempered by fear of being exposed as a fraud. I "learned to teach" by fakery, pretending that I knew what I was doing and keeping the pretense up until at some point, after many years, it stopped feeling like one.

When I began to teach my own courses, first as a teaching assistant at Stanford (1961–1962), then as an assistant professor at the University of New Mexico (1963–1966) and Northwestern University (1966–1970), I felt that I was still mentally an undergraduate in many ways who was hoping to fool students into confusing me with a real professor. Fortunately for me, the same forms of academic mystification that left me in the dark as a doctoral student also led my freshman students to believe that all college instructors know everything and must be trusted as authorities until they prove otherwise. I would have been grateful for an opportunity to discuss these anxieties and the other challenges of teaching with a faculty member or a more experienced graduate student, but except for the weekly staff meetings about the freshman course—a combination of composition and introduction to literature—there was no structured discussion of teaching. In these staff meetings, what passed for a discussion of how to teach tended to be an analysis of the text to be taught, of Andrew Marvell's "To His Coy Mistress" or Robert Frost's "The Road Not Taken."

In other words, what discourse there was about teaching took the form of an exposition of interesting things an instructor could say—or try to get students to say—about a literary work. The psychology and sociology of one's particular students—who they were, what their past experiences were, and what assumptions they had about studying literature or being part of an intellectual culture—didn't figure in the discussion. Nor did the psychology and sociology of the instructors themselves: Who were we, and why were we doing this? When my classroom was observed by a professor in the "visitation" I was required to have as a teaching assistant (and again until I became a tenured professor, after which it was assumed that nothing could be done about me), the only suggestions my senior colleague offered were that I close the door to my classroom and speak a little louder.

Clearly, questions of teaching were not thought to be intellectually interesting the way, say, the structure of a metaphysical lyric or a shift in the history of ideas was interesting. This was odd in a way, as faculty members and graduate students spoke informally of how their teaching helped them work out the ideas that went into their scholarly and critical writing. The assumption that your dissertation, suitably translated for undergraduates, would have some payoff in your undergraduate teaching was a standard one in job interviews. Some scholars even claimed that being forced to explain their ideas to freshmen had a healthy influence on their published writing. In an era when, as I have noted, consensus on principles and methods was breaking down, the commitment to teaching could have provided a countervailing sense of common ground. It still could provide that sense of common ground today, as I suggest in the proposals with which I conclude this essay.

In the fifties and sixties, however, teaching, unlike scholarship, was not seen as "intellectual work"—something that, as Mariolina Rizzi Salvatori and Patricia Donahue rightly argue, should be seen as an activity "that can be theorized, work whose parameters and conditions of possibility can be analyzed and evaluated in accordance with formally articulated standards" (2002, p. 84).

Though I absorbed this condescending attitude toward teaching, it was probably the experience of classroom failure that jarred me out of it. As early as my first teaching experiences, I was struck by a classroom dynamic that would become familiar to me over the years. The students early on sorted themselves into two distinct groups. The high-achieving insider few usually sat in the front rows, carried the class discussions, and comported themselves like would-be professors, or at least people who wanted to talk and were beginning to talk the same kind of analytic and argumentative discourse I did. The more or less silent majority sat in the back, fearful of being called on, seemingly disengaged, either unable to play the language game of literary analysis (an obsessive search for "hidden meaning" that they complained of as "overanalyzing") or unsure why the game was played at all. In my experience, this two-tiered student pattern has remained intact, even as the methodologies, theories, approaches to literature, and the canon of literature itself have exploded and proliferated after the late 1960s, as I described earlier. If "English" has become an elusive subject for graduate students in the wake of "theory," cultural critique, and other intimidating new trends, one can only imagine how much more elusive it has become for undergraduates.

The split between literature and composition has made this elusive subject—English—even more mystifying. As a new teacher, I noticed that the struggling students seemed to tie themselves in knots trying to mimic the unfamiliar moves of critical argument, and I increasingly came to feel that there is something frivolous about trying to teach undergraduates to write *literary* argument when all but the insider few needed more guidance on writing argument about *any* subject. These students needed more work in basic composition before moving to literary criticism, the special conventions of which tend to befuddle students for whom the conventions of public discourse itself are new and intimidating enough. But the status and incentives that had long elevated literature over composition made it unlikely that undergraduates would get the basic composition work they needed.

When I began teaching in 1963, professors of English were still expected to teach composition and did so, however unenthusiastically. But in order to cope with the increased enrollments of the expanding university, English departments increasingly shifted the burden (as it was seen) of teaching composition to graduate teaching assistants. By the early seventies, it was common for interviewers at the MLA convention to assure candidates that if they got the job, they would not "have to" teach comp (or not much) but would immediately teach mostly literature courses. The assumption was that any smart, ambitious young graduate student or instructor would naturally want to be free from the albatross of composition teaching as soon as possible. Who wouldn't?

One might have expected a different kind of thinking to prevail, as the late 1960s was a period in which the problem of student writing, which had been seen as chronic since the founding of departments of English, was making one of its periodic reappearances in public attention. But the late sixties was a period of "sink-or-swim" thinking about chronic educational problems. The high schools, it was said, were the proper place for students to learn to read and write; if college students were showing up with deficiencies in these areas, it was not the responsibility of the colleges to do something about the problem. With status and enrollment pressures going in the opposite direction, it was not a promising time to expect a recommitment by faculties to teach basic expository writing. Mina Shaughnessy made a stir with her 1977 book *Errors and Expectations*—a study of the problems minority students encountered in basic composition courses in open-admissions universities—but by that time, composition was so marginalized in programs taught by underpaid and overworked graduate students and adjunct faculty that these problems were not taken seriously or addressed in a bold way. Today the disconnection between "comp" and "lit" has become progressively more severe and more deeply institutionalized, even though the newest intellectual trends in the field exalt the importance of rhetoric and reject (at least in theory) the sharp antithesis the New Critics had drawn between literary and nonliterary discourse. Here again, as with the commitment to teaching, a potential area of common ground went unnoticed: the common commitment to argumentative writing.

In a book titled *What Is English?* that reported on the 1987 English Coalition Conference (which included high school as well as college teachers), the compositionist Peter Elbow virtually concluded that the question posed by his title was unanswerable: "This book," he wrote, "is trying to paint a picture of a profession that cannot define what it is" (1990, p. v). The observation was hardly unprecedented, for the identity of English has always been notoriously shaky. As early as 1911, one educator had observed that "even the general prescription of English is an agreement in name only; what actually goes under this name is so diverse as to show that we have not yet discovered an 'essential' course in English" (Graff, 1987, p. 100).

In *Professing Literature,* I show that there is something mythical about the notion of a past golden age in which a consensus had existed on the nature of English and the humanities (1987, pp. 1–14 and passim). Nevertheless, though earlier generations may have been unable to formulate the unifying principles of English, until around the mid-sixties there was still a vast amount of unspoken common ground about what constituted literature, which literature was worth studying, and how it should be studied and by whom; this common ground provided a relatively stable background against which disagreements were played out. "Scholars" might feud with "critics," to mention one of the fiercer civil wars that intersected my graduate study, but at the end of the day, one imagines, the parties drank whiskey together and lit up cigars. It is this relatively stable intellectual and social set of background understandings of "the profession" that has come apart since the late sixties.

Stephen North captures the post-sixties situation well in *Refiguring the Ph.D. in English Studies*—a recent study of the English doctoral program. North observes that under the new dissensus, departments were hard-pressed to determine what graduate students in English should cover in their studies. Indeed, departments "found themselves having to decide again and again what it meant to 'cover the field' when, on the one hand, that field—conceived in terms of both the constituent areas of expertise *and* the bodies of those who populated it—had diversified beyond anyone's experience." Moreover, with the economic recession of the early 1970s, "the resources available for carrying out any such coverage either remained the same or became scarcer" (2000, p. 59). North quotes *The Future of Doctoral Study in English,* the official proceedings of the 1987 Conference of Graduate Study, and the Future of Doctoral Study in English in Wayzata, Minnesota, in which editors Andrea Lunsford, Helene Moglen, and James Slevin (1989) conclude that "[N]o unanimity on any significant issue emerged during the conference," where the participants could agree only that "neither 'historical coverage' nor 'canonical unity' could 'guide our conceptualization of curricula. As a consequence, the editors conclude, 'there was little certainty about what our graduate students should know both as developing scholars and as apprentice teachers'" (2000, p. 63).

North gets at the heart of the matter when he observes that the new dissensus "rendered peaceful coexistence by compartmentalization increasingly untenable." His hypothetical scenario helps us see the problem in concrete terms:

> When a department's Miltonist/eighteenth century person/Emersonian/director of first-year composition retired, should it hire another Miltonist, etc., or a deconstructionist, a fiction writer, a scholar in African American literature, someone expert in computers and writing, a postcolonialist, etcetera, etcetera? Both this decision making process and the subsequent search came to be further complicated by demographic (not to mention ethical and legal) considerations: man or woman? Ivy League, land grant university, or smaller niche program? U.S. citizen or not? White, Hispanic, African American, Asian American, Native American? (2000, pp. 58–59).

As North points out, there is no clear way to compromise in such decisions, especially when diminishing funds take away the traditional pluralist option of appeasing all groups by hiring one of each.

North cites my own analysis, which I summarized earlier, of how the old additive method of avoiding conflicts lost its usefulness once the conflicts of English became too frequent and disruptive, and the financial resources for creating new space by expanding the playing field had dried up. Until the seventies, departments had been able to preserve peaceful coexistence in the face of deepening conflicts by simply adding new components to the aggregate and keeping the warring parties in separate courses or programs where they wouldn't be at each other's throats. Now this expensive option was disappearing, and deepening the problem further were the intensifying culture wars in and about education that had been festering since the antiwar protests of the sixties. These culture wars broke out in a spate of conservative attacks in the 1980s and 1990s on higher education and especially on the alleged political correctness of literary studies. It was much harder to prevent the conflicts of literary studies from erupting into public view now that these conflicts were in the news every day and were described in the latest best-selling book alleging that politically correct terrorists were silencing dissent in classrooms and faculty meetings.

I began this essay by suggesting that, though there is far less consensus about the nature and identity of English as a field of study than there was when I began my doctoral work more than forty years ago, English graduate programs still fail to confront the contested nature of "the profession" directly, leaving their graduate students to figure things out on their own. But I have also tried to suggest that, in failing to confront its conflicts, English studies have failed to recognize and take advantage of those elements of consensus that remain, specifically, the consensus on the fundamental importance of teaching and writing. However polarized we may be over theories and methodologies—and over issues of politics and ideology—I believe that few of us would disagree on the centrality of undergraduate teaching and writing, especially the writing of argument or literary criticism, both to teaching and research.

This assumption—that a latent consensus has, after all, underlain the conflicted domain of English and continues to do so today—is reflected in the seven proposals with which I conclude this essay. These proposals represent an attempt to take advantage of these underlying areas of consensus in our commitment to teaching and writing. I offer these proposals as provocations rather than as dogmatic prescriptions—as ways of making the process of socialization into professional culture more open and less mystifying.

Seven Proposals for Change

The following proposals take advantage of those areas of consensus that have been there all along, particularly the commitment to teaching and writing.

Organize Introductory Graduate Courses Around Contested Issues

Virtually all English departments have recognized that the old "Bibliography and Methods" course of the kind I took at Stanford, with its assumption of consensus and of fixed and well-defined foundations of scholarship, criticism, and the literary canon, no longer reflects, if it ever did, the way intellectual work in the field is done. Not all departments have evolved more suitable introductory courses, however, and some have evaded the problem by having no general introductory course at all. Yet it is important to help graduate students get access more directly to the shifting disagreements—and agreements—that represent the background of working knowledge that is necessary for getting their bearings in English studies.

The most direct way for English doctoral programs to accomplish this goal is to establish required, preferably year-long, introductory courses that survey major debates, past and present, in the field. Such courses might start with broad questions like "What is English?"; "Is English a discipline, and, if so, in what sense?"; and "How are English studies related to other disciplines and to students' lives?" They might then move on to other questions, like the following:

> Why read literature? What is the difference between reading for pleasure and reading analytically for complex meanings?
>
> How do we resolve the conflict or tension between respecting the work itself on its own terms and contextualizing or appropriating the text for various moral, social, personal, pedagogical, or other purposes?
>
> What are the differences between the new and old ways of historicizing literature?
>
> Are literature and literary studies inevitably "political"? In what sense? If so, what then?
>
> How did the publish-or-perish system evolve? What is its rationale? What objections have been made to it? What, if anything, should be done about it?

As Stephen North argues (he wrongly imagines that he differs from me on this issue), graduate students need to be active participants in these debates, not spectators, even if (*especially* if) they question the terms of the debate or wish to change the subject. The course needs to be open, that is, to questions like "Why are we arguing about *this* issue as opposed to that one?" or "Why should we care?"

Such courses must not duck the questions that make us most uncomfortable and therefore most need airing, such as the bitterly contested question of graduate student unions. My own view, for example, is that graduate teaching is obviously work and needs to be recognized as such. I am not persuaded by the argument that extending collective bargaining and other union rights to graduate students weakens the bond of trust between student and mentor. If anything, that bond is now most seriously threatened by the feelings of exploitation that teaching assistants often experience. There are arguments on the other side, however, some coming from graduate students themselves, and they need to be openly and frankly joined.

Contested issues courses could make use of visiting speakers who bring viewpoints from outside the department or that are not represented by the local faculty. Most departments have a modest budget for visiting speakers, but visiting talks tend to be underused pedagogically, usually being treated as extracurricular add-ons that compete with course work and other parts of the program. Yet with a bit of planning, such presentations could be integrated into courses and used to knit the curriculum together. Several years ago, I took part in an exemplary visiting speakers' series at Miami University of Ohio that served as the basis of a course. When I arrived, the students had read, discussed, and written papers on my work and compared my approach with those of other speakers in the series. The challenging questions and criticisms they raised made for an unusually intense and focused discussion that felt more satisfying to me than the usual post-lecture Q&A. I was so impressed with the Miami course as a model for introductory courses that I borrowed from it when I became director of the Master of Arts Program in the Humanities at the University of Chicago.[3] Other English departments that organize central graduate courses around contested issues include ones at the State University of New York at Albany and Illinois State University (North, 2000, p. 87; Broad and others, 1999, pp. 17–48).

Establish Required Courses and Workshops on Teaching

If it is important to recognize that there is no consensus in English studies on many fundamental issues, it is also important, as I have stressed in this essay, to recognize the two major areas in which there is considerable agreement: the central place of teaching and writing. Teaching is the common enterprise of academic English scholars, and it needs to be treated as the intellectually challenging topic it is, with its own important controversies. Future English teachers need to be exposed, for example, to debates between New Critical and more contextually oriented pedagogies, as well as to debates between contrasting teaching styles:

- Lecturing versus discussing
- The pros and cons of breaking the class into small groups (an issue that mirrors larger questions about authority and individualism)
- The pros and cons of politically committed, "critical" pedagogies, feminist pedagogies, and so forth
- Liberal versus vocational justifications for teaching English
- The tensions between composition and literature teaching and the arguments for and against bridging the gap
- The erotics of the classroom, including the kinds of rules or codes, if any, that should regulate romantic or sexual relations between teachers and students

Bring the Regular Faculty Back into Freshman Composition

Just as courses on teaching would recognize that pedagogy is part of the common ground of the discipline, bringing members of the regular faculty back into the teaching of composition would recognize that persuasive argument is also part of that common ground. As long as professors are expected to write and publish, it is reasonable to ask them to reflect on writing issues, to take those issues seriously as intellectual work, and to share their views on those issues with students. Indeed, because many professors have interesting things to say about writing, to exclude them from teaching the subject is perverse. On the other hand, assigning professors to teach composition courses is not necessarily the most productive (or cost-effective) use of their time and talents. An alternative would be to identify those professors—not just in the English department or even the humanities but across all the departments—who have the most interesting ideas on writing and are willing to share them, and then institute a large lecture supplement to freshman composition in which these professors would interact with each other and with graduate teaching assistants. The English Department at my university has experimented with such a supplementary first year composition lecture this past year.

Departments should also institute a regular writing workshop in which faculty members and graduate students present work in progress for discussion by the group. Students beginning their dissertation proposals would submit them for discussion at this workshop.

The main point should be to move beyond seeing writing and the teaching of writing as burdens that distract professionals from the "real" work of content—research. Though it may not seem surprising to encounter this crude form of content separation in the sciences, its persistence seems extremely odd in English, where, since the rise of the New Criticism, a virtually unchallenged premise has been that in any complex communication, form and content are inextricably linked. To recognize that reflecting on and teaching writing is not a burdensome add-on to the work of English scholars but a central part of their work would be simply to honor the principle of form-content unity that has guided the discipline for the last fifty years.

Link Graduate Study with Undergraduate Research

Traditionally, the consensus has been that undergraduate and graduate study in the humanities should be kept sharply separate. At its most reasonable, this view recognizes that most undergraduates do not aspire to become academics. But one of its unfortunate byproducts is an extreme and educationally crippling isolation of undergraduates from the research interests of faculty members and graduate students. Undergraduates end up being sheltered, not only from the work their faculty and graduate instructors care most passionately about, but from the core conversations of the discipline, which is to say, from the discipline itself. The result is the wide gulf that I first noticed as a teaching assistant at Stanford between the vast struggling majority of students in my courses and the small, high-achieving minority. In the process of being protected from professionalization, undergraduates are kept in the dark, as I had been as a college student, about the nature of the discipline they are studying.

In literary studies (and the humanities generally), the most glaring symptom of this withholding of secrets from students is the habit of assigning only primary texts in undergraduate courses, with little or no literary criticism (much less literary theory). The bizarre consequence of this practice is that undergraduates are denied access to the critical discourse they are expected to produce in course papers and class discussion, and then they are penalized at grading time for producing that discourse badly. If "taking literature" means writing critical essays about poems and novels rather than (or in addition to) writing poems and novels, then students need to read some samples of the discourse they are supposed to write. It makes sense for some of those samples to be drawn from the most provocative and accessible academic research.

A promising countertrend in today's university is the growth of undergraduate research programs, which make undergraduates co-participants with faculty members and graduate students in advanced research, thereby closing the traditional gap between undergraduate and graduate students. Having been involved myself in a college undergraduate research program at my university, I am pleasantly struck by the way bringing undergraduates into advanced research dissolves the traditional alienation of students by making students and instructors part of the same team devoted to common intellectual objectives. To date, however, the humanities have lagged far behind the sciences in developing undergraduate research programs, and even in the sciences such programs tend to be set aside only for graduate-school-bound honors students. There should be ways by which English departments can bring their majors and even their general education students into the most interesting research conversations of the discipline without narrowing their perspectives or prematurely imposing professional models on them.

Some will object that this is a prescription for dumbing down faculty research, and this may indeed be a danger in some cases. Arguably, however, undergraduate research can do as much to improve the quality of research as to dumb it down. It figures that faculty members and graduate students would write more accessibly and with an eye to broader contexts if they were challenged to explain themselves to undergraduate students. In this and other respects, the potential benefits of undergraduate research are as great for researchers as for undergraduates.

Bring Creative Writing into the Departmental Conversation

Creative writing programs too often form a kind of ghetto—a place for students to escape "overanalyzing" and boring scholarship and for creative writing faculty to screen themselves from literary theorists and postcolonialists. As D. G. Myers points out in his history, *The Elephants Teach: Creative Writing Since 1880,* "in the hallways of the English department, exchanges between poets and scholars are marked by mutual hostility. The poets complain that literary study has 'no point of contact with the concerns of most working poets,' the scholars dismiss creative writing as 'pseudo-literature'" (1996, pp. 4–5). As Myers observes, this isolation "is a far cry from what the founders of creative writing envisioned" before World War II, when creative writing programs were established in the hope of bridging the gap between academic literary study and contemporary creative practice (pp. 4–5).

Such isolation obviously prevents the emergence of a fruitful exchange between the creative and the scholarly halves of the faculty brain. Departments should establish courses in which creative writing instructors and students engage with literary critics and compositionists. Just as Proposal 3 (bringing the regular faculty in) would build a bridge between the literature and the composition programs, this one would build a bridge between creative writing and literary criticism on the one hand and expository writing on the other. "Creative Writing," "Scholarship," and "Theory" could each be a major unit in the "Contested Issues" introductory courses I proposed earlier. Such a unit could explore the numerous points of intersection and overlap, as well as of tension and conflict among scholars, theorists, and creative writers, perhaps by focusing on texts that blur genre distinctions such as Jorge Luis Borges' *Labyrinths,* Roland Barthes' *S/Z,* Umberto Eco's *The Name of the Rose,* and others.

Establish Joint Programs with Colleges of Education for High School Teachers

Both disciplines' scandalous neglect of (and condescension toward) the schools has long been widely recognized and deplored. Hoping to reverse this trend, the Modern Language Association (Franklin, Laurence, and Wells, 1999) published a collection of essays surveying university English teacher education programs: *Preparing a Nation's Teachers: Models for English and Foreign Language Programs.* English departments that lack sufficient social conscience (or sense of shame) to take seriously their responsibility to train schoolteachers may begin having their hand forced by economic necessity, as the demand for high school teachers remains far in excess of that for college professors. The wall of isolation must be breached that has prevented us from exploring the potential common ground between the research and pedagogical aims of English doctoral programs and of English teacher education programs in Colleges of Education.

A relatively simple way to begin creating such common ground would be to offer jointly taught courses by faculty of English and education. The courses and workshops on teaching that I propose would be obvious candidates for such joint teaching, but so would other kinds of courses, including intro courses in "contested issues." Also of value would be to institute versions of the same course to be simultaneously taught in colleges and high schools by professors, graduate students, and high school teachers working together. This practice of learning by teaching together figures to be more effective than staff development workshops in which professors and high school teachers talk about pedagogy (Graff, 2000).

Establish Alternatives for Nonacademic Employment

The Woodrow Wilson National Fellowship Foundation, led by Robert Weisbuch, has been at the forefront of a national movement to encourage graduate programs to open alternative career tracks for doctorate holders, especially those in the humanities (Magner, 1999). These efforts come up against resistance, as they challenge the traditional view that a Ph.D. is wasted unless it is crowned by a college teaching position (if God wanted English Ph.D. holders to go to work in advertising, why did He make us hate making money?).

When the University of Chicago inaugurated its Master of Arts Program in the Humanities in 1995, it formed a working partnership with the university's Office of Career Planning and Placement and secured internship agreements from several local alumni businesses. These steps were virtually unheard-of for graduate programs in the humanities at the time. As it happened, about half our students (in classes of seventy to over a hundred per year) chose to pursue academic tracks, while the other half set their sights on jobs in corporations, publishing, galleries, museums, public relations, and other nonacademic areas. Employers proved to be surprisingly receptive to the idea that graduate work in the humanities is excellent preparation for a wide range of jobs outside academia. But per-

haps this is not so surprising, seeing how widely the importance of critical thinking skills is recognized by the corporate world (Adams, 1997;
Schneider, 1999).

It is tempting to be cynical about such ideas and make charges of "sell-
ing out" and "co-optation." But there has always been something affected
and unhealthy about the pretense that the humanities are superior to the
crass and fallen world of getting and spending, whether that pretense took
the form of old-fashioned mandarinism or new-fangled oppositionality.
After all, co-optation can cut both ways: when the corporate world
absorbs humanities graduates, it is true that the graduates can be corpo-
ratized, but it is also true that the corporate world can be humanized.

Proposals for Transforming "English"

Given the resistance to institutional change that has characterized English
departments (like most academic disciplines), even if one concedes the
merits of my seven proposals, one may question the practical likelihood
of their being implemented. The notion seems especially improbable that
faculty traditionalists and avant-gardists, scholars, theorists, creative writers, compositionists, and partisans of other rival approaches, methods,
and assumptions will ever consent to air their differences for and with students, as I've been suggesting they do.

Yet it is worth noting that members of these groups already *do* frequently engage in open controversy at academic conferences and in the
pages of professional and general-interest journals. It is only within the
curriculum at our home campuses that openly debating differences seems
unusual, unseemly, and out of place. Evidently, we have become so accustomed to polite evasion of differences being the norm in local departmental life that we fail to notice that such a state of affairs is actually at
odds with the way we do our work. Arguably, courses that dramatize the
interplay of rival perspectives on contested issues would better represent
the reality of intellectual life in English studies than any set of disconnected offerings can do. What is more, greater recognition of the elements
of agreement that underlie these differences—agreement on the importance of teaching and writing—might provide the sense of shared ground
that would make it easier to air the differences.

Furthermore, even the proposals that may seem most unrealistic—
regular faculty members involving themselves in the teaching of composition, increased interest in the intellectual challenges of pedagogy, and
more collaboration between university faculty and high school teachers—
have a basis either in already-established practices or in emergent ways of

thinking. School-college collaborations have become increasingly common across the country, as educators on both sides of the divide recognize their common ground. And there seems to be growing recognition that a profession that officially claims to value writing and teaching has to be willing to commit itself institutionally to these enterprises. I have argued in this essay that English studies need to be rethought from the ground up, but such a rethinking has already been under way for decades. Ultimately, then, transforming "English" is a matter not of breaking completely from what is but of giving better institutional expression to what is already envisioned or done—and this means recognizing that we may not be as far apart as we think we are.

Acknowledgments

I want to express my special appreciation for editorial work beyond the call of duty to Ellen Wert and Chris Golde. Both put in many hours to make the composition and revision process easy and pleasant for me, and I am most grateful to them.

NOTES

1. For Winters' central formulations, see his *In Defense of Reason* (1947).

2. For more extended discussions of this add-on method of department building and its consequent evasion of conflict, see Gerald Graff's *Professing Literature: An Institutional History* (1987, pp. 88ff and passim) and *Beyond the Culture Wars: How Teaching the Conflicts Can Revitalize American Education* (1992, pp. 125–143).

3. For an account of this program's "contested issues" introductory course, see "Jumping into the Culture Wars" (Adams, 1997).

REFERENCES

Adams, J. "Jumping into the Culture Wars." *University of Chicago Magazine,* Oct. 1997, 24–28.

Broad, B., Fortune, R., Harris, C. B., Neuleib, J., Nourie, B., and Parker, K. "Renewing the Nexus: Strengthening Connections Across the English Education Program." In P. Franklin, D., Laurence, D., and Welles, E. B. (eds.), *Preparing a Nation's Teachers: Models for English and Foreign Language Programs.* New York: Modern Language Association of America, 1999, pp. 17–48.

Elbow, P. *What Is English?* New York: Modern Language Association of America, 1990.

Franklin, P., Laurence, D., and Welles, E. B. (eds.). *Preparing a Nation's Teachers: Models for English and Foreign Language Programs.* New York: Modern Language Association of America, 1999.

Graff, G. *Professing Literature: An Institutional History.* Chicago: University of Chicago Press, 1987.

Graff, G. *Beyond the Culture Wars: How Teaching the Conflicts Can Revitalize American Education.* New York: W. W. Norton, 1992.

Graff, G. "Working with the Schools: Project Tempest." *PMLA,* Dec. 2000, *115*(7), 1968–1971.

Greenblatt, S., and Gunn, G. (eds.). *Redrawing the Boundaries: The Transformation of English and American Literary Studies.* New York: Modern Language Association of America, 1992.

Lunsford, A., Moglen, H., and Slevin, J. (eds.). *The Future of Doctoral Study in English.* New York: Modern Language Association of America/National Council of Teachers of English, 1989.

Magner, D. K. "Finding New Paths for Ph.D.'s in the Humanities." *Chronicle of Higher Education,* Apr. 16, 1999, p. A16.

Myers, D. G. *The Elephants Teach: Creative Writing Since 1880.* Englewood Cliffs, N.J.: Prentice Hall, 1996.

North, S., and others (eds.). *Refiguring the Ph.D. in English Studies: Writing, Doctoral Education, and the Fusion-Based Curriculum.* Urbana, Ill.: National Council of Teachers of English, 2000.

Salvatori, M. R., and Donahue, P. "English Studies in the Scholarship of Teaching." In M. T. Huber and S. P. Morreale (eds.), *Disciplinary Styles in the Scholarship of Teaching and Learning: Exploring Common Ground.* Washington, D.C: American Association for Higher Education and The Carnegie Foundation for the Advancement of Teaching, 2002.

Schneider, A. "Master's Degrees, Once Scorned, Attract Students and General Revenue." *Chronicle of Higher Education,* May 21, 1999, A12.

Shaughnessy, M. P. *Errors and Expectations: A Guide for the Teacher of Basic Writing.* New York: Oxford University Press, 1977.

Tompkins, J. *A Life in School: What the Teacher Learned.* Cambridge, Mass.: Perseus, 1996.

Winters, Y. *In Defense of Reason.* Chicago: Swallow Press, 1947.

20

WORDS AND RESPONSIBILITIES[1]

GRADUATE EDUCATION AND THE HUMANITIES

Catharine R. Stimpson, New York University

IN JANUARY 1998, I TOOK OFFICE as the graduate dean of arts and science at New York University—a private university. Shortly afterwards, I unexpectedly became co-acting humanities dean. For nearly two years, I found myself parked at the intersection of graduate education and the humanities. Trained in English literature, an early practitioner of women's studies, previously a graduate dean at a public university, long a participant in humanities organizations, I thought I had some understanding of the traffic patterns at this particular intersection. More fool I. I confess that I found myself thinking, more than once, that humanities are a mess—a real mess—a chaotic, irresponsible, and word-riddled demolition derby. On occasion, I even indulged in the "blank slate fantasy," capriciously dreaming of what graduate education in the humanities might be like if one could start from scratch—the scratch of a pen against a blank sheet of paper.

o

Crucially, the word *mess* has two great clusters of meaning. Both apply to the humanities. In one cluster, *mess* means bad things: confusion, muddle, spillage, dirt. But in the second, *mess* means good things: food, sustenance, a group of people sitting and eating together. The same contradictory meanings apply to *messy* and *messiness*. On the one hand, *messy* and *messiness* can signify clutter and turmoil and disorder. But on the other hand, *messy* and *messiness* can signify a healthy complexity, which the constancy of change helps to create. In 1980, the report of a national Commission on the Humanities approvingly cited a lecturer who had declared that the humanities were a "mixed economy," with links to "reason, logic, and the systematic procedures of scholarship on one side; to the insights of imagination, intuition, emotion and fantasy on the other" (Commission on the Humanities, 1980, p. 15). In addition, the preconditions of creativity are often messy. Think of the apothegm, "You can't make an omelet without breaking eggs."

The humanities are at once a muddle and our sustenance—food for our minds and souls. One reason my blank-slate fantasies about graduate education were so capricious was my inability to write on a blank slate, to erase my long-held conviction that the humanities are food for our minds and souls. Fortunately, I was aware of individual humanists of brilliance, élan, and depth; humanistic work of insight, truth, and eloquence; and humanistic fields of energy and perceptions.

The hands of American graduate educators are plunged deeply into this mess with a double meaning. For graduate schools are a primary place in which advanced humanistic inquiry takes place, in which professional humanists do their work, and where the next generation of professional humanists get their training. The existing reform movements in graduate education (in graduate education in general and in specific disciplines) are inevitably influencing the humanities.[2] How far-flung that influence will be and how it will shape confusion and nurture our sustenance depends, in part, on the wisdom of contemporary graduate educators.

The Messiness of the Humanities

All academic fields are, of course, full of conflict and change. They must be if they are not to stagnate and die. Individuals and fields grow and change.[3] Expanding beyond their established borders, they disrupt existing taxonomies. (In the life sciences today, for example, graduate programs, drawing on the resources of several academic departments, do not always map neatly onto these departments.) External circumstances press down on and reshape thought's formal, public contours. However, this flux in the humanities is more disagreeable to many than flux in the sciences or social sciences because of a pervasive belief, vocalized assertively during the culture wars, that the humanities should be a repository of unchanging, "canonical" values. A corollary of this belief is that the humanities must burnish and explore the good, the true, and the beautiful that are already there. Indeed, their very "thereness" is proof of their goodness, truth, and beauty. They ought not to be the consequence of a fallible process of incessant reinvention and discovery. A corollary of this corollary is that dramatic change in the humanities may prove to be corrosive rather than rejuvenating.

The humanities have also changed because of the ways in which they have partaken of the transformations of the American research university. Thomas Bender's essay "Politics, Intellect, and the American University, 1945–1995" (1997) reminds us that immediately before World War II, academic culture became far more secular. This meant that the hold of Christians had to be broken. For example, before World War II, no Yale College department employed any Jews. Symbolically, in 1936 Harvard altered its university seal, eliminating "Christo et Ecclesiae" but leaving "Veritas." Liberalization was a democratic good, but before its displacement, religion had "provided the moral authority and basis of cultural unity for higher education, even for the new research universities" (Bender, 1997, p. 28). Now other sources of authority and unity would have to be sought. One that would inspire ambivalence in the humanities might be objectivity and the scientific method. After World War II, U.S. higher education entered into what many now call its Golden Age—a period of enormous institutional expansion and success, spurred in part by federal funding of university scientists and justified by an appealing rhetoric that linked democracy, freedom, growth, and education. The study of Western traditions was to strengthen democratic freedoms and to serve as an antifascist, anticommunist force. The academic disciplines were also redefined, but, as Bender writes,

> [The disciplines] increasingly became an end in themselves, the possession of the scholars who constituted them. To a greater or lesser degree, academics sought some distance from civics. The increasingly professionalized disciplines were . . . openly or implicitly drawn to the model of science as a vision of professional maturity (1997, p. 22).

Then, in the 1960s, the humanities became strenuously, visibly, noisily, unusually messy—the consequence of the confluence of a number of well-known forces. Much of the unhappiness of the mess is economic in origin. In general, public financial support for higher education is far less robust and far more fragile than it was before the 1960s. More specifically, public and private funding for the humanities outside higher education itself seems on a downward trajectory (D'Arms, 1997). Compounding this extrinsic difficulty, for over three decades newly minted doctorates in the humanities have faced an academic job market so difficult that it is routinely labeled "a crisis." In 1980, the Commission on the Humanities was prophetically examining the crisis of the 1970s and then-nascent efforts to plan alternative careers for Ph.D.'s. Its fourteenth recommendation was "that graduate schools and departments reassess their purposes and curricula, and consider how the training they offer in the humanities might be better adapted to both academic and non-academic employment" (1980, p. 88). The Commission's report explicitly linked such steps to the well-being of the humanities: "[Their] continued vitality . . . depends on the successful adjustment . . . to the job crisis" (1980, p. 90).

Any crisis has many interactive causes. So does the job crisis in the humanities. Loosely managed graduate programs enrolled too many students and graduated, eventually, too many doctorates. Perhaps more significantly, although higher education grew dramatically during the twentieth century, undergraduates became less interested in liberal arts degrees. Academic democratization and the expansion of the liberal arts did not prove to be partners in a merger. Undergraduates majored instead in business (20 percent of all baccalaureates now), education, the health professions, and parks, recreation, leisure, and fitness studies. In 1970, English majors represented 7.6 percent of all baccalaureate degrees; in 1997, 4.2 percent. The absolute number of English majors declined from 64,342 undergraduates to 49,345. Higher education needed fewer faculty members in many liberal arts fields (Menand, 2001). The faculty that were wanted were often for teaching service courses—remedial work in reading and writing and communications—not advanced seminars in Proust or meanings of the myth of Procrustes and his bed.

Perhaps undergraduates have voted with their feet because graduate schools have produced faculty members in the humanities who are far too arcane and specialized, who might know about the myth of Procrustes in one historical period but nothing about Proust. Or perhaps undergraduates have acted as they have because of their experience of the humanities in high school. Or perhaps undergraduates are unconsciously carrying on those grand American traditions of anti-intellectualism, philistinism, yahooism, and Babbittry. Perhaps. But I find it even more likely that many undergraduates are being pragmatic, especially if they are new to the United States or new to higher education or new to both. To survive and thrive they must be economically secure. If a college certificate or degree is a credential that enhances economic security, and higher education has promised that it is, then get that certificate or degree in an area that has a demonstrable connection to a job or to a career.

The economic insecurity of the humanities has helped to generate a collective mood of anxiety, suspicion, and frequent depression, which graduate programs both embody and resist. However, even if the humanities were more economically secure, they would still feel overshadowed by the sciences and, to a lesser extent the social sciences—those disciplines that have assumed economic, social, and cognitive power in the modern world. In his important essay on the humanities, "The Sokal Affair and the History of Criticism," John Guillory (2002) analyzes the rise of the challenge of science to the nineteenth- and twentieth-century humanities and the celebrated conflicts between humanists and scientists: S. T. Coleridge and Thomas Carlyle against Jeremy Bentham and John Stuart Mill; Matthew Arnold against Thomas Huxley; F. R. Leavis against C. P. Snow (a novelist as well as a scientist). The humanists feared "much more than the machine, regarded as the mere avatar of scientific or industrial civilization. [They] . . . went on to take utilitarian philosophy, instrumental reason, and ultimately reason itself as the objects of critique" (Guillory, 2002, p. 479).

In the contemporary university, humanists have an additional reason for their antagonism to science, a fear of the "scientific monopoly on truth . . . the fear that criticism will be relegated to mere opinion, a discourse that cannot claim to be knowledge" (Guillory, 2002, p. 479). According to historian Lynn Hunt, the self-justifications of the humanities in response to the sciences have been mutually contradictory. We can say that we are like the sciences—a science of man, the human sciences—and produce new knowledge, but if we do so, we empty the notion of tradition of meaning, and, commonly identified as defenders of tradition, are left holding an empty bag (Hunt, 1998).

The comparative weakness of the humanities within the U.S. academy manifests itself every day. The sciences and the social sciences are simply bigger. I recently gazed at a table of the production of Ph.D.'s over the five-year period from 1999 to 2003 in the arts and sciences, engineering, and agriculture, in which research is rapidly converging with the life sciences. The life sciences generated 41,681 doctorates; the physical sciences, mathematics, and engineering 56,542; the social and behavioral sciences 34,378, and the humanities (including history) 27,475 (Hoffer, 2004). Moreover, the sciences and the social sciences are richer than the humanities—a fact literally brought home every time a faculty member compares the salaries of professors in business, computer science, economics, and Slavic Studies, or a graduate student compares the fellowship stipends of students in chemistry and comparative literature, or radiology and religion.

Given such realities, the humanities may seem a reversal of the story of Cinderella, the abused stepdaughter who married the prince. In the early modern period, kings and princes and affluent merchants often reveled in the humanities. The humanities provided counsel, intellectual companionship, and guidance for a worthy, fluent public life. They dwelt in palaces and mansions. Now, for complex reasons, the humanities may no longer be the friends of kings and princes and affluent merchants and presidents. At best, they may be under the guardianship of the enlightened corporate executive or the wife of a powerful man. In brief, the humanities have reverted to the condition of being an abused stepdaughter, doing the household chores of Comp 101. When graduate programs accept this narrative of their plight, no matter how unconsciously, they inexorably salt the mood I noted earlier with pinches of self-pity, irritability, and anger at "them"—whether "them" is the administration or the sciences or "conservatives" or "capitalism."

However, size and power need not trump significance. Nor can size and power always batter down the smaller and less powerful. Since the 1960s, the humanities have shown intellectual and social growth. They have famously became more diverse, global (or transnational), and multiplicitous—in their faculties, students, areas of study, curricula, and methods.[4] Those ideas lumped together as "theory" have forced greater self-consciousness about the nature of humanistic work. A 1966 conference at Johns Hopkins University, funded by the Ford Foundation, on "The Languages of Criticism and the Sciences of Man," was instrumental in establishing a significant cross-Atlantic traffic in concepts and intellectual personalities. "Theory" has proved provocative, for aspects of it undercut fundamental assumptions that the human person—the human subject—is the central figure in history and that subjects share "universal" capacities and values. As the work of such thinkers as Michel Foucault became more powerful, "the human subject tended to disappear, trapped in existing 'epistemes' and external linguistic structures" (Bender, 1997, p. 26).

Mary Poovey, the literary critic and historian, summarizes the development of the academic humanities between the 1960s and the mid-1980s:

> By 1985, a language that stressed universal values was no longer capable of attracting scholarly consensus or external funding. Throughout U.S. higher education, academic projects tended to be more specialized, in focusing more narrowly on specific problems; more theoretically self-conscious, in subjecting their methodologies to the kind of scrutiny associated with a heightened sensitivity to race, class, gender, and sexuality and with post-structuralism; and more product-oriented, as an expression of the speed-up of scholarly production the digital revolution facilitated (2001, pp. 302–303).

This evolution has been morally admirable and academically important. Even the most hidebound of stodges among "traditional humanists" will admit that the study of African Americans or of women is necessary, that human beings and groups have their differences, and that "The Other" must engage our respect. The study of marginalized and powerless groups has also tended to democratize the humanities curriculum and to restore "civics" to programs (albeit of an ardently progressive variant)—a dislike for oppressive structures of power and hegemony, an empathy for the damaged and hurt and dominated.

Significant though the evolution within the humanities has been, it has exacted mess-making costs. The return to a progressive civics, when unmoderated, has politicized departments. Next, if there is no human subject, where, then, are the humanities—the scholarship of the human subject? Finally, the multiplicity of areas of study and methods, combining with the post–World War II stress on specialization as a badge of professionalism, has fragmented fields. In a superb essay about changes in literary studies, Catherine Gallagher might have been speaking about the humanities in general. While useful, methodological flexibility, fluidity, and eclectism dissolve any "underlying consensus about the general benefits that derive from unique specialization" (Gallagher, 1997, p. 151). More negatively, a fragmentation in which the parts lack a sense of the whole may lead to a situation in which the parts regard each other suspiciously and belligerently.

As the parts quarrel among themselves, outside observers, who might once have found the scene interesting, wash their hands of the whole affair.[5] The politics, the antihumanism, the language of theory (unfairly maligned), the fragmentation—none of this helped to build bridges between the academic humanities and large sections of the "educated public." This permitted the humanities to become easily enmeshed in the "culture wars," which began in the 1960s and were fought most ferociously over the arts and humanities during the 1980s and their conservative Republican presidencies.

As I have written elsewhere, the contemporary roots of the culture wars were in the 1960s. They were fought over four great, linked issues: (1) the nature of the United States and its role in the world—a passionate dispute that the Vietnam War violently provoked, (2) race and racial discrimination, (3) gender and gender discrimination, and (4) sexual norms. Higher education was prominent in the culture wars, "at once a source of dissent and experimentation, a strategic target, and a provider of warriors for the Right, Left, and center" (Stimpson, 2002b, p. 36). Higher education mattered because "it maintains and produces . . . intellectual capital and because it recruits and trains human capital, including a national and international elite" (p. 36).[6]

Within higher education, the humanities were a primary battleground—in part, because they had so aggressively raised questions about the nature of the United States, race, gender, and sexual norms; in part, because they are the disciplines that teach culture, concepts of truth and identity, theories of the beautiful, and values, and, in part, because, like the arts, they were economically vulnerable. Although the culture wars brought the humanities publicity and brought out the warrior spirit in many humanists, they also made the humanities even more defensive.

Two publishing events, both in 1996, crystallize for me the humanities mess and its implications for higher education and, thus, graduate education. One gave form to doubts about the contemporary humanities that had been voiced both from without and within; a second gave form to doubts about the humanities that had been voiced largely from within. The first is the so-called Sokal Affair. The Spring-Summer 1996 issue of *Social Text* (a journal associated with the academic left), taking as its theme the "Science Wars," published an article by Alan Sokal, a member of the Physics Department of New York University; the article had the deliberately mind-numbing title, "Transgressing the Boundaries: Toward a Transformative Hermeneutics of Quantum Gravity." Initially welcomed as a contribution by a "real" scientist who understood how the up-to-date, postmodern, interpretive humanities could penetrate science and deflate its claims to epistemic superiority, "Transgressing" was then revealed to be a hoax, a pastiche of postmodern authorities designed to show how ridiculous and dangerous their thought and jargony language was, how fallible their advocates were, and how wrong these advocates were to assert that they knew anything about science.

The Sokal Affair took on the dimensions of a scandal and of yet another chapter in the culture wars, resonating within academic life, the mass media, and the Internet. John Guillory writes of the consequences of Sokal's gambit for the literary academy and other "humanistically oriented enterprises": "public ignominy"; being construed as left-wing, politicized, and oh-so-politically correct; being demonized as denying the presence of "reality" and asserting that all is "socially constructed" (2002, pp. 473–474). "Look," some strong voices within the humanities said, among them philosophers, "this is what happens when you get slack, when you don't know what you're talking about." "And who," asked other commentators, largely outside the academy, "would pay for their child to study such garbage?"

The second event was the posthumous publication of *The University in Ruins* by Bill Readings, which has circulated through the U.S. humanities as a sophisticated explanation of their trauma and unhappiness. I find the book an example of romantic and apocalyptic thought, which squeezes much of the complexity out of history and inflates a picture of the sensitive, solitary soul in the wilderness, but some of our finest humanists accept it. I think of J. Hillis Miller, a literary scholar and critic of learning, subtlety, and great probity. His essay, "Literary and Cultural Studies in the Transnational University," paraphrases and ornaments Readings' argument that the university is changing radically. "Something drastic is happening in the university. Something drastic is happening to the university. The university is losing its idea, the guiding mission that has sustained it since the early nineteenth century" (1998, p. 45). It was to serve the nation-state by being the site of critical thinking and research (Wissenschaft) and a site of education (Bildung), forming the subjects of the state through philosophy or, in Anglo-Saxon countries, through literature. However, the state is now weakening, giving way to global economic and cultural systems. University training is being placed in the service of "transnational corporations" (Miller, 1998, p. 45). Funders no longer believe that the nation needs the old university as it once did; the new university no longer needs the humanities as it once did. As for humanists, they have become unreliable conveyors of whatever values a nation has left. "The cat," Miller writes, "is out of the bag. These academic bureaucrats and legislators are by no means stupid . . . they know . . . that you can no longer trust professors to teach Chaucer, Shakespeare, Milton, and the rest in the old ideological ways" (1998, p. 53).

Also reshaping the humanities are still more profound shifts. Correctly, Miller notes that the United States has become a multicultural, multilingual nation. No single work reflects this "complex, nonunifiable whole" (1998, p. 55). The new communications technologies—computers, e-mail, fax, videos, CD-ROMs, hypertext, the Internet—are altering the way "humanist scholars are related to one another and do their work" (1998, p. 50). Moreover, around 1980, a generation of university teachers and critics appeared who had been brought up with television and "new forms of commercialized popular music." They turned "spontaneously and . . . massively to cultural studies," reflecting a move from the "age of the book to the age of hypertext" (1998, pp. 60–61).

Some of what Miller proposes is true; some, like the obituary for the nation-state, is exaggerated. But if Readings and Miller are right, what are graduate programs in the humanities to do? They are to seek a university rooted in "respect rather than of knowledge, one based on dissensus rather than the search for consensus . . . and a universalized truth" (1998, p. 64). If a more corporate transnational university prevails, the struggle for the humanities will be to keep from "becoming vestigial, no more than an assembly of programs teaching the communication skills needed by educated technocrats in the service of transnational corporations" (1998, p. 65). Miller offers no road map for building the university of dissensus or for the more despairing struggle against the corporate transnational university. Instead, like Readings, he represents the world sweepingly and sketches an ethical position for the humanities that might serve as consolation for their plight.

In the midst of the culture wars, I once heard a leading humanist shout out, "We have no power, but we will tell truth to power." His sloganeering was more militant and aspirational than the encouragement to dwell respectfully and honestly in the ruins, but I find them both symptoms of an incomplete response to the mess of the humanities—too passive, too enthralled by alienation, too confined to the humanities as a site of analysis and critique rather than as a site of analysis, critique, and affirmation. The humanities are hardly an activity that encourages only the Little Mary Sunshines of any gender to enroll in graduate school. They have rarely done so. They have appealed to old fogeys and young cranks, to the shy fantasist and the dawdling escapist, to the acerb and the cruel, to the passive-aggressive and manic-depressive.

However, when compelling, the humanities have the strength to dissipate the confusing messes in which they are enmeshed. The most revered and formidable of humanistic texts and humanists shatter the bricks of our complacency and the glass of our most benevolent certitudes. They can also blast through the most heavily titanium-and-steel-reinforced chambers of our indifferent minds and hearts and lead us to new worlds. What compels these texts and people? A passion for the subject is one thing. At a graduate school dean's day, at the turn of the millennium, I heard one of the leading medievalists of her generation say, "I teach Chaucer. Nobody could be a deader white male. I love him, and my students learn to read and like him."

Another is an irrepressible passion for learning itself. In 1998, Yi-Fu Tuan, who describes his field as systematic human geography, outlined his intellectual autobiography:

> I have always wondered . . . perhaps to a neurotic degree, about the meaning of existence: I want to know what we are doing here, what we want out of life. Big questions of this kind, which occur to most children as they approach puberty, have never left me. . . . My almost

pathological need to find meaning presses me to ask, again, and again, What else is there? What goes beyond—even far beyond—coping and survival? (Tuan, 1998, p. 3).

The survival of the humanities depends on their ability to prove that survival entails going beyond survival.

The Unity of the Humanities

The messy humanities are not a discipline but a set of disciplines that apparently have no unifying method whatsoever. I remember the meetings of leaders of the humanities departments and programs that my co-acting humanities dean—a classicist—and I once facilitated. There was the logician, there the creative writer, there an ethnographer of new technologies, there a European historian, there the global historian, there the critic of Latin American literature, there the friend of Jacques Derrida, there the enemy. Some were more akin to the sciences or to the social sciences than others were. Possibly, this messiness, this lack of disciplinary purity, is a vital sign of the messiness of our human lives themselves. Except for the most obsessive and regulatory of academics, very few of us spend every iota of our ordinary lives within the borders of the academic disciplines. But how can one talk seriously and comprehensively about "what constitutes knowledge and understanding in the humanities"? Is it possible to talk seriously and comprehensively about what humanists know and how they know it? Possibly not, but humanists have to try and give a plausible account of what it means to be a humanist—no matter what the specific discipline or area within a discipline or method. If we cannot generate even a minimal description of the humanities, they will dissipate into vapors, and graduate education in the humanities will have no common bonds except that anxious sense of institutional marginality. If there are the always inevitable conflicts about the meaning of the humanities, we must follow Gerald Graff's now canonical and binding injunction: "Teach the conflict."

Two gravitational forces pull contemporary humanists together. One is a loose commitment to a particular method. Some humanists do rigorously formal work and now computer-aided work. A philosopher thinks through a problem in logic; a musicologist analyzes a Bach fugue or a Beethoven symphony. However, humanists do not base their work in mathematics, nor do they design laboratory experiments that can be replicated.[7] Humanists offer other forms of evidence to persuade their audience that they are reliable, that they are plausible, that they ought to be believed. One is the extent and depth of their awareness of the materials relevant to their inquiry—the appropriate archives, texts, historical developments, languages, works of art and architecture, cultural institutions, and conflicts. I am far more apt to trust a critic of contemporary Egyptian literature if he or she knows Arabic, English, and French, or, at the very least, Arabic. A second is the quality of sensibility, how subtle and original, how capable of creating a spacious argument or narrative and yet of doing finely textured analyses. A third form of evidence interweaves awareness of materials and sensibility—the capacity for interpretation.

John Guillory rightly laments the current interpretations of interpretation in the academy. Either it has been downgraded to a species of mere opinion, or, alternatively, it "has been reconceived as an instrument for the skeptical critique of knowledge-claims." Simultaneously, and unfortunately, some of the humanistic disciplines have become a kind of theology, "allegoriz(ing)" the disciplines as representatives of "inherent political or philosophical positions" (2002, p. 505). To put the matter more vulgarly than Guillory does, if the humanities are interpretive activities, they are in trouble because of what interpretation now means, either one person blowing off mental steam, or, alternatively, biased humanists pushing a position, or, still another alternative, a skeptic warning that what other people say is false rather than exploring the true. Certainly, in an age of massive globally distributed propaganda and sales pitches, skepticism is invaluable, but, Guillory reminds us, interpretation is also a means of "producing knowledge" (2002, p. 498). The humanities will produce knowledge most effectively when they conceive of themselves as an interpretative "human science," bridging both naturalistic and interpretative methodologies. Which discipline might be the strongest bridge? For Guillory, it is history. Like Guillory, I assign philosophy the task of providing oversight for the epistemological claims of the other disciplines.

The second gravitational force is the subject matter of the humanities: the activities of human beings. Significantly, each humanistic discipline either represents a human capacity performing at the highest level of complexity, or, alternately, studies a human capacity performing at both its most routine and at its highest level of complexity. So philosophy represents our capacity for thinking at its most complex, history our capacity for remembering at its most complex. So, in its way, does psychoanalysis. Alternately, literary criticism studies us as language-makers at both our most routine and our most complex; art history studies us as picture-makers at both our most routine and our most complex; musicology studies us as sound-makers at both our most routine and our most complex; ethics studies us as just and moral beings, again at both our most routine and our most complex. Being a humanist is to be constantly torn between admiration and horror at human activities, between being in the presence of the ethics of the New Testament and the tortures of the Inquisition, made in the name of the New Testament. The array of fundamentally influential decisions about the very meaning of being human, which we have created, also provokes both admiration and horror. They have fluctuated radically over time and vary from culture to culture. These are such "duh" comments that I hesitate to write them.

Today, many humanists describe our condition as "posthuman."[8] This term means that one Western definition of humanity, common since the early modern period, is breaking down, in great part under the pressure of modern technologies. Human beings were named as one of two poles in a set of binary oppositions, and by far the better of the two. We were human, not animals; we were human, not machines. However, these oppositions are now collapsing. The strict borders between human and animal, between human and machine are being erased. What is the difference between human and animal if we can exchange body parts? What is the difference between human and machine if the mind and a computer might replicate each other? Or if I might have a computer chip implanted in my eye or brain? The humanities, in league with the sciences, take on these questions.

However, humanists have to choose a moral as well as a disciplinary perspective as they do their work. Ardent nationalists, from the United States and elsewhere, argue that the task of the humanities is to burnish the values and achievements of a national culture. They have their parallels in various religious and ethnic groups. However, the perspective that is most apt for a pluralistic, multicultured world—a world so aware of its global ties, its localisms, and their relations—is less particularistic and far more spacious and generous. For me, it derives from anthropology—the discipline whose dictionary definition is the science or study of man. Clifford Geertz, one of the greatest of contemporary humanistic scholars, writes of a triple task of seeing: first seeing others, then of seeing ourselves as others see us, and finally of seeing ourselves among others. Geertz writes:

> To see ourselves as others see us can be eye-opening. To see others as sharing a nature with ourselves is the merest decency. But it is from the far more difficult achievement of seeing ourselves amongst others, as a local example of the forms human life has locally taken, a case among cases, a world among worlds, that the largeness of mind, without which objectivity is self-congratulation and tolerance a sham,

comes. If interpretative anthropology has any general office in the
world it is to keep reteaching this fugitive truth (1983, p. 16).

If humanists can achieve this "largeness of mind," we may, I believe, even
achieve a common picture of what being human means. I again turn to
Geertz. In his famous essay, "Thick Description: Toward an Interpretative
Theory of Culture," he offers all humanists, not just anthropologists, such
a picture: "[M]an," he writes, "is an animal suspended in webs of significance he himself has spun." Culture is "those webs, and the analysis of it [is]
. . . therefore not an experimental science in search of law but an interpretative one in search of meaning" (1973, p. 5). What Geertz calls "cultural
analysis" I take to be the work of the humanities. It investigates "the symbolic dimensions of social action—art, religion, ideology, science, law, moral-
ity, common sense." However, we spin away in a world that consists not
only of symbols but also of social structures and natural necessities. Cultural
analysis cannot lose touch "with the hard surfaces of life—with the political, economic, stratificatory realities within which men are everywhere
contained—and with the biological and physical necessities on which those
surfaces rest. . . ." (1973, p. 30). Acting in this way, we in the humanities
will "plunge into the midst" of our "existential dilemmas" (1973, p. 30).

Word-conscious humanists, inside or outside of graduate schools, will
chew over that metaphor of man as "an animal suspended in webs of significance he himself has spun." In part, it is a posthuman reminder of connections between humanity and animalism—a truth many cultures have
already known. In part, it embodies a contradiction, and contradictoriness
is as much a part of being human as our desire to construct and construe
laws. On the one hand, being suspended in a web of significance is fright-
ening; we are prisoners hanging over a void. On the other hand, spinning
webs is the task of the spider, naturalistically one of the four main arachnid
orders, but mythically quite a creature. The narratives of Greek mythology tell of Arachne, a great weaver, who had the temerity to challenge the
mighty goddess Athena. At once wise and tumultuous, Athena transformed
Arachne into a spider. She continued to weave—a symbol of the persistence of creativity. Many centuries later, E. B. White, in his children's book
Charlotte's Web, re-invented her as Charlotte, a wily and kind old spider,
aware of the terrible fragility of webs, and in her communities of people
and insects and beasts, a source and sign of wisdom itself.[9]

To be a humanist, then: to seek to understand, to interpret, and to teach
our webs, worldwide and in the dustiest corners of a village in the dunes
of the past.

Words About Responsibilities and Stewardship in the Humanities

After April 2003, no one can think about "stewardship in the humanities" without grief and bitterness. For we then witnessed the rampaging through the National Museum in Baghdad, the Iraqi National Library and archives, the Mosul museum. The deepest of human histories have been burnt, smashed, looted, and robbed. We have lost irreplaceable records of the birth of writing, agriculture, law, religion, the state. Everyone living today is a descendent of the cultures of ancient Mesopotamia. We can assign blame for our losses to organized rings of thieves and their markets, anonymous looters, remnants of a tyrant's regime, and to the U.S. government. They will (or, more probably will not) accept legal and moral responsibility. Even the most contrite acknowledgment of culpability will not bring art, history, and books back. They are gone and, with them, our heritage. Of the paltry, paltry good that might come from this colossal disaster is a sharper awareness of what we pillage when we refuse to steward the humanities: nothing less than ourselves.

Being a steward means embodying a profound concept and doing often mundane tasks. Etymologically rooted in Old English, the word *steward* first referred to the person who regulated a household and supervised the table. The association of stewardship and eating has persisted, even as stewards took on responsibilities for management of land and in the Universities of Oxford and Cambridge, for judicial duties. Although a steward is neither a titan nor a queen nor a president, he or she is responsible for central aspects of our well-being. Not surprisingly, given the decentralization of culture and education in the United States, the stewards of the messes in the humanities are dispersed. No single institution authoritatively speaks for the humanities as a whole, although some have national scope and significance. I think, for example, of the National Humanities Center in North Carolina; the American Council of Learned Societies, the umbrella organization for many disciplinary societies; the American Academy of Arts and Sciences, an American version of the European academies that have been a primary conduit of humanistic learning since the early modern period; and Phi Beta Kappa, an honorary society of liberal arts baccalaureates that sponsors a significant magazine, *The American Scholar*. Fortunately, this diffusion prevents the sclerosis from which overly centralized institutions suffer. Less fortunately, it means the humanities lack a greatly powerful champion and advocate, and a voice that can clarify the contests and arguments that give the humanities their zest, salt, rawness, and flavors.

Some of the stewards are individual voices: figures who have the talent and force to set new directions in the humanities, accomplished leaders from the private sector who give moral and philanthropic support, or singular creators who have earned the public trust. Like Bill Moyers, who appears largely on public television and publishes with trade houses, these figures often work outside of academic life. This is ironic, because the institutions most responsible for the humanities are academic ones—universities and liberal arts colleges. Like all of American higher education, they are both public and private. They support research, hire humanists for their faculties, standardize the humanities through setting the curriculum, maintain research libraries, educate the next generation of professional humanists in graduate schools, disseminate the humanities in the undergraduate classroom, create humanities centers (a healthy development in the last part of the twentieth century), and operate the university presses that have been a primary outlet for academic monographs. Higher education has been the primary life support system for the humanities, and this is almost wholly to the good. The gap between writing "almost wholly" and "wholly" exists because the humanities are saturated with the identity of higher education, its bureaucratic structures, and its processes of evaluation. A brilliant young humanist might not say, "I am a humanist and want to write as passionately and coherently as possible about the history of the American West," but rather, this humanist might say, "I am a historian, and I have to finish my second book about this border town in Nevada so I can pass muster with my department and get tenure."[10]

Traditionally, stewards of the disciplines have judged newer academic humanists—the extent and breadth of their awareness of relevant materials, the quality of their sensibility, and their capacity for productive interpretation—through their publication of a book or monograph. This remains the standard for tenure in research universities and, usually, for a solid reputation. Today, however, several forces are putting pressure on this standard. The first, paradoxically, is the demand for books for tenure in institutions other than research universities. This has led too often to quick, thin books read by only a handful of people and usually without much influence. Simultaneously, the economics of scholarly publishing are now perilous. The outlets for academic books are diminishing, threatening the good and the indifferent alike. Finally, digital technologies are changing the dissemination of information and knowledge. The humanities should be following the sciences in establishing "more inclusive networks of intellectual dialogue [and] . . . open archives" (Lewis, 2002, p. 1224). The open but urgent question is how to evaluate a humanist's work if scholarly articles are to supplement the monograph, if a range of rhetorical styles is to become more acceptable, and if more publishing is to be done electronically.

Powerful though higher education institutions are, they are not self-sustaining. They exist within a number of networks on which they feed and which, in turn, feed on them. Some of these are the "disciplinary organizations," such as the American Historical Association and the Modern Language Association. Consisting primarily of faculty members and research scholars, with some graduate student participation, they define the problems of a discipline as a whole and establish its protocols. Their flagship journals set the norms and parameters of accepted scholarship (Tomlins, 1998). Educational institutions concerned with the liberal arts form their own associations and affinity groups. Private foundations, such as the crucial Mellon Foundation and the Woodrow Wilson National Fellowship Foundation, fund projects and, through fellowships, individual scholars. Great private research libraries—the New York Public Library, the Newberry Library in Chicago, the Huntington Library in Pasadena— are invaluable repositories of manuscripts, maps, books. Independent academies provide a home for advanced inquiry.[11] To a degree that many academic scholars refuse to acknowledge, public broadcasting brings humanistic scholarship, especially in literature, drama, and history, to a wide public. The Web sites for such programs as "Masterpiece Theatre" on PBS would put many a college classroom and its syllabi to shame.[12]

Notably, federal and state governments are minor, often reluctant stewards of the humanities. In 1965, Congress authorized two organizations that were to support the arts and the humanities: the National Endowment for the Arts (NEA) and the National Endowment for the Humanities (NEH). Each endowment was to help support state councils, which have been extraordinarily creative in invigorating the arts and humanities on a local level, in bringing together academic humanists and nonacademic audiences, and in inspiring the public humanities movement—self-conscious efforts to weave the humanities with the life of American citizens. Each endowment can correctly claim a record of achievement, but they have never attained the status as stewards that the National Science Foundation, their model, has for the sciences. The endowments have been too small, too underfunded, their ability to underwrite such major "traditional" projects as the publication of the papers of important cultural and political figures too skimpy. On the one hand, they have been a battleground of the culture wars, their more liberal activities subject to vitriol, scorn, ridicule, and charges of America-hating. On the other hand, their more conservative activities have been subject to deep suspicion and charges of liberal-hating. It is far better to have the endowments than not to have them at all, but their lamentable vulnerability to political pressures renders their record of stewardship erratic.

In addition, and often unrecognized by the formal stewards of the humanities, are informal stewards and practitioners of humanistic inquiry. They may partake of the self-conscious public humanities movement, but they are far greater in number than these worthies. They simply do the humanities in their everyday life. They include the man or woman looking up a family genealogy, the members of a book club or discussion group, the audience of a state humanities council project, a listener to jazz who compares performances he or she has heard, or the solitary reader of a book of history or poetry. I once scoffed at people who, when they were introduced to a professional philosopher, would say, "I have a philosophy of life," but my laughter was cheap and superficial. A person with a philosophy of life has been a practical humanist, has thought teleologically and ethically.

To be sure, the individuals and institutions that formally support the humanities need more coordination and more facilitators who might help them network more effectively. (My use of bureaucratic jargon is ironic.) The purpose of a more coherently organized stewardship would be to make a powerful and public case for the humanities and greater funding for them. If it came to be, such a stewardship could measure its success quantitatively. Were there more fellowships for scholars? Was the NEH more immune from political posturing? A second test would be harder to design but would be as important. Would the informal stewards and practitioners have become a part of a national effort at stewardship? Would they be recognized as stewards? Would the members of the book club in my hometown feel as responsible for the humanities, and as much in debt to them, as the English department of the local university?

Questions for Graduate Programs in the Humanities[13]

Early in this essay I remarked that the hands of graduate educators in the humanities are plunged deeply into the mess, for they are engaged in the work of the humanities, as well as the training of the next generation of humanists. This training is a primary form of stewardship and responsibility. It can be conducted carelessly, routinely, or in a spirit of self-consciousness and self-questioning. Significantly, humanists pride themselves on their capacity for asking questions, for probing and anatomizing, for pushing aside formulaic, conventional, superficial answers. What questions should graduate educators in the humanities now ask themselves?

The most crucial question, of course, is Why? Why are we recruiting, admitting, and educating doctoral students? Perhaps some answers will be too selfish or cutely playful to be widely distributed. Perhaps some answers will be too fatuous even for a "mission statement"—that fast-food purveyor of the fatuous. However, unless a program can cogently say why it exists, others will ask why it must.

I have six more platters of questions for graduate programs. I believe they are vital queries, but because of the wide circulation of ideas about reform in graduate education, they are hardly nouvelle. Their pragmatism also would have surprised me when I was an idealistic graduate student too out of touch to realize how wet I was behind the ears.

First, who should the next generation of graduate students in the humanities be? What demonstrable talents should they have? And how diverse should they be? And if we believe in diversity, both nationally and internationally, as I do, how will we achieve it? However active graduate schools may now be in recruiting students from undergraduate colleges, they do far too little in reaching a broad range of high school students and their families. As Lynn Hunt writes, humanities faculties have failed to make their case, "especially to students from families in which the parents did not go to college" (1998, p. 8).

Second, once students are within programs, how do we want them to learn and what do we want them to know? A graduate degree, an economist keeps telling me, is a research degree. But what, in an age of information overload, does this mean? And is research to be deep but narrow or broad but shallow? This question may set up a false binary opposition, but it points to a hard issue: Is graduate education disciplinary or interdisciplinary? Interdisciplinarity has become a fetish and a touchstone, but no one can do interdisciplinary work well unless they have a home plate of knowledge from which they can run and to which they can return. A little learning is a dangerous thing. Graduate school both trains one's general intellectual capacities and nurtures a specialization—a strong understanding of something. Graduate education should not be a smattering of this and that.

Although Marjorie Sabin is more hostile to contemporary theory than I, she has a point when she writes:

> Young literary scholars . . . cruelly caught between the pressure to rush into print with their amateur forays into economics, psychology, anthropology, and so forth and their need—possibly even their desire— to advance their reading of literature beyond its undergraduate limits.

> The students of this poorly educated faculty, in turn, will be inevitably deprived of the literary experience necessary to test the hostility to literature promulgated by much advanced theory (Sabin, 1997, p. 98).

Yet graduate education must cultivate curiosity and the ability, which curiosity waters, to make connections between a specialty and other fields. These connections are the lines that make up the webs of interdisciplinary work. Graduate students must become suspicious of the mere evocation of the term *interdisciplinary* as if it were a prayer. They must be able to grasp what this work entails, which begins with the ability to understand one's own disciplinary roots and explain them to others. Students must also learn how many different ways there are of being interdisciplinary.[14] Is not one way of achieving this end a common course in a doctoral student's first year, what I have called "general education for graduate education" (Stimpson, 2002a). A shared intellectual experience would introduce graduate students—diverse in nationality, background, discipline, language, and training—to each other, to their intellectual homes, and to the university.

Third, organizationally, do the structures into which graduate students are admitted enable genuine learning with a flexible mixture of disciplinary and interdisciplinary approaches? Catherine Gallagher speculates that we may be in the midst of "an enormous institutional shift away from the traditional departments even though we continue to locate our professional training inside those structures. Perhaps our most difficult task now is to give our intellectual adventures the kind of secure institutional footing that would allow us to develop once again as a discipline" (1997, p. 170). The life sciences display a similar disjunction between departmental structures and the sites where research and teaching are actually being done, which results in an overlay of interdisciplinary programs over departmental structures.

If humanities departments were to be re-aligned, which would join with which? What might be peeled off and discarded? And would the social sciences need to be split between the "narrativizing" or "discursive" fields and the more quantitative and mathematical? So would political theory split off from politics, cultural anthropology from anthropology, and such subfields as historical sociology and sociology of culture from sociology? Would they and the humanities then drift toward each other and form a new academic continent with new contours? This would not happen at once—an Instant Transformation—but would take place incrementally over time. Slowly, graduate students would enter institutions in which closer fit would exist between departments and our "intellectual adventures" (Wallerstein, 2003).

Fourth, how are we to create academic citizens, members of a public? Intellectually, humanists have tended to work by themselves. The heroic and original humanist has been a solitary one. To be sure, humanists have had friends, spouses, partners, and assistants. They have spoken about their work in classrooms and conferences. But, significantly, their publications have tended to bear only their name. Collaborative practices, common to the sciences, must now take hold in the humanities.[15] It can be done within a field, or among fields, or among arts and sciences and the professions. Medical anthropology and law and literature are but two examples of these fusions. Collaborations are increasing because good interdisciplinary work so often demands collaboration, because the dramatic increase in knowledge makes it difficult for one person to master a field independently, and because of the long overdue recognition that much intellectual and artistic work is communal in nature. Some grand, formidable polymath geniuses do exist. I think, for example, of Susan Sontag in criticism and the arts and Stephen J. Gould in the sciences, both recently deceased. I would not want to force such minds into enforced companionships and false group signatures. For others, be they as brilliant as Sontag and Gould or not, should graduate programs not encourage collaborative as well as independent work? Research and teaching can be a potlatch as well as a table set by and for one.

Another meaning of participation is being involved in governance. How can we train graduate students in fair, effective, transparent governance? The refusal or inability to become genuinely engaged in governance and the habit of substituting rhetorical outcries for the work of governance help to guarantee the marginality of humanists. To do governance means to enroll in rudimentary lessons about budgets instead of complaining, "I'm not quantitative," doing competent administrative work beyond the department instead of enforcing a victim's distance between "us," the humanists, and "them," the administrators.

Fifth, after the doctoral defense is over, what do we want our students to do and be? As scores before me have pointed out, doctorates in the humanities will need decent employment. If they are going to become teachers, and most will, they will need to know how to design a curriculum both on-site and online, how to transform research into a cogent, appealing, teachable subject for students at many different levels.[16] How are we preparing them? Graduate students will need to be reassured that a variety of jobs will be appropriate outside the research university, be they in other educational institutions or outside academe altogether. How are we telling our students that they are not failures if they do not become a clone of their dissertation adviser? In a compelling autobiographical essay about her discoveries after the only job she could get was in a two-year institution, Jennifer W. Stolpa concludes:

> [W]e should examine carefully how long-standing assumptions about two-year institutions may prevent people from considering such positions as professionally sound choices. As I hear of my graduate school colleagues finishing their doctorates and entering the job market, I hope they too will confront the assumptions they may hold about two-year institutions. I know I am better for having done so (2001, p. 91).

How are we speaking to a Dr. Stolpa and, as we do so, tamping down a pernicious elitism about institutions? Realistically, we also know that some educational institutions are wretched, academically remote, governed by timeservers and petty-minded control freaks. How are graduate institutions connecting with our graduates who do hard duty in such places conscientiously?

Sixth, and finally, how are graduate programs modeling the appropriate relations between traditional learning and its new technologies that are transforming the ways in which we read, write, and learn, or, as Carla Hesse writes, the "foundational assumptions of the humanities and the nature of the libraries that sustain them." Computer scientists can teach the humanities about these new technologies. Neuroscientists and psychologists can teach humanists more about the processes of perception and cognition. Sociologists can teach humanists about our social adaptation and use of the new technologies. Humanists can remind themselves and teach others about the rhetorical nature of learning. What sort of a hybrid will we, so educated, generate from the encounters between tradition and the new? Hesse argues:

> It is not insignificant . . . that at the heart of the Xerox Corporation's Palo Alto Research Center . . . [PARC is the birthplace of the personal computer and developer of many technologies] . . . there lies a traditional library composed of tables and chairs, as well as books and serial stacks, so that researchers can engage in long, silent reading and reflection on where they are going and what they are doing (1997, p. 119).[17]

No doubt, current and subsequent generations of graduate students, who were born with a mouse in their hands, will create this hybrid far more imaginatively and usefully than my generation. But all of our efforts will be full of mistakes. Some of our hybrids may be misshapen. How will we do what we must do, ably and imaginatively?

Why the Humanities Matter

My essay began with a comment about the doubleness of the word *mess*, accusing the humanities of being a mess in the more pejorative of the two senses and praising them for being a mess in the more affirmative. I also worried that the humanities in the United States had dismissed or forgotten about the affirmative meaning of the humanities, had become defensive and obsessed with their marginality. Let me end by returning to the reasons why the humanities matter. I take them from the recent publications of an Iranian literary scholar, Azar Nafisi, who now lives and teaches in the United States. During a mess of historic proportions—the Iranian revolution, the installation of a theocracy there, the Iranian-Iraqi war—she taught literature. Belonging to a tradition of humanists and artists who have worked while literally under siege and fire, she writes that "it is precisely during such times, when our lives are transformed by violence, that we need works of imagination to confirm our faith in humanity, to find hope amid the rubble of a hopeless world" (2003a, p. A25, expanded on in 2003b). Humanists in American graduate schools, as teachers or students, may experience economic anxieties and political alienation. Even so, they can do no less to affirm the humanities than their colleagues who are in greater peril, whose breath and life are in danger, and who continue to speak with great ardor and persuasiveness of the worth of humanistic activities and learning.

Acknowledgments

I am indebted to Tom Bender, Chris Golde, Marjorie Perloff, and, deeply, to George Walker and Ellen Wert for their comments on this essay.

NOTES

1. The title of this essay comes in part from Adrienne Rich's poem "North American Time."

2. Literature about the reform movement in graduate education in general is now extensive. Of the various humanistic disciplines, the modern languages (through the Modern Language Association) and history (through the American Historical Association) have been notably active. In January 2004, the University of Illinois Press published a report of the American

Historical Association's Committee on Graduate Education, "The Education of Historians for the 21st century" (Bender, Katz, and Palmer, 2004).

3. See Hilary Putnam, "A Half Century of Philosophy, Viewed From Within" (1997), for an exemplary autobiographical account of intellectual change, here of a leading philosopher. Her essays are reliable guides to deep changes in twentieth-century American academic fields.

4. One mark of this growing diversity: the Commission on the Humanities consisted of thirty-two worthy citizens, only four of whom were women, only one of whom belonged to an American racial minority. It would be astonishing if an equivalent commission, established today, were as lacking in gender and racial diversity.

5. I am paraphrasing Franklin (1992, p. 218).

6. Stimpson (2000) and Stimpson (1993) are among my other explorations of education and the humanities.

7. Professor Jeffrey Schnapp at Stanford has implemented the pilot phase of a model of research in the humanities that is based on the MIT Media Research Lab and others. The Stanford Humanities Lab is an independent entity within the university; it funds competitively selected collaborative research projects that involve faculty, postdoctoral students, graduate students, and others from across the university, such as from the library or arts centers (www.stanford.edu/group/shl).

8. See, for example, the work of N. Katherine Hayles (1999).

9. Nancy K. Miller in "Arachnologies: The Woman, the Text, and the Critic," (1988) uses the figure of Arachne as a trope for a feminist poetics.

10. The Association of American Universities (AAU), the organization of leading research universities, has published a report about humanities on their campuses, which demonstrates far more vitality and innovation than one might have thought from gloomier accounts of the ongoing crisis in the humanities (Mathae and Birzer, 2004).

11. The American Academy of Arts and Sciences is responsible for one of the most important recent reports about the humanities, focusing on its data needs, "Making the Humanities Count" (Solow and others, 2002).

12. The culture wars generated two mutually compatible private organizations: the National Association of Scholars and the American Council of Alumni and Trustees, the common purpose of which is to label and combat the putative radicalism and "politicalization" of the liberal arts and their institutions.

13. After outlining this section, I attended a conference on "The Future of Criticism" at the University of Chicago, sponsored by *Critical Inquiry*, one of the liveliest and most consequential of humanities and social science journals.

Conference participants were asked to submit statements that briefly reflected their perception of the future of theory and criticism (www.uchicago.edu/research/jnl-crit-inq/main.html). My essay, "Myths of Transformation: Realities of Change" (2000) also outlines five principles that I believe ought to serve as a foundation for all graduate education.

14. For two different perspectives, see Renato Rosaldo (2001) and Mary Poovey (2001).

15. A good description of the possibilities of collaborative work is in the essays that derive from the 2000 Presidential Forum of the Modern Language Association, organized by Linda Hutcheon, then the MLA president (Presidential Forum of the Modern Language Association, 2001).

16. Peter N. Stearns (1993) speaks forcefully to the need for a revitalized humanities, especially history, that takes its curricular responsibilities seriously.

17. The literature on this subject is growing, but the work of Jerome McGann and Richard A. Lanham has been especially helpful to me. See, for example, Lanham's "The Extraordinary Convergence: Democracy, Technology, Theory, and the University Curriculum" (1992).

REFERENCES

Bender, T. "Politics, Intellect, and the American University, 1945–1995." In T. Bender and C. E. Schorske (eds.), *American Academic Culture in Transformation*. Princeton, N.J.: Princeton University Press, 1997.

Bender, T., Katz, P. M., and Palmer, C. *The Education of Historians for the Twenty-First Century*. Urbana: University of Illinois Press/American Historical Association, 2004.

Bender, T., and Schorske, C. E. (eds.). *American Academic Culture in Transformation: Fifty Years, Four Disciplines*. Princeton, N.J.: Princeton University Press, 1997.

Commission on the Humanities. *The Humanities in American Life: Report of the Commission on the Humanities*. Berkeley: University of California Press, 1980.

D'Arms, J. H. "Funding Trends in the Academic Humanities, 1970–1995: Reflections on the Stability of the System." In A. Kernan (ed.), *What's Happened to the Humanities?* Princeton, N.J.: Princeton University Press, 1997.

Franklin, P. "The Academy and the Public." In D. J. Gless and B. H. Smith (eds.), *The Politics of Liberal Education*. Durham, N.C.: Duke University Press, 1992.

Gallagher, C. "The History of Literary Criticism." In T. Bender and C. E. Schorske (eds.), *American Academic Culture in Transformation*. Princeton, N.J.: Princeton University Press, 1997.

Geertz, C. "Thick Description: Toward an Interpretative Theory of Culture." In *The Interpretation of Cultures: Selected Essays*. New York: Basic Books, 1973.

Geertz, C. "Introduction." In *Local Knowledge: Further Essays in Interpretative Anthropology*. New York: Basic Books, 1983.

Guillory, J. "The Sokal Affair and the History of Criticism." *Critical Inquiry*, 2002, *28*(2), 470–508.

Hayles, N. K. *How We Became Posthuman: Virtual Bodies in Cybernetics, Literature, and Informatics*. Chicago: University of Chicago Press, 1999.

Hesse, C. "Humanities and the Library in the Digital Age." In A. Kernan (ed.), *What's Happened to the Humanities?* Princeton, N.J.: Princeton University Press, 1997.

Hoffer, T. B., and others. *Doctorate Recipients from United States Universities: Summary Report 2003*. Chicago: National Opinion Research Center, 2004.

Hunt, L. "Tradition Confronts Change: The Place of the Humanities in the University." *The Humanist on Campus: Continuity and Change*. ACLS Occasional Paper, No. 44. New York: American Council of Learned Societies, 1998.

Lanham, R. A. "The Extraordinary Convergence: Democracy, Technology, Theory, and the University Curriculum." In D. J. Gless and B. H. Smith (eds.), *The Politics of Liberal Education*. Durham, N.C.: Duke University Press, 1992.

Lewis, P. "Is Monographic Tyranny the Problem?" *PMLA*, 2002, *117*(5), 1222–1224.

Mathae, K. B., and Birzer, C. L. (eds.). *Reinvigorating the Humanities: Enhancing Research and Education on Campus and Beyond*. Washington, D.C.: Association of American Universities, 2004.

Menand, L. "The Charms of College." *New York Review of Books*, 2001, *48*(16), 44–47.

Miller, J. H. "Literary and Cultural Studies in the Transnational University." In J. C. Rowe (ed.), *Culture and the Problem of the Disciplines*. New York: Columbia University Press, 1998.

Miller, N. K. "Arachnologies: The Woman, the Text, and the Critic." In *Subject to Change: Reading Feminist Writing*. New York: Columbia University Press, 1988.

Nafisi, A. "Words of War." *New York Times*, Mar. 27, 2003a, p. A25.

Nafisi, A. *Reading Lolita in Tehran: A Memoir in Books*. New York: Random House, 2003b.

Poovey, M. "Interdisciplinarity at New York University." In J. W. Scott and D. Keates (eds.), *Schools of Thought: Twenty-Five Years of Interpretative Social Science*. Princeton, N.J.: Princeton University Press, 2001.

Presidential Forum of the Modern Language Association. "Creative Collaboration: Alternatives to the Adversarial Academy." *Profession 2001,* 2001, 4–38.

Putnam, H. "A Half Century of Philosophy, Viewed from Within." In T. Bender and C. E. Schorske (eds.), *American Academic Culture in Transformation.* Princeton, N.J.: Princeton University Press, 1997.

Readings, B. *The University in Ruins.* Cambridge, Mass.: Harvard University Press, 1996.

Rich, A. "North American Time." In *The Fact of a Doorframe: Poems Selected and New 1950–1984.* New York: W. W. Norton, 1984.

Rosaldo, R. "Reflections on Interdisciplinarity." In J. W. Scott and D. Keates (eds.), *Schools of Thought: Twenty-Five Years of Interpretative Social Science.* Princeton, N.J.: Princeton University Press, 2001.

Sabin, M. "Evolution and Revolution." In A. Kernan. (ed.), *What's Happened to the Humanities?* Princeton, N.J.: Princeton University Press, 1997.

Sokal, A. "Transgressing the Boundaries: Toward a Transformative Hermeneutics of Quantum Gravity." *Social Text,* Spring-Summer, 1996.

Solow, R. M., Oakley, F., Franklin, P., D'Arms, J., and Jones, C. C. *Making the Humanities Count: The Importance of Data.* Cambridge, Mass.: American Academy of Arts and Sciences, 2002.

Stearns, P. N. *Meaning Over Memory: Recasting the Teaching of Culture and History.* Chapel Hill, N.C.: University of North Carolina Press, 1993.

Stimpson, C. R. "The Postmodern Element in the Postmodern Humanities." *Weber Studies: An Interdisciplinary Humanities Journal,* 1993, *10*(2) 41–56.

Stimpson, C. R. "General Education for Graduate Education." *Chronicle of Higher Education,* Nov. 1, 2002a, pp. B7–10.

Stimpson, C. R. "The Culture Wars Continue." *Daedalus,* 2002b, *131*(3), 36–40.

Stimpson, C. R. "Myths of Transformation: Realities of Change." Conference on the Future of Doctoral Education. *PMLA,* 2000, *115*(5), 1142–1153.

Stolpa, J. M. "Settling for a Great Job." *Profession 2001,* 2001, 85–91.

Tomlins, C. L. "Wave of the Present: The Scholarly Journal on the Edge of the Internet." ACLS Occasional Paper, No. 43. New York: American Council of Learned Societies, 1998, 1–24.

Tuan, Yi-Fu. "A Life of Learning" (Charles Homer Haskins Lecture for 1998). ACLS Occasional Paper, No. 42. New York: American Council of Learned Societies, 1998, i–ix, 1–16.

Wallerstein, I. "Anthropology/Sociology and Other Dubious Disciplines." *Current Anthropology,* 2003, *44*(4), 453.

White, E. B. *Charlotte's Web.* New York: Harper, 1952.

PART FOUR

CONCLUSION

21

THE QUESTIONS IN THE
BACK OF THE BOOK

*George E. Walker, The Carnegie Foundation
for the Advancement of Teaching*

*It is, in fact, nothing short of a miracle that the modern methods
of instruction have not yet entirely strangled the holy curiosity of
inquiry; for this delicate little plant, aside from stimulation,
stands mainly in need of freedom; without this the plant goes to
wrack and ruin without fail. It is a very grave mistake to think
that the enjoyment of seeing and searching can be promoted by
means of coercion and a sense of duty.*

—Albert Einstein, *Autobiographical Notes,* 1979, p. 17

IT IS VERY DIFFICULT for those of us who are senior scholars in our disciplines to envision the possibilities and need for truly revolutionary changes in graduate education. The scholars who contributed the essays in this volume, like other successful graduate faculty members, have thrived under the current system. Indeed, the self-same training and success that brought these scholars to our attention also perpetuates certain assumptions and can blind them to certain kinds of questions.

The essayists map out the intellectual history of their fields, identifying the challenges facing the discipline, and offering concrete suggestions for improving doctoral education in the field. They tell us that the approach and execution of Ph.D. education needs attention in the areas of, among others, interdisciplinary and collaborative research, improvement in the diversity of the student population, and the development of professional skills. The essayists consistently tell us that our current system is not optimal and that the context of both teaching and research is changing.

But in general, the suggestions they make for addressing these concerns are not revolutionary. Because the scholars we asked to write these essays all want, more than anything, to be of service to their disciplines, they fall into the trap—perhaps one that we inadvertently set—of being realistic. In offering ideas to improve doctoral education, they propose solutions that can be implemented by making small, incremental changes. In this regard their perspective and approach is mirrored by the faculty in the departments that are working with us in the Carnegie Initiative on the Doctorate (CID). This grounded and responsible approach is natural. Indeed, some might argue that for these disciplinary leaders to respond differently, either as essayists or as departmental leaders, would be to put their current students and well-respected programs at some risk and would therefore be irresponsible.

Common to all the essays is the assumption that the disciplines should remain organized as they are. All of the essayists take as given that the prevailing general structure of intellectual study and the Ph.D. degree are necessary to certain careers or career levels. These assumptions focus the authors on the quality and effectiveness of existing programs to the exclusion of more radical re-envisioning.

As a result, they are silent on many areas of doctoral education. For example, none of the authors suggest a radical overhaul of graduate education in their discipline. Nor do any of the essayists question the need for the Ph.D. degree. Moreover, as they look ahead, the essayists seem to see future opportunities and challenges in their fields that are not substantially different from those existing in the present. Yet some fields are facing rapidly changing opportunities in the globalized world, whereas others are facing considerable new challenges of competition for students.

The tragedy is that faculty members have invested so much and become so used to the current environment that it is difficult to realize that today's graduate students are struggling to breathe. We are so accustomed to the forces at work around us that we are no longer aware that they are limiting us. We need, instead, to find new vantage points from which to observe our disciplines and programs.

But, to borrow a few words from Yehuda Elkana's essay, "How best to do that?"

Asking New Questions About Doctoral Education

If we take seriously the charge to start *de novo*; if we violate the tacit assumption that disciplines, knowledge, and universities will stay fundamentally as they are today; if we do not for a moment strive to be "realistic"—then new questions emerge.

The Carnegie Foundation proposes that the central purpose of doctoral education, broadly taken, is to produce "stewards of the discipline"—highly skilled, deeply knowledgeable men and women who teach, lead, and discover not only in our own country but all over the world. We believe that the way to realize this purpose is to build and maintain doctoral programs that are centered squarely on students. Responsibility for student-centered doctoral education is a shared responsibility of the faculty, students, and administrators in the university and the practicing members of the discipline. Indeed, the essays and commentaries in this volume all assume this goal of student-centered doctoral programs. The changes they argue for, both explicitly and tacitly, are designed to support students in becoming stewards of the discipline.

Moreover, we believe that this responsibility requires us to relinquish some old habits of mind, leave excessive caution behind, and start *de novo* to build programs that meet the needs and opportunities that students now face.

These goals bring up new questions about and increased responsibility for the design and efficacy of Ph.D. programs. Thinking in terms of developing stewards of the discipline raises significantly different ideas about the features of the program, teaching in the program, and the nature of support for the program. When we think about the role of the faculty in different ways, we are able to define success for doctoral programs in new ways. We ask difficult but important questions that focus on developing responsible lifelong learners and discoverers who also facilitate the learning and discovery of others. We diligently and creatively pursue the answers to those questions.

Consider first what we should ask about the discipline. What does it contribute? Does it do so effectively? Can it justify its existence, and can it do so in language that is not defensive but that reveals a full understanding of the role it plays and roles it might play in the future? Is the discipline keeping up with the evolving nature of knowledge, discovery, and communication?

We should also ask about the Ph.D. programs in individual departments. Do they contribute effectively to the university and society? Can they justify their ongoing existence, in the university and in the field, as producers of Ph.D.'s?

Knowing that intellectual curiosity and leadership require ongoing cultivation, no matter the field, we could ask if programs invest in preserving—even increasing—the passion that drew students to their field of study. Students (and faculty) talk about losing the passion that originally drew them to their field of study during doctoral study. Is such a loss unavoidable? Why does it occur? What experiences in graduate school would ameliorate this situation?

Students (and the biographies, both formal and informal, of successful scholars) tell us that being part of a robust intellectual community is critical to the development of researchers and scholars. How should Ph.D. programs be structured to purposefully integrate students into vibrant intellectual communities?

Often neither faculty nor graduate students can explain the rationale for the various pieces of their graduate program or how the pieces fit together over time to develop a steward of the discipline. Do programs make transparent all the reasons behind the various components of the program or expectations of the discipline? This lack of transparency represents a lost opportunity for students to engage consciously in their own maturation as scholars. A lack of transparency also makes it difficult to review the Ph.D. program and determine its success in meeting student and faculty goals. How is a program to know if it is missing the mark when it does not know where the mark is?

The interests, expectations, cultural backgrounds, and academic preparation of American students have changed considerably over the past fifty years. We should ask if our doctoral programs are adjusting appropriately to attract and serve today's students. Are the programs fully realizing their potential to contribute to and enrich the field by attracting and retaining a diverse student body? As Angelica Stacy points out in her essay, in these days of two, three, four careers over a lifetime, programs would benefit from the rich experience that older students bring. In fact, graduate-level education is remarkable for its lack of effort to learn and adjust to changing student goals, talents, and motivations. Many of the approaches to coaching top-level athletes used thirty years ago would not be effective today. So why do most faculty members still mentor as they were mentored?

Other questions for the programs have to do with students' futures. Do most faculty in the program really know what the students, whether they complete the Ph.D. or not, go on to do in their professional lives? Are Ph.D. programs fully exploring and developing their students' potential for the diversity of careers that await them?

We should also think about attrition differently. We already know that large numbers of students who begin doctoral study do not complete it. In some fields, attrition rates approach 50 percent, and in some programs they exceed that. We doubt this is ever acceptable and is certainly not efficient. What is a reasonable rate of attrition? Do we know why students leave programs? What happens to these potential teachers, leaders, and discoverers? Is it possible that some of the same factors that cause students to leave also permanently handicap those who survive a doctoral program? How can we imagine changes that might lower attrition rates if we really do not know *why* people leave our programs, and if we do not determine whether these are factors within the control of a program? How can we evaluate a department's attrition rate until we debate what constitutes desirable and undesirable ("good" and "bad") attrition?

At this point, the reader may have wearied of all these questions. But these are crucial questions that, for all their importance, do not receive serious examination. And so we must find ways to get out of the trap of incremental change when what is really needed is wholesale change in the face of changing contexts, people, and politics. The way out of the trap lies, not in these specific questions but in the habit of mind that leads to asking and working together to answer them.

We must develop a deep sense of shared responsibility for our doctoral programs. We must make developing "stewards of the discipline" our highest priority and understand that other goals, such as pursuing resources and prestige, are in the service of this cause. We must learn to assess the quality of our programs with the same critical minds we bring to our disciplinary research. We must be willing to engage in the process of thinking carefully about creating student-centered graduate programs that prepare our students for the future.

But where to start, in an enterprise unused to the level of examination necessary to truly reform doctoral education? How can we move toward the kinds of questions we should be asking—and answering—regularly about our disciplines and our programs?

Building a New Model of Doctoral Education

The challenge we face is one we know well from our work as scholars: how to be knowledgeable about a field without letting the existing paradigms limit our ability to help the field evolve. Of course, we cannot truly overcome this basic human difficulty, but there are approaches that may move us past our self-imposed constraints. This is exactly the goal of the CID—to foster deliberations by participating departments that will lead to new models of doctoral education. The power of collective critical reflection by departments is currently being demonstrated by departments that are putting in practice the approach outlined in this section.

To take a first step toward a new way of thinking about doctoral education, I offer a strategy from physics. Let us approach the problem by first suspending a complex and complicated reality and then engaging in a simple thought experiment—*gedankenexperiment*—where we set up a simple, idealized, and perhaps solvable model to understand the essential properties of the problem and its solution. From this exercise perhaps we can understand better what parts of the model are useful and what parts are untenable. Ultimately, we can reintroduce reality (what physicists think of as "complicating forces") into our thinking. But the compelling vision we have created may inspire us to find creative strategies to overcome the obstacles we see.

And so, I suggest, as Galileo did with air resistance, that we at first ignore some powerful, complicated, and competing forces, such as the pressures of research and reputation and the constraints of time and money. We will instead concentrate on building a program that will fulfill the purpose of doctoral education.

I offer this four-step process as a way to design a doctoral program *de novo*. Together, the program faculty and students (and even alumni) can use it to build a simple, idealized model of student-centered doctoral education—a model that concentrates on developing stewards of knowledge and wisdom.

> Step 1: *Look ahead for the discipline.* Together, the students and faculty carefully deliberate and answer in detail the following question: What are likely to be the important opportunities and challenges for conserving, creating, and transforming knowledge and enriching the discipline and its many disciplinary neighbors over the foreseeable future?
>
> Step 2: *Identify what a Ph.D. in the discipline must know and be able to do.* In this next step, the students and faculty address this question in some depth: What content knowledge, experiences, skills, and habits of mind will be important for a new Ph.D. to meet the challenges and take advantage of new opportunities?
>
> Step 3: *Construct the goals of the program.* With the answers to these questions, the program's faculty and students construct a series of common goals and desired outcomes for Ph.D. students who complete that particular program—graduates who will enter different careers and subdisciplines.
>
> Step 4: *Design the program.* Now department members are ready to design their Ph.D. program in detail, assigning resources, creating the particular elements and requirements such as course work, assessments, and mentoring.

For example, an important part of the new doctoral program might involve a content domain, much of which can be learned independently or in seminar settings. Introductory lecture courses might be kept to a minimum and include only what is necessary to start developing in students the habits of mind, judgment, ability to communicate effectively and professionally, creativity, and tolerance and understanding of risk that come from experience.

As Yehuda Elkana and Gerald Graff advocate, learning that takes place while attempting research is powerful. As the saying goes, good judgment comes from experience, and experience comes from bad judgment. This observation implicitly points out the important role that purposeful risk taking plays in learning. Therefore, the program might decide to offer the kind of hands-on experience that allows failure, thus fostering in students a habit of critical reflection and development of professional judgment. It might embrace an understanding of the wonderful power of true intellectual controversy and the ability to set priorities—all habits, attitudes, and skills that are essential to scholars who are lifelong, effective (as Angelica Stacey says, "expert") learners who can start again and again at the bottom of a new learning curve. The program could be designed to develop students who not only understand the advantage of occasionally working with scholars from other intellectual tribes but who have learned to trust other deep ways of knowing from disciplines different from their own. As Yehuda Elkana also suggests, the new graduate program would encourage risk taking and intellectual adventurousness while fostering the importance of precision and rigor.

In this *gedankenexperiment,* it would be possible to distinguish a second-year student from a fourth-year student by asking each student a series of questions. Without resorting to simple questions that reveal how long a student has been enrolled, a faculty questioner ought to be able to discern a student's developing maturation as a scholar in the field. The faculty member ought to be able to accurately determine how far along the developmental trajectory student has traveled—to the second year, to the fourth year? This simple test would also reveal whether the faculty members have developed the ability to ask discerning questions and whether they understand how students develop. At the same time, it would yield information as to how the program systematically helps students to develop, that is, whether it is meeting its stated goals. Ideally, in such a program the faculty would have created a set of experiences for students that model and develop the ability to engage in fertile, frisky forums of oral and written discussions that stimulate and illuminate the scholarly mind.

Of course, it is critical that each department deliberate and collectively develop its vision and dream. Faculty and students must detail the goals of the program with sufficient specificity to yield appropriate programmatic elements: formal courses, mentoring and advising, professional development activities, pedagogically motivated testing, skill-developing experiences, and expected performances such as idea generation, judgment, thinking like a member of the discipline, and (of course? or maybe not?) a capstone document called "the dissertation." As a result of its deliberations, the department might decide that some currently cherished programmatic elements require radical changes or could be dropped all together. New programmatic elements, not currently imagined, might be added.

Imagine a department that has developed its Ph.D. program having considered these questions, so that the rationale for the program's elements is collectively understood by the faculty and graduate students. The resulting program will be *purposeful* (P) and *assessable* (A). The program's stewards and stakeholders would engage regularly in *reflection* (R) about the program's design, function, and efficacy. And thus the rationale for the various ingredients and processes in the Ph.D. program would be *transparent* (T) to faculty and graduate students. (In the CID, we use the acronym PART to summarize these desirable features of a doctoral program.)

The habit of critically evaluating progress in meeting departmental goals for the Ph.D. program is essential for improvement. The program (and its pieces) can and should be assessed in terms of its success in achieving its stated purposes. As one concrete example, tracking all students who enroll in the program and gathering meaningful feedback from those who leave the program, as well as from alumni and employers, provides data that can be reviewed and used in decision making about further program changes.

Imagine, then, that the department follows these four steps routinely as a way to review its graduate program, and that the process and its outcomes are regularly presented to the graduate students (in fact, they participate in it). That is, the Ph.D. program evolves through a continuous process of iterative, collective reflection.

In short, this is a program that can address the kind of tough questions posed in the opening of this commentary—and do so regularly.

Sustaining the Vision

What is the greatest threat to a department's vision of a student-centered Ph.D. program? An over-veneration of and undue deference to competing priorities. I maintain that if a program (and, indeed, a discipline) has a clear and shared purpose, and it can defend the design and operations of the program according to this vision, with data on outcomes, it is much less susceptible to the distortions of competing priorities. By keeping what is best for the students front and center, the pulls of human friction, finite energy, limited time, and "conflict of interest" lose much of their power.

With a purposeful, assessable, transparent program that is subject to continuous reflection, we will know which aspects of our Ph.D. programs are inviolable, and why. We will know more precisely how to invest our resources of time and energy and how best to deploy people and facilities. With a clear goal, with solid information about our progress toward that goal, we can act in enlightened self-interest and learn to assess competing priorities, fruitfully exploiting, ignoring, or accepting them.

But none of this can happen without a profound change in *faculty attitudes and habits*. In the absence of a strong, compelling vision for Ph.D. programs, faculty spend their time in ways that are consistent with their own comfort zone or sense of priorities derived from their habits and training. Too often, this skews decisions toward maintaining the status quo, which is not necessarily to the advantage of their doctoral students. Thus faculty resist enrichments of graduate programs that they perceive as intrusive on faculty time or a competing use of resources.

In fact, this natural resistance to change is a real challenge to our programs. To overcome this requires us to envision wonderful, unnatural, unthinkable acts: student-centered Ph.D. programs do not necessarily require more faculty time, only faculty spending time with students in *different, purposeful, and more effective ways*.

We must be willing to relinquish some old habits and ways of mind. We need a collective will. We need to accept our shared responsibility to engage in this process. And we need to act with strong leadership and an understanding of the need for change. The power of our vision for doctoral education can help sustain us and should provide the impetus for creative problem solving.

Considering Where We Go from Here

Today's Ph.D.'s have extraordinary new opportunities to lead efforts to extend human knowledge. They already enjoy new possibilities for educating the next generation of scholars and citizens and for doing so in a wide spectrum of institutional settings. They are also called upon to provide expert opinion in a dizzying array of high-profile public areas. They have a special opportunity and responsibility to inform the public about their disciplines and, ultimately, to shape the public's attitude about the importance of their fields and the attendant habits of mind of an informed, engaged, and ethical scholar.

Perhaps now, more than ever, our world needs the contributions of life-long learner-scholars. Developing these important world citizens requires that we examine and redesign our doctoral programs with these new responsibilities in mind. The quality of the collective thought that goes into structuring Ph.D. programs must be outstanding. So must the collective responsibility for continuing to monitor and reform our Ph.D. programs so that they truly prepare Ph.D.'s for the challenges of the times. This is an intellectual challenge as serious as any we face at the frontiers of disciplinary investigation.

Our first step into this future is to envision a student-centered purpose for our programs and then to engage in making that vision a reality.

The good news is that this approach is already being taken by the eighty-four participating departments in the CID. Together, graduate students *and* faculty (both as individual departments and nationally as a group of departments) are thinking about their programs and learning from and constructively criticizing each other. This is leading to both partial and holistic improvements in these graduate programs. The essays in this book have been important catalysts in their deliberations. Whether or not the rest of us take similar steps and act is up to the faculty and graduate students in our programs. Even if a few departments make significant progress in making their Ph.D. programs more focused on student learning, there still remains the challenge of moving the rest of the doctoral education community in this direction.

There have been many calls for reform over the last few decades, and yet the kind of actions we believe are important have not occurred. Why should the present situation be any different? Perhaps because present global dynamics, economics, and wider choices for potential graduate students make the need clearer and may finally move us to seriously grapple with this issue. As "stewards of our disciplines" (and of the commonality of human learning), we can do no less.

I am optimistic.

REFERENCES

Einstein, A. *Autobiographical Notes: A Centennial Edition* (P. A. Schilpp, ed. and trans.). Southern Illinois University at Carbondale. LaSalle and Chicago: Open Court Publishing Company, 1979.

NAME INDEX

A

Adams, J., 387, 388
American Academy of Arts and Sciences, 25, 404, 413
American Association for the Advancement of Science, 24
American Chemical Society (ACS), 24, 136, 144, 152, 170–171, 174
American Council of Alumni and Trustees, 413n12
American Council of Learned Societies, 404
American Educational Research Association, 270
American Historical Association, 293, 406, 412–413n2
American Mathematical Society (AMS), 118n7
American Psychological Association, 270, 271
Anderson, P., 68, 70
Anderson, P. W., 105
Appleby, J., 16, 18, 19, 27, 57–58, 293–294, 311–326
Arnold, M., 394
Association of American Colleges and Universities, 152
Association of American Universities (AAU), 413n10
Ausable, D., 279

B

Ball, D., 3, 260–263

Barber, E., 80, 93n13
Barker, K., 164n14
Barnes, B., 92
Barone, T., 269
Barthes, R., 385
Bass, H., 16, 17, 18, 19, 27, 31, 58, 82, 90–91, 99, 101–119, 288
Beard, C. A., 297, 309n2
Becker, C., 317
Behrens, J. T., 274, 276
Bender, T., 16, 17, 18, 19, 27, 291, 293, 294, 295–310, 309n3, 392, 395, 413n2
Bentham, J., 394
Berliner, D., 16, 18, 19, 27, 51, 248, 268–289
Biddle, B. J., 284
Biddle, S., 84, 85
Birzer, C. L., 413
Bloor, D., 92
Borges, J. L., 385
Boyle, R., 69
Bradley Foundation, 324
Breslow, R., 16, 18, 19, 31, 34, 51, 52, 137–138, 167–186
Bruner, J. S., 88, 277
Burroughs Wellcome Fund, 54, 164
Bush, V., 128
Bushman, R., 314

C

Calfee, R. C., 287
Carlyle, T., 394
Caro, R., 329

SUBJECT INDEX

A

Academic careers: for chemistry students, 150–151; history monographs and, 341; job crisis for humanities, 392–394; limited positions in, 47, 48–51; for mathematics students, 108–110; in neuroscience, 208–209, 221; nonacademic vs., 25–26; oversupply of historians for, 299–300; preparing English students for, 352, 353; student preparation for classroom teaching, 81–82; teaching assistantships as preparation for, 324, 345–346

ACS Directory of Graduate Research, 171

Admission policies, 362, 368n2

Adviser-student relationship, 200–201

Age, 192–193

American Heritage Dictionary, 252

American Higher Education (Beard), 309n2

American Scholar, The, 404

"American Scholar, The" (Emerson), 298

"Analysis and the Complex Problem of Intellectual Influence" (Zuckerman), 92n1

Apprenticeships: graduate education as, 141; "master"/"apprentice" concept, 305; not working in English, 372; postdoctoral, 48, 49, 50, 158; retained in history doctorate, 346–348; suggestions for teaching, 153–154

"Are There Too Many Ph.D.'s in Mathematics?" (Duren), 117n2

"Art as a Cultural System" (Geertz), 88

"Assessing Research-Doctorate Programs" (Ostriker and Kuh), 94n21

At Cross Purposes (Golde and Dore), 94n21

At the Helm (Barker), 164n14

Attrition: questions about, 422–423; student, 5, 187, 193; women and minorities in English programs, 360

B

Behaviorism in educational psychology, 278

Beliefs and misconceptions, 258, 266

Beyond the Culture Wars (Graff), 388

Beyond the Molecular Frontier (National Research Council), 167

Big ideas in educational psychology, 277–279

Bioengineering, 222–223

Biological sciences, 92n2

British Ph.D. programs, 59, 147–148, 163n5

C

Career counseling, 130, 131

Career paths: academic vs. nonacademic, 25–26; in doctoral programs, 49–50; education, 246; educational psychology, 282–285; employment in neuroscience, 208–209; English, 352, 353, 386–387; history,

175–176; preparing students for faculty career, 150–151; profiles of students in, 191–193; proposed changes for program, 195–200; research on substances, 172; research proposals in, 179–180; reward systems in programs, 202–204; shortening time-to-degree in, 149; stimulating creative research, 179, 195–196; strategies for implementing change in, 157–162; student research in, 178–179; subfields within discipline, 171; suggested enhanced curriculum for, 161, 162; suggested reforms for future faculty, 152–162; taking nontraditional paths in, 187–188; teaching vs. research, 149–150; transformation of substances, 172–173; viewing education as profession, 153

Chemists: students joining lab of, 136–137; time-to-degree for, 136, 145–150

Children, 193, 205n1

Chronicle of Higher Education, 362

Classical Mechanics (Goldstein and others), 72

Collaborative practice, becoming team players, 53

Collaborative practices: benefits of, 131; in English, 365, 366; in humanities, 410; research groups, 131–132, 155, 159

"Common Sense as a Cultural System" (Geertz), 88

Communication skills: communicating profession to public, 80–81, 82; grant writing, 157, 159, 231–232; importance of theses, 53; needed by chemistry students, 144; oral and written, 182–183; providing students with, 52–53; writing for publication, 266. *See also* Professional skills; Writing

Community of practice: creating guild of historians, 334–338; doctoral training as entering, 275; guild definition and, 337

Competition: among faculty, 83; between faculty and students, 39–40

Comprehensive exams, 78, 89–90

"Conference on the Future of Doctoral Education," 366

Conflict: obscuring areas of, 370; organizing courses around, 380–382, 400; wrestling with, 373–374

Conflict of interest, 156

Conservatism: conserving important ideas, 10–11; studying discipline's innovation and, 82–84; tenure and faculty, 35–38

Context: education and cultural, 271–273, 279–281; historical research into, 330, 331

Contradictions: cultural influences leading to, 69–70; incomplete paradigms and theories in sciences, 71–72; scientific method and, 71; within disciplines, 67, 68, 69–71, 92nn3, 4

Controversy: contested issues in English, 370, 373–374, 380–382; in history, 325–326; over unified scientific method, 71

Creativity, stimulating in research, 179, 195–196

Critical Inquiry, 413–414n13

Critical thinking: art of synthesis, 306; crucial element in education discipline, 261; learning to improve arguments, 344; risk and rigor in natural sciences, 73–76; training students in, 87. *See also* Independent thinking

"Crucial Elements of Scholarly Inquiry and Student Learning," 261–263

E

H

I